Tenth Edition

YOUR CAREER

How to Make It Happen

Lisa M.D. Owens

Dean of Learning Sciences, Emeritus, *Procter & Gamble*;
President, *Training Design Strategies LLC*

Crystal Kadakia

Organizational Consultant & TEDx Speaker; CEO, *Kadakia Consulting*

Lauri Harwood

Instructor, *Miami University*;
Business Consultant and Trainer, *Cincinnati, OH*

 CENGAGE

Australia • Brazil • Canada • Mexico • Singapore • United Kingdom • United States

CENGAGE

Your Career: How to Make It Happen, **Tenth Edition**

Lisa M.D. Owens, Crystal Kadakia, Lauri Harwood

Senior Vice President, Higher Education & Skills Product: Erin Joyner

Product Director: Matthew Seeley

Product Manager: Katie McGuire

Content Manager: Manoj Kumar, Lumina Datamatics, Inc.

Product Assistant: Kimberly Klotz

Marketing Manager: Scott Chrysler

Digital Delivery Lead: Amanda Ryan

Intellectual Property Analyst: Ashley Maynard

Intellectual Property Project Manager: Kellianne Besse

Production Service: Lumina Datamatics, Inc.

Designer: Erin Griffin

Cover Images:
iStock.com/Hispanolistic
kathayut kongmanee/ShutterStock.com
red mango/ShutterStock.com
Rawpixel.com/ShutterStock.com
Shift Drive/ShutterStock.com

Design Image: Ewa Studio/ShutterStock.com

Library of Congress Control Number: 2020918525

ISBN: 978-0-357-36135-1

Cengage
200 Pier 4 Boulevard
Boston, MA 02210
USA

Cengage is a leading provider of customized learning solutions with employees residing in nearly 40 different countries and sales in more than 125 countries around the world. Find your local representative at **www.cengage.com.**

To learn more about Cengage platforms and services, register or access your online learning solution, or purchase materials for your course, visit **www.cengage.com.**

Notice to the Reader

Publisher does not warrant or guarantee any of the products described herein or perform any independent analysis in connection with any of the product information contained herein. Publisher does not assume, and expressly disclaims, any obligation to obtain and include information other than that provided to it by the manufacturer. The reader is expressly warned to consider and adopt all safety precautions that might be indicated by the activities described herein and to avoid all potential hazards. By following the instructions contained herein, the reader willingly assumes all risks in connection with such instructions. The publisher makes no representations or warranties of any kind, including but not limited to, the warranties of fitness for particular purpose or merchantability, nor are any such representations implied with respect to the material set forth herein, and the publisher takes no responsibility with respect to such material. The publisher shall not be liable for any special, consequential, or exemplary damages resulting, in whole or part, from the readers' use of, or reliance upon, this material.

Printed in the United States of America
Print Number: 02   Print Year: 2022

Contents BRIEF

Contents

PART 3 Apply for Jobs

PART 4 Shine at Interviews

PART 5   Connect, Accept, and Succeed

Preface

Among the good things in life, a good job doing work you enjoy and building a fulfilling career is one of the best. The single purpose of this book is to help you achieve this goal. You'll find practical, useful, and realistic advice to help you get interviews and job offers and become a valued employee.

Your own career is a journey, and each journey begins with one step out of the front door and into the world. You've likely taken many steps out of that figurative door. Now it's time to map out your journey of many steps so that you can reach a destination of your choice. This textbook can help you choose your next destination—where you can contribute your talents while continuing to strengthen your skills for the next part of your journey. Think of the *Job Search Journey* as one leg of the longer *Career Journey*. You may go on multiple Job Search Journeys throughout your Career Journey.

A successful career no longer needs to be with a single company. However, a successful career is more than a string of jobs. A successful career is one in which each successive job builds strengths and skills to give you greater opportunities to contribute to the world, your community, the company you work for, your family, and yourself.

You are responsible to lead and direct your Career Journey, but many others will provide essential support. Although you will use the Internet to help you find jobs, your most powerful tools are the people you know, the people who know you and your career goals, and the people who are in your Career Network. Start now to build the network of people who will be beside you on your Job Search Journey, the next leg of your Career Journey.

ORGANIZATION OF THE TEXT

As with any journey, it happens one step at a time, and it goes more smoothly if some planning is done before the journey begins. This textbook lays out the *Job Search Journey* in five phases, with two or three steps for each phase. As you review the table of contents, you will see that each phase is a part, and each step correlates to a chapter in the textbook. The map on page xiii shows the steps and the ultimate destination: the beginning to a successful career.

All along the way, this text provides help during each phase and at each step, in the form of side bars. Each phase starts with advice from two real people. One of these is a career expert and the other is a person who recently went through his or her own Job Search Journey. In addition, each chapter contains:

- motivational statements,
- encouragement to form good work habits,
- a cautionary note,

- typical scenarios that people face,
- guides for how to form and use a career network,
- how to harness social media during the job search,
- advice about your job search online, and
- activities and templates to help ensure a successful journey.

PHASE 1: Prepare for the Journey. This phase is all about getting ready for the journey ahead—both physically and mentally. It's like mapping out a trip. **Chapter 1, *The Job Search Journey*,** introduces the concept of a Job Search Journey as a way to more easily achieve a successful career. It encourages physically preparing systems to file and store the materials needed for this journey, such as educational and work records, samples for a portfolio, information about job openings, and contact information for people who are part of an individual's Career Network. **Chapter 2, *Know Yourself to Market Yourself*,** is about how to market an individual's skills and talents. It leads you, the readers, through a self-analysis of what you have to offer an employer and how to describe it in a way that makes you a desirable employee for the right jobs. **Chapter 3, *Picture Yourself in the Workplace*,** explores different work environments to guide you to look for destination jobs that are more suited to your personality and lifestyle, and explores how to tap into in-demand industries and occupations for a broader array of job openings.

PHASE 2: Create Your Resume. This phase is like packing a suitcase with the essentials for the trip. It focuses on the resume as a primary tool for introductions to potential employers. When the resume is successfully honed, it is the foundation for job applications, interviews, and communicating the readers' personal brand and character. **Chapter 4, *Plan Your Resume*,** starts by describing how the resume can be used effectively with Warm Introductions—that is, with your Career Network contacts—or with Cold Leads. It goes on to describe what goes into a resume and helps you gather the necessary information. **Chapter 5, *Write Your Resume*,** gives very practical and up-to-date advice on how to write a resume, including what types of words to select (action verbs, keywords, etc.), editing tips, and formatting advice. Together, these chapters help you craft a powerful resume that shares your unique personality and gets employers' attention.

PHASE 3: Apply for Jobs. This phase moves outside the classroom and outside of your head and into the world of work. It's the equivalent of putting money down for travel tickets and packages. **Chapter 6, *Find Job Openings*,** describes how to build a Career Network and use it and other sources to find job openings that are a good career fit. **Chapter 7, *Write Job Applications*,**

gives detailed advice and tips for filling out applications, both online and on paper, so that the application is accepted into employers' recruiting systems, plus tips on cover letters such as when to use them and how to write them. The goal of this phase is to apply for jobs in a way that will lead to interviews.

PHASE 4: Shine at Interviews. With the ultimate destination farther ahead, it's time to explore some places of interest along the way. This phase focuses on the all-important interviews, and stresses the importance of practice and preparation. **Chapter 8,** *Know the Interview Essentials*, gives insight into the employer and recruiter expectations around interviewees' attitude, dress, body language, conversation, and etiquette. With the ground rules established, this chapter goes on to describe actions that attract interviews and methods for keeping the *Job Search Journey* energized in between these exciting and stressful interviews. **Chapter 9,** *Prepare for Your Interview*, describes the many types of interviews and interview questions, with up-to-date tips on how to succeed all along the way. **Chapter 10,** *Interview Like a Pro*, focuses on the next level of preparation—building confidence through practice, doing homework before each interview, getting physically prepared to climb the summit, and closing the interview on a high note.

PHASE 5: Connect, Accept, and Succeed. Now the destination is in sight. This is not the time to lose energy; rather, it is a time to stay connected and energized until the end goal is reached. Then it's time to enjoy the destination … until it is time for the next journey on a fulfilling lifetime career. **Chapter 11,** *Stay Connected with Potential Employers*, describes how to follow up after interviews to help snag a job offer. Then it describes how to evaluate job offers and respond professionally—either yes or no thank you—to each offer. **Chapter 12,** *Dealing with Disappointment*, helps deal with the realities of rejection and long waits between interviews and offers. **Chapter 13,** *Take Charge of Your Career*, provides up-to-date advice on what to do during the first hours, days, weeks, and months at this new career destination. It wraps up with advice on how to stay for the long term or identify signs that it is time to choose a new destination to further enhance the Career Journey.

APPENDIX: *Your Career: Making It Happen*. These pages pull together the most critical tools and reminders for each phase of the job search journey. Encourage students to tear out these pages and keep them on hand as a quick reference guide whenever they embark on a job search journey during their careers.

NEW TO THIS EDITION

This tenth edition has been significantly updated to reflect the changes in the marketplace, the increasing use of web-based tools in the recruiting process, and the recognition that many jobs are filled without ever getting posted publicly.

Beyond the general update and change in tone, overall, there are five highly notable changes, described next. This edition integrates technology and online tools into each chapter, provides practical steps for networking, simplifies planning for success, addresses modern use of cover letters, updates stories and profiles, includes more diversity of students, and covers a broader range of careers.

Technology is rapidly changing the basics of how to find, and get, a job. The authors' research reflected in *Your Career, 10e* helps you stay in the know by introducing up-to-date practices and resource links for help as the career industry continues to evolve.

Online tools are no longer relegated to an appendix that can interrupt the flow of your lesson plan. Instead, this edition takes the online elements—concepts, resources, how-to instructions—and introduces them in context throughout the job search process. This is reflected in the instructor notes so you can guide students in today's online job search practices. Online elements range from video interviews to using online job boards to social media networking and more.

Real-life stories help students learn more deeply. To supplement your own stories and experiences, this edition adds real-life stories within each major phase of the job search. These are purposefully written in a way that can help each of your students see themselves as a person who can successfully craft their career as they seek a job.

Networking is one of the best ways to find and get top jobs. Yet myths about how to network abound. The authors have partnered with networking experts to bring to you and your students those techniques that are proven to develop a network that serves during the current job search, and for subsequent success on the job. Don't be surprised to learn a few tips yourselves; the authors learned a great deal from this partnership that we put to good use on a daily basis. For those who claim shyness and introversion as barriers to networking, this book is ideal, as it teaches techniques to turn networking from the uncomfortable "talk and take" mentality to a "teach and give" mentality that introverts can successfully embrace.

A wider range of career types were intentionally incorporated into the edition, providing a good balance of advice to succeed in today's broadening industries. This book offers insights that work across such industries as the construction industry, medical careers, accounting, small business, Fortune 500 jobs, automotive industry, software and computer technology, and the creative arts. Your class may focus predominantly on one industry or might cover a range of industries. Either way, this edition is more likely to minimize your need to supplement or translate the job search process so that it works for your unique group of students.

Updated personal profiles are featured at the start of each of the five sections of this edition. The profiles were chosen to reflect greater diversity so that more students can see someone more like themselves in at least one of the ten profiles. And while some profiles remain timeless, others were updated with stories and advice that is more upbeat, current, and relevant for your students.

The Plan for Success feature has been updated to include motivational quotes and to point students to helpful online planning templates.

Use of cover letters in today's digital world has changed dramatically. There is much less focus on these, and yet, in some situations, they are a crucial part of the job search process. In this edition, the topic of cover letters is folded into the chapter on writing resumes. This is consistent with the point in time that job seekers will be faced with the decision to add or exclude a cover letter as they apply online. Modern protocol is described to help readers make this decision, and focus the cover letter on just those elements that recruiters and potential employers want to spend time reading.

Chapter 7, "Write Job Applications," now includes advice and instruction on cover letters. The tenth edition's Chapter 7 and 8, "Write Job Applications" and "Write Effective Tailored Cover Letters," has been combined into Chapter 7, reflecting the current trend to use cover letters sparingly.

FOR THE READER: HOW TO USE THIS TEXT

Your Career: How to Make It Happen is more than a text. It is a simulation or practice session for the real event: finding a job that meets your needs.

If you have nearly completed your degree program and graduation is around the corner, use the activities in this text to get you ready for the upcoming Job Search Journey. This text will walk you through every step of the way. Use the early chapters of self-assessment to better understand what elements in your field of study give you the most pleasure and to what kinds of jobs within your field you will most enjoy applying your skills. Use the middle chapters to get peer feedback to help you hone your resume and Personal Brand Statement.

If, on the other hand, you are a few years from graduation, use this text and course as a way to explore your field more broadly. Figure out what you need to add to your life experiences and your portfolio in the next few years to help you land a job that is a good career fit after graduation. Begin now to build your Career Network. You are lucky to be getting a head start on this. Consider practicing to use the Job Search Journey process by applying it as you search for a summer job or internship, or even a volunteer role that will add to your resume.

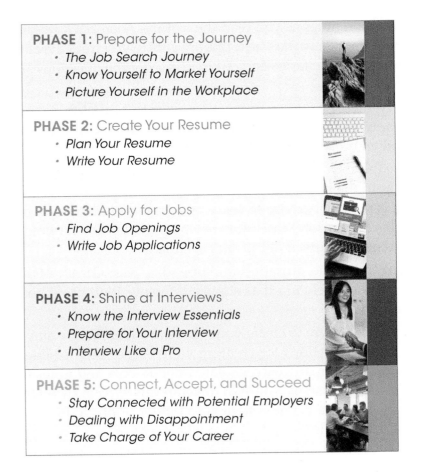

PHASE 1: Prepare for the Journey
- *The Job Search Journey*
- *Know Yourself to Market Yourself*
- *Picture Yourself in the Workplace*

PHASE 2: Create Your Resume
- *Plan Your Resume*
- *Write Your Resume*

PHASE 3: Apply for Jobs
- *Find Job Openings*
- *Write Job Applications*

PHASE 4: Shine at Interviews
- *Know the Interview Essentials*
- *Prepare for Your Interview*
- *Interview Like a Pro*

PHASE 5: Connect, Accept, and Succeed
- *Stay Connected with Potential Employers*
- *Dealing with Disappointment*
- *Take Charge of Your Career*

To get the most out of this text, we suggest that you post the Job Search Journey map, described in detail in Chapter 1. Then follow these steps for each chapter to maximize your benefits from the text and class:

1. As you start each of the five parts, use the steps in *plan for Success* to set you up for success.

2. With each chapter, review the outcomes before you start. When you complete a chapter, confirm that you can accomplish these outcomes by answering the questions in the end of chapter section called *Chapter Checklist*. Each question has a number beside it that tells which outcome section contains the related information, should you want to review the material.

3. Complete the Career Action Worksheets. These give you a chance to practice and get feedback so that you become a pro. Some worksheets will require you to interact with people you do not know. Expect to feel a degree of discomfort. Be brave and get out there to meet new people and expand your Career Network.

4. Take personal notes as you read the features such as *Overcoming Barriers* and *Your Career Network*. These tips are gifts to you from the authors. Read the Real World Scenarios and strive to answer the questions at the end of each one.

5. Actively incorporate online activities into your Job Search Journey throughout each chapter with a special focus on *You, Online*. Search online and find your own resources to supplement concepts in the book.

6. Because the journey is often long, stay inspired. Find your favorite quotes throughout the book. Reread your favorite stories about real-life people and their personal advice to you at the start of each section of the book. Then check your Job Search Journey map to see how far you have come and to remind yourself of the final destination.

7. Tear out the guide provided in Appendix, *Your Career: Making It Happen*, and proactively use it as a quick reference tool throughout your Job Search Journey.

In addition, make sure to create your Career Builder Files to stay organized. The detailed instructions for creating your Career Builder Files will help you organize your many career-related documents and notes to create an extremely useful system. You will develop this system through an online portfolio tool, or as a paper system via a binder or portfolio. Through practical, hands-on application, the personal content of the Career Builder Files will motivate you to take on the challenge of the Job Search Journey now and for your entire career.

From your authors,

"We wish you lifelong success in your Job Search Journey."

KEY FEATURES

Part Opener Content

Plan for Success

Each of the five parts begins with a *Plan for Success* feature to help students plan specific completion dates for the steps they will accomplish in that part, with a reminder to take into account the other things going on in their busy lives.

PART 1

Prepare for the Journey

PART 1 Your job search is like a journey, and each journey begins with one step out the front door and into the world. Successful job searches tend to have five phases. The first phase, "Prepare for the Journey," begins with organizing for what's ahead, assessing yourself to market yourself more effectively, and visualizing yourself as a successful employee in the workplace.

CHAPTER 1	The Job Search Journey
CHAPTER 2	Know Yourself to Market Yourself
CHAPTER 3	Picture Yourself in the Workplace

PLAN for Success

Success is more likely when you have a written plan. Use the online template *Plan for Success* to create your own written plan for successfully completing Part 1, Chapters 1–3.

"All you need is the plan, the roadmap, and the courage to press on to your destination"

—Earl Nightingale

ADVICE FROM THE EXPERT

With over 20 years of experience in coaching and developing others, Allen Zink has invaluable advice for those starting and growing on their career journey. "The most important aspect of finding a best fit career is to really, truly know yourself. Being honest with yourself regarding who you are, what drives you, and what your purpose is, are critical elements to truly being happy in a career." To understand your strengths and determine your career goals, Allen suggests, "take a little reflection time" and "think about a time when you were operating at your best and consider where you were, who you were working with, what you were doing, and how you were feeling." During that reflection time, define your strengths and goals based on discovering "the sweet spot of things you not only do well, but are passionate about."

Then connect these strengths with a company's need or role. Find a best fit company by considering if "the company's culture, values, and business proposition" align with your values. Also consider "growth opportunities and ways to further develop your skills and capabilities."

When it is time to find the job, Allen says that "networking plays a huge role in the job search!" It's important to have identified your personal brand, the words or statement that describes "how others perceive you or would describe you." Allen suggests asking yourself, "What do I want to be known for? If I could only use one word to describe me, what would that word be?" When you know what you want and who you are, you can "maximize your network" by "giving your contacts something to work with and ultimately to be able to act on." Even though "your contacts typically really want to help you," without clarity, you may not be using your network well. "Always remain positive when interacting with your contacts. Circle back to your contacts periodically and share your progress, as they may continue to have suggestions for you."

Keep positive during the job search by "planning networking meetings with people you are very comfortable with each week to help balance out the more difficult and energy draining meetings with others." It's also important to "celebrate the wins and debrief the losses from an objective point of view." Lastly, stay energized during your job search by "mixing in some activities that you enjoy and finding other people who are currently looking for a new role. It will be comforting to know that your feelings and emotions are normal!"

ALLEN ZINK
Vice-President Senior Development Consultant, Fifth Third Bank

STORIES FROM THE JOB SEARCH

EDWIN TORRES
Registered Nurse, Surgical Progressive Care Unit

Edwin is passionate about his new role as a registered nurse (RN). Initially, he just wanted a job to pay the bills, but during his first job at a hospital as patient transporter, he discovered his passion: medicine and helping people. Over the course of several years, Edwin continued his education to gain better roles in medicine.

Edwin wanted to be an RN. The barriers: money, time, and the fact that no one in his family had ever gone to college. Edwin's dad helped; he used his network. His chiropractor contact agreed to hire Edwin as a massage therapist if he would get certified. Edwin completed the one-year program in six months while continuing work as a patient transporter. When Edwin started the massage therapist job, he also enrolled in a nursing school. While on the new job, Edwin noticed some practices that felt unethical. He was asked to leave. He was happier at a different chiropractic office, until state licensing laws changed and caused his role to be eliminated. To pay nursing school bills, he took a job with a less respected organization; but at least it came with flexible hours and benefits. These jobs helped him hone a valuable skill: how to make vulnerable people feel comfortable.

The school of nursing was tough. This first cohort of 40 students quickly dwindled to 5. A new cohort of 15 was formed. To get through classes, clinicals, study, and exams, Edwin says these 15 people practically lived together. He achieved his degree! Next, he would have to take the Nursing Boards exam.

Meanwhile, life had intervened. Edwin met the love of his life, got married, bought a house, and got a dog. Then one day, he got the phone call from his mother: something was wrong with his dad. Edwin rushed to his parents' house, and there his training kicked in. He got his dad to the emergency room and quickly realized from the EKG that his dad had a massive heart attack. Doctors confirmed it. Through months of hospitalization, Edwin stayed at his dad's side. The background noise and commotion of the hospital actually helped him study. He was immersed in the medical environment and meeting others with similar interests. He had thought he wanted a role in surgery, but a nurse in the Surgical Progressive Care Unit (SPCU) convinced him to switch his focus. "Come see me when you pass your Boards. I'd like you on my team," she said.

There was a two-year gap before Edwin passed his Nursing Boards. He wanted that SPCU job at the hospital where his dad was so well cared for. Edwin prepared his resume, applied online, and created a cover letter, which explained upfront why there as such a gap. When he walked into the interview, his interviewer was the recently promoted nurse who had said, "I want you on my team." He got the job.

When asked later what he saw as next in his career, Edwin said, "I'm a medical geek now. I've just discovered a YouTube about virtual reality to reduce opioid use. My study just got funded! My career has become my vocation." Edwin's advice to others: "Don't let situations stop you from achieving what you want. No matter how long it takes, go for that goal—that dream goal." He says, "My career has been a journey that continues. Each of us can make a difference if we follow our passions and interests."

Advice from the Expert

In the five "Advice from the Expert" sections, get advice from real people, including a recruiting manager and career coach. These professionals discuss career management and real-world issues when moving forward on the Job Search Journey.

Stories from the Job Search

Learn from five real people who have been recent job seekers. They include a new hire, a mid-career job seeker, and a recently graduated job seeker. These people share the job search issues that they experienced and solutions to common challenges that students can immediately relate to.

Chapter Opener Content

Learning Outcomes

At the beginning of each chapter, a list of learning outcomes provides a set of concise learning goals. Each learning outcome is addressed in a main chapter heading. Outcomes are also tied to the end-of-chapter worksheets, questions, and activities.

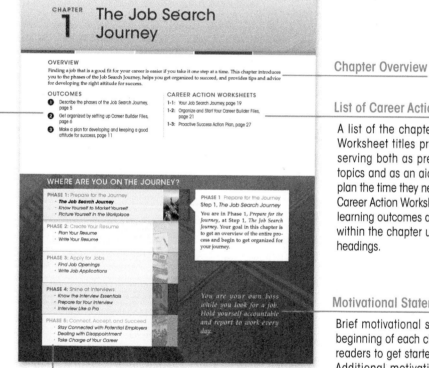

Chapter Overview

List of Career Action Worksheets

A list of the chapter's Career Action Worksheet titles provides a preview, serving both as pre-exposure to the topics and as an aid to help students plan the time they need for this course. Career Action Worksheets are linked to learning outcomes and are introduced within the chapter under the relevant headings.

Motivational Statements

Brief motivational statements at the beginning of each chapter encourage readers to get started on the chapter. Additional motivational statements throughout the chapter encourage students to continue through the end of the chapter.

The Job Search Journey

Upbeat language and achievable, concrete small steps help keep students in a positive frame of mind in the class and on the Job Search Journey. A colorful graphic repeated at the beginning of each chapter helps students recall the steps and track their progress as they work through the course.

Chapter Interior Features

FEATURE BOXES

MAKE IT A HABIT
Start with a Positive Attitude

Your Job Search Journey will be an exciting and challenging time. You will be managing new tasks on top of an already busy schedule, while at the same time feeling the thrill of taking power into your own hands for your future. Every day, make it a habit to reaffirm feelings of excitement and confidence as you move forward on this journey. Post your favorite affirmations in places where you will see them often. Here are a few affirmations to get you started:

- I have the power to succeed.
- I will create happiness and success.
- I can make my own choices and decisions.
- I can choose to make changes in every area of my life.
- I am satisfied that I have done my best.
- I have a plan for the future, and my plan is open to change.
- I will not give up on myself.
- I have the power to succeed. (End your pep talk by repeating the first sentence—it says it all.)

Don't be shy about starting your day with a pep talk. Add your own sentences and repeat them to yourself throughout the day. Forming this habit will help you during challenging times throughout life.

Keep it fun. Try a habit-forming mobile app or website, such as MindSet, Way of Life, Done, Strides, and Habitify. Search online for the latest mobile apps.

hfng/Shutterstock.com.

Make It a Habit

This feature spotlights winning behaviors and strategies for growing professionally.

Overcoming Barriers

This feature (formerly titled Caution!) alerts students about behaviors to avoid or how to plan in advance for good results.

Every chapter highlights important tips for using online tools and technology, including the Internet and social media, throughout the Job Search Journey. These tips go beyond the activities within the chapters that do such things as guide students to create a LinkedIn® profile, clean up their online social media so they present a professional face to potential employers, and assess the top-rated online tools for job searches.

OVERCOMING BARRIERS
Take Charge of Your Career Right Now

Many factors in your job search are not under your control, but one thing certainly is—the effort you make to stand out from the crowd every step of the way. To get an edge over other job seekers, (1) set personal goals for this class and for your job search, (2) believe in your drive and commitment to achieve your goals, and (3) use this class and textbook to succeed.

Your Career: How to Make It Happen is filled with practical, realistic advice and actions. When you read each chapter, think about how you can apply the information and advice to your goals and situations. Complete the Career Action Worksheets and be sure to set up and maintain your Career Builder Files. Use the websites that support the textbook.

Set a goal today to use all the resources available to you and to take charge of your career!

metamorworks/Shutterstock.com

Real World Scenario 1-1

Jamie is finishing her associate's degree and has a part-time job. As she starts to look for a full-time job, she realizes that her desk is *very* disorganized. She missed paying a bill for her apartment and finally found it buried under some important class notes she thought she'd lost. (The business cards she'd been looking for since the career fair two weeks ago were also in the pile of paper.) Keeping up with follow-up phone calls for her job search, juggling her class and work schedule, and taking care of her day-to-day needs is harder than she thought it would be. She knows she needs a system to stay on top of everything.

What suggestions do you have for Jamie as she organizes her desk?

Real-World Scenarios

Each chapter includes one or two real-world scenarios that give insights into how chapter concepts work in real-world situations and pose thoughtful questions that can be great for kicking off class or group discussions in order to personalize the learning.

Your Career Network: Who's in Your Network?

Between 70% and 85% of jobs are identified through the job seeker's network. So this is a good time to take a look at your network. Networking specialist Lynne Waymon of Contacts Counts, LLC, says that we all have four networks:

- **Work Net:** people you currently work with. Consider who you know at a paid or volunteer job or from your school project teams and classes.
- **Org Net:** people you know who are part of bigger organizations that you belong to. Consider the company you work for, the school you attend, a religious organization, or sports team you are on. You already have one thing in common—your org—and that gives you a good start at a networking connection.
- **Industry Net:** People who are in your industry. If this list is short, join a professional or industry organization and start building your Industry Network! For example, those in the nursing profession can join the American Nurses Association. Try to get a LinkedIn connection.
- **Life Net:** Your friends and family. They may be friends on your favorite social media platform, or your neighbors, or your family members' friends.

Make a list of the people in your four networks. Career Action Worksheet 6-1 provides a template to help you create your networking lists. During your Job Search Journey, add to this list. Keep contact information current so that you can reach out to these people. Each step of your Job Search Journey can benefit by reaching out to one or more of these four networks.

Source: Make Your Contacts Count: Networking Know-How for Business and Career Success," 2nd edition, 2007, by Anne Barber and Lynne Waymon, publisher AMACOM, a division of American Management Association

Your Career Network

New to this edition: Because networking is so critical to finding the right job as part of a career journey, a new feature on how to network is included. So many people talk about networking, but few know how to do it well. And many students feel uncomfortable when trying to network face-to-face with people they don't know. The new advice in these sections will help overcome these barriers, for students of all ages and experience levels.

End-of-Chapter Content

Chapter Checklist

Check off each item you can do. Reread sections in this chapter to help you complete the checklist.

- ☐ Name and explain the phase that best describes where I am today in my Job Search Journey. Name and describe the next job search phase. ❶
- ☐ Plan and organize my job search by collecting and organizing my records and choosing a method to keep track of communications. ❷
- ☐ Describe my plan for further developing and maintaining a good attitude during my Job Search Journey. ❸
- ☐ Put my long-term and short-term goals in writing, with concrete steps to achieve each goal. ❸
- ☐ Describe a few tips to help me manage my time even better during my Job Search Journey. ❸
- ☐ Practice proactive skills that demonstrate a positive attitude and a focus on solving problems. ❸

Critical Thinking Questions

1. What is the value of knowing about the phases and steps for a job search? ❶
2. Why is it important to organize your records for your job search? ❷
3. How will your Career Builder Files help you succeed in your Job Search Journey? What tools will you use? How will you get started? ❷
4. What effects do positive and negative thoughts, images, and self-talk have on performance? ❸
5. How would you rate your ability to set goals, manage your time, and be proactive? Would you rate your skills as excellent, good, or needing improvement? What specific actions can you take to stay strong or improve these skills? ❸

Trial Run

Get Off to a Good Start ❸

The beginning of your job search is a good time to evaluate some of the skills and attitudes that will help you have a successful journey. Read these statements and rate yourself using the following scale:

Chapter Checklists

These checklists of questions help students confirm that they have achieved the major goals from each chapter's action steps. These checklists are keyed to the chapter outcomes. Students are encouraged to review a section if they struggle to answer a Chapter Checklist question.

Critical Thinking Questions

Critical Thinking Questions encourage students to reflect on each chapter's learning outcomes, and how the students will use those outcomes in the Job Search Journey.

Trial Run

Interactive and role-play activities are provided in *Trial Run* at the end of each chapter. These provide opportunities to practice desired outcomes of the chapter. Each activity requires peer or self-evaluation.

Career Action Worksheets

More than 50 Career Action Worksheets help students apply chapter content and advice to their own unique situations. Extremely flexible, the worksheets can be used individually or in groups, in class or as homework.

Students create personal documents that can be used as they search for jobs, now and in the future. Guided assessments prompt students to consider a good career fit beyond matching skills and qualifications, to include their preferences, personal traits, lifestyle, personal goals, and preferred work style. All this is clearly aimed at helping students find jobs that are a good fit for them and their desired career path.

Self-assessment tools built into the worksheets enable readers to easily evaluate their progress on their Job Search Journey. Students are instructed within the chapter when they should complete each worksheet; the worksheets themselves are located at the end of each chapter.

▶ CAREER ACTION WORKSHEET

1-3 Proactive Success Action Plan ❸

Take this time to set goals that inspire and excite you for your Job Search Journey.

My job search goal:

Why is this goal important to me? What will happen if I don't achieve this goal?

Steps I will take to achieve this goal:

Action Steps	Date
1. Schedule time to assemble my Career Builder Files.	
2.	
3.	
4.	
5.	

What two or three people from my Career Network can provide support during this journey?

Career Action Worksheet Callout Boxes

Boxes are placed strategically within the text to suggest at what point the reader can jump to an activity. This encourages student to do a few activities at a time rather than be overloaded with activities at the end.

> ▶ CAREER ACTION
> **Complete Worksheet 1-1**
> Your Job Search Journey, page 19

SUPPLEMENTAL MATERIALS

For Instructors

Instructor Companion Site

Everything you need for your course in one place! This collection of book-specific lecture and class tools is available online via www.cengage.com. Access and download Microsoft® PowerPoint lecture slides, the Instructor Guide, course management forms, and more.

Instructor Guide. Expansive yet focused, the powerful Instructor Guide helps busy instructors create a cohesive learning experience for students.

For Students

Student Companion Site

Visit www.cengage.com to access useful web links and an explanation of common workplace terms.

Acknowledgments

The authors are grateful to the people who shared their real-life stories for the profiles. Thank you to Gina Arens, Molly Cramer, Leslie Kirkland, Lisa Mark, Dedra Perlmutte, Jenn Pirino, Nichole Sims, (Jacob) Eli Thomas, Edwin Torres, Allen Zink.

The authors would like to thank several people. First and foremost, thank you to Vern Schellenger (Principal Consultant, Contacts Count) for his insights, review, and advice on the networking components added to this edition. Thank you to Mara Vuillaume (Learning Designer, Cengage Learning), who assured that all the content is clearly connected with the learning objectives for each chapter. Thank you to Doug Bergman (Manager Recruitment, Lee Health), for spending several hours demonstrating the hiring-side of the online recruitment process.

Finally, thank you to Anastasia Bandemir, Brad Wolfenden II, and (Jacob) Eli Thomas for providing additional insights into our target readers' experiences both during the job hunt and as they read and use this textbook.

About the Authors

Lisa M.D. Owens

Ms. Owens is a learning expert who approaches learning programs in a systemic fashion, applying current best practices emerging from recent neuroscience findings. Following a decade in the engineering field designing chemical plants, recruiting young women engineers, and doing consumer and market research, Lisa shifted into a role as a full-time corporate training manager at Procter & Gamble. In this position, she created P&G's first online global training programs, including a new hire web-based training in 1998 called Experience the Journey. She has also worked on training for P&G interviewers. In 2000, partnering with a P&G recruiting leader, she created the first online internal job posting system for over 80,000 employees and their managers at over 200 sites around the world. Following retirement after 30+ years with P&G, Lisa founded Training Design Strategies LLC (TDS) in 2012 and continues doing what she does best: working with the doers and the movers of the world to help them achieve their goals by using powerful training and training strategies. Beyond her current work with clients, she was on the advisory board for Ohio University's instructional design certificate program, GC-ASTD's Executive Advisory Board, and CorpU's Leaders-as-Teachers Executive Council. Her publications include *Designing for Modern Learning: Beyond ADDIE and SAM* (2020, ATD Press, coauthor), *Leaders as Teachers Action Guide* (2014, ATD Press, coauthor), and *Lo start-up di una Corporate University* (Italian). She has contributed to several books in the series on *Active Training* by Mel Silberman and Elaine Beich.

Crystal Kadakia

Crystal is a two-time TEDx speaker, organizational consultant, and best-selling author, known for transforming the toughest workplace changes into exciting possibilities for our digital world. As a consultant, she brings organizations into the digital age, reimagining people strategies with clients in areas such as career development, learning culture, inclusion, leadership development, and employee engagement. Past clients include General Mills, Southern Company, Monster.com, Sierra Club, and other organizations.

Her academic background includes a bachelor's degree in chemical engineering and a master's in organization development. After six years working for Procter & Gamble, she began her consulting firm where she has tackled transforming the status quo and bridging gaps between people in the workplace. For example, through her best-selling book, *The Millennial Myth: Transforming Misunderstanding into Workplace Breakthroughs* (Berrett-Koehler, 2017), and keynotes, Crystal has changed the story around the generation gap for thousands over the past decade. Along with supporting clients, her next project is a deep study of living and leading in the digital age, including practices that help create connection, emerge from burnout, and balance the role of technology in our day to day lives.

Crystal dug deep into what today's employees need to perform, to learn, and to develop on the job. Together with Lisa MD Owens, they mapped out a new instructional design model for today's workplace and share their learning and experience in the book, *Designing for Modern Learning: Beyond ADDIE and SAM (2020 ATD Press, coauthor)*.

Crystal is honored to be a Power 30 Under 30, CLO Learning in Practice, and ATD One to Watch award recipient. Originally from Austin, Texas, she is now based in Atlanta, Georgia, with her husband Jeremy, where they love immersing in nature and cultural experiences.

Lauri Harwood

Lauri Harwood is an instructor at the Farmer School of Business at Miami University in Cincinnati. She has been a consulting editor and textbook author for Cengage Learning since 1993. She was a professional writer, instructional designer, and project manager as the former owner of Vandalay Group Inc. and, prior to that, for The Oxford Associates. Lauri has a bachelor of arts degree in English literature from the University of Cincinnati, and a master's degree from Miami University in technical and scientific communication.

Dedication

To my sister, Rhoda, whose reentry into the workplace has been a model of career development. And to my late daughter-in-law, Becky, whose career helped her live a fuller life.

—Lisa M.D. Owens

To my sister, Sheryl, whose persistence at excelling in her career serves as a good role model for many. To my mother, Rashesha, whose ability to grow a successful career while overcoming her diverse background and facing many challenges inspires me. To my father, Shailesh, whose astronomical aspirations and perseverance to follow his meaningful passions guides me.

—Crystal Kadakia

PHASE 1:
PREPARE FOR THE JOURNEY

Prepare for the Journey

PART 1 Your job search is like a journey, and each journey begins with one step out the front door and into the world. Successful job searches tend to have five phases. The first phase, "Prepare for the Journey," begins with organizing for what's ahead, assessing yourself to market yourself more effectively, and visualizing yourself as a successful employee in the workplace.

ADVICE FROM THE EXPERT

ALLEN ZINK

Vice President Senior Development Consultant, Fifth Third Bank

With over 20 years of experience in coaching and developing others, Allen Zink has invaluable advice for those starting and growing on their career journey. "The most important aspect of finding a best fit career is to really, truly know yourself. Being honest with yourself regarding who you are, what drives you, and what your purpose is, are critical elements to truly being happy in a career." To understand your strengths and determine your career goals, Allen suggests, "take a little reflection time" and "think about a time when you were operating at your best and consider where you were, who you were working with, what you were doing, and how you were feeling." During that reflection time, define your strengths and goals based on discovering "the sweet spot of things you not only do well, but are passionate about."

Then connect these strengths with a company's need or role. Find a best fit company by considering if "the company's culture, values, and business proposition" align with your values. Also consider "growth opportunities and ways to further develop your skills and capabilities."

When it is time to find the job, Allen says that "networking plays a huge role in the job search!" It's important to have identified your personal brand, the words or statement that describes "how others perceive you or would describe you." Allen suggests asking yourself, "What do I want to be known for? If I could only use one word to describe me, what would that word be?" When you know what you want and who you are, you can "maximize your network" by "giving your contacts something to work with and ultimately to be able to act on." Even though "your contacts typically really want to help you," without clarity, you may not be using your network well. "Always remain positive when interacting with your contacts. Circle back to your contacts periodically and share your progress, as they may continue to have suggestions for you."

Keep positive during the job search by "planning networking meetings with people you are very comfortable with each week to help balance out the more difficult and energy draining meetings with others." It's also important to "celebrate the wins and debrief the losses from an objective point of view." Lastly, stay energized during your job search by "mixing in some activities that you enjoy and finding other people who are currently looking for a new role. It will be comforting to know that your feelings and emotions are normal!"

PLAN for Success

Success is more likely when you have a written plan. Use the online template *Plan for Success* to create your own written plan for successfully completing Part 1, Chapters 1–3.

"All you need is the plan, the roadmap, and the courage to press on to your destination"

—*Earl Nightingale*

STORIES FROM THE JOB SEARCH

EDWIN TORRES

Registered Nurse, Surgical Progressive Care Unit

Edwin is passionate about his new role as a registered nurse (RN). Initially, he just wanted a job to pay the bills, but during his first job at a hospital as patient transporter, he discovered his passion: medicine and helping people. Over the course of several years, Edwin continued his education to gain better roles in medicine.

Edwin wanted to be an RN. The barriers: money, time, and the fact that no one in his family had ever gone to college. Edwin's dad helped; he used his network. His chiropractor contact agreed to hire Edwin as a massage therapist if he would get certified. Edwin completed the one-year program in six months while continuing work as a patient transporter. When Edwin started the massage therapist job, he also enrolled in a nursing school. While on the new job, Edwin noticed some practices that felt unethical. He was asked to leave. He was happier at a different chiropractic office, until state licensing laws changed and caused his role to be eliminated. To pay nursing school bills, he took a job with a less respected organization; but at least it came with flexible hours and benefits. These jobs helped him hone a valuable skill: how to make vulnerable people feel comfortable.

The school of nursing was tough. This first cohort of 40 students quickly dwindled to 5. A new cohort of 15 was formed. To get through classes, clinicals, study, and exams, Edwin says these 15 people practically lived together. He achieved his degree! Next, he would have to take the Nursing Boards exam.

Meanwhile, life had intervened. Edwin met the love of his life, got married, bought a house, and got a dog. Then one day, he got the phone call from his mother: something was wrong with his dad. Edwin rushed to his parents' house, and there his training kicked in. He got his dad to the emergency room and quickly realized from the EKG that his dad had a massive heart attack. Doctors confirmed it. Through months of hospitalization, Edwin stayed at his dad's side. The background noise and commotion of the hospital actually helped him study. He was immersed in the medical environment and meeting others with similar interests. He had thought he wanted a role in surgery, but a nurse in the Surgical Progressive Care Unit (SPCU) convinced him to switch his focus. "Come see me when you pass your Boards. I'd like you on my team," she said.

There was a two-year gap before Edwin passed his Nursing Boards. He wanted that SPCU job at the hospital where his dad was so well cared for. Edwin prepared his resume, applied online, and created a cover letter, which explained upfront why there as such a gap. When he walked into the interview, his interviewer was the recently promoted nurse who had said, "I want you on my team." He got the job.

When asked later what he saw as next in his career, Edwin said, "I'm a medical geek now. I've just discovered a YouTube about virtual reality to reduce opioid use. My study just got funded! My career has become my vocation." Edwin's advice to others: "Don't let situations stop you from achieving what you want. No matter how long it takes, go for that goal—that dream goal." He says, "My career has been a journey that continues. Each of us can make a difference if we follow our passions and interests."

The Job Search Journey

OVERVIEW

Finding a job that is a good fit for your career is easier if you take it one step at a time. This chapter introduces you to the phases of the Job Search Journey, helps you get organized to succeed, and provides tips and advice for developing the right attitude for success.

OUTCOMES

1 Describe the phases of the Job Search Journey, page 5

2 Get organized by setting up Career Builder Files, page 6

3 Make a plan for developing and keeping a good attitude for success, page 11

CAREER ACTION WORKSHEETS

1-1: Your Job Search Journey, page 19

1-2: Organize and Start Your Career Builder Files, page 21

1-3: Proactive Success Action Plan, page 27

WHERE ARE YOU ON THE JOURNEY?

PHASE 1: Prepare for the Journey
- **The Job Search Journey**
- *Know Yourself to Market Yourself*
- *Picture Yourself in the Workplace*

PHASE 2: Create Your Resume
- *Plan Your Resume*
- *Write Your Resume*

PHASE 3: Apply for Jobs
- *Find Job Openings*
- *Write Job Applications*

PHASE 4: Shine at Interviews
- *Know the Interview Essentials*
- *Prepare for Your Interview*
- *Interview Like a Pro*

PHASE 5: Connect, Accept, and Succeed
- *Stay Connected with Potential Employers*
- *Dealing with Disappointment*
- *Take Charge of Your Career*

PHASE 1 Prepare for the Journey
Step 1, *The Job Search Journey*

You are in Phase 1, *Prepare for the Journey*, at Step 1, *The Job Search Journey*. Your goal in this chapter is to get an overview of the entire process and begin to get organized for your journey.

You are your own boss while you look for a job. Hold yourself accountable and report to work every day.

THE FIVE PHASES OF THE JOB SEARCH JOURNEY

Finding a job that meets your needs and uses your talents and skills is a journey. Like most journeys, it starts with YOU deciding to make the journey, planning for it, doing it, and finally reaching your destination, with lots of good stories to tell. Get ready for an exciting journey into your future as you search for your first or next job in your career field.

Your job search can be an exciting journey because:

- There are more options than you might realize.
- The journey itself will lead you to know yourself even more.
- The journey can lead to a job that will be a major part of your life, affecting how much you are paid, how much time you spend working, and how much you enjoy your time on the job.

Exploring career fields and job opportunities will be an important part of your work life not only for your first job but also for your entire career. Career paths are rarely straightforward. Instead, your career path will evolve as you, and your situation, evolve: your interests and passions, your skills and experience, the economy, and your situation in life.

You likely have an idea about your current **job target**—the job you want to land. As you search for open job positions, you will compare them to your job target to find a close match. This match is a **best fit job.**

So whether this is your first job search, a continuation of your career journey, or the start of a new career path, you owe it to yourself to get it right. No one will care more about your career than you do. If you are starting a new path in an existing career, review Chapter 13 to see options to grow your career in new ways. Use this textbook and this class to succeed in your Job Search Journey—and make your career happen.

The **Job Search Journey** (Figure 1-1) has five phases. The five parts of this book correspond to these phases. In each part, you'll find advice and activities to help you succeed in that phase.

Figure 1-1 The Job Search Journey

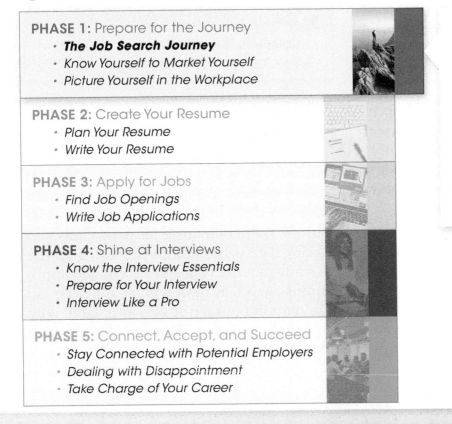

PHASE 1: Prepare for the Journey
- **The Job Search Journey**
- *Know Yourself to Market Yourself*
- *Picture Yourself in the Workplace*

PHASE 2: Create Your Resume
- *Plan Your Resume*
- *Write Your Resume*

PHASE 3: Apply for Jobs
- *Find Job Openings*
- *Write Job Applications*

PHASE 4: Shine at Interviews
- *Know the Interview Essentials*
- *Prepare for Your Interview*
- *Interview Like a Pro*

PHASE 5: Connect, Accept, and Succeed
- *Stay Connected with Potential Employers*
- *Dealing with Disappointment*
- *Take Charge of Your Career*

These are the phases and steps of a typical job search. The book is divided into five parts to match these phases, with chapters to address each step. Each chapter starts with this **Job Search Journey Map** as an indicator of what phase and step you will cover in that chapter as you proceed on your journey.

Getting Started

You are about to begin a new job search. The goal of your job search is to:

- Identify or confirm a career field that fits with your skills and interests.

- Find a fulfilling job in your career field that will use your talents.

- Seek out employers who will value your work and pay you for it.

- Form a team or network of people who will be a positive part of your work life.

Start now to gather tools that will help you discover your job target for a career that will be exciting to pursue and that will play to your strengths. If you are already experienced with the Job Search Journey, review Chapter 13 first to understand options to grow your career further.

PHASE 1: Prepare for the Journey. A little prep work understanding your goals makes for a smoother journey, whether you have already chosen your job target or are still exploring. Get organized, assess your strengths and workplace preferences, explore the breadth of jobs in your career field, and create your first marketing tools in this phase.

PHASE 2: Create Your Resume. Your resume is the image of you that potential employers will see. Planning and crafting this document takes deep thought and careful work so that you can market yourself effectively.

PHASE 3: Apply for Jobs. Network and research to find job opportunities and openings through Warm Introductions, **Career Network Meetings**, and Cold Leads. Apply for jobs using your master resume to create a picture for potential employers that shows how you can fit into their workplace.

PHASE 4: Shine at Interviews. Use strategies to get interviews, prepare and practice for different types of interviews and interview questions, and write thank-you notes that will help potential employers remember you. Be ready for pre-employment tests and follow-up interviews.

PHASE 5: Connect, Accept, and Succeed. Follow up with potential employers after your interviews to ensure they continue to see you as a possible employee. Evaluate job offers and decide to accept the job or continue to look for a better job fit. Finally, when you accept a job in your career field, be prepared to shine as you adjust to your new job and grow in your career.

▶ *CAREER ACTION*

Complete Worksheet 1-1
Your Job Search Journey, page 19

ORGANIZE YOUR JOB SEARCH

Now is the time to create systems to organize the information you need on your Job Search Journey. Gathering this information now and making it easy to access quickly will help you be ready to write your resume and **job applications** as well as meet with people who can help you in your job search and, later, with potential employers. Think of it as packing your suitcase for a trip.

What's the Difference Between a Job and a Career?

A **job** involves performing a designated set of responsibilities and duties for a specific employer.

A **career** encompasses a series of jobs in the same occupation or profession, either with the same company or with different companies. (*Career, occupation*, and *profession* mean the same thing.)

Your career is your life's work. Your major in school enables you to follow many different career paths, each with a wide variety of job opportunities. For example, Sandra is studying to become a registered pediatric nurse. She currently works as a licensed practical nurse in a nursing home (her job) and is pursuing a nursing career. Later, she could choose to train fellow nurses or work in a more administrative or management job. This series of jobs makes up her career. Leon works as a security guard (his job) while he studies criminal justice (his major). Although there are many ways he could use his criminal justice degree, his career goal is to become a federal air marshal or K9 officer.

You can read more about the differences between a job and a career, and what these differences can mean during your working life, in Chapter 13.

Dmitry Kalinovsky/Shutterstock.com.

Career Builder Files is the name for all the records you assemble and organize for your job search. These files have three sections, which are described below. See Figure 1-2 for examples.

- **About Me:** This section contains a collection of records, awards, information about you, your thoughts about jobs and your career, and drafts of your Personal Brand Statement.

- **About Jobs:** Use this section to track job leads, contact information for people you talk to, your research about career fields and job listings, and your draft job applications and resumes.

- **Master Career Portfolio:** In this section, collect documents you will share with others, especially during interviews, such as your master resume, customized resumes you have sent to potential employers, job applications, samples of your work, cover letters, and thank-you notes.

The **Career Action Worksheets** at the end of each chapter will help you gather the information you will need on your Job Search Journey. At the end of each Career Action Worksheet is a reminder to add your work to one of the three sections of your Career Builder Files.

As you pull together your Career Builder Files, both the items recommended here and others that you think are helpful, think about what these documents say about you. What picture do they paint? Where will you best fit into the workplace as you seek your next job as part of your career?

Figure 1-2 Creating Your Career Builder Files

Here are examples of what you might add to your Career Builder Files so that all of your Job Search Journey documents are in one place and easy to find for this part of your career journey. In some cases, you will keep only copies of these documents in your files.

About Me

Records of completion
- Your diploma(s) or degree(s)
- Your transcripts
- Licenses, such as for forklift operation, real estate, or cosmetology

Documentation of Performance
- Performance reviews from past employers or internship managers
- Awards, such as for perfect attendance on the job and in school, academic accomplishments, employee of the month, participation in academic or career-related fairs or competitions
- Letters of recommendation or commendation
- Notes of thanks or praise for previous work and contributions

Samples of Your Work
- Your work, captured as drawings, photographs, website, or video
- Writing samples for dramatic writing, technical writing, or general business writing

Legal or Government Records
- Proof of identity such as a copy of your social security card, birth certificate, passport, visas, and/or immigration forms such as green card or work permit
- Military records such as your discharge papers or military service awards

Personal Assessments
- Career Action Worksheets about you, from this textbook
- Results of recognized self-assessments such as the Myers Briggs Type Indicator or the O*Net Interest profiler at "My Next Move"

Experiences
- Volunteer work
- Community and school projects
- List of jobs you have held, including your job titles
- Trips you have made that have broadened your life experience
- Notes from Career Network Meetings

Your Personal Brand (see Chapter 2)
- Your contact (or business) card
- Your Personal Brand Statement
- Your 30-Second Commercials

About Jobs

People, Their Contact Information, Title, and a History of Your Interactions
- People in your Career Network, including Warm Introductions (see Chapter 6)
- Recruiters and Career fair contacts
- Private employment agency contacts
- Potential employers, human resource contacts, hiring managers
- People who might provide a good recommendation or reference
- Mentors and advisors
- Professional, trade, and industry organizations

Sources of Job Listings
- Websites that list jobs you can apply for, including your username and password
- Location of bulletin boards you can check for jobs
- Publications that provide want ads
- Names and addresses of job and career centers
- Hidden job possibilities, insider tips, and jobs suggested by your network or research

Jobs You Want to Apply for
- List of jobs that are of interest, and their location or source
- List of companies you would like to pursue
- Status of your job application process
- Job descriptions of those positions you will or have applied for

Job Application Documents
- Draft resume (see Chapters 4 and 5)
- Draft job applications and master application data sheet (see Chapter 7)
- Cover letter and customized drafts (see Chapter 7)
- Career Action Worksheets about jobs (at the end of chapters in this textbook)

Master Career Portfolio

Job Application Package (for each company and job that you apply to)
- Resume (all formats, see Chapters 4 and 5)
- Cover letter (see Chapter 7)
- Job application (see Chapter 7)

Recommendations and References (see Chapter 7)

Your 30-Second Commercials (see Chapter 2)

LinkedIn® Profile (a copy of it or your LinkedIn URL and name)

Select Samples of Your Work

Set Up Your Career Builder Files

There are many parts and items to keep track of on your job search, so take the time to set up good systems to organize, store, and track the information you will need. When you need to act quickly, you'll be glad you can find the documents you need to print or photocopy.

How you organize your Career Builder Files will depend on the current format of these documents and the way you typically access the Internet. Choose a system that you are comfortable using and that is secure and available to you at any time.

Some of the documents already exist, or are best stored, on paper. Keep these items in an accordion folder with tabs. Keep pages clean and neat (no dog hair or coffee stains) and invest in sheet protectors for certificates and other important documents that exist only on paper. Back up these documents so you don't lose them by taking a photo or scanning them and uploading to a **cloud storage site** such as Microsoft OneDrive, Apple iCloud, Dropbox, or Google Drive. These sites allow you to store and organize files online.

Whichever website, software, or app you use to organize your documents, be sure to do these things:

- Organize the documents into folders.

- Use descriptive folder names and obvious file names. Consider creating an index that will make it easy to find files and information, especially for hardcopy files.

Your Career Network: Who's in Your Network?

Between 70% and 85% of jobs are identified through the job seeker's network. So this is a good time to take a look at your network. Networking specialist Lynne Waymon of Contacts Counts, LLC, says that we all have four networks:

- **Work Net:** people you currently work with. Consider who you know at a paid or volunteer job or from your school project teams and classes.
- **Org Net:** people you know who are part of bigger organizations that you belong to. Consider the company you work for, the school you attend, a religious organization, or sports team you are on. You already have one thing in common—your org—and that gives you a good start at a networking connection.
- **Industry Net:** People who are in your industry. If this list is short, join a professional or industry organization and start building your Industry Network! For example, those in the nursing profession can join the American Nurses Association. Try to get a LinkedIn connection.
- **Life Net:** Your friends and family. They may be friends on your favorite social media platform, or your neighbors, or your family members' friends.

Make a list of the people in your four networks. Career Action Worksheet 6-1 provides a template to help you create your networking lists. During your Job Search Journey, add to this list. Keep contact information current so that you can reach out to these people. Each step of your Job Search Journey can benefit by reaching out to one or more of these four networks.

Source: Make Your Contacts Count: Networking Know-How for Business and Career Success," 2nd edition, 2007, by Anne Barber and Lynne Waymon, publisher AMACOM, a division of American Management Association

- Invest in a flash drive and back up your digital files regularly. (Password-protect the flash drive.)
- Make sure your Career Builder Files are secure and confidential. Don't share your passwords with anyone. If you own a computer, keep your virus protection program up to date. Don't walk away from a computer you use in a public place, such as your school's computer lab. Be especially cautious about visiting questionable websites that could expose your files to computer viruses (such as earn-big-bucks-by-working-at-home sites).

- Back up your files regularly.
- Use password protection to protect your personal information and avoid identity theft.

Once you start applying for jobs and going to interviews, things can move quickly. Organize your Career Builder Files so that you can manage it easily every day. Your email might offer a good option for managing some of your job search information, such as recording people's contact information, tracking which version of your customized job application you sent to each potential employer (see Part 3), employer responses, interview details, follow-up requirements, and communications. You can even take notes about your phone conversations and thoughts about a job and then send these notes to yourself in an email. Be sure to write a descriptive subject line for every email so that you can find it again.

If your email account is cluttered, or if your email address is not professional, consider opening a new account for your job search and career interactions. Be sure to:

- Use a professional name for your account (for example, nadia.basara@gmail.com, not sk8trgrl@gmail.com).

- Use labels or folders to sort the messages. Think through your organization system. For example, you might sort by company name or by month of your job search.

- Record your username and password in a secure place (not in an email).

- Check this account every day!

▶ **CAREER ACTION**

Complete Worksheet 1-2
Organize and Start Your Career Builder Files, page 21

Real World Scenario 1-1   Jamie is finishing her associate's degree and has a part-time job. As she starts to look for a full-time job, she realizes that her desk is *very* disorganized. She missed paying a bill for her apartment and finally found it buried under some important class notes she thought she'd lost. (The business cards she'd been looking for since the career fair two weeks ago were also in the pile of paper.) Keeping up with follow-up phone calls for her job search, juggling her class and work schedule, and taking care of her day-to-day needs is harder than she thought it would be. She knows she needs a system to stay on top of everything.

What suggestions do you have for Jamie as she organizes her desk?

DEVELOP A SUCCESSFUL ATTITUDE

OUTCOME **3**

A Job Search Journey is hard work, and there will be lots of bumps in the road along the way. A positive outlook and positive behaviors can help you stay focused so that you can effectively market yourself to potential employers.

Maintain a Positive Outlook

Research has shown that a positive outlook can have a powerful effect on personal performance, confidence, and even health. Follow the tips below to stay positive during your Job Search Journey.

Positive Thinking and Behavior

Positive thinking is making a conscious effort to be optimistic and to anticipate positive outcomes. **Positive behavior** is purposely acting with energy and enthusiasm. When you think and behave positively, you guide your mind toward your goals and generate matching mental and physical energy. Use positive self-talk; for example, "I did a good job on that report" or "I can do this." Avoid self-critical thinking such as "I'm really nervous about this phone call." Avoid uncommitted language such as "I'll try." Plan to do it.

Positive thinking actually causes changes in the brain that boost your ability to perform and to project enthusiasm, energy, competence, and confidence—qualities that companies look for when they hire and promote employees. A positive attitude is positively infectious!

Positive Visualization

Positive visualization is purposely forming a mental picture of your successful performance and recalling the image frequently. The act of visualizing the successful performance of a skill or an activity in detail increases learning and skill development.

MAKE IT A HABIT
Start with a Positive Attitude

Your Job Search Journey will be an exciting and challenging time. You will be managing new tasks on top of an already busy schedule, while at the same time feeling the thrill of taking power into your own hands for your future. Every day, make it a habit to reaffirm feelings of excitement and confidence as you move forward on this journey. Post your favorite affirmations in places where you will see them often. Here are a few affirmations to get you started:

- I have the power to succeed.
- I will create happiness and success.
- I can make my own choices and decisions.
- I can choose to make changes in every area of my life.
- I am satisfied that I have done my best.
- I have a plan for the future, and my plan is open to change.
- I will not give up on myself.

- I have the power to succeed. (End your pep talk by repeating the first sentence—it says it all.)

Don't be shy about starting your day with a pep talk. Add your own sentences and repeat them to yourself throughout the day. Forming this habit will help you during challenging times throughout life.

Keep it fun. Try a habit-forming mobile app or website, such as MindSet, Way of Life, Done, Strides, and Habitify. Search online for the latest mobile apps.

hfng/Shutterstock.com.

Doing what you love is a constantly changing journey that will last a lifetime.

To strengthen your performance, practice visualizing yourself achieving your career goals with confidence and ease.

Strong Self-Esteem

Projecting confidence requires healthy **self-esteem**, a belief in your abilities and your worth. It is easier to project a confident, competent image when you feel good about yourself.

To build and maintain your self-esteem, surround yourself with a positive environment (positive people, activities, hobbies, reading, and entertainment).

Taking care of your body, mind, and spirit also boosts your self-esteem. Looking and feeling your best boosts your confidence, and others are more likely to respond positively to you.

Set Goals for Your Job Search

Companies stay in business by setting and achieving goals (for example, increased sales, new product development, and lower production costs). Successful job seekers also set goals and work to achieve them. Follow these steps to focus your efforts on achieving your goals.

- **Set long-term and short-term goals.** More ambitious goals such as earning your college degree require more time and are called **long-term goals.** Your **short-term goals** are accomplishments you want to achieve more quickly, such as assembling your Career Builder Files. Short-term goals

OVERCOMING BARRIERS
Take Charge of Your Career Right Now

Many factors in your job search are not under your control, but one thing certainly is—the effort you make to stand out from the crowd every step of the way. To get an edge over other job seekers, (1) set personal goals for this class and for your job search, (2) believe in your drive and commitment to achieve your goals, and (3) use this class and textbook to succeed.

Your Career: How to Make It Happen is filled with practical, realistic advice and actions. When you read each chapter, think about how you can apply the information and advice to your goals and situations. Complete the Career Action Worksheets and be sure to set up and maintain your Career Builder Files. Use the websites that support the textbook.

Set a goal today to use all the resources available to you and to take charge of your career!

include many tasks that you need to complete to achieve a goal, typically in the next few days or next week.

- **Define your goals clearly in writing.** Experts say that writing down your goals strongly increases your likelihood of achieving them. Written goals increase your sense of commitment, clarify the steps and tasks you need to take, and help you remember important details. Use short, specific statements that you can aim for (for example, "Turn in my college application by August 1"). Avoid vague goal statements such as "I will earn more money this year." To help you clarify vague statements, ask yourself questions that define when, where, why, and how such as "How much money do I need to pay my current bills?" and "What is something I would like to use extra money for?"

- **Define the purpose and benefit of your goals.** Link your goals to a realistic, practical, and specific purpose that benefits you. Then add a stretch goal—something you want and that could become a reality if you challenge yourself. To boost your motivation, set high goals that inspire you, whose results you are really excited to achieve.

- **Develop an action plan, set deadlines, and act.** Divide each goal into logical, progressive steps. Set deadlines and priorities for completing each step. Complete the steps on time.

- **Record your progress.** It may seem simplistic, but a long series of check marks on a list can motivate you by providing a sense of accomplishment. Don't get discouraged if you miss an occasional short-term goal—stay focused on your long-term goal. Use an app to help you, such as GoalsOnTrack, Toodledo, Coach.me, and Any.do. Search online for the latest tools.

- **Reward yourself.** Rewards are motivators. Do something nice for yourself as you progress toward achieving your goals.

- **Evaluate your goals and adjust as necessary.** Evaluate your progress toward achieving your goals (see above for a list of **mobile apps** that can help). Experiment with new methods if you're not getting the results you want or if circumstances or priorities change your goals.

Here are some templates for goals that you can set.

- Spend _____ hours a day/week finding job leads.
- Apply for _____ jobs each week/month.
- Complete Phase 1 of my Job Search Journey by _____ [date].
- Complete Phase 2 of my Job Search Journey by _____ [date].
- On the first day of each _____ [week/month], review what I learned from Phases 3 and 4 of my Job Search Journey and adjust my plans based on what I learned.
- Read _____ pages of Chapter 13, "Take Charge of Your Career," every [day/week].

To help you achieve your goals, try some of the time management tips from the next section.

Manage Your Time

Your Job Search Journey may feel like a full-time job. In some ways it is! Even if you are going to school and working, you owe it to yourself to spend enough time on your job search. After all, the job you land will affect where you spend your time, energy, and talents for many years to come.

Time management is an important personal and professional skill. Everyone has 24 hours every day. Successful people learn to make the most of their time by establishing their priorities, setting goals, and using organizational strategies and tools.

- Decide which activities are important and make sure they get done. Plan ahead to avoid doing everything at the last minute.
- Break large projects into small, manageable steps.

- Expect everything to take three times longer than you think it will take.
- Use small amounts of time productively by keeping your task list with you. When you find you have an extra few minutes, take a quick look at your task list and do at least part of a task on your list. Small steps add up!
- Get into the habit of using a planner or calendar (digital or hard copy).
- Make regular appointments with yourself or with a trusted mentor or friend to review your progress and adjust your plans so that you can reach or exceed your personal goals.
- Avoid doing work that makes you feel busy but is not focused on achieving your goals. Cut back on your other commitments or free time if you need to.
- Celebrate when you reach every goal. Do something that energizes you for the next phase of the journey.

Find Positive Support Through Social Networking

Social networking, both online and offline, will be a vital tool in your successful job search. Every chapter of *Your Career: How to Make It Happen* highlights ways to use social networking and social media tools to enhance your job search. If you were an employer, whose would you look at first: the resume of the job seeker your friend or business acquaintance told you about, or one from the long list of applicants who applied through a job board?

As you start your job search, set a goal to use your social networks to maintain a good attitude for success, to motivate yourself, and to find job leads:

- Post your defined, clear **objective** for your career goals on your online **social media profiles**. Make your goals SMART: specific, measurable, achievable, realistic, and time-sensitive.

- Post questions to start conversations with your networks and get Warm Introductions to job opportunities; for example, "Does anyone know someone in this field I could talk to?" and "What qualities do you think make me unique?"

- Stay away from discussing how difficult your job search is in any forum (except in trusted, close relationships). Project an upbeat attitude.

Your social network gives you back what you put into it. It can reinforce your positive outlook—or it can drown you in negativity with well-intended empathy. Use your networks to motivate you and reinforce your own positive thinking.

Real World Scenario 1-2 | Alex knows he needs a better job, but he's overwhelmed by the idea of *looking* for a job. It seems like there are a lot of challenges working against him, including the debt he incurred paying for his family's basic needs while he went back to school. He's worried about how long it may take to find a new job—and it seems like he needed one yesterday. His cousin told him, "Just do it. Start somewhere and see where that takes you." Alex has made that his motto and is moving forward, one step at a time.

What do you think of Alex's motto? Can you imagine your Job Search Journey as a series of small, achievable steps? What resources do you have to feel positive about starting this journey?

Be Proactive

In his world-acclaimed book *7 Habits of Highly Successful People*, Stephen Covey emphasizes that the way people typically approach challenging situations and tasks is a major determinant of their career success.

People who use a **proactive approach** to situations boost their careers by focusing on solving problems, taking positive actions, and taking responsibility for their actions. People who use a **reactive approach** sabotage their success by focusing on problems instead of solutions and by avoiding difficult situations.

Proactive skills include setting goals and plans down in writing, tracking progress, and rewarding yourself for success. Today, it's easier than ever with the support of mobile apps. Using proactive skills leads to many career benefits, such as positive work relationships, improved work performance, better problem-solving skills, increased motivation, and enhanced self-esteem. Practice your best proactive thinking and behavior while you are on your Job Search Journey.

▶ *CAREER ACTION*
Complete Worksheet 1-3
Proactive Success Action Plan, page 27

Chapter Checklist

Check off each item you can do. Reread sections in this chapter to help you complete the checklist.

☐ Name and explain the phase that best describes where I am today in my Job Search Journey. Name and describe the next job search phase. **❶**

☐ Plan and organize my job search by collecting and organizing my records and choosing a method to keep track of communications. **❷**

☐ Describe my plan for further developing and maintaining a good attitude during my Job Search Journey. **❸**

☐ Put my long-term and short-term goals in writing, with concrete steps to achieve each goal. **❸**

☐ Describe a few tips to help me manage my time even better during my Job Search Journey. **❸**

☐ Practice proactive skills that demonstrate a positive attitude and a focus on solving problems. **❸**

Critical Thinking Questions

1. What is the value of knowing about the phases and steps for a job search? **❶**

2. Why is it important to organize your records for your job search? **❷**

3. How will your Career Builder Files help you succeed in your Job Search Journey? What tools will you use? How will you get started? **❷**

4. What effects do positive and negative thoughts, images, and self-talk have on performance? **❸**

5. How would you rate your ability to set goals, manage your time, and be proactive? Would you rate your skills as excellent, good, or needing improvement? What specific actions can you take to stay strong or improve these skills? **❸**

Trial Run

Get Off to a Good Start **❸**

The beginning of your job search is a good time to evaluate some of the skills and attitudes that will help you have a successful journey. Read these statements and rate yourself using the following scale:

Rating Scale: 1 to 4 (1 = not really; 2 = sometimes/somewhat; 3 = usually; 4 = definitely)

_____ A. I tend to be a positive person.

_____ B. I like spending time with positive people.

_____ C. I spend time thinking about my goals.

_____ D. I have a written list of goals with the dates I want to achieve them.

_____ E. When I have something complicated or important to do, I break the task into smaller steps.

_____ F. If something goes wrong, I try to figure out what I could have done differently.

_____ G. If I don't understand something, I'm willing to ask for advice.

_____ H. I tend to keep my files well organized at home and school.

_____ I. I use time management strategies to help me get things done and do them on time.

_____ J. I feel positive about the future.

For your high-scoring statements, consider offering your help to others in these areas.

My high-scoring statements (list from 1 to 3 statements):

Which low-scoring statements do you think will have the most negative effect on you during your Job Search Journey (list from 1 to 3 statements)?

Write a goal for improving in those areas. Find someone—friend, mentor, family member, classmate, instructor—who might be able to help you improve.

My improvement goal:

Who might help me with the low-scoring statements?

This page is intentionally blank.

▶ *CAREER ACTION WORKSHEET*

1-1 Your Job Search Journey ❶

You are on a journey to find your next job (or your first job!) in a career field that you have chosen. As with any journey, it helps to know the parts of the route you will take. Build your understanding of your route by trying this experiment.

1. Without looking in the book, name as many of the five phases of the Job Search Journey as you can remember.

2. Now grade yourself using Figure 1-1 on page 5. How many of the five phases did you remember?

3. Try one more time on a blank sheet of paper. Did your score improve?

4. Most of us get better with practice. Flag Figure 1-1 in your book. Look at the map often to see how far you have advanced on your Job Search Journey.

This page is intentionally blank.

▶ *CAREER ACTION WORKSHEET*

1-2 Organize and Start Your Career Builder Files ❷

Start your Career Builder Files. First, choose the location for your files using the following tips:

- **Online Options and Considerations**
  - o Get access to your files no matter where you are, from any Wi-Fi or web-connected computer or device.
  - o If you use a cloud storage site like Google Docs or Dropbox, you can find files faster using the search feature. Create three files and name them About Me, About Jobs, and Master Career Portfolio.
  - o Email is easy to search by name, content, and date. Even better is an email system that has additional features such as a linked calendar, contacts list, and/or filing system to organize your contact information, documents, and appointments.

- **Offline Options and Considerations**
  - o You could use an accordion folder or large three-ring binder, with tabs labeled About Me, About Jobs, and Final Portfolio sections. You'll need a three-hole punch or lots of sheet protectors for your binder. Create an index that lists the documents behind each tab.
  - o Back up your hard copy documents, such as your driver's license, by taking a photo and storing it somewhere safe where you will be able to quickly find it again.
  - o Back up your critical online files. You can print copies and file them in a safe place, or email copies to yourself so you can access them from another computer. In case of a computer virus or system hack, you want to be able to easily recreate those items that you put a lot of time and thought into creating.

Now, inventory your existing files. In the table on the following page, write down where each document is stored. Make a note of any document you do not have yet, and make a plan for obtaining that document. For some files, the Comments column tells you the chapter where you can find more information about this type of file. Throughout your Job Search Journey, add files to the appropriate section of your Career Builder Files. Your Master Career Portfolio section will likely be empty at the beginning of your Job Search Journey and will become more complete as you go through each phase.

The following table will become the Table of Contents for your Career Builder Files.

Create an inventory of documents for your Career Builder Files	Need it	Have it	Where I put it	Comments
About Me Section				
Records of Completion				
High school transcript				
College transcript				
Diplomas				
Copy of certifications or course completion				
Licenses (especially if related to your field)				
Documentation of Performance				
Awards, such as for perfect attendance on the job and in school, academic accomplishments, employee of the month, participation in academic or career-related fairs or competitions				
Performance reviews from past employers or internship managers				
References (about your skills and performance)				Chapters 4 and 5
Recommendations (about your character), including notes of thanks or praise for previous work and contributions				Chapters 4 and 5
Samples of Your Work				
Your work, captured as drawings, photographs, website, or video				
Writing samples for dramatic writing, technical writing, or general business writing				
Proof of Identity				
Driver's license				
Green card or immigration status				
Military service records				
Social security card				

Create an inventory of documents for your Career Builder Files	Need it	Have it	Where I put it	Comments
Personal Assessments				
Career Action Worksheets about you, from this textbook				
Results of recognized self-assessments such as the Myers Briggs Type Indicator or the O*Net Interest profiler at "My Next Move"				Chapter 2
Experiences				
Volunteer work				Chapter 2
Community and school projects				Chapter 2
List of jobs you have held and your job titles				Chapters 4 and 5
Trips you have made that have broadened your life experience				Chapter 2
Notes from Career Network Meetings				Chapter 6
Your Personal Brand				
Your contact or business card				Chapter 2
Your Personal Brand Statement				Chapter 2
Your 30-Second Commercials				Chapter 2
About Jobs Section				
People, Their Contact Information, Title, and a History of Your Interactions (note when and how you met them and keep track of all email and phone conversations; consider using a job search service or app or an Excel spreadsheet for keeping track of it all)				
People in your Career Network, including Warm Introductions				Chapter 6
Recruiters and career fair contacts				Chapter 6
Potential employers, human resource contacts, hiring managers				Chapters 8 through 10
People who might provide a good recommendation or reference				Chapters 4 and 5
Mentors and advisors				
Professional, trade, and industry organizations				Chapter 6

(Continued)

(Continued)

Create an inventory of documents for your Career Builder Files	Need it	Have it	Where I put it	Comments
Sources of Job Listings				
Websites that list jobs you can apply for, including your username and password				Chapter 6
Publications that provide want ads				Chapter 6
Names and addresses of job and career centers				Chapter 6
Career Fair opportunities (list date, time, place)				
Hidden job possibilities, insider tips, jobs suggested by your network or research				Chapter 6
Jobs I Want to Apply for				
List of jobs that are of interest, and their location or source				Chapters 3 and 6
List of companies you would like to pursue				Chapter 3
Status of my job application process				Chapter 7
Job descriptions of those positions I will or have applied for				Chapter 7
Job Application Documents				
Your resume (master and customized)				Chapters 4 and 5
Your job applications (master and customized)				Chapter 7
Cover letter (master and customized)				Chapter 7
Career Action Worksheets about jobs				

Create an inventory of documents for your Career Builder Files	Need it	Have it	Where I put it	Comments
Master Career Portfolio Section				
Job Application Package (for each company and job that you apply to)				
Resume				Chapters 4 and 5
Cover letter				Chapter 7
Job applications				Chapter 7
Recommendations and References (see Chapters 4 and 5)				
Your 30-Second Commercials (see Chapter 2)				
LinkedIn Profile (a copy of it or your LinkedIn URL and name) (Chapters 2 and 4)				
Select Samples of Your Work				

Add your completed work to your Career Builder Files as the first page.

This page is intentionally blank.

▶ *CAREER ACTION WORKSHEET*

1-3 Proactive Success Action Plan ❸

Take this time to set goals that inspire and excite you for your Job Search Journey.

My job search goal:

Why is this goal important to me? What will happen if I don't achieve this goal?

Steps I will take to achieve this goal:

Action Steps	**Date**
1. Schedule time to assemble my Career Builder Files.	
2.	
3.	
4.	
5.	

What two or three people from my Career Network can provide support during this journey?

What is one question I can post on my social media platforms to start exploring my career goals?

What tools (online, mobile, or offline) can I use to help stay accountable to the goals I have set?

Add your completed work to the "About Me" section of your Career Builder Files.

Know Yourself to Market Yourself

OVERVIEW

Before you start applying for jobs, take a closer look at what you are marketing about yourself. Consider what differentiates you from others who are applying for these same jobs. Next, develop your Personal Brand Statement, the one- or two-sentence statement that captures your strengths and goals. Your Personal Brand Statement becomes the central theme of your 30-Second Commercials and, later, your resume that you use to capture the attention of target employers for jobs that are a good career fit for you.

OUTCOMES

❶ Take a personal inventory of what you can offer an employer, page 30

❷ Start developing your Personal Brand Statement and your 30-Second Commercials, page 36

CAREER ACTION WORKSHEETS

WHERE ARE YOU ON THE JOURNEY?

PHASE 1: Prepare for the Journey
- *The Job Search Journey*
- **Know Yourself to Market Yourself**
- *Picture Yourself in the Workplace*

PHASE 2: Create Your Resume
- *Plan Your Resume*
- *Write Your Resume*

PHASE 3: Apply for Jobs
- *Find Job Openings*
- *Write Job Applications*

PHASE 4: Shine at Interviews
- *Know the Interview Essentials*
- *Prepare for Your Interview*
- *Interview Like a Pro*

PHASE 5: Connect, Accept, and Succeed
- *Stay Connected with Potential Employers*
- *Dealing with Disappointment*
- *Take Charge of Your Career*

PHASE 1 Prepare for the Journey

Step 2, *Know Yourself to Market Yourself*

You are in Phase 1, *Prepare for the Journey*, Step 2. Your goal in this chapter is to assess yourself so that you know what you have to offer an employer and to learn to market yourself effectively and concisely with a great Personal Brand Statement and 30-Second Commercials. You will identify what makes you unique and valuable.

You have more to offer employers than you might realize. Just ask someone else! Often, we are our own worst critics. Take time to see your strengths.

TAKE A PERSONAL INVENTORY

It is time to put together a personal inventory of what you have to offer an employer. When you see it all together, it will be easier to identify what is unique about you and what sets you apart as the preferred job **applicant**. You have already started your inventory as part of assembling the About Me section of your Career Builder Files. In Chapter 2, you will gather information about yourself that will help you learn how to market yourself. In Phases 3 and 4 of your Job Search Journey, you will learn how to share this information with potential employers. This information includes your:

- Education and professional training
- **Work experience**, skills, and accomplishments
- Transferable skills, such as your time management and communication skills

The more information you collect, the better, because you will see patterns that you may not have seen before. Look for those things that create the unique combination that describes you and is connected to your job target.

Your Education and Training

Start by using Career Action Worksheet 2-1 to list your education and training: the name of the school, dates you attended, and your degree or certificate; your career-related courses, skills, and organizational activities; your accomplishments and achievements; and any scholarships, awards, or recognition you received.

Use your own notes, records, social media posts, and memories to create your inventory. Then go deeper by asking people who knew you at the time to look at the worksheet and help you add to it. They may be able to see value in some things that you might take for granted or have forgotten. Be sure to ask your current instructors and classmates.

As you think about your accomplishments, include your specific contributions and what it took for you to achieve success. Consider these examples:

- Helped the other members of the math team to prepare and do practice testing for a competition, resulting in winning second place out of over thirty teams
- Voted treasurer of the senior class because of my strong organizational skills and experience using Microsoft® Excel
- Won Indoor Archery National championship, Intermediate class, as a result of hours of practice three times a week, diligently following the advice of my coach, and learning to keep my equipment in top shape

---

Real World Scenario 2-1 Anisha listed her educational experiences and decided to get some classmates' input. After all, they knew the "real" Anisha. Mike took one look at her list and immediately asked, "Where's the sociology project we did last year, about the health concerns of students?" As a paralegal student, Anisha hadn't thought of including this project, but as she talked about it with Mike, she realized how much work she'd done, from helping decide what questions to ask, to interviewing several students, to creating a spreadsheet to record all the responses. This project was definitely going on her list!

What's a project you spent significant time on? What skills did you develop that you can document in your Career Builder Files so that you can highlight them at a networking event or job interview?

▶ *CAREER ACTION*
Complete Worksheet 2-1
Education, Training, and Activities Inventory, page 45

Your Work Experience and Skills

The next step is to use Career Action Worksheet 2-2 to list your work and other relevant experience. Along with the dates and places, list your duties, accomplishments, achievements, and contributions; the skills and knowledge you developed; and any recognitions or commendations you received. Include internships, cooperative education placements, military career, and volunteer work such as community service projects.

▶ *CAREER ACTION*
Complete Worksheet 2-2
Experience and Skills Inventory, page 47

Your Job-Specific Skills

Job-specific skills are the skills and technical abilities that are needed to perform a particular job. For example, using accounting software to prepare a customized balance sheet for a client is a job-specific skill for a bookkeeper. Realigning brakes is a job-specific skill for an auto mechanic. Operating diagnostic equipment is a job-specific skill for a medical sonographer. See Figure 2-1 for more examples.

Employers expect job applicants to have key job-specific skills so that they do not have to provide as much on the job training. You might be required to take a test or demonstrate that you know how to use a software application or specialized tools and equipment.

Your Contributions

Be specific about your contributions to the project or company when you describe your job-specific skills and duties. For example, "raised 20% more in contributions over previous year" or "my final report was showcased in the organization's newsletter." Your past successes are the best indicator of future

Figure 2-1 Examples of Job-Specific Skills

Licensed practice nurse: Take blood pressure, give injections, apply dressings, give CPR, notate a patient's chart.

Administrative professional: Use MS Office, manage calendar for others, proofread, run copy machine, type 40 wpm.

Carpenter: Frame a house, use a power drill, read and follow building codes, set up scaffolding, read blueprints.

Truck driver: Drive a tractor-trailer truck, use GPS, perform routine vehicle inspections and maintenance, assess load stability.

Electrician: Read technical diagrams, install lighting systems, identify electrical problems, repair and replace wiring, use power tools.

Cosmetologist: Provide cosmetic consulting, understand the attributes of hair, skin, and nails, apply hair color and highlights, give manicures and pedicures, know and follow state regulations.

Sound engineer technician: Operate audio and video equipment, set up and tear down equipment, install equipment in offices and schools, convert audio and video to digital formats.

Computer security specialist: Install security software, educate users about computer security, monitor networks for security breaches, respond to cyber attacks.

successes, so be ready to share this information with potential employers.

Try using the **WHI method** to describe what you have done: what, how, importance. In other words, describe what you did, how you did it, and why the result you achieved was important to the business or organization. Here are some examples:

- A bookkeeper might describe a task as "Balanced books (*what*) using organizational and detail-oriented skills (*how*) to achieve an 'excellent' rating during annual audits (*importance*)."
- A construction supervisor might write, "Supervised a team of framers for the

OVERCOMING BARRIERS
Reveal Yourself Earlier

"It's too soon to create a LinkedIn profile!" That's what many students say. Yet now is a great time to get started as you prepare for your Job Search Journey. Here are a few benefits if you start now:

- Try out your Personal Brand Statement on your social media profiles, and get some early feedback from others about how to make it stronger. You can update your profile several times.

- Become more visible to others in your industry as you build your Industry Net (see Chapter 1). When you network, you can easily share your social media profile so others can read up on you after they meet you.

- When you write up your profile, it's easier to identify gaps that you can fill, and it gives you more time to think about how you want to be viewed by others. Adjust your profile as your view of yourself and your accomplishments grows and develops.

Can you think of other good reasons to start now? How will you use your social media profile to give you a jump start on your job search?

---

summer (*what*), leading them (*how*) to deliver ahead of schedule with only one call-back (*importance*)."

If you practice using the WHI method now, it will help you when you write your resume and cover letters later on in your Job Search Journey.

Your Transferable Skills

Transferable skills, often called soft skills, are abilities that can be applied in more than one work environment—skills that *transfer* from one job to another. Employers pay a lot of attention to a job applicant's transferable skills because they may not provide training on these skills, such as how to manage your time or do basic math or get along with your coworkers. Different jobs emphasize different transferable skills, but most employees would benefit from the transferable skills listed in Figure 2-2.

Consider, for example, a construction supervisor and a bookkeeper. Both must work well with others, manage time, solve

Figure 2-2 Examples of Transferable Skills

Adaptable and flexible	Negotiation and conflict resolution
Analytical	Plans and manages multiple tasks
Attention to detail	Problem-solving
Communication	Public speaking
Critical observation	Reading and writing
Follows directions well	Teamwork and collaboration
Leadership	Time management
Manages deadline pressures	Works independently
Math	

Figure 2-3 Examples of Demonstrating Transferable Skills

School/Volunteer Activity or Part-Time Job	Transferable Skill This Activity Demonstrates
Receiving an A in a business writing course ...	Shows workplace writing skills
Being elected treasurer of the student government ...	Shows that you are trusted and have financial skills
Selling the most advertisements for a soccer tournament program ...	Shows that you have marketing skills and persevere at tasks
Receiving a perfect attendance award ...	Shows that you are dedicated and reliable
Receiving positive comment cards from several customers ...	Shows that you have good interpersonal and customer service skills
Participating in a committee to solve a campus parking problem ...	Shows that you have experience working with others to solve problems
Working on a school or community newspaper ...	Shows that you are accustomed to deadline pressures

problems, read, and communicate effectively. All of these are transferable skills. Both employees will be competent in these areas, even though framing a house and balancing a set of books (a job-specific skill for each field) are not related. See Figure 2-3 for ideas about how you can use your activities and experiences to demonstrate that you have developed a transferable skill.

Employers know that employees who have strong transferable skills are more likely to adapt to new situations and roles. Also, a job-specific skill in one career field might be a transferable skill in a different field. For example, typing 40 words per minute (wpm) is necessary for an administration professional and is a bonus for a lab technician who enters lab results into the computer. When you apply for jobs (Chapter 7), for each job you apply for, you will review and adjust your job-specific skills list to be consistent with what is required for each job. Then you will add the transferable skills that might be a bonus for that job opening (see Figure 2-4).

Identifying your transferable skills is especially important if you have limited work experience or if there are many applicants for a job opening. Think hard about the transferable

Figure 2-4 Examples of Job-Specific Skills Used as Transferable Skills

Welding skills: Be a welder, weld inspector, or welding equipment salesperson.

Teaching or mentoring skills: Teach in public or private schools, provide training to others in a workplace or design training for a workplace, design or deliver online education, manage others.

Healthcare experience and skills: Be a nurse, lab tech, senior companion, online training designer for healthcare workers, healthcare inspector.

Engineering skills: Be an engineer, project manager for technical work, sales tech, government inspector, specifications writer, technical witness for court and insurance cases.

Cosmetology skills: Work at a salon or spa, sell cosmetics to shoppers or to stores, work for a magazine or company that provides reviews of cosmetics, apply makeup for theater, movie, or TV shows.

skills you have developed and demonstrated in your school and volunteer experiences. These "soft skills" may seem unrelated to your job goals, but they help you build valuable transferable workplace capabilities that you can use to market yourself to employers.

Real World Scenario 2-2 Emilio works as a radiology technician but has started to be interested in medical equipment sales after interacting with the sales representatives who call at the clinic. As Emilio thinks about his experience as a radiology technician, he realizes that he has several transferable skills that will help him in sales. He has the technical background and knows the equipment from the technician's perspective better than the sales reps, in some cases. Positive feedback from patients speaks to his customer service skills. He also has fundraising skills from raising money for the community garden.

What are your strongest transferable skills, and how will they help you in different jobs and careers you've considered?

Some of your transferable skills are simply a natural outcome of who you are. They define you. Are you, by nature, punctual? Friendly? Intensely focused? Curious? These natural qualities can be strengths on the job and are qualities that an employer will value. Complete Career Action Worksheet 2-3 to help you inventory your personal qualities.

▶ *CAREER ACTION*

Complete Worksheet 2-3
Personal Qualities Inventory, page 49

It takes courage to grow up and become who you really are.

—*E. E. Cummings*

Tools for Deeper Self-Assessment

Many self-assessment tools and resources are available to help you assess your career

interests and **values** and match the results not only to appropriate careers but also to groups of jobs within a career field. A self-assessment tool can provide insights that can be a powerful aid when you write your Personal Brand Statement (page 55). You can find self-assessments through:

- **Your school's career services counselors.** These counselors can help you take aptitude and interest tests and guide you to information about career fields and jobs in your local job market. The career center may have a license for self-assessments that charge a fee.

- **Government websites.** All levels of government have a strong interest in assuring that employers can find employees and that job seekers know what skills are needed in today's workplace. Explore federal government websites such as Career One Stop (careeronestop.org) sponsored by the U.S. Department of Labor, the Bureau of Labor Statistics' Occupational Outlook Handbook (bls.gov/ooh), and O*NET Online (onetonline.org), as well as your state's employment website.

- **Online.** The Internet has many online self-assessments. We're not talking about the quizzes on Facebook. Try searching online for "Career self-assessment tools online free" and look for links from reputable sources. While the Keirsey Temperament Sorter and Myers-Briggs assessments are extremely helpful and popular, there are several versions online that vary in quality. In this case, your school's counselor might be your best resource to get a good, quality assessment.

Your Online History

Employers will search you online where they will see your online image or brand. Search for yourself on the Internet. What do you see? Here are some questions to consider and act upon as you review your history.

- **What is your brand?** Objectively read your posts and profiles. Can you see patterns that describe who you are, what is important to you, and how you interact with others? These are part of your brand. Which of these do you want to capture in writing and formally add into your Personal Brand Statement?

- **Are you hard to find?** For example, perhaps you have a common name or share a name with a famous or infamous personality. Figure out how to help employers, recruiters, and people in your network find the "real you" online.

- **Can you find your successes?** We often post our successes online. Use your online history to job your memory about things that might demonstrate your skills and showcase your character.

- **Does your history need a cleanup?** It is common for employers and recruiters to search for you online. What will they see? Many companies have expectations regarding your social media presence. Clean up items that do not reflect well on you or are potential in conflict with the company's values. Remove references to inappropriate behavior

- **Are you up-to-date?** Review and update your social media profiles before starting your job search. Recruiters look for total consistency between your resume, application, and online profiles and commonly reject applications if there are inconsistencies. Even something as simple as an inconsistency for dates of employment can set off red warning flags for recruiters and hiring managers. Make sure your profiles are accurate and demonstrate ethical attitudes that are acceptable to potential employers.

MAKE IT A HABIT
Build Greater Self-Awareness

Strong candidates for a job can talk convincingly about their strengths, of course—and they can also demonstrate how a so-called weakness can actually be a strength for a particular job. They do this by focusing on specific skills and personal traits they have.

To be able to communicate about yourself positively and effectively, you have to know yourself! Self-awareness is defined as understanding one's own knowledge, abilities, skills, and personality. To build your self-awareness, think about the process and skills you use to stay organized and accomplish a task or larger project on time—while you are doing the work. Take the time to reflect afterward on what made the project successful. For example, suppose you are going to host a party for your parents' thirty-fifth anniversary, with out-of-town guests, a video of their lives together, a catered dinner, and a DJ.

What skills would you need to use to plan and host a great party?

Learn how to reflect on the things you do well—and learn from the things that don't go as planned. Look at your work objectively and think about what you did well. Practice accepting compliments graciously and speaking confidently about your achievements. These habits will help you prepare for interviews later on in your Job Search Journey.

Danie Nel/Shutterstock.com

▶ *CAREER ACTION*
Complete Worksheet 2-4
Self-Assessments and Career Planning, page 51

DEVELOP YOUR PERSONAL BRAND STATEMENT AND 30-SECOND COMMERCIALS

OUTCOME **2**

Now that you have completed your personal inventory, you are ready for the next step: using the information you collected to develop your **Personal Brand Statement**, a summary of the benefits you offer to an employer. **This power-packed statement describes YOU: it's a tagline or slogan for marketing yourself.** You can use it in conversations and interviews, and you can use this finely crafted statement in your resumes, job applications, and as part of your online presence. It is also the foundation of your 30-Second Commercials.

A strong Personal Brand Statement showcases your strong points and differentiates you from other job applicants. It will be a central theme of your "marketing campaign" to find and get the best fit jobs in your career field. Do not settle for the first statement you write. Many people hone their Personal Brand Statement over several weeks or months as they get new ideas for describing themselves and what they have to offer. You may want to talk to people who know you well to see what they think are your unique strengths. Here is one way to create your Personal Brand Statement:

Step 1: Start with a word or two that describes **you.** Think of things that people say about you or that come naturally to you. For example, you might be a thinker, doer, innovator, educator, caring person, organizer, actor, designer, or salesperson.

Step 2: Next, jot down phrases that describe how you do things or what you are known for. For example, you might be known for delivering results despite challenges, balancing multiple priorities, knowing the right flavor combination, having an eye for color, helping the team work together in harmony.

Step 3: List a few of your personal traits. Think about traits that set you apart from others in the way you do things or the way you approach other people. Examples include doing things with speed, thoroughness, kindness, gentleness, or logic. The personal qualities in Career Action Worksheet 2-3 can help you make this list.

Step 4: Weave the words in Steps 1, 2, and 3 together to create a few lines that describe you. Try out lots of combinations. Change the words and phrases until you feel that the statement describes **you.**

Think of your Personal Brand Statement as your "secret sauce." It describes the ingredient you bring to the team and the workplace. Do you spice things up? Tone things down? Blend with the recipe? Add a splash of color? Are you the specialty spice for specific recipes? Or the go-to spice for every dish? Try to capture those things that you uniquely bring to the table—and that others will want. See the examples in Figure 2-5.

Your Personal Brand Statement should be directly or indirectly connected to your field of study or career field. If you don't see the connection between your statement and what an employer would need, talk to your friends and family members or to a school counselor. Take the first example in Figure 2-5. A person who is a harmonizer and helps people get along together would be great as a team member or team leader in a wide variety of jobs. The best fit careers link a person (their interests, preferences, skills, and personal traits) and their work. Your Personal

Brand Statement is a way to help you see this link more clearly so that you can convince prospective employers that you are the right person for the type of job you want. Use Career Action Worksheet 2-5 to develop your Personal Brand Statement.

▶ **CAREER ACTION**

Complete Worksheet 2-5

Develop Your Personal Brand Statement, page 53

Prepare Your 30-Second Commercials

Think about getting hired as "making the sale." In this case, you and your capabilities are the product. You complete the sale by telling prospective employers what you can uniquely bring to their company that is of value to them. When you can describe how your capabilities will benefit an employer, you are more likely to spot job openings and land jobs that are a good career fit for you. Your Personal Brand Statement is the core of what you are selling.

▶ **CAREER ACTION**

Complete Worksheet 2-6

Make Your Social Presence Job Ready, page 55

To help make the sale, incorporate your Personal Brand Statement into several 30-Second Commercials that you can use in a conversation or interview. A 30-Second Commercial is a "clincher" speech that highlights your strongest qualities and shows how they will benefit the employer. Each commercial will be slightly different depending on who you are talking with and what that person is looking for. As you tailor your commercial to your listener, showcase your good qualities, but do not exaggerate, even a little! Be ready to give an example of a time when you demonstrated each quality.

Figure 2-5 Examples of Personal Brand Statements

I am ...
- A harmonizer who helps people get along together
- A healthcare worker who wants to increase joy among those who struggle to find it
- A highly competitive individual who likes to win at everything I do
- A history nut who wants to help everyone know state and local history and understand how our city got to where we are
- A futurist who applies new technology to make things better and faster
- A person who sees beauty everywhere and tries to capture it in ways that others will appreciate
- A researcher who appreciates the challenge of discovering how things fit together
- A persuasive salesperson with a passion for matching products with people's needs
- A teacher at heart, whose passion is to help other people be the best they can be
- A technically minded person who enjoys a wide variety of technical problem-solving challenges
- A welder who is expert at matching the right welding rod and electrode for every job, whether for sheet metal or aerospace construction
- An entrepreneur who helps businesses succeed and expand
- A lover of the outdoors who likes to help people challenge themselves and stay safe
- A person who loves to keep things organized

Your 30-Second Commercials will be useful in many situations, such as networking events, practice and real interviews, and thank-you notes. You can draw from a commercial for 45-second and even 15-second "spots."

Drafting Your 30-Second Commercials

Career Action Worksheet 2-7 will help you create several 30-Second Commercials. Here is a description of the steps:

Step 1: Personal Brand Statement. Write your Personal Brand Statement at the top of a sheet of paper or key it into a document. This statement is the core of your message, so you should keep it in front of you as you draft your commercial.

Step 2: Education and skills. Write a brief summary of your education, experience, and skills that equip you to do a specific job successfully.

Step 3: Employer needs. List several things you think an employer would need from an employee like you. Beyond experience and skills, there are several things that all employers need, for example, employees who can follow directions; who work well with others and on their own; who are careful and accurate and will not make too many mistakes; and who are flexible, trustworthy, and dependable. Before you draw up your list, learn what employers in your career field seem to be looking for. Read job descriptions and talk with your mentor or people who work in the field. O*Net Online (onetonline.org) has up-to-date, survey-based feedback from many employers in the same career fields about jobs in that field, including the skills, interests, and work styles employees need to have.

Step 4: Put it all together. Draft your 30-Second Commercial so that in a few sentences, you describe who you are, what your education and skills are, and how you will meet an employer's needs. The examples in Figure 2-6 can help you get started. Like Nicole and Brad, you should craft a different commercial for each prospective employer. A good 30-Second Commercial will emphasize different elements of who you are and what you can offer that make you the ideal person for a specific job.

Step 5 Optional: Record it. Consider making a video of your 30-Second Commercial. Not only does this help you practice saying it smoothly, but also you can share it in your own voice with others on social media sites so people see the real you. Some job sites even let you upload this for recruiters and potential employers to see. It can take several hours to get a good 30-second video. Carefully choose the following for your 30-second video project:

- Professional attire, such as you would wear on your first day on the job
- Lighting so that your face is visible and not in shadow
- Background that is plain and simple so there are no distractions
- Sound level that is audible and not overpowering
- What you say with both your words and your body language. Stand tall. Be confident. Say your Personal Brand Statement, but don't read it. Be natural.

You'll want to record your commercial several times. Listen to it; watch it. Have a friend check it out too, with fresh eyes. Each take can get better. Don't shoot for perfection; target for good enough.

Find a job you love and you will never have to work a day in your life.

—Confucius

Figure 2-7 shows the outline of a 30-Second Commercial and shows how Shane delivered his commercial at a professional meeting. Shane's conversation with Lillian probably lasted more than 30 seconds, but notice how Shane uses examples that focus on the employer's needs and that emphasize his results-oriented accomplishments and his transferable skills. Because his outline is short and to the point, he can hone in on the information that will interest Lillian and convince her to take a closer look.

Figure 2-6 Examples of 30-Second Commercials

Example 1: Nicole

Personal Brand Statement: I am a teacher who cares deeply for teenagers and the struggles they go through on their life journey.

Education and Skills: I have a bachelor's degree in education from Central University. I did my student teaching in the eleventh grade at a downtown school where half the students were recent immigrants who did not speak English as their first language. I developed and taught a successful curriculum for beginning composition with an 85% pass rate (high for this school).

Employer's Need	Nicole's 30-Second Commercial
A public school in the inner city that wants someone who understands the challenges in this environment and will stay for at least two years	I am a teacher who cares deeply for teenagers and the struggles they go through on their life journey. My education degree from Central University prepared me well for student teaching in the inner city of Hanover, where half of my students were recent immigrants who were learning to speak English. My passion for helping them helped me relate at their level. Together we achieved an 85% pass rate for basic composition, something that is nearly unheard of at this school. Several students and their parents gave me gifts and thanked me for being their teacher. I would like to make a similar impact at your school.
A private school that seeks teachers who can create curriculum that meets new standards	My education degree from Central University prepared me well for developing curriculum for inner-city high school students. It wasn't easy to teach basic composition to EOL students, but I did it and got praise from my staff teacher as well as from the students. I look forward to the challenge of writing and delivering curriculum to meet the needs of your students because I care deeply about teenagers and their success at this point in their life journey.
A suburban school that wants excellent teachers for its college-bound students	My bachelor of education from Central University plus my own high school education at a premier high school have prepared me to deliver a high-quality program at your high school. While your students are very different from the inner-city students I worked with when I did my student teaching at Hanover High School, I've seen that high schoolers face similar challenges no matter what their economic status: the challenge of discovering who they are and what they will do with their lives. I look forward to helping your students discover these things about themselves in the context of developing their academic skills.

Example 2: Brad

Personal Brand Statement: Creating something from a few pieces of wood, some hardware, and stain still makes me happy. Seeing customers smile when they see my work makes it all that much better.

Education and Skills: I have an associate degree in carpentry from Monty Tech, have passed the U.S. Green Building Council's LEED Green Associate exam, and have a license to practice carpentry in the tristate area. I've built high-end furniture for family members, and I put myself through school working summers and weekends as a framer.

(continued)

Figure 2-6 *(continued)*

Employer's Need	Brad's 30-Second Commercial
A home builder who builds for high-end clientele and wants employees who are flexible enough to do framing and high-end cabinetry	Working with wood is the best thing in the world, in my mind. I've framed houses to put myself through school. And I've built high-end furniture for family members as gifts. I got my LEED Green Associate certificate because I like using the most environmentally friendly materials and design practices. I would like to work on your team and with your customers. In my experience, they are the kind of people who will appreciate taking care of our world, one piece of wood at a time.
A remodeling firm that wants carpenters who do a good job and keep the customers happy so that the firm gets good reviews and repeat business	When I can work with wood, it's a good day. When I can create something from wood that others appreciate, it's a great day. I appreciate your company's focus on cabinetry, and I look forward to making your customers happy. My associate degree in carpentry and my LEED Green certification, plus my experience building high-end furniture as gifts for my family, have helped me build the skills I need to do a great job for you and your customers.
A furniture-building company that needs dependable workers who consistently show up for work so that customer furniture orders are delivered on time	It's so nice to know that there is a company where I could work with wood every day. I enjoy cutting, sanding, shaping, fitting, gluing, and staining wood. My associate degree from Monty Tech has taught me how to work with wood so that what I make not only looks great today but also will last for your customers for decades to come.

Start Building Your Career Network NOW!

It is to your advantage to have numerous people in your network who are in the same industry. They might be in the same job that you are targeting, or are somehow working with people in these jobs, such as managers or team members. These people can:

- give better advice on your resume and job applications,
- provide insights into what to expect in an interview or on the job, and
- offer tips and leads for potential job openings.

Start building your career network now. It takes more than clicking on a "Connect" link to get these people to agree to spend time with you to help you in your job search. Here are things you can do to expand your knowledge of your chosen industry and your career network, especially your Industry Net (see Chapter 1, page 10).

- **Follow** people and companies in your industry.
- **Stay current** in your industry by reading related online posts.
- **Comment** on these posts. You can complement people for their insights, thank them for their perspective, ask a thoughtful question to help you gain deeper insight, or add your own perspective if you are confident on the topic.
- **Connect** with people. Whenever you attend a live professional meeting, meet people and ask if you can connect with them on social media.
- **Search** for people who you think you could learn from, and contact them using social media. (See Chapter 6 for more on Career Network Meetings.)

Over time, you will have a greater online presence among those in your profession, which can build trust and respect.

Figure 2-7 Outline and Delivery of a 30-Second Commercial

Outline	Delivery
Job target: Sales representative with Axion Group, an office technology company **Personal Brand Statement**: I'm an IT technician and sales consultant who enjoys designing customized systems that help businesses run more efficiently. **Experience**: Four years developing small business solutions at Computer Logistics, Inc. **Education**: Associate degree in information technology and certificate in business management **Achievements**: Received "excellent" customer performance ratings at Computer Logistics Voted Most Helpful Clerk by customers at Ralston Pharmacy Increased school newspaper revenues by 20% as advertising assistant **Related job skills and preferences**: Business math Business computing (hardware, networking, data storage, cloud computing, off-the-shelf and proprietary software) Enjoy travel; open to relocation **Transferable skills**: Strong communication and interpersonal skills; highly organized	**Shane** (reading Lillian's name tag with her company name): Hi, I'm Shane Bradley. You're with Axion Group? I read about the opening for a sales representative in the office technology solutions group, and I think I'd be a good fit. **Lillian**: Nice to meet you, Shane. What's your background? **Shane**: I've been with Computer Logistics' small business solutions group for four years. I have hands-on experience in customized solutions, and I have an associate degree in information technology and a certificate in business management. **Lillian**: Do you think you can make the transition from a small business to consulting with Fortune 1000 customers on enterprise-wide solutions? **Shane**: I do. I recognize that there are differences, and I've wanted to move to larger-scale solutions for a while. I keep up with the industry, and I'm strong on the technical side and the sales side. Selling any technical solution is a team effort, and I've been called the ultimate utility player. **Lillian**: That group has a reputation for being tough on new hires. They throw you into the deep end, and it's up to you to sink or swim. **Shane**: The listing says that the reps are on the road about 25% of the time, and that sounds great. You're right, but my career network is only a phone call or LinkedIn message away. And my family has gradually moved away from this area, so I'd jump at the chance to relocate to help turn around an underperforming district. **Lillian**: Do you have a business card? **Shane**: Here it is. My LinkedIn profile has more details. May I give you a copy of my resume? **Lillian**: Could you email it to me? Here's my card with my email address. It was nice meeting you, Shane. **Shane**: Likewise. You'll have my resume tomorrow, Lillian. Thanks again. It was great talking with you.

Showcase Your Personal Brand Statement Online

Your Personal Brand Statement, when written well, serves as "bait" to "hook" the people you network with into a conversation about your current job search goals. Make your Personal Brand Statement visible in as many places as possible online. Consider using a segment or shortened version of your Personal Brand Statement in these places:

- As your email signature to close every communication you send
- In the About section of your Facebook profile
- As your Twitter tagline
- In your LinkedIn summary or headline
- In your standard bio when posting blog posts
- On your business card or contact card (see Chapter 4)

Many social media websites have places for you to showcase your Personal Brand Statement and 30-Second Commercial video. They each have their own audience and benefits. Use Career Action Worksheet 2-6 to help you create a good image on LinkedIn and other social media sites.

> ▶ **CAREER ACTION**
> **Complete Worksheet 2-7**
> Create Your 30-Second Commercials, page 59

Chapter Checklist

Check off each item you can do. Reread sections in this chapter to help you complete the checklist.

- ☐ Document my education, work experience, job-specific skills, and transferable skills. ❶

- ☐ Identify my personal qualities so that I can build some of them into my Personal Brand Statement. ❶

- ☐ Research online self-assessments to help me better understand myself so that I can market myself. ❶

- ☐ Say my Personal Brand Statement out loud. I can read it for now, but eventually I will want to memorize it so I can more easily and comfortably talk to employers about who I am and what I have to offer them. ❷

- ☐ Be prepared to make the sale by delivering at least one polished 30-Second Commercial—written script or video—that emphasizes my qualifications and includes either a WHI statement (what, how, importance) or a measurable accomplishment. ❷

Critical Thinking Questions

1. Why is it important to assess and document your education, work experience, skills, and accomplishments? ❶

2. How are job-specific skills different from transferable skills? Give three examples of each. ❶

3. Why is it useful to identify your personal qualities? ❶

4. Why is it important to be able to talk about your strengths confidently? ❶ ❷

5. Describe at least three ways you can use your Personal Brand Statement. ❷

6. How is a 30-Second Commercial different from a Personal Brand Statement? ❷

7. Why do you need just one Personal Brand Statement and several 30-Second Commercials? ❷

Trial Run

My Dream Job ❶

After you complete Career Action Worksheets 2-5 and 2-7, do this activity with a partner or group.

Pretend you are on a game show and the host asks you to describe yourself. Use your Personal Brand Statement to introduce yourself.

Briefly describe your dream job. Then imagine telling the recruiter at My Dream Job Company why you are the ideal person for this job. You have 30 seconds to make your case.

1. What is the job called?

2. Briefly describe the job.

3. Write your 30-Second Commercial for your dream job, then say it aloud.

4. Now imagine that you are making a YouTube video commercial. Deliver your commercial again, out loud, using your best body language and delivery.

5. If you can, video or record yourself delivering your commercial!

This page is intentionally blank.

▶ CAREER ACTION WORKSHEET
2-1 Education, Training, and Activities Inventory ❶

Complete the sections of this inventory that apply to you: (1) High School Inventory, (2) Post-secondary Education Inventory, and (3) Seminars and Workshops Inventory. Be as thorough as you can. You will use this information again in Part 2 when you plan and write your resume.

HIGH SCHOOL INVENTORY

Name of School: _____

Address: _____

_____

Dates of Attendance: _____ to _____ Date of Diploma: _____

Grade Point Average: _____

Career-Related Courses: List the career-related courses you completed.

Career-Related and Organizational Activities: Describe your involvement in school, extracurricular, community, and other activities (examples: clubs, sports, organizations, volunteer work).

Career-Related Skills: List the skills you developed through your classes and other activities. Include job-specific skills and transferable skills (examples: using MS Office, calculating numbers, using specific tools/equipment, working on a team, persuading others).

Achievements and Awards: List (1) special accomplishments and achievements and (2) awards, recognition, or honors you received in school and through other activities (examples: selected to perform in musical production, second place in marketing competition, award for perfect attendance). Summarize praise you received from instructors, classmates, and others.

POSTSECONDARY EDUCATION INVENTORY

Complete one form for each postsecondary school (beyond high school) you attended.

Duplicate the form if you attended more than one postsecondary school.

Name of School: _____

Address: _____

_____

Dates of Attendance: _____ to _____ Date of Diploma: _____

Grade Point Average: Overall: _____ In Your Area of Study: _____

Career-Related Courses: List the career-related courses you completed.

Career-Related and Organizational Activities: Describe your involvement in school and extracurricular activities, in professional or other associations or organizations, in community activities, in volunteer work, and in other activities.

Career-Related Skills: List the skills you developed through your classes and other activities. Include job-specific skills and transferable skills (examples: preparing oral and written communications, marketing, analytical skills, persuading and leading others, working as a team member).

Achievements and Awards: List (1) special accomplishments and achievements and (2) awards, recognition, or honors you received in school and through other activities. List any scholarships you earned. Summarize praise you received from instructors, classmates, and others.

SEMINARS AND WORKSHOPS INVENTORY

Name of Seminar/Workshop: _____

Offered by: _____ Date(s): _____

Career-Related Concepts or Skills I Learned: _____

Name of Seminar/Workshop: _____

Offered by: _____ Date(s): _____

Career-Related Concepts or Skills I Learned: _____

Name of Seminar/Workshop: _____

Offered by: _____ Date(s): _____

Career-Related Concepts or Skills I Learned: _____

Add your completed work to the "About Me" section of your Career Builder Files.

▶ CAREER ACTION WORKSHEET

2-2 Experience and Skills Inventory ❶

Duplicate the worksheet for each position or project (cooperative work experience, internship, volunteer/paid work experience, military experience) and complete the sections that apply to your situation. Specific and detailed information will help you create your Personal Brand Statement and 30-Second Commercials. You will also use some of this information in your resume.

POSITION (or ACTIVITY) TITLE _____

Name of Organization/Committee _____

Address _____

Phone Number _____ Salary (if paid experience) _____

Circle Type of Experience: (1) Cooperative   (2) Volunteer   (3) Internship   (4) Paid Work

Dates of Employment or Involvement _____

Manager Name/Title _____

JOB DUTIES AND RESPONSIBILITIES

Career-Related Skills

Job-Specific Skills

Transferable Skills

Accomplishments and Achievements. Describe your accomplishments in this position using the WHI (what, how, importance) method (examples: reduced order processing time by 15% by developing more efficient processing methods that enabled the company to take more orders; named employee/volunteer of the month because of punctuality and being helpful to customers; supervised evening shift of five employees independently and allowed the senior manager to take a vacation).

Praise Received. Summarize praise received from managers, coworkers, committee members, and customers.

Job Transition. Why did you stop working here?

Performance rating from manager (circle one):

Excellent   Very Good   Good   Needs Improvement   Poor

Career Builder Files. Add any evidence of your skills, accomplishments, and praise to your Career Builder Files (examples: written performance appraisal, job description, certificate for attending a workshop).

Add your completed work to the "About Me" section of your Career Builder Files.

▶ CAREER ACTION WORKSHEET

2-3 Personal Qualities Inventory ❶

Use this worksheet to identify your strongest personal qualities and work performance traits. These characteristics will help you as you craft your Personal Brand Statement and 30-Second Commercials. Remember, there are no wrong answers when you are defining what is important to you.

Rate yourself on each item by circling high (H), average (A), or low (L).

Add characteristics not listed here that you would give yourself a high rating for.

Respond to the statements at the end of this worksheet.

Personal Quality/Work Performance Trait	Your Rating (High, Average, Low)		
Dependable/responsible	H	A	L
Hard worker	H	A	L
Flexible	H	A	L
Creative	H	A	L
Patient	H	A	L
Perseveres	H	A	L
Punctual	H	A	L
Takes initiative/resourceful/self-starter	H	A	L
Diplomatic	H	A	L
Intelligent	H	A	L
High energy level	H	A	L
Works well with a team	H	A	L
Sets and achieves goals	H	A	L
Plans, organizes, prioritizes work	H	A	L
Outgoing personality	H	A	L
Ability to handle conflict	H	A	L
Optimistic	H	A	L
Realistic	H	A	L
Enthusiastic	H	A	L
Confident/high self-esteem	H	A	L

(Continued)

(Continued)

Personal Quality/Work Performance Trait	Your Rating		
	(High, Average, Low)		
Willing to take on new assignments	H	A	L
Orderliness of work	H	A	L
Attention to detail	H	A	L
Ability to manage time well	H	A	L
Honest, high integrity	H	A	L
Ability to multitask	H	A	L
	H	A	L
	H	A	L
	H	A	L
	H	A	L

Highlight the five high-rated items that best describe you.

Describe five examples of how you have used or demonstrated some of these high-rated qualities and traits in the past.

For each of your top five high-rated items, describe why an employer might want to hire a person with this quality or trait.

Add your completed work to the "About Me" section of your Career Builder Files.

▶ CAREER ACTION WORKSHEET

2-4 Self-Assessments and Career Planning ❶

Complete a self-assessment about your career interests and/or your personal traits. Start with the O*Net Interest Profiler, a self-assessment tool, by visiting www.mynextmove.org and clicking the "Start" button found in the block "Tell us what you like to do." You can also explore your state's employment website. Consider using the free online version of the mini Myers-Briggs Type Indicator quiz and/or the Keirsey Temperament Sorter. (Your school's career center may have a license for self-assessments that require a fee.)

List at least two things you discovered after taking a self-assessment.

Explain why your career choice is a good match with your personality and interests.

Add the results of the online self-assessments to the "About Me" section of your Career Builder Files.

Add your completed work to the "About Me" section of your Career Builder Files.

This page is intentionally blank.

▶ *CAREER ACTION WORKSHEET*

2-5 Develop Your Personal Brand Statement ❷

Use the information in Career Action Worksheets 2-1 to 2-4 to answer these questions.

1. What one or two words describe what you do in general terms? (examples: thinker, doer, innovator, educator, caring person, organizer, actor, designer, worker)

2. What are you known for? (examples: delivering results despite challenges, balancing multiple priorities, being driven to finish tasks, knowing the right flavor combination, having an eye for color, helping the team work together in harmony)

3. What sets you apart from your peers? (examples: speed, thoroughness, kindness, gentleness, logic)

Weave these words into a short statement that describes you in a way that is appealing. See the examples in Figure 2-5 on page 37.

Share your statement with two people whose point of view you respect and value. Ask them these questions:

- Does this statement describe me accurately? How could I improve it?
- Can you think of situations when you have seen me demonstrate this statement?
- If I were to write another statement, what characteristics should I include?

Rewrite your Personal Brand Statement based on what you learned from these discussions.

Add your completed work to the "About Me" section of your Career Builder Files.

This page is intentionally blank.

▶ CAREER ACTION WORKSHEET

2-6 Make Your Social Presence Job Ready ❷

Because employers will look at your online presence, it's important to get it Job Ready.

A. Create or update your LinkedIn Profile.

B. Create or update your profile on one other social media site of your choice.

C. Share your updated profiles with your instructor.

D. Answer the questions at the end of this worksheet.

A. YOUR LINKEDIN PROFILE

LinkedIn was launched in 2003 with the mission of being a place where members can showcase their professional identity and gain insights into the professional world. Today it is the job seeker's most useful **social media platform**. Because over 90% of recruiters rely on LinkedIn, according to data from the Society of Human Resource Management, this worksheet focuses on starting to build your LinkedIn profile.

Set up an account or access your current account. Begin or revise your profile using the following guidance.

- **Headline:** The headline is located under your name and summarizes your brand, your expertise, and what sets you apart from others. It's critical because it's the first thing people see on the search results page when searching LinkedIn and should be compelling enough that viewers are enticed to click and view your profile. Use a few short phrases pulled from your Personal Brand Statement separated by a comma, or vertical | separator. Use search-optimized **keywords. Instead of thinking of what words to describe yourself, think about what words employers and recruiters will search on, and use those so that they find you!** See Figure 2-8 below for an example.

- **Industry:** By specifying the industry you belong to, you are naming your job market and your competition! Make sure your choice is accurate.

- **Summary:** This section contains a compelling summary of your professional story, incorporating industry-specific keywords, and is more than 40 words. A great way to start your summary is by using your full Personal Brand Statement. You can also upload documents and videos to your summary. If you have filmed your 30-Second Commercial (Worksheet 2-7), this is a great place to include it.

Figure 2-8 Image of LinkedIn Profile Page

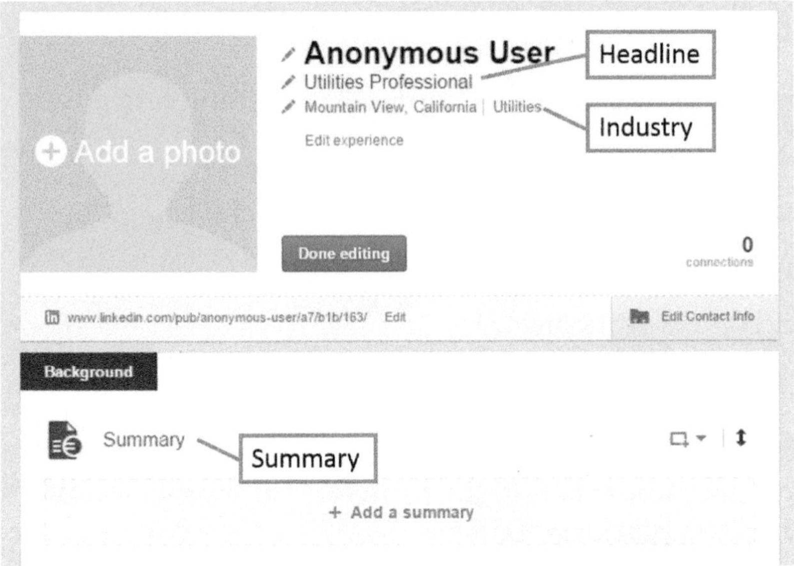

- **Photo:** Serious LinkedIn users include a photo. While it's not required by recruiters, a photo can help build trust, and help people recognize and remember you when you are meeting face to face. If you use a photo, choose a high-quality, high-resolution headshot photo with a neutral background in which you are wearing professional clothing like what you might wear every day on your target job.

B. OTHER SOCIAL MEDIA PLATFORMS

This worksheet provides some guidance on Facebook and Twitter only. There are many other sites that have their own audience and benefits. Choose one that is likely to be popular in your career field.

Which other social media site will you create or review? _____

FACEBOOK

Historically Facebook was primarily a personal social media site, instead of professional. However, Facebook has added a "Jobs" section and features that help connect employers and job seekers. Reinforce your Personal Brand Statement over time on your Facebook profile by sharing industry-related content and status updates. Tell your network about your job search through positive, clear status updates. Categorize your relationships by using the drop-down menu next to an individual's name and adding them to a specific list, such as Close Friends, Acquaintances, or Work Related, so that you can target your status updates as needed.

TWITTER

On Twitter, your personal brand can shine through in your profile description. Use a concise version of your Personal Brand Statement to describe your abilities and goals. Also include relevant hashtags by placing the symbol # before a phrase. A *hashtag* is a way to track conversations between users by organizing and grouping tweets on similar subjects. For example, for the field of technician, you can search #technician and see profiles and comments related to the topic of technician.

C. SHARE YOUR REVISED SOCIAL MEDIA PROFILE WITH YOUR INSTRUCTOR.

D. ANSWER THESE QUESTIONS:

1. What does your professional email signature say today? What changes will you make to it to showcase your Personal Brand Statement?

2. Where will you showcase your Personal Brand Statement? (check the boxes)
[ ] Facebook? [ ] Twitter? [ ] Instagram? [ ] Others? _____

3. Do an Internet Search on your name.

a) Do you see any inappropriate or unexpected information?

b) Are there items online about you that are either unprofessional or contradict your personal brand? What will you change or remove?

c) Check your privacy settings on social media sites. What is hidden from recruiters? What can employers view about you?

This page is intentionally blank.

▶ CAREER ACTION WORKSHEET

2-7 Create Your 30-Second Commercials ❷

Challenge yourself to write three 30-Second Commercials. Follow these steps for each commercial. Do your work on a blank sheet of paper or in a text file on a computer.

Personal Brand Statement: Write your Personal Brand Statement at the top of the page or key it in at the top of the file.

Employer Needs: List skills and traits an employer or interviewer might need or want. You can find these right now by searching online for a few job postings that you might be interested in. You can ignore the location; simply read these real job postings and pick three or four things the employer needs that match your strengths (examples: excellent communication and interpersonal skills; ability to work collaboratively in a team environment and independently; high level of energy and drive to accomplish goals; strong PC skills, including MS Word, Excel, and PowerPoint).

Education and Skills: Briefly summarize your education and skills that relate to the employer's need.

A Draft Commercial: Describe how you can meet the employer's need, backing up that statement with your education and your experience, work performance, and accomplishments. Where possible, use data—numbers or percentages—to describe your successes. Be your authentic self. "Sell" only what you can deliver.

Conciseness: Review your draft and find ways to shorten it. Ask others for ideas and input.

Practice: Practice delivering your commercial out loud for several prospective employers. The goal is not to memorize it word for word, but to have the best words ready in your head when you need them. Strive to sound enthusiastic about what you offer and about your qualifications.

Save your best commercials in your Career Builder Files. As you prepare for interviews, scan these and practice ways to tailor your commercials for each job interview.

Repeat this exercise with two other employer needs (#3 above).

Add your completed work to the "About Me" section of your Career Builder Files.

When one of your 30-Second Commercials is complete enough to share during an interview or important networking meeting, add it to the "Master Career Portfolio" section of your Career Builder Files.

This page is intentionally blank.

Picture Yourself
in the Workplace

OVERVIEW

Chapter 3 expands your perspective on possible target jobs and employers. You will consider how differences between one company and another impact your career success and personal fulfillment.

OUTCOMES

1. Recognize differences in workplace cultures, page 62
2. Explore and describe career fields and workplace possibilities, page 69

CAREER ACTION WORKSHEETS

WHERE ARE YOU ON THE JOURNEY?

PHASE 1: Prepare for the Journey
- *The Job Search Journey*
- *Know Yourself to Market Yourself*
- **Picture Yourself in the Workplace**

PHASE 2: Create Your Resume
- *Plan Your Resume*
- *Write Your Resume*

PHASE 3: Apply for Jobs
- *Find Job Openings*
- *Write Job Applications*

PHASE 4: Shine at Interviews
- *Know the Interview Essentials*
- *Prepare for Your Interview*
- *Interview Like a Pro*

PHASE 5: Connect, Accept, and Succeed
- *Stay Connected with Potential Employers*
- *Dealing with Disappointment*
- *Take Charge of Your Career*

PHASE 1: Prepare for the Journey
Step 3, *Picture Yourself in the Workplace*

You are in Phase 1, *Prepare for the Journey*. Your goal in Step 3 of this phase is to explore career fields. In the exploration process, you will assess yourself to better understand what you want from a job and what you have to offer an employer. Ultimately, this will help you better market yourself for your job target.

Picture yourself on the job. Not just on the first day, but doing the everyday work. Most jobs are one part wonderful and two parts drudgery. That's why they call it WORK. When you can envision a real day-to-day workplace, and see yourself smiling in that future, then you have a goal. That is the job you want to find.

RECOGNIZE DIFFERENCES BETWEEN WORKPLACES

OUTCOME **1**

In the last chapter, you did some self-assessment to see what you had to offer an employer and how you could package this and market yourself. Now let's consider what you are looking for in an employer that will help meet your career desires.

Lifestyle Difference

Consider Sara, Chris, and Jason. Each was graduating with a degree in accounting, but each landed in very different job situations. During a small group exercise in their Career Search class, they noticed that accounting jobs fell into different groups. There were jobs with corporations, small firms, and government agencies. There were jobs related to taxes, payroll, billing, and finance.

Sara was interested in advancing in her career so that one day she could be a manager of others, so her mentor encouraged her to spend more time looking for and applying to accounting positions for corporate and government job openings. In these roles, she would learn from others, work hard to excel, and have opportunities to be a manager within three to five years.

Chris, on the other hand, was more interested in a job that was stable and would allow him to spend time with his family. So Chris avoided jobs related to taxes and payroll because these jobs have big end-of-the-month and tax season periods that often require overtime for people working in the finance and accounting departments.

Jason wanted to be adventurous and travel. He eventually found a job working for a company that does audits of other companies' books across the United States. He had to work as an apprentice for two years and take additional certifications paid for by the company. It was all worth it to him to be able to be in San Francisco this month, in Minnesota

next month. He was rarely home, so he shared an apartment with a friend. His costs were low, and he could save for that sports car he always dreamed of having.

What lifestyle are you looking for? Look at Career Action Worksheet 3-1, "Career Lifestyle Preferences to Consider." Do you want to jet around the country or stick to one place? Do you need defined hours or a flexible schedule to meet responsibilities with children or aging parents? Or do you prefer long hours and possible overtime? Do you need insurance or education payments to get an advanced degree in the future?

As you read **job postings**, try to read between the lines to determine what your employer will need from you if you apply for and get this job. If you are not certain, make a list of questions and try to get answers. You could network with an employee of that company or research the company online using sites like Glassdoor.com, Indeed.com, or Careerbliss.com, where you can see ratings and reviews of companies from employees who work there.

Take time now to think through what you really need. As you begin your job search, look for those things that will best fit with your desired lifestyle. By pursuing companies that best fit your lifestyle, you will be more excited throughout the Job Search Journey, and that excitement will be noticed and rewarded by potential employers.

▶ *CAREER ACTION*
Complete Worksheet 3-1
Career Lifestyle Preferences to Consider, page 75

Preferences on the Job

Most of us think simply about getting a job with fair pay, healthcare benefits, and a nice manager. If you think a little deeper, you are more likely to find jobs that will bring you greater satisfaction.

Unlike Sara, Chris, and Jason, Trevor did not get the advice he needed to help him think deeply about his needs. Trevor wanted to change careers. He was dispirited and wanted to get out from being a fast-food restaurant manager, a job that not only had him leading and motivating his team but also had him working at all hours of the week. He wanted an 8 a.m. to 5 p.m. job doing computer work. He graduated from night school with high honors in computing and landed a great job with a local software firm. However, once he was in the new job, he quickly discovered that his new work was very solitary. Not only was he lonely during the day, but also he had difficulty not bringing work home when he wanted to spend time with his family.

Within a year, Trevor started a new job search. This time, he knew more about what he needed to be happy at work and in life. He moved to a larger firm, where he did computer software repairs with a team of software experts. Knowing there was a team allowed him to focus on his family during his evening hours. Now he is more satisfied with life, both on the job and after hours.

> ▶ *CAREER ACTION*
> **Complete Worksheet 3-2**
> Job Environment Preferences, page 77

Culture: Yours and Theirs

What type of company do you want to work for? Here are a few things to consider:

- Size
- Location of headquarters
- Diversity of employees
- Mission, values, and purpose

Size

Small businesses are the heart of the American economy, large companies make a big impact, and midsize companies have room for growth. You can research the pros and cons for the various sizes of companies—small, midsize, large, international, global, start-up, franchise. Start your research with this article: "Fortune 500 or Startup? How to Tell What Size Company Is Right for You" (www.time.com/money/3834486/big-company-small-company-career/). Small companies have small staffs and may rely heavily on a few employees, often asking them to do things outside their normal job that broaden their skill set quickly. Midsize firms are likely to reinvent themselves every five years or so and may ask you to reinvent yourself and grow with them. Large firms tend to have more well-refined procedures and policies simply to manage the large number of employees, products, customers, and government requirements. All three types of companies can have good jobs to offer and can be good places to work. The question is, where will you find your best fit job? Are you willing to deliver what this size company will need?

Headquarters

The location of the headquarters provides one clue to the reputation and culture of the company. A company based in Sweden (for example, IKEA) or Japan (for example, Toyota) is likely to have a different view of hierarchy, work standards, and procedures than, say, a company based in the Midwest or New York City. For example, European firms tend to have great vacation policies but demand hard work and long hours at other times. Japanese firms tend to value relationships before execution when it comes to decision making, and this can cause culture shock for some U.S. citizens. A company with a Midwest culture might emphasize politeness and friendliness, while a company in New York City could be faster paced. Think about the impact the company's culture will have on you. Will you fit in, will you grow and develop, or will you feel stress as a result of the culture in which you spend your time while you are working?

Diversity of Employees

Try to find clues about the diversity of employees within the company. Ethnic diversity may be mentioned on the company website. For example, some companies post blogs and articles saying that ethnic diversity is something they value because diversity helps them achieve their business goals. You can also do other research online. For example, *Fortune* magazine publishes an annual list of the 100 Best Companies to Work For. You might be surprised by the names of the companies that show up on this list! Many states and cities have similar "Best Companies" listings too. Do the research and then think about how you will fit in.

The Mission, Values, and Purpose

Most company websites state the company's purpose, values, goals, and/or mission statement. Be sure to read these, not only so that you are prepared for an interview but also so that you can decide if this is the type of company you want to be associated with. Which company mission statement appeals to you more: "Combines aggressive strategic marketing with quality products at competitive prices...." or "Provides the best to enable business to excel"? These mission/values/purpose statements may seem like just nice words on a page, yet they provide insight into what is important to the company and how the culture and work environment are on a day-to-day basis. In the first example, employees are likely working in a competitive, sales-driven environment, where performance is measured by reduced costs and increased sales. In the second example, employees may be measured by less tangible business goals such as training hours completed or customer service quality goals. Make sure there is a fit between what enables your productivity and the company's approach to business.

> **Real World Scenario 3-1**   Carol is excited and proud to be graduating this year. She is the first person in her family to graduate with more than a high school degree. It took a lot to achieve this goal. When considering a workplace, she wants a company that will support her as she strives to achieve her life dreams. She has a lot of outside commitments and looks for a company and role that will provide flexibility. She wants to continue growing, so she is looking at companies with strong mentorship programs and maybe an education program. Carol knows that she is a persistent person and good at leveraging all her resources to achieve her goals. She believes her personality will be a good fit with a company that values hard work, diversity, and transparency.
>
> *What company programs and cultural traits do you feel support your personal values?*

Discovering Your Ideal Workplace

Now that you've thought about what your preferences are, how can you discover what companies are a good fit for you? You can find the answer online and through conversations with current employees. Start by looking at well-known companies in your industry or in your location. Then look at two types of sources for information:

- **Company websites and channels:** If you go to the company's website, you can usually find a page about their culture and values. It might be under the heading of "About Us" or under a header for job seekers. Next, look at the company's social media channels, typically LinkedIn or Facebook. This will differ by industry.

- **External reviews:** First, search the web for "best places to work in 20_ _" [enter year]. You'll find lists from many reputable sources. You may be surprised by what you see. It's not just big city companies on

Your Career Network: Ask Your Network, What's It Really Like?

Social media says one thing about a company, the company website says another. What are you to believe? Are the negative social media comments just from poor employees, or does the company say one thing but act differently? A good way to find out is to grow your networks to include people who are closer to the industry and companies where you might be employed. While everyone's truth is different, you can start to gather enough information to spot patterns that will help you decide if a company might match your needs. Here's a short list of questions you can ask people about their workplace to help you understand what's real at their company.

- Tell me about your day today, or tell me about a typical day for you.
- What do you like most about working there?
- How would you describe the environment at work?
- What are the typical personality traits of successful people there?
- What is it like to be on a team?
- How much advancement or training and development are available?
- What's it like for new hires? How long are new hires treated like "new hires"?
- How is the topic of work-life balance treated there?
- How is conflict between people handled? Who resolves conflict?
- What do you wish someone told you before you started working there?

the list. Next, look at websites that collect and share reviews and comments from current and ex-employees. For example, see Glassdoor, Indeed, and CareerBliss. Search on the companies in your areas or on those companies that you are interested in working for.

The Employer/Employee Relationship

There is a two-way relationship between companies and employees. This relationship is a big commitment for both parties.

Companies rely on employees to operate their business, produce high-quality products or services, meet the needs of customers, and help make a profit. Companies invest a great deal of time and money in training, developing, and paying workers. In the United States, costs for employees commonly double or triple the cost of the goods a company sells.

Employees invest considerable time and energy in performing their job duties every day. They expect to be paid for their work; have a safe, healthy work environment; be given the equipment and supplies they need to do their jobs; and have an **immediate manager** who provides just enough direction and support to do the job. Many employees also seek additional training and development on the job so that they can improve their skills.

For the relationship to be successful, the expectations of the company and the expectations of the employee must be met. Be prepared to do your part to understand what is needed of you. Then use the skills you developed—academic, technical, interpersonal, communication—to deliver the job. One company was known for making sure that the relationship was clear and that expectations worked both ways. At the bottom of every paycheck statement were these words: "Now we are even."

> ▶ *CAREER ACTION*
> **Complete Worksheet 3-3**
> Employer/Employee Relationship, page 79

Workplace Behavior and Conduct

Within each company's culture, there are expectations for employee conduct, and there are workplace rules that must be followed. Typical expectations include the following:

- Be courteous to others—customers, workers, your boss—no matter your own mood.
- Be productive, punctual, and reliable.
- Follow health, safety, and security rules.
- Behave ethically, and especially follow the company code of conduct.

Courtesy

Use your network to get the inside scoop on the expected professional behavior before you go for an interview. You will learn more when you are on the job. Here are some examples:

- In many workplaces, there are rules against employees dating and, in all workplaces, sexual harassment is illegal.

- Always treat the customer with respect, no matter what.
- Represent the company well when talking to people outside the company.
- Watch out for unwritten rules. For example, be aware of the proper way to address people, such as in some restaurants, where the senior cook prefers to be called chef. There are lots of rules for talking with managers. Proper etiquette is especially important when navigating the hierarchy, especially related to suggesting changes, expressing your desires, and meeting with upper management without your immediate manager's agreement.

You can learn more about cultural norms and unique workplace manners by observing others and seeking advice from trusted coworkers.

Productivity

A strong work ethic and an inner drive to do a good job go a long way toward a successful career. Here are ways you can demonstrate a strong work ethic. Consider starting to practice these things now, in your current work or school environment, if you are not doing so already:

- Proactively set goals, preferably with your manager, and persistently meet these goals.
- Make sure you understand assignments, know what success looks like, and stick with tasks until they are finished, even when you have little or no supervision.
- Develop efficient work processes and check your work before you turn it in.

Health, Safety, and Security

To protect the company and its employees, the company puts in place many health, safety, and security regulations. Some of

Respect Diversity

An ethical organization is committed to diversity. The ethical employee:

- Understands that the world is diverse and that it will continue to grow more diverse in the future

- Accepts and respects diversity in all people—diversity of ethnicity, race, gender, age, physical ability, and lifestyle

- Understands that there is no place in the workplace for telling or listening to jokes that have racial, ethnic, gender, or lifestyle overtones

The workplace should be an inclusive space. Diversity is about learning from others and showing respect for everyone.

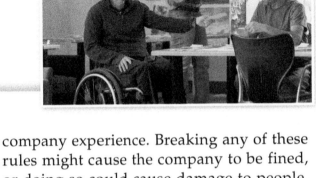

Huntstock/yes/Disability Images.

these are government or other regulatory requirements. Others are requirements from the company's insurance company. Other rules are just common sense or are based on company experience. Breaking any of these rules might cause the company to be fined, or doing so could cause damage to people, equipment, and/or the environment.

Why Teams Work

Teamwork plays an important role in the workplace. It leads to a more productive as well as a more pleasant work environment. Teamwork benefits both employees and companies. Here is how good teamwork looks:

- **Collaboration.** People work together and support one another to achieve team goals.

- **Communication.** Coworkers share information freely to help each other perform effectively.

- **Sharing strengths and resources.** Team members apply themselves willingly. When one member lacks certain skills, another team member is there to fill the gap.

- **Better decisions and solutions.** A team can generate more discussion, ideas, and solutions than a single individual can. Each member adds a unique point of view.

- **Quality.** Team members take pride in the team effort and ensure that each member gets what he or she needs from other team members to turn out the best possible work.

Monkey Business Images/Shutterstock.com.

OVERCOMING BARRIERS
Be Careful with Sensitive Information

iDEAR Replay/Shutterstock.com

At one time or another, every employee has access to sensitive company information or knows things about the company that are not intended to be made public. Be as careful with company information as you are with your personal information. Information your boss shares with you might be confidential, so do not divulge it without permission.

Here are some examples of common actions employees take to secure sensitive information:

* Password-protect confidential documents.

* Do not leave your computer with open documents on the monitor. Close the files before you leave your station.

* Never leave sensitive documents out on your desk for passers by to see.

* When you leave work for the day, store sensitive documents in a locked file cabinet.

* If you use a laptop, password-protect the system. Use a security cable or put your laptop in a locked drawer to avoid it being stolen.

* Keep your company smartphone in a safe location. Use a sign-on password to protect the data, just in case the phone is stolen.

Security rules also serve a purpose. Be sure to wear your company identification badge as required and be cautious about losing it or loaning it out. This also applies to computer equipment and passwords or security codes. Protect the company by protecting its security. Don't be like the intern who left a company computer unsecured in his car. It was stolen. The thieves got access to customers' personal data. It cost the company money to fix the issue and created a lot of bad press and a loss of trust with its customers.

Ethical Expectations

Ethics are guidelines or accepted standards about what is right or wrong. **Business ethics** is the application of ethical principles in a business environment. The principles apply to individual employees and to the entire organization. Many companies publish their **code of ethics** online. When you start work, the company may ask you to sign a statement saying you agree to follow these ethical guidelines. Many companies ask all employees to reread and sign these guidelines annually as a general reminder of expectations. Ethical guidelines are good for you and for the business. Ethical guidelines may touch on legalities and company policy, and they are listed to provide full disclosure about how the company operates. Guidelines often include the following:

* Keep accurate, honest records and accounts.

* Follow local, state, and federal laws.

* Treat employees equally without regard for their sex, age, ethnicity, race, religion, physical ability, or lifestyle.

* Be trustworthy. Conduct business honestly.

As an employee, being honest and ethical includes the following:

* Give a full day of work. This includes showing up on time, not taking long breaks, and not conducting personal communications (text, phone, or Internet use) during work time.

* Do not steal or borrow from your employer. This starts with not taking office pens or

copy paper and includes being trustworthy with money and financial matters.

- Be a trusted team player. For example, don't take credit for a coworker's idea or leave the dirty work, like a jammed printer or copier, for your coworkers.

- Be honest. If you make a mistake, own up to it quickly. Be especially honest on your resume by not exaggerating your **qualifications**, age, or experience.

Consider the job applicant who indicated on her resume that she was fluent in Spanish. Imagine her dismay when the interviewer spoke to her in Spanish until he realized that she didn't understand what he was saying!

You can see some of the best examples of Codes of Conduct here: www.i-sight.com /resources/18-of-the-best-code-of-conduct -examples/. If you want to see the code of conduct for companies before you apply, use their website. Typically, it's under the heading of "About Us" or "Careers." If not, try using the *Search* feature for the website, or the *Contact Us* feature.

Note that many companies run credit checks on job applicants. A good personal credit rating is a sign that an employee knows how to manage money. A poor credit score is a sign that an employee is financially irresponsible or takes financial risks. So consider fiscal responsibility even before you get that job.

Ethical decisions boil down to this: do the RIGHT thing. Because of the consequences, doing the right thing often takes courage. If you don't know the right thing to do, that's a clear sign that you should talk with an immediate manager or trusted mentor.

> ▶ *CAREER ACTION*
> **Complete Worksheet 3-4**
> Internet Research on Corporate Codes of Ethics, page 81

EXPLORE CAREER FIELDS AND WORKPLACE POSSIBILITIES

OUTCOME 2

Your education is a major factor in determining the industry or field in which you will work. Whether you are just starting out or getting close to graduation, you can view career fields and your field of study more broadly to open up a wider range of job opportunities. Job possibilities that match your skills and education are likely to be found in a broad range of workplaces. Figure 3-1 shows a few examples.

In-Demand Industries and Occupations

At any given time, certain industries are growing, while others are declining. If you can link your chosen field and an in-demand industry, you may find more job openings. For example, can you tap into the burgeoning movie-making industry in the Atlanta area? This industry needs more than actors, directors, and camera crews. They need costumers, computer specialists, set builders, electricians, and more.

The United Stated Department of Labor keeps track of which jobs are in demand and average wages for jobs. You can see this in the Occupational Outlook Handbook at www .bls.gov/ooh/. This handbook is free and is revised by the Bureau of Labor Statistics every two years. It has the latest employment projections for the decade and can help you find career information on duties, education and training, and outlook. Here are a few things to see on this website:

- Browse occupations by highest paying, fastest growing, and most new jobs.

- Search for your career group or target job title, or browse occupation groups.

- Search for Occupations (see "Select Occupations" by pay, education, etc.).

Figure 3-1 Common and Possible Job Environments

Education	Most Common Job Environments	Possible Job Environments
Nursing	Hospitals, medical offices	Clinics at schools and industrial settings, healthcare research, medical insurance
Construction	Residential and commercial construction, remodeling	Set building for movies and theater, specialty shipping container construction, building maintenance supervisor, industry in-house construction team
Historian	Schoolteacher, museum	Librarian, corporate archivist, researcher, media fact checker, publications reviewer or writer

In general, jobs in the medical field are likely to continue to increase due to the aging population and the increase in the number of medical research breakthroughs. Computer and information technology (CIT) occupations are growing faster than any other occupation (13%, 2012–2016), due to an emphasis on cloud computing, the collection and storage of big data, and information security. The median annual wage for CIT jobs was $84,580 (2017), which was higher than the median annual wage for all occupations of $37,690. Look for the fields that are growing. How might your chosen career field link to one of the growth industries where there are more opportunities?

MAKE IT A HABIT
Expand Your Perspective

When exploring workplaces, many people make the mistake of believing that what they have experienced in the past or the knowledge that they currently have defines the possible opportunities they can obtain in the future.

On the contrary, the world of work is continually changing based on economic, political, and societal changes, on both a global and local level. Here are some tips to continually expand your perspective:

- Focus on what careers you can do or workplaces you can find instead of what you can't do or can't find.
- Make a habit of questioning your own understanding of your field, including questioning what you've learned from your professors, instructors, and career center. Things change too fast for even our experts to keep up.
- Avoid making assumptions. Check your assumptions against the latest facts and data.

Those who challenge their perspectives find more unique and positive opportunities than those who limit themselves by what was possible in the past.

Elena Elisseeva/Shutterstock.com.

Real World Scenario 3-2 John had originally chosen the field of welding technician because he enjoyed working with his hands. Nearing completion of his degree, he was glad to find that the BLS *Occupational Outlook* showed that welding is a growing field. This reassured him that he had chosen the right field. However, the BLS information also showed that welding technicians were more in demand in places other than where he lived. He decided he would try to find a job in his local area first, and, if absolutely necessary, to look for jobs in other areas even if he had to move to a different state.

Have you looked at the projections for your field? What factors influence the ability to find a job easily and successfully in your field?

As human beings, we tend to seek out varying levels of status, certainty, autonomy, relatedness, and fairness. Seek a job that can provide these elements at a level that you find satisfying.

Explore Online Resources for In-Demand Careers

Finding career information and jobs online has never been easier. Here are some top government resources and commonly used websites that can help you identify a career or job.

Government Websites

- CareerOneStop, www.careeronestop.org/
- USAJOBS, www.usajobs.gov/
- USAgov, www.usa.gov/job-search

Nongovernmental websites

- Careerbuilder.com
- Dice.com
- Glassdoor.com
- Google Careers
- Idealist.com

- Indeed.com
- LinkedIn.com
- LinkUp.com
- Monster.com
- SimplyHired.com

▶ **CAREER ACTION**
Complete Worksheet 3-5
Internet Research on In-Demand Careers, page 83

Explore Possibilities for Hidden Jobs

Most people know how to find jobs in the obvious places. Accountants search among accounting firms or accounting departments. Computer techs might look to computer repair or sales companies. Teachers look for jobs at schools. However, there are **hidden jobs** that you can find.

There are two types of hidden jobs: those that are never posted or advertised and those that are obscure niche jobs. See Chapter 6 to learn more about finding jobs before they are posted by tapping into your **Career Network**. Niche jobs are found by looking for jobs in unexpected places.

Here is one way to broaden your thinking. Search online for a list of companies in your area. Now choose five companies and start brainstorming how you might fit in that company. For example, an accountant might find a job with a lawn cutting service that needs help with billing, accounting, and maybe even taxes and scheduling. Or a biologist might find a job with a microbrewery that needs help in the laboratory with managing and running beer chemistry analysis. Likewise, a psychologist could land a job with a medical insurance company counseling clients with special situations.

Think about your hobbies and interests that go beyond your career choice. Maybe you can combine your interests and career. A person interested in outer space, but with a career in computer hardware repair, could focus his or her job search on companies that build aircraft or that supply products for the U.S. Air Force and NASA. A person with education in carpentry and an interest in art can become the managing supervisor responsible for packing art for shipping at a museum or art warehouse. If you are involved in a club related to your interests, talk to other members for more ideas about jobs that combine your career and interests. Here are a few more examples:

- Brandon's chosen career is in biology, and he is fascinated with food. He started searching for jobs in laboratories that work with food products, food production, and food inspection.

- Megan chose a career in teaching and had an interest in religion. She focused her search on teaching roles at parochial schools, nursery schools run by religious organizations, and the seminary in her town. She also explored teaching at high schools that offered classes in comparative religion.

- Didier loved archery and learned how his muscles worked to make him a better archer. His fascination with muscles for his sport led him to a career in massage therapy that morphed into a career in physical therapy.

Be excited about the possibilities. Your excitement and the resultant energy will be helpful as you continue on your Job Search Journey. By considering your goals for lifestyle, company culture, and job skills—as well as your personal values—you can uncover a much larger pool of jobs that more closely match your needs and interests.

> ▶ *CAREER ACTION*
> **Complete Worksheet 3-6**
> Exploring Possibilities for Hidden Jobs, page 85

Chapter Checklist

Check off each item you can do. Reread sections in this chapter to help you complete the checklist.

- ☐ List some of the lifestyle differences I might experience if I take a job with one company versus another, such as a large, midsize, or small company; or a government, corporate, or not-for-profit organization. ❶

- ☐ Describe the type of things I prefer when working on a job. Consider the physical atmosphere, the emotional atmosphere, the people, and the level of challenge on the job. ❶

- ☐ Describe how I can learn about the differences in culture between potential companies. ❶

- ☐ Considering that the relationship between employee and employer is a fair exchange, make a list of what I can give the employer (beyond spending time), and what my employer might give me in return (beyond a salary or paycheck). ❶

- ☐ Describe why ethical behavior at work is valuable and important for both me and my company. ❶

- ☐ List the types of jobs that I originally thought I was qualified to do. Now add to that list at least three additional jobs based on my research. ❷

- ☐ List what I might be qualified to do in one of the growth industries or in-demand career fields. ❷

Critical Thinking Questions

1. The employer/employee relationship works both ways. Brainstorm some responsibilities the chapter did not list for both the employer to the employee and the employee to the employer. ❶

2. People can grow their skills and experience; however, personality and interests are not as changeable. Your particular personality and interests will be an asset for some jobs and a hindrance for others. For what types of jobs will your personality and interests be an asset? A hindrance? ❶

3. Who else is affected when an organization acts unethically? Who is affected when an employee acts unethically? List at least three groups and explain how each group is affected by unethical actions by an employer and an employee. ❶

4. Why is it important to consider growth industries when exploring careers and thinking about your job prospects? ❷

5. What is the value of considering jobs that are outside of the growth industries and job markets common for your career field? ❷

Trial Run ❶

That's Entertainment! Relationships

Working alone or with a partner, watch a movie or television show centered on a workplace (such as a hospital, an office, a police station, a laboratory, a restaurant, a television station, a hair salon, a coffee shop, a school, or another workplace). Identify and discuss the employee/employer relationships in the movie or TV show that you watched. Then select one character who is an employee. Evaluate that employee on the expectations and skills listed below. For each item, provide an example to explain how the character earned the score.

Rating Scale: 1 to 4 (1 = poor; 2 = okay; 3 = good; 4 = exceptional)

Meets employer's expectations   Score: _____

Example:

Is reliable   Score: _____

Example:

Is prompt and timely   Score: _____

Example:

Performance on the job   Score: _____
Example:

Demonstrates a positive attitude   Score: _____
Example:

Behaves appropriately for this workplace   Score: _____
Example:

Demonstrates thinking and problem-solving skills   Score: _____
Example:

Demonstrates communication and teamwork skills   Score: _____
Example:

Demonstrates technology-related skills
(for example, using technology, equipment, and medical skills)   Score: _____
Example:

Shows a strong work ethic   Score: _____
Example:

Is appropriately attired and groomed for the job   Score: _____
Example:

What advice would you give the character to improve his or her score in any areas of weakness? How could the person improve workplace competencies to be successful on the job and in the future?

▶ CAREER ACTION WORKSHEET

3-1 Career Lifestyle Preferences to Consider ❶

For each item below, mark how important each lifestyle preference item is to you and your job, and jot down your thoughts on why.

My Lifestyle Preferences	Level of Importance			My Thoughts (such as *why* you chose this answer or your experience related to this topic)
	High	Medium	Low	
Stability: My job isn't expected to change much.				
Security: This company will always be here for me, and I will be able to work here for a long time.				
Purpose: This job helps me be part of something bigger to help the world or other people.				
Independent: When I work, I can do it my way with minimal direction.				
Entrepreneurial: I have a large amount of ownership and ability to innovate and implement new ideas. I will take risks to find new markets, products, and profit.				
Competence: I have the chance to do good work every day and improve my skills with experience and training.				
Challenge: This job gives me tough problems and issues that I can solve using my skills and knowledge.				
Balance: When I leave the job, I can leave it behind and focus on my life outside of work.				
Advancement: I have the opportunity to advance to manage more people and business.				
Flexibility: I have the ability to define how I get the results of the work, including when and where I best work.				

List your two most important career lifestyle preferences, and describe why these are important to you.

1.

2.

Jot down your thoughts about what types of industries or jobs might provide this lifestyle.

Add your completed work to the "About Me" section of your Career Builder Files.

▶ *CAREER ACTION WORKSHEET*
3-2 Job Environment Preferences ❶

For each item below, mark how much of this job environment item you would like in your workplace and jot down your thoughts on why.

Description of Job Environment	None 1	2	Some 3	4	A Lot 5	My Thoughts (such as *why* you chose this answer, or where you have seen or experienced this environment)
The Work						
Predictable, structured						
Free to do good work (minimal supervision)						
Intellectually stimulating, contemplative						
Work with people (versus things)						
Hands-on work						
Work with data or ideas (versus people)						
The Interaction with People						
Work together in harmony						
Work together in healthy competition						
Lively, energetic (versus quiet, calm)						
The Emotional Nature						
High risk, edgy						
Get-it-done						
Sense of completion						
Long-term goals						

(Continued)

(Continued)

Description of Job Environment	None 1	2	Some 3	4	A Lot 5	My Thoughts (such as *why* you chose this answer, or where you have seen or experienced this environment)
Creative						
High pressure						
Cutting-edge technologies or thinking						
The Physical Environment						
Orderly and aesthetically pleasing						
Relaxed, easygoing						
Changes regularly						
Lively, upbeat, energized						
Outdoors (versus indoors)						

Jot down your thoughts on a few types of jobs or industries to avoid, based on what you don't want in a job environment.

Jot down your thoughts on a few types of jobs or industries that could provide you with a job that somewhat matches your preferences.

Add your completed work to the "About Me" section of your Career Builder Files.

▶ *CAREER ACTION WORKSHEET*

3-3 Employer/Employee Relationship ❶

Think about a successful employer/employee relationship you have experienced or observed. List the expectations for the job.

Employer's Expectations	Employee's Expectations

Why was it a successful relationship?

Now think of an unsuccessful employer/employee relationship you have experienced or witnessed. Describe the expectations for the job.

Employer's Expectations	Employee's Expectations

In your opinion, was there a mismatch of expectations? How could the situation have been improved or avoided?

Add your completed work to the "About Me" section of your Career Builder Files.

This page is intentionally blank.

▶ CAREER ACTION WORKSHEET

3-4 Internet Research on Corporate Codes of Ethics ❶

Find and report on two organizations in your career field that have posted their codes of ethics online.

Example: Search words are company name + "ethics" OR "code of conduct"

Career Field: _____

Organization 1: _____

What are the key topics covered in the code of ethics?

Organization 2: _____

What are the key topics covered in the code of ethics?

Both Companies

How are the codes of ethics different? Are the differences significant? Explain.

Summarize the code of ethics for this career field.

Based on its code of ethics, which organization would you rather work for? Why?

Add your completed work to the "About Me" section of your Career Builder Files.

This page is intentionally blank.

▶ *CAREER ACTION WORKSHEET*

3-5 Internet Research on In-Demand Careers ❷

Use the CareerOneStop website to research two in-demand jobs that interest you. Write a brief summary of your findings in the areas provided below. Then add to your findings below by repeating your search using a nongovernment website of your choice.

OCCUPATION 1

Job title:

Description:

Tasks:

Skills:

Median salary:

Education required:

Technology skills required:

OCCUPATION 2

Job title:

Description:

Tasks:

Skills:

Median salary:

Education required:

Technology skills required:

Add your completed work to the "About Me" section of your Career Builder Files.

This page is intentionally blank.

▶ *CAREER ACTION WORKSHEET*

3-6 Exploring Possibilities for Hidden Jobs ❷

Your Career Field: _____

List companies in your area in the first column, then use the right column to brainstorm about careers and jobs you might not have considered. See Figure 3-1 for examples.

Companies in your area	Brainstorm, then write down how you might use your skills in this company

Other interests you have that are outside of your career	Brainstorm, then write down how you might combine this interest with your career

In-demand industries	Brainstorm, then write down how you might use your skills in this industry

Add your completed work to the "About Me" section of your Career Builder Files.

This page is intentionally blank.

PHASE 2:
CREATE YOUR RESUME

Create Your Resume

PART 2 Learn how to plan and write winning resumes that capture potential employers' attention and lead to interviews.

LISA MARK

MA Career and College Counselor, Employment Coach

ADVICE FROM THE EXPERT

Your Career Direction, LLC

After 20 years in the recruiting industry, Lisa Mark launched her business, Your Career Direction. Her coaching and counseling practice helps students, recent graduates, and professionals discover and achieve their career direction. Her services include step-by-step career exploration, interview preparation, resume review, networking skills, and more.

From her extensive experience with resumes, Lisa emphasizes marketability over simply cataloging job history and says that "an effective resume is not a data dump of job responsibilities. It is a marketing document that presents your information in a professional, engaging, and easy to read manner." Among the most common errors Lisa sees are "resumes that only list job responsibilities and lack accomplishments, are without any personal style, or make claims without specific facts to back up statements."

Previously, as a corporate recruiter, her process included "a quick scan of about 40 seconds, scanning the top, looking for a Professional Summary, then Job Titles, Company Names and technical skills, and career or industry related keywords. Currently, most resumes are submitted digitally and are searched by computer software for key words. In smaller businesses, employers scan resumes in only 4–6 seconds." Therefore, resumes must be easy to read and well formatted. Employers recruiting recent grads and junior candidates screen out resumes written with poor grammar and typos. On the subject of cover letters, she again emphasizes the importance of expressing your personality, professionalism, and confidence in as few words as possible due to very short attention spans. "The cover letter can be thought of as an appetizer to the main course, which is the resume. If the starter is tasteless, one would have no appetite for the entree."

When sending resumes to job boards or job search engines, Lisa warns job seekers to be sure to apply in a timely fashion. "When using Internet posting sites, apply within 1–3 days of their posting, especially with aggregator sites such as Indeed.com." Lisa recommends that "niche and industry job boards are best, as are jobs posted on LinkedIn" Applicants can increase their chances greatly by applying directly to companies via company websites and by networking.

Lastly, if seeking help with writing your resume, Lisa cautions you to do your research. "Only hire a professional who has knowledge of the current job market and the job search process. Be wary of 'free' resume writing scams and those who market themselves solely as 'Resume Writers' who will lack the comprehensive expertise most job seekers need in order to produce an effective resume."

PLAN for Success

Success is more likely when you have a written plan. Use the online template *Plan for Success* to create your own written plan for successfully completing Part 2, Chapters 4 and 5.

"A goal without a plan is just a wish."

—*Antoine de Saint-Exupéry*

STORIES FROM THE JOB SEARCH

LESLIE KIRKLAND
CPC

Abstract Coder

After a long career in pharmaceutical sales, Leslie felt it was time for a change. Because she felt burned out and wanted to shift to a more personally meaningful career, she sought additional education and achieved the Certified Professional Coder certification in the medical billing and coding field. However, she found the right education wasn't enough to land a job in her new career direction.

So she looked for assistance in writing her resume. She says having assistance helped her "identify my key skills and abilities and write my skills to fit the requirements of the job" as well as "write my accomplishments and how they will benefit a potential employer." Talking to an expert helped her gain an objective outside perspective and display her history in an engaging way to potential employers.

After her revisions, she received compliments from interviewers on her resume, including that it "was easy to read and understand." She also felt her resume "grabbed your attention."

She also used LinkedIn during her job search and used her resume to create her profile. "I updated my entire profile for the job search," she said. She also went one step further to build her credibility and asked for recommendations. "My old manager wrote me a recommendation as well as a former client."

The best piece of advice Leslie received about resumes is to "keep it simple and remember it's a sales tool to sell yourself." Leslie finally landed a job in the medical billing department at a local hospital and feels one huge step closer to having a meaningful career.

OVERVIEW

Creating a winning resume takes effort but will pay off when you are applying for jobs. Your resume will be organized, written, and formatted so that it represents your personal brand and passes screening by software, and by recruiters and Human Resources personnel. Chapter 4 helps you plan and gather the right information for each section of your resume and describes alternative uses for your resume.

<table>
<tr><td>

OUTCOMES

1. Identify the purpose and role of a resume, page 91
2. Describe the main sections of a winning resume, page 93
3. Prepare and request materials related to your resume, page 101

</td><td>

CAREER ACTION WORKSHEETS

4-1: Collect the Right Information, page 107

4-2: Resume Outline, page 109

4-3: Your Qualifications, page 111

4-4: Your Work Experiences, page 113

4-5: Organize Your Experience, page 115

4-6: Enlist References, page 117

4-7: Investigate Winning LinkedIn Profiles, page 119

</td></tr>
</table>

WHERE ARE YOU ON THE JOURNEY?

PHASE 1: Prepare for the Journey
- The Job Search Journey
- Know Yourself to Market Yourself
- Picture Yourself in the Workplace

PHASE 2: Create Your Resume
- **Plan Your Resume**
- Write Your Resume

PHASE 3: Apply for Jobs
- Find Job Openings
- Write Job Applications

PHASE 4: Shine at Interviews
- Know the Interview Essentials
- Prepare for Your Interview
- Interview Like a Pro

PHASE 5: Connect, Accept, and Succeed
- Stay Connected with Potential Employers
- Dealing with Disappointment
- Take Charge of Your Career

PHASE 2 Create Your Resume

Step 1, *Plan Your Resume*

You are in Phase 2, *Create Your Resume*, at Step 1, *Plan Your Resume*. Your goal in this chapter is to understand the sections and purpose of a resume and to gather the right information to write your resume.

Resumes that win are planned. Nothing is typed without thought put into it—just as you should think before you speak, in the virtual world you must think before you type.

WHAT IS A RESUME? OUTCOME 1

A **resume** is a brief document, typically one or two pages, that details your qualifications for a particular job target. It is a record of your relevant work experience and education, and it is a tool for showcasing your personal brand to target employers and for getting job interviews. Your resume is an evolving document that you will revise and rewrite as your experience and job target change over time. Along with a strong networking strategy, a good resume is your key to getting an interview. (See Chapter 6 for more on networking.)

The Role of Resumes in Warm Introductions versus Cold Leads

As you network or conduct Career Network Meetings as described in Chapter 6, you may generate a **Warm Introduction** to a target employer. A Warm Introduction is a two-way connection between you and a potential employer made by a live person. Through Warm Introductions, not only are you introduced to a job opportunity that may not be listed publicly yet, but also a potential employer is introduced to you in a more personable way—from someone they know and trust already. When a member of your Career Network is ready to make a Warm Introduction on your behalf, they expect you to follow up by sending your resume after your meeting. Your resume can then be passed on to the potential employer, along with personal comments from your networking contact about your interaction.

When your Warm Introductions share your resume with others, you get the added benefit of people who not only speak on your behalf to target employers but who also can provide more personal information that simply doesn't appear in a written resume or submitted job applications. The format of your resume plays a very important part in making your Warm Introductions feel proud to share your resume to their coworkers and managers. Often, job seekers build great rapport in person but then write an average or inconsistent resume. It's important to provide a resume that your contacts feel confident to share with others in their companies.

If you learn about and apply to a job opening through an online job board or **job search engine**, this is called a **Cold Lead**. Resumes are even more important because Cold Leads don't have a warm-bodied person who can intercede on your behalf. The resume is the primary tool that captures and presents your qualifications to target employers. According to research conducted by Glassdoor[1] the average job opening attracts 250 resumes! Consider the following steps that a typical large company uses to process resumes received from job postings or Cold Leads, and how they determine which applicants to interview:

1. According to Capterra,[2] 75 percent of employers use **applicant tracking systems (ATS)**, software that automates recruiting processes and tracks applicants. After posting a job opening, employers rely on the software to search each applicant's resume and application for predetermined keywords that match the job description and requirements. Then, the software flags and ranks resumes that appear to be a good fit. The software can also eliminate resumes that do not meet the requirements of the job description. ATS are getting more and more sophisticated every day in an effort to help recruiters process the large quantity of applicants efficiently.

2. Human resources staff members or external recruiters review the resumes selected by the software program. Resumes of the

---

1 www.glassdoor.com/employers/blog/50-hr-recruiting-stats-make-think/
2 www.capterra.com/recruiting-software/impact-of-recruiting-software-on-businesses

most qualified applicants are forwarded to departmental hiring managers. The other resumes are stored for future consideration and are typically deleted after six months.

3. The hiring managers review the resumes and choose applicants to interview based on the applicants' qualifications and whether they appear to be a good fit with the department's needs.

By the end of Phase 2 of your work in this book, you will have an effective resume that can be used in both Warm Introductions and Cold Leads.

Winning Resumes

Employers are always looking for the best match between their needs and applicants' qualifications when they select just a few people to interview. Your resume needs to compel the reader to want to learn more about you and to contact you for an interview. Try to get as many Warm Introductions as you can. The more methods you use to build personal connections with a target employer, the more likely you will be contacted for an interview.

Real World Scenario 4-1 Diana asked for feedback on her resume from a recruiter who mentioned that she needed more industry keywords. Diana did some research and made some updates. She also practiced verbally using the keywords when describing her skills and work experience. At her next Career Network Meeting, she made sure to mention her experience in the context of these keywords. She was happy to be copied on an email sent to the contact's manager that stated, "Diana is very knowledgeable and up to date on the challenges and skills we need. Her resume is attached and shows experiences that I think would potentially make her a great fit with our company."

How can you improve your resume as a tool to be used in both Warm Introductions and Cold Leads?

A compelling, winning resume often does the following:

- Introduces elements of your Personal Brand Statement and 30-Second Commercial that you developed in Chapter 2

- Tells a story, concisely and in compelling language; at a glance, a reviewer should be able to get a feel for your personal brand, strengths, and accomplishments

- Quickly shows that you have the qualifications for the job and can meet the employer's needs

- Contains **search-optimized keywords** and phrases that you think applicant tracking systems and human reviewers will look for to easily filter applicants

- Offers a professional image and an example of good written communication skills

Just as no two resumes are the same, resume guidelines vary widely and are constantly changing. The Internet is a rich resource for staying on top of resume trends and locating additional resume writing and formatting suggestions. As you continue to revise and fine-tune your resume, use your favorite **search engine** to:

- Research resume strategies.
- Find answers to specific resume questions.
- Search for writing and formatting guidelines.
- Find examples of power words and industry keywords.
- Access sample resumes, content ideas, and templates from different careers.
- Locate resume consulting services.
- Investigate quality sites that offer useful resume development advice. See the sample resumes at the companion website.

Well-established sites like Indeed, Monster, CareerBuilder, and About also have helpful articles related to resume writing strategies.

A successful resume generates interviews for both Warm Introductions and Cold Leads.

PLAN YOUR RESUME CONTENT

Writing a great resume typically does not happen on the first try, and you want to write a great resume, one that gets you interviews. You begin by planning and developing a master resume that you can customize for different job openings, relationships, and events. In this section, you will learn about the most common organizational structure and sections used in resumes today.

Your goal is to create a professional-looking document that can be skimmed quickly for key information and read critically to reveal impressive details. You do not have to include everything. In fact you should NOT include everything! It is more important to be purposeful and focused on the top three or four things you want target employers to know about you and your experience. This shows your ability to articulate your strengths clearly and your respect for the employer's time.

In this chapter, you will gather your resume information and create a plan for what to include. In Chapter 5, you will write your resume.

In many situations, your resume can be part of a **Job Application Package** that could include a cover letter, social media profile, recommendations, and a business card. Packages work well to get attention for both Cold Leads and Warm Introductions. Part 3, "Apply for Jobs," discusses using your Job Application Package to help you find job openings and apply.

▶ *CAREER ACTION*
Complete Worksheet 4-1
Collect the Right Information, page 107

Organize Your Resume

The way you organize your resume sections and details helps an employer quickly identify your most important skills, qualifications, and experience. The most common resume organization combines a focus on skills and timeline of work experience. Throughout the resume, including search-optimized keywords is important when you apply through an automated process. For an overview of the sections and general layout, see Figure 4-1.

View Figure 4-2 on page 96 for an example of a resume. Learn more about each component of the resume in the next section.

▶ *CAREER ACTION*
Complete Worksheet 4-2
Resume Outline, page 109

Your Resume Sections

The following sections will fulfill the resume needs of most job seekers. Modify the section headings to best fit your experience and qualifications.

Contact Information

At the top of your resume, list your name, phone number, and email address. Follow these tips:

- Do not use the heading *Resume* or *Contact Information*. The contact information is the only section of a resume that does not have a heading.

Figure 4-1 Resume Outline

- Contact Information
- Professional Profile
- Qualifications
- Work Experience
- Education
- Optional Sections
  - Related Experience
  - Military Service

Figure 4-2 Sample Resume Layout

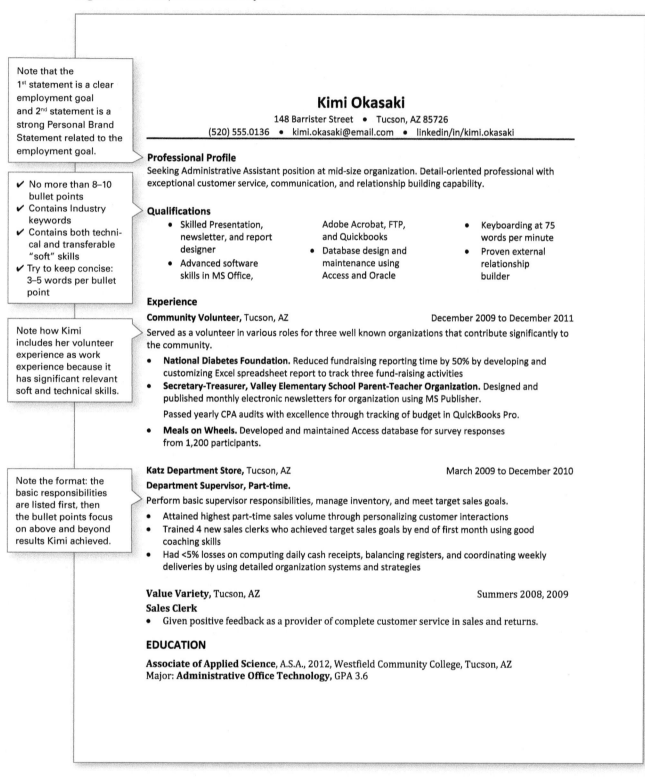

Note that the 1st statement is a clear employment goal and 2nd statement is a strong Personal Brand Statement related to the employment goal.

✔ No more than 8–10 bullet points
✔ Contains Industry keywords
✔ Contains both technical and transferable "soft" skills
✔ Try to keep concise: 3–5 words per bullet point

Note how Kimi includes her volunteer experience as work experience because it has significant relevant soft and technical skills.

Note the format: the basic responsibilities are listed first, then the bullet points focus on above and beyond results Kimi achieved.

Kimi Okasaki

148 Barrister Street • Tucson, AZ 85726
(520) 555.0136 • kimi.okasaki@email.com • linkedin/in/kimi.okasaki

Professional Profile
Seeking Administrative Assistant position at mid-size organization. Detail-oriented professional with exceptional customer service, communication, and relationship building capability.

Qualifications

- Skilled Presentation, newsletter, and report designer
- Advanced software skills in MS Office,

- Adobe Acrobat, FTP, and Quickbooks
- Database design and maintenance using Access and Oracle

- Keyboarding at 75 words per minute
- Proven external relationship builder

Experience

Community Volunteer, Tucson, AZ   December 2009 to December 2011
Served as a volunteer in various roles for three well known organizations that contribute significantly to the community.

- **National Diabetes Foundation.** Reduced fundraising reporting time by 50% by developing and customizing Excel spreadsheet report to track three fund-raising activities
- **Secretary-Treasurer, Valley Elementary School Parent-Teacher Organization.** Designed and published monthly electronic newsletters for organization using MS Publisher.

  Passed yearly CPA audits with excellence through tracking of budget in QuickBooks Pro.

- **Meals on Wheels.** Developed and maintained Access database for survey responses from 1,200 participants.

Katz Department Store, Tucson, AZ   March 2009 to December 2010
Department Supervisor, Part-time.
Perform basic supervisor responsibilities, manage inventory, and meet target sales goals.

- Attained highest part-time sales volume through personalizing customer interactions
- Trained 4 new sales clerks who achieved target sales goals by end of first month using good coaching skills
- Had <5% losses on computing daily cash receipts, balancing registers, and coordinating weekly deliveries by using detailed organization systems and strategies

Value Variety, Tucson, AZ   Summers 2008, 2009
Sales Clerk

- Given positive feedback as a provider of complete customer service in sales and returns.

EDUCATION

Associate of Applied Science, A.S.A., 2012, Westfield Community College, Tucson, AZ
Major: **Administrative Office Technology,** GPA 3.6

- Center justify the information.
- Use the name you are best known by, such as Michael Hardesty, not Michael J. Hardesty III.
- Choose whether you want to include your mailing address. If you are applying for jobs locally, include your address below your name. If you are applying out of city or state, consider whether you expect the potential employer to pay relocation expenses. If yes, include your address. If not, it may be wise to exclude your address.
- Provide one reliable phone number. Put the area code in parentheses to indicate that it is optional depending on where the user is calling from. (While it's on your mind, listen to your voice mail greeting. Do you state your name as you use it in your job search? Does your greeting sound professional?)
- Use an email address that won't get tossed out by an employer's spam filter. An address such as john.waters@email.com is professional and appropriate. Sk8trBoy@email.com is not.
- Consider including your LinkedIn URL or personal website URL if you have space.
- Omit a fax number. Fax machines have been largely replaced by email. If a potential employer wants to fax a document later in the interview or hiring process, you can provide a number then.
- Avoid crowding your contact information, and avoid making it so prominent that the rest of the resume looks compressed. Size 14 font should be the maximum used.
- If your resume is two pages, put your name, email address, and page number at the top of the second page.

See Figure 4-3 for examples of how to format contact information.

Professional Profile

The **Professional Profile** is a two-sentence section that states your job target and the Personal Brand Statement that you developed in Chapter 2.

The job target:

- Can be stated as a job title or the type of work desired. For example: Medical Laboratory Technician; Office Supervisor for a travel agency.
- Should reflect the job title stated in the job posting to help applicant tracking systems highlight your resume. For example: Health Information Technician position requiring the ability to perform detailed clerical tasks, to change priorities quickly, and to communicate well; Server position in an exclusive restaurant where knowledge of international cuisine is an added value.
- Can include one or more of your most important job-specific skills and areas of specialization. For example: Information

Figure 4-3 Contact Information Examples

Appropriate Formatting	Inappropriate Formatting
Michael Hardesty	Michael J. Hardesty III
(871) 424-9873	(871) 424-9873 (home)
781 Right Road	(871) 547-2434 (cell)
Iowa City, IA 52246	Iowa City, IA 52246
mhardesty@gmail.com	greathire@gmail.com
linkedin.com/in/michaelhardesty	

Systems Analyst I position in a financial environment requiring system design, programming, investigation, reporting skills. When worded accurately, these skills could be the search-optimized keywords that applicant tracking systems are looking for.

The second statement is the Personal Brand Statement you developed in Chapter 2. Recall that your Personal Brand Statement showcases your greatest strengths, top transferable skills, and personal qualities that you bring from your varied experiences and achievements throughout your career journey. This statement should clearly distinguish you from other applicants for the job. This statement typically remains the same for each job application, though you can choose to highlight different transferable skills for a specific job. See some examples in Figure 4-4.

Qualifications

The *Qualifications* section is an easy-to-read, bulleted list of skills that ties together your work, volunteer, and education experience into a cohesive picture to highlight why you are the ideal **candidate** for the job. The goal of this section is to support your Personal Brand

Statement by concisely identifyir skills, and capabilities. The Quali tion should contain a bulleted list of the skills you believe you have that set you apart from other applicants. Limit yourself to the top 8 to 10 skills. Each skill should be described in no more than three to five words.

Keep in mind that you will have to prove in the remainder of the resume that the qualifications you listed are valid. If you're struggling, take a look at job postings for your job target. Try to use words from the job description to help include search-optimized keywords that represent your personal brand. Because this section is a quick focal point for employers, use it to emphasize specific and relevant skills, capabilities, and related accomplishments such as the following:

- **Experience-based skills.** This would include tangible skills directly related to the job target's field, like Balancing Ledgers, Top Rated at Customer Service, and Precision Welder.

- **Transferable skills.** Briefly describe how the skills gained on previous jobs are relevant to the current job target. This would include soft skills such as Project Management, Customer Service, Strategic Decision Making, and Marketing Material Design.

- **Software skills.** Most jobs require use of software. If appropriate for the position you are applying for and your experience, list several applications you can use and your level of expertise with each. If your list is long, consider grouping the applications into categories labeled Master, Intermediate, and Basic, or by types of software with just a few examples of each. Employers today assume basic computer skills such as typing and word processing or keyboard skills, so if possible, don't list these. Instead, highlight knowledge you have in specialty applications such as Adobe Photoshop, WordPress, or SAP. (Better yet, set

Figure 4-4 Examples of Well-Written Professional Profiles

> Note how both of these examples follow the format discussed: job target followed by the Personal Brand Statement.
>
> **Example 1:** Gain employment as a master chef at a four-star restaurant. Experienced master chef that excels in a high-stress, multiple-priority environment and adds new creative energy and flavor with knowledge of international cuisine.
>
> **Example 2:** Seeking to serve as a welding technician in the utilities industry. Detail-oriented welder known for not only fixing the problem but also identifying additional needs, with a strong passion for customer satisfaction.

aside time during your job search to take free online tutorials to increase your skills.)

- **Language skills.** Many employers value employees who can communicate in more than one language. If English is not your first language, list your first language as one in which you are fluent. For example: Multilingual: Fluent in English and Spanish, limited conversational French, and reading-only Italian. You can also list TOEFL scores for any language, be it your first or adopted language.

Look back at your completed Career Action Worksheets 2-2 and 2-3 to review your qualifications, skills, and key personal traits. List them in order of importance as they relate to your job target. For example, if you are applying for a position with a doctor's office, start with skills you have learned in your medical courses and your emergency medical volunteer work.

Alternate titles for the *Qualifications* section are Qualifications Summary, Skills Summary, and Career-Related Skills; or, for business and technical careers, Core Competencies. Regardless of the name, spend time crafting a list of concise statements of your skills that let the employer know you are capable of doing the job.

▶ *CAREER ACTION*

Complete Worksheet 4-3
Your Qualifications, page 111

Work Experience

In the *Work Experience* section of a resume, list the jobs you have held, starting with the most recent one, and go backward. Show how both your career has developed and how you have built skills over time. This section serves as the proof or evidence of your Professional Profile and Qualifications. Follow these steps to create a well-written summary for each of your work experiences:

1. First, list your job title and dates of employment.
2. On the next line, list the name of the company.
3. Starting on the third line, write a brief results-oriented description of your basic job responsibilities in one to two sentences.
4. Then create bullet points that focus on what you accomplished above and beyond the base expectations. They should not focus on the *tasks you did*, but *how you contributed to the results*. Follow these tips for writing strong bullet points:

- **Use the WHI method to provide consistent structure.** In Chapter 2, you learned the WHI method: *what* you did, *how* you did it, and its *importance*. Each bullet point should describe a single achievement using the WHI method. In a single sentence, describe the importance of the achievement you made using quantifiable business results, describe what the task was, and end with how you specifically contributed or delivered the result.

- **Think carefully on the How You Did It.** The "how" is what sets you apart from other job seekers. Your unique strengths and personal brand should shine through as you describe how you achieved a result or made a contribution through your job at the company.

- **Measurable examples.** Give specific, measurable examples of your accomplishments—such as increased sales, decreased costs, and reduced errors— ideally with a percentage, a specific dollar figure, the number of items sold, and so on. For example: Increased sales by 45% through skillful negotiation and sales ability with automotive clients. Note the use of WHI. The *what* and *importance* are combined in the statement "Increased sales by 45%"; the remainder focuses on the *how*.

5. After writing your work experiences, skim through all of them. Do you repeat details or tasks in multiple different experiences? Try to remove examples of the same skill and highlight different things you learned in each position you have held.

MAKE IT A HABIT

Keep Your Skills Inventory Up to Date

During your job search and throughout your career, you will want to update your inventory of skills. Get into the habit of reassessing your skills and accomplishments twice a year. As you develop new skills and gain more experience, training, and education, your goals will change or expand.

Repeating the self-analysis activities in this chapter at turning points in your career will also help you identify your skills and see where you could strengthen your skills to set you apart from other job applicants. You can then seek the training and experience you need to help ensure that you will continue to be an asset to employers and will grow in your career.

logoboom/Shutterstock.com

- **Your role in teamwork.** If you worked as a part of a team and do not have a specific result attributed to you as an individual, state your role on the team, what the team's result was, and what you specifically did to aid in achieving the team's result.

- **Highlight promotions or multiple jobs with same employer.** If you have held increasingly more responsible jobs with one employer, show this to demonstrate your reliability and your ability to learn and achieve on the job. List only new responsibilities and accomplishments for each promotion or job title.

See Figure 4-5 for an example of well-written and organized work experience.

All your examples should demonstrate work experience, transferable skills learned, and initiative. Employers consider these qualities real pluses, particularly for entry-level applicants. Furthermore, they demonstrate work ethic, an important quality discussed in Chapter 3.

Review Figure 4-2: Sample Resume Layout on page 96 one more time. This time, pay close attention to the language used in the *Professional Profile, Qualifications,* and *Work Experience* sections and how well they follow the guidelines you just learned.

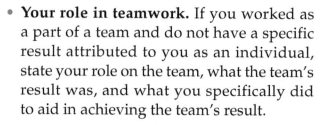

> ▶ *CAREER ACTION*
> **Complete Worksheet 4-4**
> Your Work Experiences, page 113

Education

List your education in reverse chronological order (most recent first). List the technical schools, colleges, and universities you have attended, the years of attendance, and the degree(s) you earned. Include relevant certifications, specialized training, and seminars.

Figure 4-5 Work Experience Example

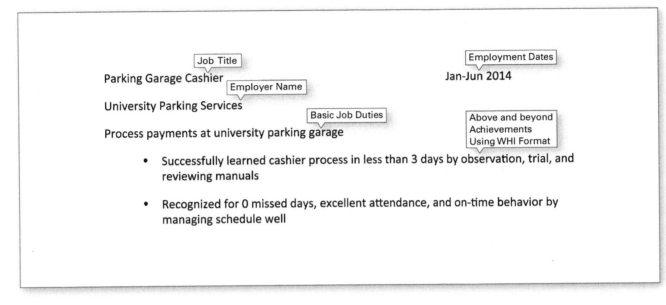

If your overall GPA or your GPA in your concentration area is high and you graduated with honors, include this information on your resume.

Optional Resume Sections

Add the following sections if they are appropriate for your situation.

Related Experience

Use this section to highlight other experience that relates to your job objective. Include activities such as memberships, awards, and leadership positions earned in professional or trade associations; honorary groups; and social, service, and school organizations. Use similar formatting as in the Work Experience section. For the bullet points, highlight the role and key projects you were involved in.

Instead of the heading Related Experience, consider a heading that may be more appropriate for your achievements and experiences, such as Awards and Honors, Volunteer Work, Community Service, Certificates, Activities, or Professional Associations.

Military Service

Include any military experience that is relevant to your job target, emphasizing relevant training, responsibilities, and accomplishments. Highlight any rapid progressions, significant promotion(s), and special commendations.

OVERCOMING BARRIERS
Never Lie or Stretch the Truth on Your Resume

If you can't prove it, it doesn't belong on your resume.

It is *never* acceptable to lie or stretch the truth about your work experience. Employers can and do verify facts on your resume (including degrees, job titles, and dates of employment) and will contact your references. If you are caught in a lie, you will gain a bad reputation and will have no chance of being hired.

Even if you get away with a lie and are hired, the truth has a way of coming out. When your employer discovers the truth, you can be fired.

Consider listing your military record in its own section if it is significant; you can also list it in the Work Experience section. Translate any military jargon into terminology that your readers will understand—and that showcases your relevant qualifications. Make sure to define acronyms and focus on the skills you learned, instead of the specific tasks. Many civilians cannot relate to or understand specific military tasks but can easily understand leadership, strategic decision making under pressure, teamwork, and other skills as being important to the workplace.

Personal Information

In most cases, resumes should not include personal information such as your age and marital status. Fair employment laws prohibit employers from requesting such information. Do not include your photograph; to avoid charges of discrimination, many employers will not consider a resume that includes a photo. The only exception to this rule is a position that requires a certain appearance, such as modeling.

If your job target is in the field of nutrition, physical fitness, or sports and you want to provide relevant information about your own health consciousness, fitness level, or suitability for an active job, do so in a Related Experience section with the name Activities and Awards or something similar. In that section, you can list hobbies and/or accomplishments such as these:

- Completed two marathons in 2011
- Finalist in Eat Your Veggies Recipe Competition, Charleston WV, 2011
- Cofounded running team at Northside Montessori, 2010

What if I Don't Have Enough Experience?

Many first-time job seekers struggle writing their resume because they might not have a lot of work experience. Taking short cuts like increasing font size to fill up the page is not the only (or best!) option. Here are a few tips to help:

- List your part-time and summer work, internships, school projects, volunteer work, and community involvement. Even if the title does not relate directly to your job target, emphasize the transferable accomplishments and skills you developed.
- Consider applying for a freelance or project-basis position in your profession. Websites such as Upwork, Snagajob, and even Craigslist can help you find non-fulltime opportunities to gain some experience.
- Explore obtaining specific certifications or skills not included in your degree program

that you commonly see in job postings. Websites like Skillshare and Udemy as well as professional associations in your field can help you close the gap.

Remember, you have something valuable to offer your target employer! Even though it may not always be easy, use positive visualization, your Proactive Success Action Plan (see Career Action Worksheet 1-3), and your Career Network to help you identify your strengths.

PREPARE RELATED MATERIALS

Your resume is the foundation for the many tools used to find job openings and apply for jobs. Now that you understand the sections of the resume, you are ready to prepare all the materials you will need to write your resume in Chapter 5. You can also be proactive in gathering supporting materials like references, recommendations, and business cards. Getting your resume right allows you to solidify your message to potential employers and repackage it for multiple uses.

Gather Information

How can you get your resume right? Now that you understand the purpose and sections of the resume, start collecting the right data as you begin writing. Follow these strategies as you gather information:

- **Organize and prioritize.** As you review the Career Action Worksheets, note which experiences, skills, projects, and capabilities have the most "wow" factor.

- **Revise language.** Do your descriptions present your experience in the best, most concise way? Take time to draft more powerful language.

- **Collect evidence.** For the experiences and skills you want to highlight, find any

Your Career Network: Find Resumes

In addition to doing online research, a great way to get examples specific to your job target is to use your Career Network. Think about who is in your Career Network. Is there anyone in your major, career field, or related to your job target? Consider connections you feel close or comfortable with. Try asking them for a copy of their resume. Especially if they already have a job in the field you are interested in, you can pick up some tips! Make sure that you reach out in polite, expectation-free language and to thank them later. It's also a way to show that you are serious about your job search and the progress you are making.

iStock.com/Jovanmandic

related documents or presentations. Use these to help remind you of important details that you can add to your resume.

Group your best information for each section. When you gather and organize the right information, writing the resume is a faster, easier process.

> ▶ *CAREER ACTION*
> **Complete Worksheet 4-5**
> Organize Your Experience, page 115

References

When you are selected for a job interview, your potential employer will likely check your references. A job **reference** is a person who can and will vouch for your capabilities, skills, and suitability for a job. References are typically people who have been your instructors and coaches in school or your managers or coworkers in volunteer and paid work environments.

Identify people with whom you have a good relationship and who can confirm (from firsthand observation) your performance on the job, in school, or in other activities. Relatives and classmates are not appropriate references.

The more references you have available, the better prepared you will be for your job search. Many employers request three references they can contact before making a job offer. With a large list of references, you can use the most helpful references for each job you interview for. For example, if one of your references knows someone at a company you are targeting, you can use that person as a reference when you apply for a job there. If you are qualified to work in two career fields, such as retail sales and accounting, ask people in each field to be your references.

Do not assume that a person will agree to be a reference for you. Always ask (and get) permission before using anyone as a reference. Ask if it is okay to share their email and/or phone contact information with employers. Collect the information you find in Career Action Worksheet 4-6.

Your references do not belong on your resume. It is unnecessary to state "References available upon request." However, make sure to plan ahead because it can take time to find contact information and get their agreement! Make a list of your references' names, titles, and phone numbers and take it to interviews. To protect your references' privacy, do not put your references' names or contact information on your resume or a job application. A typical reference sheet is available on the companion website for this textbook.

▶ *CAREER ACTION*

Complete Worksheet 4-6
Enlist References, page 117

Get Effective Recommendation Letters

Written letters of recommendation are an impressive addition to your Job Application Package. Ask the people who agree to be a reference for you and who are most enthusiastic about your job performance, qualifications, skills, and/or abilities if they are willing to write a recommendation letter.

You are more likely to get a positive answer if you can give the person written starter information for the letter. Give the person your resume and a summary of strengths or skills you would like them to cover so that they have concrete information to work with.

File your recommendation letters in the Master Career Portfolio section of your Career Builder Files.

Align Your Business Card

This is a great time to prepare for social networking to find job leads. It often takes 7 to 10 business days to print and receive business cards. Using your business card during networking shows professionalism and can be another place to showcase your personal brand. Sites like Vistaprint and Moo offer a variety of business card templates. View the inspiration gallery at Moo to get some ideas for how to make your business card impactful. Also consider the examples shown in Figure 4-6.

This is also a great time to review social media profiles and see what others are doing to increase their visibility in search results. You can get ideas on how you want to display your skills and write your Professional Profile so it stands out.

> ▶ *CAREER ACTION*
> **Complete Worksheet 4-7**
> Investigate Winning LinkedIn Profiles, page 119

By now, you should understand the value of a resume for use with both Warm Introductions and Cold Leads. You should also understand the sections of a resume and have organized your information enough to begin (in Chapter 5) writing this all-important part of your Job Application Package.

Figure 4-6 Sample Business Card

Chapter Checklist

Check off each item you can do. Reread sections in this chapter to help you complete the checklist.

- ☐ Describe how to use my resume differently with Warm Introductions and with Cold Leads. **❶**
- ☐ Know the requirements for a winning resume. **❶**
- ☐ Describe the overall layout and sections of a resume. **❷**
- ☐ Understand the format and content needed for each section of the resume. **❷**
- ☐ Gather the appropriate information from my Career Builder Files to prepare for writing my resume. **❸**
- ☐ Request references from the right people in my Career Network. **❸**
- ☐ Start researching top-ranking profiles and noting ideas for my LinkedIn profile. **❸**
- ☐ Plan to order business cards. **❸**

Critical Thinking Questions

1. Why are Warm Introductions more effective than Cold Leads? **❶**
2. What characteristics of your resume are reviewed by applicant tracking systems when you pursue Cold Leads? **❶**
3. Why is having a Professional Profile recommended over a simple Objective statement? **❷**
4. What skills should be highlighted in the Qualification section? **❷**
5. What is the purpose of the bullet points in the Work Experience section? **❷**
6. Why is it important to be purposeful about the experiences and strengths you highlight on the resume? **❷**
7. What other ways can you use the information in your resume to showcase your personal brand? **❸**

Trial Run

Review Online Resumes ❷

To write a powerful resume is a difficult task. As you write your resume, get inspiration by reviewing resumes from your industry or job target. However, these samples are only guidelines and are not intended to be used as shown. Search the Internet for "Sample Resumes for {insert your job target here}." Look at the image results and pick one resume to look at.

Copy and paste the text of the sample resume into a word processing file and make the necessary revisions. If more comfortable, print out these resumes and take out your red pen. Put yourself in the shoes of a recruiter or hiring manager.

Edit the revised resume for mistakes and typos. List the changes you would make to improve the resume. Pair up with a classmate and exchange resumes for peer editing.

Evaluate resumes on the following elements:

Rating Scale: 1 to 4 (1 = not really; 2 = sometimes/somewhat; 3 = usually; 4 = definitely)

_____ A. The Objective or Professional Profile includes the job title or required abilities specified by the employer.

_____ B. Qualifications contain keywords that match requirements for the job.

_____ C. Qualifications are concise with three to five words per bullet point.

_____ D. Qualifications are relevant to the stated job objective. Major strengths are included.

_____ E. Work Experiences use the WHI method.

_____ F. Work Experiences focus on quantifiable achievements and results.

_____ G. Work Experience bullet points do not include long run-on sentences or unnecessary words.

_____ H. If work experience is limited, relevant paid and nonpaid internships and volunteer or other pertinent activities are included.

_____ I. The job seeker emphasizes courses, internships, degrees, certificates, and so on that best support the objective.

_____ J. The overall GPA or GPA in the concentration area is included (if impressive).

_____ K. The job seeker emphasizes involvement in professional and other organizations that support the job objective.

_____ L. Relevant awards, achievements, and offices held are included.

_____ M. The overall design is appealing.

_____ N. When you skim the resume for 30 seconds you get a feel for who the applicant is.

_____ O. The content is correct (grammar, spelling, and punctuation).

This page is intentionally blank.

▶ *CAREER ACTION WORKSHEET*

4-1 Collect the Right Information ❶

Use the checklist below to collect all the right files from your Career Builder Files for planning your resume. Read through them and update if needed.

☐   CAW 2-1 Education, Training, and Activities Inventory

☐   CAW 2-2 Experience and Skills Inventory

☐   CAW 2-3 Personal Qualities Inventory

☐   CAW 2-5 Develop Your Personal Brand Statement

List below other information you want to collect and read before you begin writing your resume.

This page is intentionally blank.

▶ *CAREER ACTION WORKSHEET*

4-2 Resume Outline ❷

You are about to create your draft resume.

PART A: Create an outline—resume sections and headings only—for your resume using this worksheet (here or on the product website) or on a word processing document.

PART B: Fill in as much of your information as you can from the documents you collected in Career Action Worksheet 4-1. Don't fill out the Qualifications or Work Experience sections yet. You will focus on these critical sections in later worksheets.

Name _____

Mailing Address _____ (Optional)

Email Address _____ LinkedIn URL _____

Phone Number _____ Website URL _____

PROFESSIONAL PROFILE (*State your current job target and the Personal Brand Statement you developed in Chapter 2.*)

QUALIFICATIONS (*Use terms and keywords that are related to your target job to describe your capabilities and accomplishments.*)

WORK EXPERIENCE (*State your accomplishments in measurable terms whenever possible. Start with the most recent job and list each job in reverse chronological order, ending with your earliest work experience. If you have little actual work experience, list internships, volunteer work, and school projects in this section. Adjust the headings as needed, for example, substituting the school, class, or organization name in place of company name.*)

Company Name _____

Dates of Employment _____

Job Title _____

Company Name _____

Dates of Employment _____

Job Title _____

Company Name _____

Dates of Employment _____

Job Title _____

Company Name _____

Dates of Employment _____

Job Title _____

EDUCATION (*If you have attended more than one school, list the schools in reverse chronological order—the most recent one first. Do not list high school if you have higher-level schooling, unless the high school is considered very prestigious.*)

Name of School	Major(s)/ Minor(s)	Overall GPA/ GPA in concentration area	Degree(s)/ Certificate(s)	Years Attended
_____	_____	_____ _____	_____	_____
_____	_____	_____ _____	_____	_____
_____	_____	_____ _____	_____	_____

RELATED ACTIVITIES/EXPERIENCE (*Include internships, volunteer work, service clubs, organizations, tutoring, class projects, honor groups, internships, leadership positions, awards and honors, associations and memberships, and so on. List the name of the program or organization and the dates you were involved. Briefly summarize your experience, accomplishments, and activities.*)

MILITARY SERVICE (*List branch of service, highest rank, training, areas of specialization, major duties, skills and knowledge developed, honors, location of service, and discharge status.*)

Add your completed work to the "About Jobs" section of your Career Builder Files.

▶ CAREER ACTION WORKSHEET

4-3 Your Qualifications ❷

PART A: Create an initial list of your strengths that could be included in the Qualifications section. Select strengths that you believe would set you apart from other job seekers and/or uniquely define you.

List 10 to 15 areas in which you have expertise and then summarize each area concisely in three to five words.

Strength, Capability, or Expertise Area	Concise Three- to Five-Word Description
Example: For an administrator—Looking at large amounts of data and organizing it so it is easy to read	Logical Visualizer of Data
Example: For a sales professional—Talking to people in a way that makes them feel comfortable to tell me their real problems	Empathetic, Persuasive Marketer
1.	
2.	
3.	
4.	
5.	
6.	

7.	
8.	
9.	
10.	
11.	
12.	
13.	
14.	
15.	

PART B: Revise the outline of the resume you created in Career Action Worksheet 4-3 to include your qualifications.

Add your completed work to the "About Jobs" section of your Career Builder Files.

▶ CAREER ACTION WORKSHEET
4-4 Your Work Experiences ❷

PART A: Practice writing your work experience using the WHI format. Choose three previous experiences, either work experiences or experience from a school project or organization if you have little work experience.

Example:

Department Supervisor, Part-Time

Katz Department Store   March 2012 to December 2012

Perform basic supervisor responsibilities, manage inventory, and meet target sales goals.

- Attained highest part-time sales volume through personalizing customer interactions

- Trained 4 new sales clerks who achieved target sales goals by end of first month using good coaching skills

- Had <5% losses on computing daily cash receipts, balancing registers, and coordinating weekly deliveries by using detailed organization systems and strategies

Create three bullets for each work experience using this formula:

Achieved (important result) _____ for (project or company) _____ by (how did you do it) _____

Work Experience #1:

Job/Role Title: _____

Company Name: _____

Basic Job Duties or Assigned Task: _____

- Achieved _____ for _____
  by _____

- Achieved _____ for _____
  by _____

- Achieved _____ for _____
  by _____

Work Experience #2:

Job/Role Title: _____

Company Name: _____

Basic Job Duties or Assigned Task: _____

- Achieved _____ for _____

  by _____

- Achieved _____ for _____

  by _____

- Achieved _____ for _____

  by _____

Work Experience #3:

Job/Role Title: _____

Company Name: _____

Basic Job Duties or Assigned Task: _____

- Achieved _____ for _____

  by _____

- Achieved _____ for _____

  by _____

- Achieved _____ for _____

  by _____

PART B: Revise the outline of the resume you created in Career Action Worksheet 4-3 to include your work experiences.

Add your completed work to the "About Jobs" section of your Career Builder Files.

▶ *CAREER ACTION WORKSHEET*

4-5 Organize Your Experience ❸

PART A: Look at each of your work and related experiences collected in Career Action Worksheets, 4-1, 4-2, and 4-4 in greater detail. Identify which achievements you would like to highlight for each work experience and put them in order by "wow" factor. Note any evidence you have to support the achievement. Evidence can be presentations, reports, positive feedback received, and so on.

Work Experience 1: _____ **(Job title)**

Project Achievement 1: _____

    Evidence: _____

Project Achievement 2: _____

    Evidence: _____

Project Achievement 3: _____

    Evidence: _____

Work Experience 2: _____ **(Job title)**

Project Achievement 1: _____

    Evidence: _____

Project Achievement 2: _____

    Evidence: _____

Project Achievement 3: _____

    Evidence: _____

Work Experience 3: _____ **(Job title)**

Project Achievement 1: _____

    Evidence: _____

Project Achievement 2: _____

    Evidence: _____

Project Achievement 3: _____

    Evidence: _____

Add your completed work to the "About Jobs" section of your Career Builder Files.

PART B: Revise the resume outline you started in Career Action Worksheet 4-2 to include all of your work experiences, in chronological order. Each bullet point under each experience should be prioritized by what you want the employer to see first and written using the WHI format. Later, when you are preparing for interviews, your list of evidence will help you collect the right documents to take to an interview so that you have physical evidence to support your achievements as you discuss them with an interviewer. **You should now have a draft of your resume.**

Add your updated first draft resume to the "About Jobs" section of your Career Builder Files.

▶ *CAREER ACTION WORKSHEET*

4-6 Enlist References ❸

List at least three people who would recommend you to potential employers. Consider possible references from your education/training and work experience along with respected people who can be personal references. Record their names and information below. Plan to contact each person and ask him or her if they would serve as a reference.

Reference #1:

Name:_____

Title and Organization:_____

Mailing Address:_____

How I know this person:_____

Telephone Number(s):_____

Email Address:_____

Permission to use as reference? (yes/no):_____

Possible to write a formal recommendation letter? (yes/no): _____

Reference #2:

Name:_____

Title and Organization:_____

Mailing Address:_____

How I know this person:_____

Telephone Number(s):_____

Email Address:_____

Permission to use as reference? (yes/no):_____

Possible to write a formal recommendation letter? (yes/no): _____

Reference #3:

Name:_____

Title and Organization:_____

Mailing Address:_____

How I know this person:_____

Telephone Number(s):_____

Email Address:_____

Permission to use as reference? (yes/no):_____

Possible to write a formal recommendation letter? (yes/no):_____

Reference #4:

Name:_____

Title and Organization:_____

Mailing Address:_____

How I know this person:_____

Telephone Number(s):_____

Email Address:_____

Permission to use as reference? (yes/no):_____

Possible to write a formal recommendation letter? (yes/no): _____

Add your completed work to the "About Jobs" section of your Career Builder Files.

▶ CAREER ACTION WORKSHEET

4-7 Investigate Winning LinkedIn Profiles ❸

In preparation for finishing your LinkedIn profile, take some time to review LinkedIn profiles in your career field or job target.

1. Using the search tool on LinkedIn, search for people in your career field. Can you find one or two people in your field?

   a)

   b)

2. Find an example of a LinkedIn profile you like. What makes it a good profile?

3. Find an example of a LinkedIn profile you feel needs improvement. What would you improve?

4. Do another search on your field and look at the results page.

   a) What shows up in the search page from the profile?

   b) Pay special attention to the summary and tagline. What type of words do people use who show up at the top of the page?

Add notes relevant to your resume to the "About Me" section of your Career Builder Files.

This page is intentionally blank.

OVERVIEW

Now that you have gathered the right information, Chapter 5 shows you how to transform the evidence of your experience, skills, and achievements into an effective resume that tells a personal story. Use the activities in this chapter to prepare and evaluate a resume draft, revise it, and format your print and plain text resumes. You will then be ready to apply for jobs through both Warm Introductions and Cold Leads.

OUTCOMES

1 Write your resume following the guidelines for each section, page 122

2 Edit your resume, page 127

3 Format your resume for web, social, and print, page 129

CAREER ACTION WORKSHEETS

5-1: Revise Your Qualifications List, page 145

5-2: Strengthen Your Work Experiences, page 147

5-3: Resume Action Verbs and Keywords, page 149

5-4: Write a Stronger Professional Profile, page 151

5-5: Create Your Draft Master Resume, page 153

5-6: Create Your Plain Text Resume, page 155

5-7: Finish Building Your LinkedIn Profile, page 157

WHERE ARE YOU ON THE JOURNEY?

PHASE 1: Prepare for the Journey
- *The Job Search Journey*
- *Know Yourself to Market Yourself*
- *Picture Yourself in the Workplace*

PHASE 2: Create Your Resume
- *Plan Your Resume*
- **Write Your Resume**

PHASE 3: Apply for Jobs
- *Find Job Openings*
- *Write Job Applications*

PHASE 4: Shine at Interviews
- *Know the Interview Essentials*
- *Prepare for Your Interview*
- *Interview Like a Pro*

PHASE 5: Connect, Accept, and Succeed
- *Stay Connected with Potential Employers*
- *Dealing with Disappointment*
- *Take Charge of Your Career*

PHASE 2 Create Your Resume
Step 2, *Write Your Resume*

You are in Phase 2, *Create Your Resume*, at Step 2, *Write Your Resume*. Your goal in this chapter is to write a powerful, effective master resume.

You are the expert on yourself. What could be easier than writing about something you know about very well? It's up to you to decide how to show the best of yourself.

WRITE YOUR RESUME

Once you have determined the appropriate sections and gathered all the data for your resume, the next step is to thoughtfully write each section and create a **master resume**. A master resume is your perfected resume that is the basis for any customized resumes you create for particular job postings, job applications, or social media platforms. Your goal is to demonstrate convincing evidence of your experience, highlight your unique personality, and provide a concise, cohesive picture of what an employer should expect of you as an employee. You will learn the following four strategies to write a powerful master resume:

1. Be purposeful.
2. Use specific examples.
3. Use action verbs.
4. Optimize keywords for search.

You will then edit and strengthen your draft resume until you are proud to call it your master resume. Finally, you will format your resume for web, print, and social media platforms and by the end of this chapter, you will be ready to apply for jobs in Phase 3 of your Job Search Journey.

Think about the different sections of a resume (Chapter 4). Each of the four strategies can be used in each section. For example, you can use action verbs in both the Qualifications section as well as when discussing your Work Experience. Consider how each strategy can be applied to each section of your resume. Start by writing your Qualifications, Work Experience, and Education, and any Optional sections and apply each of these four strategies. At the end, when all your achievements and strengths are fresh in your mind, write your Professional Profile section.

Be Purposeful

Don't include in your resume every task you were ever assigned to do. Instead, be purposeful about what you will include—and more importantly, what you will exclude—from each section. Review the notes you wrote through the Career Action Worksheets in Chapter 4. For example, if you are targeting a job for a career in accounting, you probably don't need to mention the marketing display design skills you've picked up in your retail jobs, but you might want to include the organization, prioritization, and customer service skills.

For each of your Work Experiences and Related Experiences (education, volunteer, organization, etc.), select just three to five bullet points of the most relevant, impactful experiences that showcase your skills and strengths. As you purposefully choose your bullet points, look for common themes in skills, strengths, and capabilities. Do certain skills come up in multiple work or project experiences? List these skills and strengths and compare them to what you included in Career Action Worksheet 2-2 and Career Action Worksheet 4-3. These skills and strengths form a great start to a purposefully created Qualifications section, especially because you know they are supported by Work Experience examples.

Remember, this is a time for you to craft what you want a potential target employer to see of your history. You can craft this story to highlight successes you've had in both school and work and separate your achievements from mundane, ordinary tasks. That is what will help you stand out from other applicants!

> ▶ *CAREER ACTION*
> **Complete Worksheet 5-1**
> Revise Your Qualifications List, page 145

Use Specific Examples

Once you know what examples you will focus on and highlight for the Work and Related Experience sections, use specific terms to describe your accomplishments. Notice how the specific statements below are more impactful:

General/Vague	Specific
Reduced costs significantly	Reduced costs by 20%
The leading producer	Top producer of 30 employees

The most persuasive resumes describe the job seekers' accomplishments with numbers, percentages, and dollar amounts to emphasize how the accomplishments can meet the potential employers' needs. Use numbers whenever possible to enhance the credibility of your achievements.

It also helps to describe how those results were achieved. Notice how the numbers and further explanation in the example below strengthen the accomplishments further:

- Processed more orders than any other member of the 10-person work team

- Processed 40% more orders than any other member of the team of 10 by creating an efficient process and by leveraging organizational skills

Remember the WHI format you learned in Chapters 2 and 4: **What** you did, **How** you did it, and the **Importance**. Use the WHI format as you finalize the Work Experience section of your resume. It may help to review Career Action Worksheet 4-4.

> ▶ *CAREER ACTION*
> **Complete Worksheet 5-2**
> Strengthen Your Work Experiences, page 147

Use Action Verbs

Review what you've written so far for your Professional Profile and Work Experiences. For each bullet point, have you used action verbs? **Action verbs** suggest a *state of powerful motion* in comparison to "Being" verbs that suggest a *state of existence* (*am, is, are, was, were*).

For example, for a nurse position, try saying "saw patients" instead of "patients were seen." Taking it a step further, try using powerful action verbs such as "provided care to patients," not "saw patients" or "patients were provided care." Action verbs show that YOU took the initiative, and they convey a stronger image of your achievements and contributions. Notice how both examples below use quantifiable results, but the second example with active verbs is more impactful.

- With zero errors, calculations were completed by using Excel software

- Completed calculations with zero errors using Excel software

By using action verbs, you call the reader's attention to the actions and skills you are demonstrating through your experience.

Also avoid "Helping" verbs such as *have, had, may,* or *might*. For example, say "managed" instead of "have managed." Helping verbs sound weaker and can hurt your credibility. They imply you have done something in the far away past, instead of still having a skill today.

Figure 5-1 has a list of common action verbs. Select verbs that convey your qualifications most *powerfully*. Look at the bullet points you wrote using the WHI format. Now, look at the verbs you used. Are there more powerful, active verbs you can use?

Compare the first two examples below and notice the use of more specific action verbs in the second example.

Okay: **Started** inventory tracking system, saving time and increasing efficiency

Stronger: **Designed** and **implemented** inventory tracking system, saving time and increasing efficiency

Designed and *implemented* clearly describe the job seeker's scope of responsibility and convey a greater sense of accomplishment. Here are two more strong examples:

Strong: **Raised $55,000** and **organized** and **trained** volunteers for citywide elder-help campaign

Strong: **Reduced** final ballot processing time by 25% by coordinating school's student body elections

---

▶ *CAREER ACTION*

Complete Worksheet 5-3
Resume Action Verbs and Keywords, page 149

Optimize Keywords for Search

As introduced in Chapter 4, applicant tracking systems are used by employers to narrow down the number of resumes they receive. Employers program the system to look for specific keywords, usually based on the job posting and job description. The software combs through resumes to surface the applicants with the required skills, knowledge, and capabilities for a position. When you take time to reflect and include these keywords in your resume, you are optimizing your resume for search.

Figure 5-1 Examples of Resume Action Verbs

accomplish	conduct	evaluate	manage	prove	select
adapt	consolidate	examine	monitor	provide	sell
administer	control	execute	motivate	publish	serve
advise	coordinate	expand	negotiate	purchase	setup
analyze	create	expedite	obtain	raise	solve
approve	customize	forecast	operate	rate	specialize
arrange	delegate	formulate	order	recommend	start
assemble	deliver	generate	organize	reconcile	streamline
assess	demonstrate	guide	originate	record	strengthen
audit	design	handle	overhaul	redesign	structure
budget	detect	identify	oversee	reduce	study
build	develop	implement	participate	reorganize	summarize
catalog	diagnose	improve	perform	repair	supervise
change	diagram	increase	plan	report	support
clarify	direct	inspect	prepare	represent	teach
coach	discover	install	present	research	test
collaborate	distribute	instruct	process	resolve	track
collect	draft	integrate	produce	respond	train
communicate	earn	introduce	program	review	update
compile	edit	investigate	promote	revise	upgrade
complete	eliminate	lead	propose	schedule	validate
compute	establish	maintain	protect	screen	write

iQoncept/
Shutterstock.com

OVERCOMING BARRIERS
Save It for the Interview

Be careful not to put yourself out of the running for an interview by placing something unnecessary on your resume. It is not necessary to volunteer negative information about yourself. For instance, if you were fired from a job, do not indicate this fact on your resume. If necessary, discuss it during an interview, where you will have an opportunity to explain the situation.

Likewise, reserve any discussion of salary, wages, or compensation until you have had adequate opportunity to discuss your qualifications in an interview. Placing a monetary requirement on a resume could eliminate you from a job or seriously weaken your negotiating position. If employers ask for and insist on your compensation expectations, use broad numbers (the mid-thirty thousands, for example) and indicate that this is negotiable. Look at Chapter 10 to learn more about answering difficult questions.

Employers will also search for these keywords when they read resumes. Think of keywords as the magnets that pull employers' attention to your resume. Strive to include as many appropriate keywords in your Professional Profile, Qualifications, and Work Experience sections as possible. Appropriate keywords for your job target include industry terminology and specific words or short phrases that are in job descriptions and ads. Use the following list of sources to help identify appropriate keywords to include in your resume.

- Job Posts and descriptions for positions you are considering (print or online)
- Websites of employers you are considering
- Government publications such as the *Occupational Outlook Handbook* (print or online)
- Job titles
- Skills and specialties
- Education, certifications, licenses, and course work
- Computer/software/hardware skills and specialized tools
- Industry buzzwords, jargon, and acronyms
- Professional associations in your field (check their websites, publications, newsletters and meetings)

Include keywords throughout your resume and repeat critical keywords.

Employers may use different terms in their search criteria, so use synonyms for keywords (for example, *budget* as a synonym for *forecast* and *supervisor* for *manager*). Include the abbreviation and the full name of your degree, as in *B.A.* and *Bachelor of Arts*.

Real World Scenario 5-1

Ben was struggling with writing his Professional Profile. He felt like there was so much he could say about his strengths and experience that it was difficult to be concise. He wanted to demonstrate how hard and fast he worked by listing all the things he does at his current part-time job. His advisor reminded him that he should focus on the most important things and look for what words could be eliminated. So Ben brainstormed with a few friends to come up with a general description of what he does that would tell the reader that he works hard and fast. He was happy with his final statement: "Consistently recognized by employers and coworkers for integrity, speed, quality of work, and ability to handle multiple responsibilities."

How can you describe your strengths in a powerful, concise statement?

Applicant tracking systems typically seek nouns. For example, in searching for AutoCAD drafters, the software may look for nouns (and noun synonyms) such as *CAD, engineer, AA degree, certified drafter, Computer-Aided Drafting, AutoCAD, wiring diagrams,* and *physics.*

Figure 5-2 has examples of typical keywords used to select resumes to fill two positions.

Now that you have applied the four strategies to the Qualifications, Work Experience, Education, and Optional sections of the resume, think about your Professional Profile. Review Career Action Worksheet 4-2. What unique strengths were common across the sections of your resume that could improve your Personal Brand Statement? Remember, this is one of the first parts a recruiter will review. Take time to revise your Professional Profile and make it stand out!

▶ *CAREER ACTION*

Complete Worksheet 5-4
Write a Stronger Professional Profile, page 151

Your Career Network: Trusted Reviewers

There are probably people in your Career Network who can help you see your strengths. They might be old coworkers, previous classmates, mentors, or family members. Ask them to review your resume. Ask them to think about and jot down answers to the following questions:

- Do they think it represents you well?
- Are there any strengths or unique personality traits that make you a valuable employee they think are missing?
- Do they see evidence of your Professional Profile in your Work Experience and Qualification sections?
- Is there anything that gives them a pause when they are reading?
- Are there any grammatical errors or typos?
- Would they hire you?

The people you trust to advocate for you can support you during this stage of the Job Search Journey. Don't be afraid to ask for help!

Figure 5-2 Sample Keyword Search Terms

Position Title	Sample Keywords	Position Title	Sample Keywords
Accountant	CPA, audit, accounting, accounts receivable/payable, statistics, spreadsheet, finance, systems training, computer, database, team player, B.B.A. Accounting, accurate, project leader, customer relations, accounting database, tax code, ethics, Sarbanes-Oxley compliance, data integrity	Web-based training developer	e-learning, WBT, instructional design, distance learning, synchronous, asynchronous, ADDIE, training, project management, Lectora, Flash, SharePoint, Dreamweaver, CourseBuilder, Centra, SCORM, Section 508, DeBabelizer, Director, Captivate, Acrobat, LMS, SABA, SumTotal, Illustrator, Photoshop, PageMaker, Persuasion, Fireworks, Premiere, Sound Forge, Movie Maker, JavaScript, SQL, Lingo

EDIT YOUR RESUME

By now, you should have completed a strong first draft of your resume. Now it's time to review, clean up any errors you see, and learn how to customize it for particular job postings and social media platforms.

Common Grammar Mistakes to Avoid

The worst feeling is to spend hours writing a resume only to be rejected because of typographical errors. Remember the comment from Lisa Mark in the Advice From The Expert section—just two errors stopped her from moving forward with an applicant. Grammar mistakes are easy to make, but easy to avoid with adequate proofreading. Make sure to look out for the following common errors, then get others to help you find any that you may have missed.

Homophones

Homophones are words that sound the same but have different spellings and meanings. Here are some common homophones to watch out for when you write your resume:

- Two, To, and Too—*Two* refers to the number; *To* is a preposition usually expressing direction or motion toward a place, person, or time; *Too* is an adverb meaning additionally.

- They're, Their, and There—*They're* is a contraction for *they are*. *Their* is a possessive meaning belonging to them. *There* refers to a place.

- A lot and Allot—*A lot* refers to a large quantity or extent; *Allot* refers to distributing something between people or groups. *Alot* is not a word.

Possessives versus Contractions

Don't confuse words of possession and words that are contractions. Here are some examples:

- Your and You're—*Your* is a possessive meaning something that belongs to you. *You're* is a contraction of *you* and *are*.

- Its and It's—*Its* is a possessive meaning belonging to him or her. If you can replace *it* with *him* or *her*, there is no need for an apostrophe. *It's* is a contraction for *it is* or *it has*.

In general, be careful when you use apostrophes. Besides incorrect use of contractions, make sure you are not making a plural word, such as *employees*, into a possessive term incorrectly, such as *employee's*.

Inconsistent Tense

Use the past tense only for previous jobs or positions, and use the past tense consistently. Never write about a current job experience using the past tense. Switching between tenses like *managed* to *managing* to *manage* appears unprofessional.

Misspelled Words, Abbreviations, and Capitalization

Always use spell check. Then proofread to make sure spell check caught all the errors and didn't mistakenly switch *we're* for *were*. Remember to stay away from abbreviations, even when they are career specific, unless it is

---

Real World Scenario 5-2 Cara had been over her resume again and again. She was sure it was right. The night before the interview, she printed out a few copies to take with her. She looked at this version so that it would be fresh in her mind. Suddenly she noticed that she had made two errors! She had misspelled the company name with an *ie* rather than an *ei*, and she had used *too* instead of *to*. She quickly fixed both mistakes and was thankful that, despite the errors, she was still getting an interview. She would give the interviewer and any new job leads the new version of her resume.

How could Cara have avoided the errors?

MAKE IT A HABIT
Proofread, Proofread, Proofread

Make it a habit to proofread all your documents and make sure you are following grammar rules. The slightest grammatical error can make you appear unprofessional and unqualified for the job. As one recruiting manager said, "If they can't pay attention to detail in their own resume, how can I expect them to pay attention to details on the job?" Use these tactics to help you catch any errors:

- Print important documents such as applications and resumes, and review with a red marker to highlight any errors.

- Read text aloud and listen for any errors or awkward sentences.

- Ask someone else to review your work.

- Use the spell and grammar check in your word processing software or use a service like Grammarly.com or the latest grammar help online.

Stay cautious and don't forget to proofread all your communications.

Pixsooz/Shutterstock.com

a term you know is used industry wide. If the recruiter doesn't understand the acronym, they won't appreciate the skill or competency you are trying to describe. Use capitalization consistently throughout your resume. Only capitalize proper nouns and the first word of each sentence or phrase.

Review your draft resume with these grammatical rules in mind.

Be Clear and Concise

Even for companies that use applicant tracking systems to select the most promising resumes, deciding which applicants to interview is time consuming. With over 50 resumes to scan a day, you can expect most recruiters to spend 30 seconds or less on your resume. Presenting an easy-to-read, clear, concise message and format is critical for making the most of the limited time your resume will receive. Follow these rules and tips to keep your resume concise:

- **Use phrases,** not complete sentences, and omit *I, me,* and *my.* The reader knows the resume is about you.

- **Be focused and concise.** Eliminate wordiness and complexity by focusing each section, bullet, or line on just one idea. If using full sentences, keep them short!

- **Eliminate articles *the, a,* and *an.*** Instead of saying "balanced the budget," simply say "balanced budget."

A resume for a recent graduate should be one full page. If you have extensive work experience, two pages are acceptable. In this case, use logical page breaks and repeat the current heading at the top of the next page followed by "(continued)" so that the reader can follow the flow.

► *CAREER ACTION*
Complete Worksheet 5-5
Create Your Draft Master Resume, page 153

Keep Track of Your Resumes

Unless you get very lucky and are offered the first job you apply for, you will develop several versions of your resume during your job search. For example, you may need to change the job target, emphasize different skills and capabilities in the Qualifications section, or add specialized keywords based on different job postings you find. You may also have different formats of the same resume, such as a PDF file and a Word document. The information between different formats should match. You need a system that keeps all versions in sync so that you can respond quickly and accurately to job postings.

Develop a naming convention for each customized Job Application Package (Chapter 7).

To be organized and able to respond to job postings quickly, for each job you apply for create a folder on your computer or in the Cloud (backed up on a flash drive reserved for your job search and Career Builder Files). Keep a copy of the job posting, any versions of the resume you used, any cover letters (Chapter 7), copies of all emails related to your application, and—if you get an interview—your interview notes and the text of your thank-you letter.

Elena Elisseeva/Shutterstock.com

FORMAT YOUR RESUME

Now that you have reviewed the content, grammar, and language used in your resume, pay attention to the format. Up to this point, you may have been using a word processing program. However, when you submit your resume, you may not have a choice about the file type, especially online. To assure that your resume can be seen, it is very important to follow any formatting instructions included in the job posting. Read the post carefully to make sure you haven't overlooked any detailed submission instructions. You need to be ready with the following resume formats:

- **Microsoft® Word's .doc or .docx file format**—.doc or .docx is currently the best format to use as you create and edit your resume. It may also be requested as the

preferred file format for online applications because it is easier for applicant tracking systems to search for keywords.

- **Adobe Acrobat's .pdf file format**—.pdf is the best format for emailing or otherwise sharing your resume because it shows only the finished product without all the formatting and editing that you did and cannot be modified easily by the recipient.

- **Notepad's .txt file format**—.txt files have no formatting (no bullet points, tables, bold font, etc.) and are used to copy and paste your resume data directly into online application fields.

Print Resume

You will use printed resumes to hand to Warm Introductions and at networking meetings. You'll want your printed resume—to be:

- Visually appealing
- Capable of being scanned accurately into a resume database

Using your word processing program to make edits, review the Formatting Dos and Don'ts on pages 130–131. After you have drafted and formatted your print resume, print it out and review it again, paying careful attention to every detail. Mark areas for improvement and then revise it.

To save your final version, simply click *Save*. To save your final resume in .pdf format, click *Save As* and select *.pdf* from the file type drop-down menu.

Creating a Plain Text Resume

You also need a **plain text resume,** a text file (.txt file) that has no formatting (no bold, no tables, no bullets, no quotation marks, dashes, asterisks, etc.). The main purpose of this text file is to serve as the source file for copy and paste online applications.

- At some sites, you paste the entire plain text resume into one text field.

- At other sites, you paste sections of the resume into labeled text fields such as "Work Experience 1" or "Education."

Other sites use the headings in your resume to fill in fields automatically; you then check each field and correct any errors (for example, if the program puts your job duties in the skills field). Start with the final version of the print resume you are using to apply for a job. Then follow these steps to create your plain text resume.

1. Save the print resume as a .doc file with a different name.
2. Format the file so that it will convert to a clean .txt file:
   a. Replace bold text with all caps and bullets with hyphens.
   b. Remove the tabs and start every line at the left margin.
   c. If your resume has two pages, delete the page break and the header at the top of the second page.
3. Save the "stripped down" Word file as a .doc file and a .txt file. Close both files.

Formatting Dos for Print Resumes

- Use the whole page effectively. Space sections to fill the entire first page with an attractive layout framed by one-inch margins on all sides.

- Create a visual hierarchy in each section. Draw attention to headings by using larger text font as well as bold and italicized text to emphasize items. Do not use all capitals, however, because this gives your resume an alarming tone and feel.

- Use a standard font. Keep the font size between 11 points for body text and 14 points for headings.

- Place the most important information at the top left of the page or section—where readers naturally begin reading.

- Use bulleted lists instead of paragraphs.

- Be simple and consistent. Format the same elements the same way.

- Use one space after periods and add a line break between sections and experiences.

- Use color sensibly, if at all. For example, try dark blue for the contact information and section headings. Experiment with color before you send your resume, and don't make color a "feature." Most resumes are simply black and white, but if you are applying for a job in a creative field, color and design may be important.

- Print your resume on a laser printer on one side of white or cream-colored paper. If the paper has a watermark, print with the watermark facing up and toward the reader.

Formatting Don'ts for Print Resumes

- Don't use the headings *Resume* or *Contact Information* at the top of a resume.

- Don't use excessive decorative fonts and formatting. These elements look unprofessional and do not scan well.

- Don't crowd the text to fit everything on one page. Check your writing again and see where you can be more concise. If the text still doesn't fit, end the first page at a logical stopping point near the bottom of the page. If a section carries over, repeat the heading on page 2 (for example, *Education, continued*).

- Don't use a newsletter layout or multiple columns. Applicant tracking systems assume that the text reads from left to right across the page in one column.

- Don't adjust the spacing between characters. Use standard left-margin alignment for body text. (Headings can be centered.)

- Don't use formatting that can blur or corrupt the scanned image. Avoid the following:
  - Light-colored text
  - Shadow effect
  - White text on a black background
  - Boxed text
  - Vertical lines (you can use a single horizontal line as a separator between sections if you leave enough space above and below the line so that it doesn't touch any letters)

- Don't fold or staple the resume. (Creases and staple marks can cause scanning errors.)

- Don't print page 2 on the back of page 1; use two sheets of paper attached with a paper clip.

---

4. Open the folder with the .txt file and double-click the filename to open it. Windows opens the .txt file in the text editor program Notepad. *Do not open the .txt file in Word.* Check the format of the .txt file to make sure you didn't miss anything when you formatted the .doc file in Step 1.

5. If necessary, add blank lines to make the resume more readable. Notepad ignores automatic line breaks in the .doc file and displays paragraphs, such as a description of job duties, as one continuous line of text that runs off the screen. Divide these long lines into lines of 65 characters, including spaces, by inserting a hard return at the end of each new line.

6. Always finalize the *format* of a plain text resume (and cover letter) in Notepad, not in Word. To keep both versions of the current resume in sync, make *text changes* in the formatted print resume and re-create the unformatted .doc file and .txt file.

Look at the sample plain text resume in Figure 5-6 on page 136.

▶ *CAREER ACTION*
Complete Worksheet 5-6
Create Your Plain Text Resume, page 155

Customize Your Resume

Do not send the same resume to every potential employer. A customized resume is more effective at showing how you meet the requirements for a particular job posting and can significantly increase your chances of getting an interview.

Start with your master resume, the one you are working on in this class. Make sure it is as perfect as you can get it. Ask others to review it and give you feedback, then revise it. Using this final master resume, customize it for specific job titles, job postings, and target employers.

- Customize the Job Objective statement of your *Professional Profile* section for different job targets and industries.

- Customize your list of *Qualifications* based on the skills and requirements described in the job posting.

- Prioritize bullet points based on relevance to the job posting's responsibilities and skills in the *Work* and *Related Experience* sections of your resume.

- Use search-optimized keywords throughout your resume that match the terms in the job posting.

- Use appropriate industry terminology.

Figure 5-3 shows excerpts from a resume for a service manager position along with changes made to customize the resume for a position as an automotive insurance adjuster. Notice how the same person can show how he or she is qualified for different jobs by purposefully choosing what to share about his or her experience and qualifications. (For a side-by-side comparison of a resume customized for two different jobs, view Figure 5-9 on page 139–140.)

When the jobs you are applying for are quite similar, the adjustments may be minimal. If you are applying for different types of jobs in a similar industry or if you are applying to jobs in two or more career fields, you will need to revise your resume to fit each new job target. Try these steps to make it easier to customize your resume.

Figure 5-3 Customized Resume Example

"Before"	"After"
Objective: Service manager in multiline dealership	**Objective:** Insurance adjuster in automotive collision repair industry
Auto Repair Customer Service Scheduled appointments, performed preinspections, achieved upgrade sales on 95% of accounts, quoted estimates, wrote work orders, performed post-repair inspections, explained statements to customers, and increased referrals from customers by 40%	**Modified to Focus on Claims Management** Scheduled client appointments, determined mechanical and auto body damages within 45 minutes, negotiated repairs with clients and insurance companies, prepared job documentation (pictures, work orders, billing), performed post-repair inspections, and explained statements
Parts Management Managed ordering and stocking of mechanical and auto-body parts inventories, selected suppliers and negotiated vendor discounts that averaged 25% to 30% below wholesale, reconciled shipping invoices to billing statements, and approved payments	**Modified to Focus on Cost Containment** Obtained clients' permission to use appropriate aftermarket and/or rebuilt parts on 95% of jobs; located replacement parts; negotiated price, delivery, and discounts, averaging 25% to 30% below wholesale; returned unused parts for credit; reconciled billing discrepancies; approved payments

1. Open a copy of your master resume in a window on the left side of the screen.

2. On the other half of the screen, use your browser to read about the new career field and read several job postings, including listings for jobs you are not considering.

3. Compare your resume against the industry terminology for the new field.

4. Highlight text in your resume that you can modify, and then paste the new terminology into your resume where appropriate.

5. Look for ways to increase the number of keywords that match the career or job.

For example, you might list different courses you have taken if a course title includes a keyword that you cannot use when describing your work experience. A teacher who is applying for jobs as a corporate trainer would use the terms *trainer, instructor, presenter*, and/or *facilitator* instead of *teacher*.

Your Resume Online

Post Your Resume on Social Media

Both LinkedIn and Facebook let you share your resume with your online network. On Facebook, fill out the Work and Education portion of your profile by cutting and pasting from your plain text resume. Make sure to check the final version for readability. Add spaces and line breaks where needed.

LinkedIn is designed for job seekers, and there are a variety of ways to make sure your experience is showcased effectively. Take time to finish building your LinkedIn profile with the content from your master resume.

> ▶ *CAREER ACTION*
> **Complete Worksheet 5-7**
> Finish Building Your LinkedIn Profile, page 157

Create a Resume Website

With today's technology, setting up a website is easier than ever. There are both free and paid options that walk you through setting up a site that showcases you, your resume, and, if appropriate, your portfolio. This resume format is more flexible than the others because it supports more sophisticated elements, such as animated graphics, sound clips, and video clips. Web resumes can also be creative sales tools for people who want or need to display their artistic abilities, such as photographers, artists, singers, models, architects, and graphics and computer specialists. A resume website can also be a great place to include a filmed version of your 30-Second Commercial (see Chapter 2). Note that a web resume should be used in addition to—not as a substitute for—your print and plain text resumes. Figure 5-10 on page 141 is the first page of a web resume.

There are several categories of personal sites.

- **Simple landing page site:** This is a single page site that showcases your basic information, including an *About* section and links to your social media profiles. Some examples are About.me, Enthuse.me, and Strikingly—make sure to search for the latest sites to help you create a powerful landing page.

- **Full website:** A full website provides you with several different pages, including a blog, portfolio, resume, and more. A *blog* is a website with articles you've written listed in reverse chronological order. Several popular options that offer both free and premium templates to help you build your site are Weebly, Wix, and SquareSpace. Each has step-by-step documentation and makes it easy for you to manage your site without a lot of computer technical knowledge.

- **Infographic sites:** A new trend has emerged where a visual site is created based off your LinkedIn profile. They translate your profile into a visual history that can be grasped quickly. A site like this may be useful if you have a long career history and want to "boil down" a lengthy resume to its essentials. Sites to consider for this include Vizualize. me and Re.vu. See an example in Figure 5-4.

Having your own website is a great addition to your marketing materials and allows you more control over the information about you that is visible on the Internet. In contrast, social media profiles have to be monitored for what your network was contributing to your profile. Your website can also be listed on your business card and resume when networking.

Congratulations! You have completed a big part of the Job Search Journey. Now that you have created your master resume, you are ready to apply for jobs and proceed to Phase 3 of the Job Search Journey.

Sample Resumes

The following sample resumes are on pages 135–141:

Print Resumes for Different Career Targets

- Figure 5-5: Sample Resume, Private Security Guard
- Figure 5-6: Sample Resume, Health Information Technician
- Figure 5-7: Sample Resume, Registered Environmental Technician

Resumes in Other Formats

- Figure 5-8: Plain Text Resume, Registered Environmental Technician
- Figure 5-9: Web Resume, Art Teacher

Customized Resumes

- Figure 5-10: Side-by-Side Comparison of Customized Resumes

Additional resumes highlighting other job targets can be found on the Student Resources site.

Figure 5-4 Example of an Infographic of a Profile

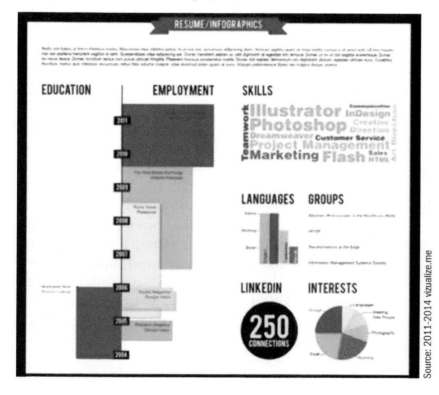

Source: 2011-2014 vizualize.me

Figure 5-5　Sample Resume Private Security Guard

THOMAS STANLEY

tom.stanley1066@email.com　　　　　　　　　linkedin.com/in/tomstanley1066
(716) 555.2457　　　　　　　　　　　　　123 Forest Drive, Springfield, NY 14201

> Thomas' professional profile highlights important competencies in a personable way.

Professional Profile

Private Security Guard position requiring ability to perform safety, security, and surveillance procedures. Observant, careful individual with up to date license, known for excellent communication and interpersonal skills.

> Although he uses more than 3–5 words, he limited the total number to 3 to highlight the most impactful qualifications.

Qualifications

- Well trained and certified through multiple training avenues
- Practical experience in closed-circuit video surveillance and switchboard operations
- Experienced in working with juvenile offenders

> Notice his use of the WHI format and action verbs.

Relevant Work Experience

Buffalo Juvenile Justice Center, Buffalo, NY　　　　　　　September 2014–November 2014
Juvenile Corrections Intern
Monitor and enforce security at facility.

> He highlights the broad criminal justice experience. He gained. He places emphasis on safety and security procedures by listing them as the first job duty.

- Monitored and ensured safety and security of 50 juvenile detainees.
- Successfully enforced facility safety and security rules including managing 3 conflicts
- Escorted juvenile offenders to classes, counseling sessions, and work-release programs.
- Conducted security checks, searches, and pat downs

Erie County Sheriff's Department, Hamburg, NY　　　　　　　Summer 2012, 2013
Assistant Supervisor, County Fairgrounds Grounds and Maintenance
Supervised groundskeeping and maintenance crew of eight work-released juveniles for the County Sheriff's Department.

> He emphasizes his conflict resolution and interpersonal skills, which are important qualifications for security guards. He also describes his ability to complete and submit essential paperwork.

- Quickly resolved multiple worker disagreements and scheduling issues using training in conflict resolution techniques
- Evaluated work crew weekly and submitted thorough and timely paperwork to the Sheriff's Department

Baker Sporting Goods, Buffalo, NY　　　　　　　　　　　April 2011–May 2012
Security Guard, Part-time
Monitored customers and employees to maintan internal and external loss-theft control.

> Although part-time, this position gave him practical experience in a variety of common security guard tasks.

- Conducted closed-circuit video surveillance of store and building exterior.
- Recognized for swift response to employee and customer security and safety requests.
- Identified new security actions through submission of daily loss prevention reports.

Certifications and Training

- New York State Security Guard License, 2011
- Carrying Concealed Weapons License, 2010
- First Aid and CPR Certification, 2007

- Physical Fitness Specialist, 2008
- Fire Prevention and Safety Training, 2009
- Burglary Prevention Training, 2009

> Note the Optional Section Thomas included. Because security guard positions can have several certification requirements, he lists his training, certificates, and licenses with dates to show that they are current. He uses industry keywords and stresses safety, fitness, and security.

Education

Crown Community College, Associate of Applied Science, 2014
Major: Criminal Justice　GPA: 3.75

Figure 5-6 Sample Resume Health Information Technician

SONYA REID

2332 Clovis Boulevard • Savannah, GA 31401 • (912) 555.0109
Sonya_reid@email.com • linkedin/in/sonya_reid

PROFESSIONAL PROFILE

Health Information Technician position requiring the ability to perform detailed tasks, change priorities quickly, and communicate well. Excellent customer service rep and team member, known for helping people feel at ease and working efficiently.

QUALIFICATIONS

- RHIT, Registered Health Information Technician, 2014
- Family practice receptionist, 1.5 years
- Awarded Superior Service Certificate twice
- Five-month internship as assistant to Health Information Technician, Community Hospital

EDUCATION

Associate of Science, A.S., 2014, Savannah College of Georgia, Savannah, GA
Major: **Health Information Technology**, GPA 3.6
Related Courses and Skills
Medical Terminology • Clinical Classification Systems • Health Information Management
Health Delivery Systems • Health Data • Introduction to Health Law and Ethics
Human Disease Mechanisms • Health Care Reimbursement • Alternative Health Care Settings
Business Communications

CERTIFICATION

Registered Health Information Technician, 2014

EXPERIENCE

Community Hospital, Savannah, GA   January 2014–May 2014
Clinical Intern

Shadow Health Information Technician and assist in basic duties.

- Reduced Health Information Technician's workload by 25% by end of internship in reviewing and assigning diagnosis codes and DRGs and coding Medicare/Medicaid billing items.
- Abstracted appropriate information and retrieved medical records from records department using appropriate procedures.

Family Practice Partnership, Savannah, GA   July 2012–December 2013
Evening Receptionist2

Manage patients' needs and reception area.

- Provided cheerful, efficient service to patients; awarded Superior Service Certificate in 2012 and 2013.
- Checked in patients, obtained insurance and billing information, and pulled charts for nurses.
- Copied requested records for transport to other medical offices.

She emphasizes her Technician certification by placing it first because it is a primary requirement for the job she is seeking. Notice that all bulleted qualifications are repeated elsewhere in Sonya's resume to highlight her most important qualifications and to catch a human reader's attention.

Sonya puts her education and certification first because she knows employers will place more importance on this area.

Sonya includes her internship under work experience and uses the WHI format to demonstrate the capabilities she has gained.

Figure 5-7 Sample Resume Registered Environmental Technician

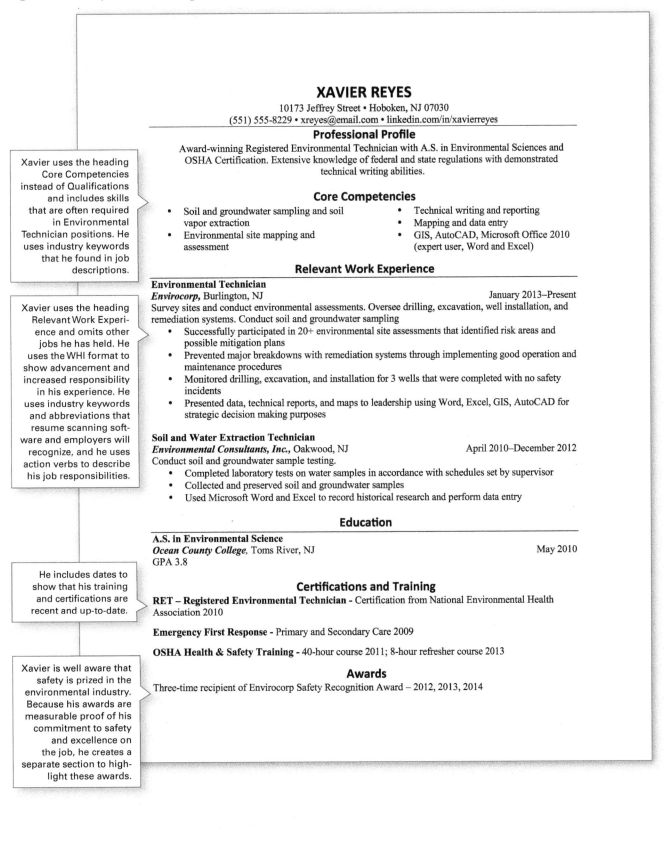

Xavier uses the heading Core Competencies instead of Qualifications and includes skills that are often required in Environmental Technician positions. He uses industry keywords that he found in job descriptions.

Xavier uses the heading Relevant Work Experience and omits other jobs he has held. He uses the WHI format to show advancement and increased responsibility in his experience. He uses industry keywords and abbreviations that resume scanning software and employers will recognize, and he uses action verbs to describe his job responsibilities.

He includes dates to show that his training and certifications are recent and up-to-date.

Xavier is well aware that safety is prized in the environmental industry. Because his awards are measurable proof of his commitment to safety and excellence on the job, he creates a separate section to highlight these awards.

XAVIER REYES

10173 Jeffrey Street • Hoboken, NJ 07030
(551) 555-8229 • xreyes@email.com • linkedin.com/in/xavierreyes

Professional Profile

Award-winning Registered Environmental Technician with A.S. in Environmental Sciences and OSHA Certification. Extensive knowledge of federal and state regulations with demonstrated technical writing abilities.

Core Competencies

- Soil and groundwater sampling and soil vapor extraction
- Environmental site mapping and assessment

- Technical writing and reporting
- Mapping and data entry
- GIS, AutoCAD, Microsoft Office 2010 (expert user, Word and Excel)

Relevant Work Experience

Environmental Technician
Envirocorp, Burlington, NJ   January 2013–Present
Survey sites and conduct environmental assessments. Oversee drilling, excavation, well installation, and remediation systems. Conduct soil and groundwater sampling

- Successfully participated in 20+ environmental site assessments that identified risk areas and possible mitigation plans
- Prevented major breakdowns with remediation systems through implementing good operation and maintenance procedures
- Monitored drilling, excavation, and installation for 3 wells that were completed with no safety incidents
- Presented data, technical reports, and maps to leadership using Word, Excel, GIS, AutoCAD for strategic decision making purposes

Soil and Water Extraction Technician
Environmental Consultants, Inc., Oakwood, NJ   April 2010–December 2012
Conduct soil and groundwater sample testing.

- Completed laboratory tests on water samples in accordance with schedules set by supervisor
- Collected and preserved soil and groundwater samples
- Used Microsoft Word and Excel to record historical research and perform data entry

Education

A.S. in Environmental Science
Ocean County College, Toms River, NJ   May 2010
GPA 3.8

Certifications and Training

RET – Registered Environmental Technician - Certification from National Environmental Health Association 2010

Emergency First Response - Primary and Secondary Care 2009

OSHA Health & Safety Training - 40-hour course 2011; 8-hour refresher course 2013

Awards

Three-time recipient of Envirocorp Safety Recognition Award – 2012, 2013, 2014

Figure 5-8 Plain Text Sample Resume Registered Environmental Technician

XAVIER REYES
10173 Jeffrey Street • Hoboken, NJ 07030
(551) 555-8229 • xreyes@email.com • linkedin.com/in/xavierreyes
Professional Profile
Award-winning Registered Environmental Technician with A.S. in Environmental
Sciences and OSHA Certification. Extensive knowledge of federal and state
regulations with demonstrated technical writing abilities.

Core Competencies
* Soil and groundwater sampling and soil vapor extraction
* Environmental site mapping and assessment
* Technical writing and reporting
* Mapping and data entry
* GIS, AutoCAD, Microsoft Office 2010 (expert user, Word and Excel)

Relevant Work Experience
Environmental Technician
Envirocorp, Burlington, NJ
January 2013–Present
Survey sites and conduct environmental assessments. Oversee drilling, excavation,
well installation, and remediation systems. Conduct soil and groundwater sampling
* Successfully participated in 20+ environmental site assessments that identified risk
areas and possible mitigation plans
* Prevented major breakdowns with remediation systems through implementing good
operation and maintenance procedures
* Monitored drilling, excavation, and installation for 3 wells that were completed with
no safety incidents
* Presented data, technical reports, and maps to leadership using Word, Excel, GIS,
AutoCAD for strategic decision making purposes

Soil and Water Extraction Technician
Environmental Consultants, Inc., Oakwood, NJ
April 2010–December 2012
Conduct soil and groundwater sample testing.
* Completed laboratory tests on water samples in accordance with schedules set by
supervisor
* Collected and preserved soil and groundwater samples
* Used Microsoft Word and Excel to record historical research and perform data entry

Education
A.S. in Environmental Science
Ocean County College, Toms River, NJ
May 2010
GPA 3.8

Certifications and Training
RET –Registered Environmental Technician - Certification from National
Environmental Health Association 2010

Emergency First Response - Primary and Secondary Care 2009

OSHA Health & Safety Training - 40-hour course 2011; 8-hour refresher course 2013

Awards
Three-time recipient of Envirocorp Safety Recognition Award – 2012, 2013, 2014

Figure 5-9 Web Resume Art Teacher

THE SHORT STORY

"I found I could say things with color and shapes that I couldn't say any other way–things I had no words for."

Georgia O'Keeffe

Enthusiastic, creative, and talented art teacher with ability to foster student curiosity, creativity, and self-discipline in a positive learning environment. Collaborative educator with outstanding interpersonal and communication skills complemented by strengths in interactive learning and differentiated instruction.

WORK EXPERIENCE

Long-Term Substitute Art Teacher

John F. Kennedy Middle School, Riverside, CA
September 2011-June 2012

Designed and implemented interactive lesson plans and units and educated on proper methodologies and techniques. Evaluated each student's progress and adjusted lessons accordingly.

- Initiated first after-school Art Club to provide students with additional opportunities to further their creative capabilities and explore new mediums.
- Selected and matted 120 pieces of student artwork for exhibition at prestigious art gallery show.

Student Teacher

J.P. McCaskey High School, Lancaster, PA
January-April 2011

- Raised student awareness and appreciation of the arts through creative lesson plans and teaching methods.
- Provided small-group instruction in basic jewelry making, water colors, acrylics, and etching.

Entrepreneur / Metalsmith

Judy's Jewelry Designs (www.judysjewelry.com), Riverside, CA

Figure 5-9 Web Resume Art Teacher *(continued)*

2009-Present

Started small business to manufacture unique sterling silver and bead jewelry. Created business plan and marketing plan, prepared budget, and purchased tools. Traveled throughout region and country to display and sell jewelry at juried craft shows and exhibitions.

- Collaborate with individual customers to design and create custom jewelry.
- Network with boutique owners, customers, and juried craft shows to promote designs.

EDUCATION AND CREDENTIALS

Certification: Art—California and Pennsylvania Permanent K–12

Bachelor of Science in Art Education, 2011
Kutztown University, Kutztown, PA

Jewelry Technician Certification, Revere Academy of Jewelry Art
San Francisco, CA, 2011

CONTACT

See what you like? Get in touch with me:

Email

Phone

Location

Figure 5-10 Side-by-Side Comparison of Customized Resumes

DONITA SILVA
Donita.silva@email.com **linkedin.com/in/donita.silva**
1247 Madison Rd Columbus OH 43216 (614) 555.5225

	Resume 1: Accounting Systems Auditor	Resume 2: Information Systems Analyst
Note the different focus for the Professional Profile: the job objective is customized.	**PROFESSIONAL PROFILE** Accounting Systems Auditor I	**PROFESSIONAL PROFILE** Information Systems Analyst I position in a financial environment requiring system design, programming, investigation, reporting skills
Note the different qualifications highlighted for the different job objective	**QUALIFICATIONS SUMMARY** • Education in accounting practices and computer systems • Programming competence in C, C++, C#.NET and Visual Basic.NET • Practical experience in EDP accounting applications • Master user: Office 2010, SharePoint 2010, Silverlight 4 • Proven interpersonal skills and team skills in an auditing environment • Experienced in IBM Power Systems, Windows Server 2008, Active Directory, Microsoft Exchange Server 2010, and Novell LAN operations	**QUALIFICATIONS SUMMARY** • Education in computer systems and accounting practices • Proven interpersonal skills and team skills in a financial setting • Programming competence in C, C++, C#.NET and Visual Basic.NET • Practical experience in EDP accounting applications • Master user: Office 2010, SharePoint 2010, Silverlight 4 • Experienced in IBM Power Systems, Windows Server 2008, Active Directory, Microsoft Exchange Server 2010, and Novell LAN operations
	WORK EXPERIENCE	
Donita left the work experience the same. She could have prioritized the bullet points within each experience if there was different relevance or importance for the differing job objective.	**Alexander & Swartz**, Columbus, OH 9/11 to Present **Part-time Assistant Staff Auditor:** Assist in audits of cash, accounts receivable, and accounts payable for midsized firms that use IBM Power Systems. Interface with clients and write audit reports as member of Business Services Assurance and Advisory team.	
	Micronomics Inc., Columbus, OH 6/08 to 9/11 **Part-time Programming Assistant:** Designed, documented, coded, and tested C program subroutines for order-entry system. Achieved 95% average program-accuracy rate on test runs. Cataloged and filed new programs and program patches for company's software library. Used Microsoft Exchange Server 2010.	
	Renton College, Columbus, OH 9/06 to 6/08 **Computer Operator Aide:** Using Windows Server 2008, copied files for backup. Verified accuracy of reports and scheduled print sequences. Implemented schedule changes that improved efficiency of backup procedures by 25%.	
	EDUCATION **Bachelor of Business Administration, B.B.A.**, 2012 Renton College, Columbus, OH Major: Computer Information Systems Minor: Internal Auditing	
She highlighted different Relevant Courses of Study	**Relevant Courses of Study:** • Analysis, and Auditing of Accounting Information Systems • Internal Auditing • Information Systems Auditing • Accounting Applications • Database Management • Advanced Corporate Finance • Cost Accounting	**Relevant Courses of Study:** • System Analysis and Design • Systems Development • Quantitative Analysis • Advanced Programming • Data Communications • Database Systems • Advanced Corporate Finance • Statistical Techniques • Information Systems Auditing

Chapter Checklist

Check off each item you can do. Reread sections in this chapter to help you complete the checklist.

☐ Write a cohesive master resume that tells a story and supports my Personal Brand Statement with relevant work experience and qualifications. ➊

☐ Write a clear, concise, attention-grabbing Professional Profile to focus my entire resume. ➊

☐ Use measurable details and accomplishment statements to market myself. ➊

☐ Use appropriate action verbs and keywords to demonstrate that I have the required skills and knowledge. ➊

☐ Edit my resume using proper grammar and eliminating unnecessary information. ➋

☐ Customize my resume to meet the needs of the employer and match my resume to the job description by using specific terms and industry terminology. ➋

☐ Format my resumes in the .doc (or .docx), .pdf, and .txt formats correctly. ➌

☐ Post my resume online. ➌

Critical Thinking Questions

1. Why is it essential to use action words and search-optimized keywords in a resume? ➊

2. It is important to be selective about what to include in your resume instead of including everything you've done. Why is it so hard for most job seekers to do this? ➊ ➋

3. Why is the WHI method such a powerful tool? What can you do if you cannot find quantifiable data to support your skills and experience? ➊

4. What difference do you think it makes to an employer if they see resumes with proper grammar and clean formatting versus ones without? ➋ ➌

5. How can you tailor your resume to target a specific job or employer? Give at least three examples from your own resume. ➋

6. Why do you need a plain text resume? What are the requirements for this resume, and how do you create it? ➌

Trial Run

Get Resume Feedback ❶ ❷

It can take a long time to write a resume. After you have finished writing the master resume, you might not want to ask for feedback because it might mean that you have to make more edits! However, getting feedback is a step you don't want to skip. It's always better to catch errors and strengthen your resume before potential employers see it.

Trade resumes with a classmate and complete the following steps:

1.　If they have a different job target, explain the research you've done and describe the job target you've chosen. Let them explain their job target. If you haven't done research, do it now!

2.　Review your classmate's resume. Put yourself in the shoes of a hiring manager. Would you hire your classmate?

3.　Highlight any search-optimized keywords you see. Take a guess if you aren't familiar with their field.

4.　What evidence do you see in the Work Experience, Qualifications, Education, and Optional sections that supports their Professional Profile? Underline or highlight these.

5.　What are the top three items you would change that you believe would get your classmate the job?

Review your feedback with your classmate. Actively listen when they share their feedback with you. And don't forget to make changes!

This page is intentionally blank.

▶ *CAREER ACTION WORKSHEET*
5-1   Revise Your Qualifications List ❶

Copy into a new file the Career Action Worksheet 4-3 table with your qualifications. Finalize your Qualifications list for use in your resume by using the following checklist:

☐   Have you selected the most important, eye-catching strengths and capabilities? Have you been purposeful and only included the top 8 to 10 strengths?

☐   Have you described your top strengths in no more than three to five words?

☐   Have you ordered your Qualifications list from most important and relevant to least important and relevant?

☐   Have you used industry-relevant keywords?

Ensure that these updates are in the "About Jobs" section of your Career Builder Files.

This page is intentionally blank.

▶ CAREER ACTION WORKSHEET

5-2 Strengthen Your Work Experiences

Copy into a new file your Career Action Worksheet 4-4, Your Work Experiences. Finalize your Work Experiences for use in your resume by using the following checklist:

☐ Order your Work Experiences chronologically, starting with the most recent experience first.

☐ Follow the correct format: Job Title, Dates of Employment, Company Title, two-sentence job description, bullet points of achievements.

☐ Strengthen your WHI-formatted achievements with quantifiable results.

☐ Eliminate unnecessary words and acronyms.

☐ Use search-optimized keywords as appropriate.

☐ Choose action verbs that are relevant to your Work Experience, using the reference list in Figure 5-1 on page 124 as a starting point.

☐ If your work experience is limited, have you included relevant paid and nonpaid internships and volunteer or other pertinent activities?

☐ Include any significant school projects, organization work, or other related experiences in this section. Significant projects would include ones where you had significant results, spent a large amount of time, and/or can demonstrate multiple skills using more than one bullet point. If you need only a single bullet point to describe the work, it is probably better to include in an Optional section such as Related Experiences or Organizations.

☐ Use your notes from the sample resumes you reviewed to ensure your resume makes the best possible impression.

Ensure that these updates are in the "About Jobs" section of your Career Builder Files.

This page is intentionally blank.

▶ CAREER ACTION WORKSHEET

5-3 Resume Action Verbs and Keywords

1. Prepare a comprehensive list of appropriate action verbs and keywords (industry terms; acronyms; terms describing your job positions, experience, education, skills, etc.).

2. Use the list from Figure 5-1 and the Internet as a primary resource in your research.

3. Print a report with (a) your lists of action verbs and keywords and (b) the resources you used to identify them.

Resources for identifying action verbs and keywords for your resume

- *Your Career: How to Make It Happen* companion website
- Job postings and descriptions for positions you are considering
- Websites of target employers you are considering
- Government publications such as the *Occupational Outlook Handbook*
- Professional associations in your field (check their websites, publications, and meetings)
- Internet searches on resume keywords, resume action verbs, resume power verbs, and resume power words
- Online encyclopedias and dictionaries

Add your completed work to the "About Jobs" section of your Career Builder Files.

This page is intentionally blank.

► *CAREER ACTION WORKSHEET*

5-4 Write a Stronger Professional Profile

Copy into a new file the Professional Profile you wrote in Career Action Worksheet 4-2, Resume Outline. Revise it using the following checklist:

- ☐ Used industry-relevant keywords
- ☐ Stated strengths in the most concise form
- ☐ Supported strengths by your work experience and qualifications
- ☐ Made Personal Brand Statement relevant to your Job Target

Send your Professional Profile to trusted colleagues, friends, or classmates for review. Ask if they are easily able to understand it and what suggestions they have for improvement. Finalize your Professional Profile using their feedback and what you have learned in this textbook. Ensure that these updates are in the "About Jobs" section of your Career Builder Files.

This page is intentionally blank.

▶ *CAREER ACTION WORKSHEET*

5-5 Create Your Draft Master Resume ❷

It is time to create your draft master resume! Copy your completed Career Action Worksheet 4-2, Resume Outline, into a new file for this activity. Make sure you have updated each section with the drafts you created above.

- ☑ CAREER ACTION WORKSHEET 5-1: Revise Your Qualifications List
- ☑ CAREER ACTION WORKSHEET 5-2: Strengthen Your Work Experiences
- ☑ CAREER ACTION WORKSHEET 5-3: Resume Action Verbs and Keywords
- ☑ CAREER ACTION WORKSHEET 5-4: Write a Stronger Professional Profile

When you've updated each section, use the checklist below to edit this file—your draft master resume!

- ☐ Ensure you have included and properly formatted all sections, including Education, Related Experiences, Awards and Honors, and any Optional sections.

- ☐ For the Education section, have you emphasized courses, internships, degrees, certificates, and so on that best support your objective? If your GPA is impressive, have you included it (overall or major/minor related to your job objective)?

- ☐ Is the length of the resume appropriate for your level of experience?

- ☐ Is the resume free of all grammatical errors, including incorrect use of homophones, tense, capitalization, contractions, and other common errors?

- ☐ Did you use sentence fragments and omit the articles *the, a,* and *an* and the words *I, me,* and *my*?

- ☐ Is the overall design visually appealing and easy to read?

- ☐ Have you used appropriate fonts; white space; and acceptable enhancements such as bold, bullets, and tabs for indenting? Have you used italics sparingly?

Now give your resume the 30-second skim test. Do you get a feel for who you are as an applicant? Does your eye flow easily toward keywords and strengths? Does your resume tell the story you want it to tell?

Add your completed work to the "About Jobs" section of your Career Builder Files.

NOTE: After review by your instructor, and possibly some final revisions, you can rename this file Master Resume and add this to the "Master Career Portfolio" section of your Career Builder Files.

This page is intentionally blank.

▶ CAREER ACTION WORKSHEET

5-6 Create Your Plain Text Resume ③

PART 1. Convert the print resume you created in Career Action Worksheet 5-5 to a plain text resume. Follow the steps below. You may want to review the sample plain text resume in Figure 5-6 on page 136.

1. Save the print resume you created in Career Action Worksheet 5-5 as a .doc (or .docx) file with a similar name (for example, *MasterResume_plain text source file.doc*).

2. Now save the new .doc file as a .txt file with the same file name. This file will have less formatting. Newer versions of Word create cleaner .txt files, so experiment with the formatting you need to change.

3. Now clean up the .txt file in Microsoft® Word so that it is a usable plain text resume. Use the following checklist:

   ☐ Start every line of contact information at the left margin (no indents).

   ☐ Replace previously bold headings with ALL CAPS to ensure the text still stands out.

   ☐ Add blank lines to emphasize sections as needed. For example, insert two blank lines before the section headings.

   ☐ Replace bullets with hyphens (newer versions of Word convert bullets to asterisks automatically).

   ☐ Format tables as lists.

   ☐ For each company in the employment section, put the dates of employment under the company name.

   ☐ If your resume has two pages, delete the page break and the header at the top of the second page.

4. Save this new "stripped down" Word file as a .doc file. Use Save As to save it again as a .txt file. Close both files.

5. Open the folder with the .txt file and double-click the filename to open it. Windows opens the .txt file in the text editor program Notepad. *Do not open the .txt file in Word.*

   Always finalize the *format* of a plain text resume (and cover letter) in Notepad, not in Word. In the future, if you update or change your resume, you will want to keep the *print* and *plain text* files in sync. To keep both versions of the current resume in sync, make *text changes* in the formatted print resume and create a new unformatted .doc file and .txt file.

6. Check the format of the .txt file to make sure you didn't miss anything when you formatted the .doc file in Step 2. If necessary, add blank lines to make different sections of the resume stand out more. Because Notepad does not wrap text automatically, look

for long lines of text that run off the screen. Insert hard returns to divide these long lines into lines of 65 characters, including spaces.

7. Save the .txt file. Repeat these steps to create a new plain text resume every time you modify your print resume.

PART 2. Email your plain text resume to yourself to confirm that the format holds up in email.

1. Open your email program and create a new message addressed to yourself.

2. Select all of the resume text, then copy and paste it into the email message window.

3. In the email subject line, enter a reference number from a job posting you have found.

4. If you have a cover letter (see Chapter 7), create a plain text version and copy and paste it into the email above your resume. Then type a line of asterisks or equal signs under the last line of the cover letter to mark the end of your cover letter and the beginning of your resume.

5. Clean up any odd spacing or other formatting problems.

6. Send the message to yourself and check the format of your resume. Repeat this process until your plain text resume comes through as a clean, attractive, and readable document.

Add your completed work to the "Master Career Portfolio" section of your Career Builder Files.

▶ CAREER ACTION WORKSHEET

5-7 Finish Building Your LinkedIn Profile ❸

Now that you have your master resume, you can complete building the LinkedIn Profile you started in Chapter 2.

- Revisit your headline and summary sections. Do you need to make updates based on your final Professional Profile?

- Copy and paste your job experience by Adding Positions under the Experience section of your LinkedIn profile.

- You can also add Awards and Honors, Education, and Organizations, using your Career Builder Files.

- When you add Skills, note that if a skill is common among users, it will appear as you are typing. Be sure to choose common skills because these skills are optimized for searchability. When your network endorses your skill set, LinkedIn organizes the skills based on those that have the most endorsements.

- Do you have any pending connection requests? Make sure to check regularly and also seek out individuals you would like to connect with.

- Search for yourself using the search function. How does your profile appear on the results? Are you at the top? If not, edit your profile URL with your most easily found name (search on the Help for the latest way instructions to update).

- Also consider asking for recommendations. When you make your request, provide a draft or a few bullet points of what you would like them to cover. This makes it easy and fast for them to help you out!

Share your updated profile with your instructor or classmate.

Your LinkedIn Profile is just one place online that you can showcase your resume. Filling it out can be the starting point for any other social media platforms you would like to use on your Job Search Journey.

This page is intentionally blank.

PHASE 3:
APPLY FOR JOBS

Apply for Jobs

PART 3 Learn how to find and apply for jobs that will match your job target. You will learn two strategies to help you find jobs using both Warm Introductions through your Career Network, and Cold Leads through job boards. You will learn how to complete job applications for jobs that closely match your job target, using either online or paper forms. You will be able to determine when a cover letter might help you land a job, and learn how to write one to get the attention of potential employers.

CHAPTER 6	Find Job Openings
CHAPTER 7	Write Job Applications

ADVICE FROM THE EXPERT

NICHOLE SIMS

Talent Acquisition Manager

Nichole has seen a wide range of job applicants and job applications during her 19 years as a Talent Acquisition Manager at a large U.S. company. She's seen which applicants succeed on the job, and which ones don't make it through the process. Her advice can help you succeed.

"The most important thing is compatibility. The job must be a good fit for you. Ask yourself, 'Is this the company I want to work for?' Maybe a friend said, 'I like working here,' but that doesn't mean that YOU will like it. Research the company and the jobs. If the job offers some of the responsibilities you have enjoyed in the past, as well as an opportunity to gain new experience, it could be a match. The company should be able to take you where you want to go and vice versa. That could be a good career move."

Nichole advises to be strategic in your job search. Start early to determine what you want from a job and what skills you need to add to get the jobs you want. For example, freshmen or sophomores can attend career fairs and tell recruiters, "I want to be strategic and gain the experience I will need for this position. What are the qualifications for your jobs?" Most will be happy to talk with you.

When it comes to job applications, Nichole says, "Follow instructions! If there is a question on the application, answer it. Do not say 'see resume.' That question is there for a reason and you need to take the time to answer it. Pay attention to details, even if some recruiters are more forgiving these days about spelling and grammar. Spell names correctly, whether you are referring to the recruiter or the company.

She advises not to put your picture on your resume because it could lead to discrimination, and to stay away from personal details. "Tell us about your job qualifications."

Companies usually want to fill positions quickly. If you are not available for several weeks, make the company aware so they can plan accordingly. Be honest with the company and with yourself about your true availability.

Nichole encourages job seekers to express your interest for the job in your application, in cover letters, in the interview. If you aren't enthusiastic, the next candidate might be. Enthusiasm can win jobs, so express yours! Then, when you get the job, be ready to prove you were the right choice with your performance.

PLAN for Success

Success is more likely when we have a written plan. Use the online template *Plan for Success* to create your own written plan for successfully completing Part 3, Chapters 6–7.

"The problem human beings face is not that we aim too high and fail, but that we aim too low and succeed."

—Michelangelo Aim high!

STORIES FROM THE JOB SEARCH

(JACOB) ELI THOMAS

Lead Data Science Instructor

Eli felt that his career had stalled. He decided to switch careers and upskill with additional education. He did his research, looking for the next "hot" in-demand jobs. An article, "Data Scientist: The Sexiest Job of the 21st Century," described a data scientist as having skills in business, math, and software. He could do that! So, he enrolled in a year-long program and spent four hours a day commuting to and from school to get the degree.

The new job search began six months into the program when companies presented summer internship projects. Eli choose to work with Litterati, a start-up company dedicated to minimizing litter in the world. Eli would work on global projects, even one for the United Nations! As an immigrant from South America, he was especially excited about working globally to make a difference. And it was a great way to expand his Organization Network. He earned the title "Head of Data Science," which looks great on his resume and LinkedIn profile.

A school career expert helped him hone his LinkedIn profile, especially the Summary Statement. The summary did more than describe Eli as a data scientist, it told Eli's story so that potential employers would see all the skills Eli would bring to their company. His resume as a subset of his LinkedIn profile and the two documents were completely aligned.

With degree in hand, the real job search began. Eli used both the Career Network strategy and Cold Leads Strategy. His Cold Leads online applications resulted in requests for interviews, but the process took months. While waiting, a network contact asked if she could recommend him for a job at Flatiron School, a company that teaches technology and was interested in creating new courses in Big Data. Eli agreed. Flatiron quickly reviewed Eli's strong LinkedIn profile, and asked him to send a resume and 20-minute YouTube video of him training a live class. After running a criminal background check, they offered him the job.

Now Eli has the best of all worlds. His pay is significantly higher, he's doing work he loves, he works virtually (no commute!) and is super excited to be writing the Big Data training courses as well as a new textbook on the topic. And he still has time to volunteer with Litterati.

Eli's advice: Use LinkedIn. Stay in touch with your network. Warm Introductions are much stronger than Cold Leads, Make sure that your LinkedIn profile shows the three-dimensional you, with all the skills you bring and the passions that drive you in your career.

6 Find Job Openings

OVERVIEW

In this chapter, you will learn how to use two different strategies to find jobs. The first is a Career Network strategy in which you will build a powerful network of people who can give you career advice and serve as Warm Introductions to help you find job openings. The second strategy uses Cold Leads and online systems to find job postings. Then you will learn to choose carefully which postings to apply for, by focusing on those that are a good match to your job target.

OUTCOMES

❶ Describe the Career Network strategy for finding jobs, page 163

❷ Describe and prepare for Career Network Meetings, page 170

❸ Describe the Cold Leads strategy for finding jobs that match your job target, page 175

❹ Identify which job postings are a good match to your job target, page 180

CAREER ACTION WORKSHEETS

6-1: Your Network List, page 185

6-2: Career Network Meeting Outline, page 187

6-3: Hold a Career Network Meeting, page 189

6-4: Research Job Postings, page 191

6-5: Compare Job Postings to Your Job Target, page 193

WHERE ARE YOU ON THE JOURNEY?

PHASE 1: Prepare for the Journey
- *The Job Search Journey*
- *Know Yourself to Market Yourself*
- *Picture Yourself in the Workplace*

PHASE 2: Create Your Resume
- *Plan Your Resume*
- *Write Your Resume*

PHASE 3: Apply for Jobs
- **Find Job Openings**
- *Write Job Applications*

PHASE 4: Shine at Interviews
- *Know the Interview Essentials*
- *Prepare for Your Interview*
- *Interview Like a Pro*

PHASE 5: Connect, Accept, and Succeed
- *Stay Connected with Potential Employers*
- *Dealing with Disappointment*
- *Take Charge of Your Career*

PHASE 3 Apply for Jobs
Step 1, *Find Job Openings*

Your goal in Chapter 6 is to learn to use and grow your Career Network, develop your strategy for finding job openings, and compare jobs so that you can apply for jobs you are most likely to get a positive response from and that are a good match to your job target.

Your network can be a key to a treasure trove of job openings on your Job Search Journey. Pick up a key from everyone you know and start opening doors.

THE CAREER NETWORK STRATEGY FOR FINDING JOB OPENINGS

You want to have a Career Network Strategy to find jobs. Numerous studies have noted that the majority of jobs—70%–85%—are found through **networking.*** Networking is the process of developing relationships with people. These people could potentially help you find jobs and help with your job search in other ways. The higher the quality of your network, the greater your chances are of finding someone who knows about a job that could be a great match with your job target.

Recall from Chapter 4 that **Warm Introductions** are personal introductions to an employer who might have a job opening that isn't even posted yet. People in your Career Network can give you or help you get Warm Introductions to job openings.

A Career Network Strategy to find jobs consists of these steps:

1. Define who is in your network.
2. Evaluate the quality and size of your network connections.
3. Expand your network as needed.
4. Put your network to work for you.

Define Who Is in Your Network

Who do you know? And who do they know? That is your Career Network. In Chapter 1, you learned about how to look at your Career Network as four separate lists of people that you know. There are people from your workplace, organization, profession, and personal life. (See "Your Career Network" box, page 167.)

It's obvious to seek help from your close ties, but it is your further connections who often provide great job leads because they travel in different circles. That friend your Aunt Kris always talks about might hold a gold nugget for you on your Job Search Journey. So treat every meeting—virtual and live—as an opportunity to create a Career Network connection that can serve as or lead to a Warm Introduction to that perfect job opening.

Employers often prefer to hire people recommended by their current employees because their employees understand the company, know what the job requires, and are more likely to know if a person is a good

---

Job Postings and Job Openings—There Is a Difference

A **job posting** is an advertisement created by an employer that alerts others to the need to fill a job opening. It describes the job responsibilities and job requirements, including experience, education, and skills.

A **job opening** is a job vacancy which an employer intends to fill, either now or in the future. The job opening may or may not be officially posted or advertised.

Why does it matter? If you can identify and apply for a job opening before it becomes a job posting, you have less competition. Only those insiders who know about it might want to apply.

*Source: https://www.payscale.com/career-news/2017/04/many-jobs-found-networking.

match with the company culture. This means that you should put effort into finding someone who works at your target employer. Make a network connection with them now, and they may be willing to provide a Warm Introduction for a job later.

Later, in Career Action Worksheet 6-1, you will create your Career Network list. By understanding who is in your network now, you can better leverage all your connections. You can ask for their help to expand your network by introducing you to others who might be helpful on your Job Search Journey.

Evaluate the Quality and Size of Your Current Career Network Connections

Look at your list. Which of your four networks is largest? Smallest? Typically, a person who is new to a career field will have a smaller number of people in their Industry Network list. Don't worry, there are ways to expand your network, especially the Industry Network.

Now look at the quality of your connections. Some ways to think about quality include how close you are to your connection, how close they are to your industry, and how big their influence is in either the industry or their workplace. In this section, you can read about improving the closeness of your connections. In the next section, Expand Your Network, you can learn how to identify connections that are closer to your industry and have higher levels of influence.

One way of evaluating how close you and your connections are is based on length of time you have known each other. According to Vern Schellenger, a principal consultant for Contacts Counts, LLC, another way is to rate the quality of your connects is by evaluating how much your connection knows and trusts you. Are you just acquaintances—knowing a little bit about each other—or are you

advocates—knowing each other's strengths, passions, goals, and a bit about your personal lives? It takes time to build high quality, trusting relationships. Ways to build closer connections include:

- Come into contact with each other more often. A few times a month is better than a few times a year, even if it's just giving a comment on social media or emailing them an article every now and then that they might find interesting.

- Let them know what you are good at and what they can count on you for, through your interactions.

- Let them see your character and competence, and look for theirs, either through shared experiences or through sharing stories about your life.

- Don't just "take" from your connections; "give" too. You might not think you have anything to give, but you do. A smile, a listening ear, a link to one of their interests like a new restaurant close to them. Listen to your connections to learn more about them and what they need or want. You'll be surprised how easy it is to find something you can offer them in return.*

People in your Career Network should feel that you will represent them well if they refer you to *their* network. Demonstrate that you are a professional who understands and follows the rules of the business world. For example, dress appropriately when you meet with your contacts in person. On voice mail, leave professional-sounding messages that are clear and to the point. Be careful not to put new contacts on the spot by asking personal questions or pushing for insider information that they are hesitant to share. Make sure to thank every person you meet, in the moment that you meet them as well as through a follow-up email.

---

*Source: The Key to Attracting Advocates Feb 2014 SMPS Marketer.pdf

Throughout *Your Career* you will read about standard workplace expectations. Look through the following list and read about these topics as needed.

- Chapter 4, personal references
- Chapter 4, business cards
- Chapters 5 and 8, writing tips
- Chapter 8, professional dress
- Chapter 8, phone etiquette
- Chapter 8, interview etiquette
- Chapter 10, professional binder or portfolio
- Chapter 11, thank-you notes

Be prepared to make a good impression by learning as much as you can about the situations you may encounter during networking—before you encounter them.

▶ **CAREER ACTION**
Complete Worksheet 6-1
Your Network List, page 185

Keep expanding your network. Your network can help you now during your Job Search Journey, and your network can be invaluable in the future when you are on the job.

Expand Your Network

The more time you spend with others who work in your career field, the more likely it is that you will learn about job postings and gain valuable information that you can use in interviews and on the job. The earlier you start, the more contacts you will gather. Do not hesitate to start building your network before you are actively seeking a job.

No matter where you are—school, grocery store, the gym—look for opportunities to initiate conversations about your job search. Be friendly and outgoing, and introduce yourself to people. If someone asks how you are doing or what you've been up to, tell them that you're busy looking for a job. Often that is all it takes for other people to ask about the type of job you are seeking. You never know—they just might know someone in your field.

Remember, quality connections are not ones that are just close, but are in your industry and have influence. High-quality in your Career Network means people who:

- **Are in your career field,** because they are likely to have more relevant leads.
- **Are in higher level positions,** because they are likely to be more aware of unadvertised job postings and may be able to connect you directly to the hiring manager.
- **Know you well,** or who know someone who knows you well, or have met you in person, because these people are most likely to want to take time to help you.

Expand Your Career Network

The point of a networking strategy is to build relationships that lead to Warm Introductions to job openings and postings. At this point in your Job Search Journey, people in your Industry Network are the most likely to be able to help. There are four ways to expand your Industry Network: ask your current network for referrals, find opportunities with new people you meet, attend professional and industry events, and build your presence online in your industry.

Reach out to everyone in your current Career Network—family, friends, former coworkers and classmates, alumni, mentors, and other people you know—by phone, text, social media, email, or in person. Let them know that you are looking for a new job and share your job search goals. For example, you might say, "I'm working on a degree as a geology technician, and my ideal job would combine outdoor work and laboratory analysis. Do you know anyone in this field or industry that can help me learn more?" Notice that you are not asking for a job or for the name of someone who can give you a job. You are in the "search" phase of your Job Search Journey, looking for network connections that might eventually lead to an employee-referred job posting.

You can also get connections by asking about other people. When you meet new people in social situations, ask what they do for a living and don't be afraid to ask how they found their job and request their advice. Asking directly is typically not as productive as saying something like this:

- What advice would you give me about finding a job in the auto mechanics industry?
- Do you have any advice for finding a job in sports medicine in this area of the country?
- Who else do you think I should talk to about jobs in our field?

This approach focuses on the word *advice* and makes your contacts more inclined to help. Don't forget that to build your connections into something of higher quality, you will need to listen closely to discover what they need. What can you offer them? Then continue to deepen the quality of the relationship by building trust, demonstrating your character, and showing that you are competent.

Seek High-Quality Contacts Whenever Possible

There are both one-time events and ongoing involvement opportunities that allow you to connect directly with people in your field. Think of these events as pre-interviews and prepare accordingly (look back at Shane and Lillian's conversation on page 41). Prepare conversation starters such as "What brings you here?" or "This location works well for this event." Practice introducing yourself. Set a personal goal to talk with a certain number of people.

Here are some places to connect with people in your field:

- **Attend career fairs.** Career fairs (also called job fairs) are excellent networking opportunities because you can connect with many potential employers at one time.

- **Attend networking events.** In a typical year, the Chamber of Commerce and other organizations in your area will hold networking events for job seekers. There might be events for veterans, for women, for job seekers in a specific career field, and so on.

- **Participate in professional associations and industry trade groups.** Join and be active in professional, industry, trade, and other relevant associations or groups, many of which offer assistance to job seekers. Nearly every career field has such a group; search for "*career field* trade group" or "*career field* professional association" (for example, "cosmetology trade group" or "cosmetology professional association"). The websites themselves are a valuable source of career information and job leads.

- **Do volunteer work.** Volunteer opportunities can be found in nonprofit organizations that have limited resources. Look for organizations that will likely need your professional skill set. For example, Habitat for Humanity needs volunteers with skills in carpentry, plumbing, and roofing, as well as the less obvious skills of volunteer coordination, meal preparation, accounting, leadership, project management, and many more. Your volunteer contacts can be a wonderful source of networking connections.

- **"Try before you buy."** Consider "practicing" in your career field to gain experience working side by side with people you can learn from. Cooperative education, internships, and volunteer positions are excellent opportunities for networking and may lead to full-time employment. Cooperative education programs place you in a paying job in your field, alternating semesters between school and work. Internships provide a period of supervised work and training in a workplace and are often scheduled during breaks in the academic calendar.

If you are shy or uncomfortable talking with strangers, consider volunteering to work at the registration table, hand out material, or help with other tasks that will help you interact with many people more comfortably. Be ready to exchange business cards and contact information. Take the time after each event to make notes about your conversations and enter the contact and job lead information into your tracking system, as discussed below.

Your Career Network: How to Network at a Meeting or Event

Attending a professional or industry meeting or event for the first time can be awkward. You don't know anyone, and it's hard to start conversations that will help you find a job. While it might be the first thing on your mind to ask for a job, you know that can turn off strangers from offering help. So what should you do?

First, take the pressure off. Networking is about relationship building, and results are not likely to happen overnight. So, don't expect it. Turning strangers into close connections is the key to getting the help you're looking for. The Warm Introduction might not happen the first time you meet, but it may happen over the next several meetings.

Next, walk in with a reasonable goal to keep you motivated and moving. Some examples: collect ten business cards or contact names in your industry, give out 20 of your business or contact cards to people you spoke with, talk to five people for at least three minutes about their view of this industry or their own job in it.

Have a short list of starter questions. Examples include, how long have you been part of this organization/professional or industry group? What have been the keys to your success in this field? What do you see as the value of being part of this group and attending these monthly meetings? I'm new in this industry; how long have you been in this field of work?

Plan and practice a few 30-Second Commercials to introduce yourself to others. For example: "Hi I'm ____. I am interested in the field of ___ and am getting my degree in ___. I would like to know more about the industry, both about what it's like on a day to day job, and about what the hot topics are in the industry. That's why I'm here today. How about you?" With networking "speeches," keep them short, and plan for a way to hand the conversation over to them. Do more listening than talking.

Listen with the intent of giving back. If you listen, you will discover things that others need that you might have. And when you listen with the intent of giving back, the entire session can feel more relaxed for you. Take notes and be sure to follow up with people after the session.

Enjoy your next networking session!

Finally, you can expand your network by building your presence online. Consider which social media platforms are used the most by your industry, if any. Then, see what opportunities they have for connecting with new people online. For example, LinkedIn offers the Groups and Companies features to expand your social network. You can:

- Join the top five largest membership groups in your field or industry in your local area, your region, and, finally, at the national level. Everyone who is in a group with you is automatically accessible to become a first-degree connection. The higher the number of members in a group you have joined, the larger your network can become.

- Look for people who have posted great discussion topics in your groups. Request to add them to your connections and set up a Career Network Meeting with them.

- Use the search function to find companies you would like to work for. Then, on the company page, look at the section How You're Connected. Request to be added as a connection to relevant employees or those who you have a mutual connection with. You can then directly message the individual.

- Respond thoughtfully to posts a company has posted or relevant discussions in Groups. You never know who will see your comments and request to be connected with you!

On Twitter, expanding your social network is easy because you can follow anyone. There is no "application process" where a user may not accept your follow. Follow relevant thought leaders, professional and industry associations, companies, and publications in your field. Retweet content you find interesting. Reply and start conversations using the hashtag feature as appropriate. You can reach out to individuals directly and message them, but it's best to wait until you've shown interest through retweeting and replying to their feed.

On any platform, it doesn't hurt to create a post asking for recommendations of people you should talk to about your job target. Social media platforms allow access to many people today that you would not know or meet locally. Take advantage of your Career Network online!

Keep Track of Your Network

You made a list of your Career Network in Career Action Worksheet 6-1 and evaluated the size and quality of your network. You've just learned about ways to expand your network. It's important to keep track of all your connections and contact information so that you can reach out to them. This includes updates and adding your new connections to the list.

In Chapter 1, you learned how important it is to keep things organized so that you can find them when you need them. This applies to your contacts too. Choose just one or two methods to keep track of people. Maybe it's in Contacts on your smartphone (which you back up regularly and protect against viruses). Maybe your email system has a good contact organization method. You might add your LinkedIn connections or one other social media platform as the most current way to reach them, but confirm that it is sufficient for recording the information you need about active contacts. Here is a list of the type of things you should track.

- **Name,** proper spelling of first and last name, nickname, and if they prefer being called by their first name or Mr./Mrs./Ms./Doctor.

- **Contact information,** as many addresses as you can find and which they prefer. This includes email, Twitter, their LinkedIn profile link, phone number, physical mailing address, street address, etc.

- **Position and company name.** If this information changes, try to be aware of it. Be sure to congratulate them if it's a promotion.
- **How you know them,** perhaps from a job fair, from high school, through an introduction by another of your connections, at a networking event, etc.
- **Their connection to your job search.** Why is this connection important to have in your network? Do they have knowledge of your career field or of local companies you're interested in? Do they have general business connections or a large network of their own? Are they someone who has your interests at heart?
- **Your last interaction and your next interaction.** Keep notes about when you last spoke (date and summary information), and notes about when you next plan to connect. If they agreed to provide a Warm Introduction to their employers on your behalf, you should make a note of it and follow up when appropriate. If you sent a thank-you note, list the date, so you never have to worry and wonder if you really did send it. If you need to update the person after you connect with someone who he or she recommended to you, make a note of it.

Keeping track of your interactions with people in your Career Network is another way to demonstrate professionalism, and to build their trust in you.

Put Your Network to Work for You

Your network connections can provide many things for you on the Job Search Journey. But to get these things, you have to ask.

What You Can Ask of Your Career Network

The first step is to let everyone in your network know that you are looking for a job in a specific field and would appreciate it if they let you know if they have any related information or contacts who might be able to help. Let them know, in general terms, about your qualifications and availability. Share your master resume with people who might have an active interest in helping you. Here are the types of things you can get from such a request:

- General career advice
- Insider information about the industry, trends, and job search methods in your field
- Information about specific target employers
- Introductions to people who are in your career field
- Job leads
- A Career Network Meeting

What You Can Ask of Your Industry Network

You can get different types of help from people in your Industry Network. Because these people share your field of interest, occupation, or profession, they will understand the situation better and are more likely to have more exact information for you. They are also more likely to provide higher quality advice. Here are the types of things you might request from someone in your Industry Network:

- Career advice specific to your industry
- Insights into a typical workday
- Discussion on common misperceptions about work in this industry
- The value of specific certifications or additional training
- An introduction to others in your industry (add them to your network!)
- Accompany you to an industry association meeting
- A Career Network Meeting
- A Warm Introduction to a job opening!

YOUR CAREER NETWORK MEETINGS

What Is a Career Network Meeting?

A Career Network Meeting is a meeting set up by you to discuss career-related topics with anyone who is in your Career Network, or who might be. When you request a Career Network Meeting from someone in your network, you are asking for something very valuable: their time and their advice. What may surprise you is that people are often very willing to give this! So, don't hesitate to ask. Whether they realize it or not, when they give to you, they get back. They might get a compliment (they may feel flattered by your request), an opportunity to reflect on their own career, a chance to do a favor for the person who suggested you contact them, or simply the pleasure of taking a break from the routine and meeting someone new—you!

Request a Career Network Meeting

You are about to request a meeting for 20, 30, or 60 minutes. It might be face-to-face at a local coffee or sandwich shop (after all, most people need coffee or lunch) or a phone or video call. Remember, at this step, you are not asking for a job; you are in a listen-and-learn mode to learn more about the industry, where good jobs might be found, and how to improve your resume, job applications, and interview skills.

Here are the steps for requesting a Career Networking Meeting:

1. **Why Connect?** Identify what this person can offer you in your job search.

2. **What's the Goal?** Select 2–3 questions or topics that can guide the discussion.

3. **How to Connect?** Request via email, phone, social media platform, or in person.

(Also see Chapter 8, *Sound Impressive by Sounding Prepared.*)

4. **Accepted or Declined?** Make it enjoyable, not an obligation.

5. **When and Where?** Have an idea, but be ready to go with their preferences.

Why Connect?

First, understand why it might be beneficial to meet with this person. Too often, people set up a meeting because someone said that this contact would be a good person to talk to. But why? Are they in the same field as you? Does their company hire people in your field? Do they give career advice as part of their daily job? If you are unsure of the answer, reconnect with the person who suggested it.

If you are setting up the meeting with someone who is already in your network, think about what they can offer you. Career insights? Grammar check on your resume or draft job application? Suggestions on how to connect with more people in your career field? Ideas about how to find a good job in your area of expertise? (Remember, you are not asking for a job at this point. You are asking for advice and direction.)

What's the Goal?

Based on why you want to meet with this person, narrow down your goal to 2–3 questions or topics to guide the discussion for this meeting. The examples above can get you started—see "What You Can Ask of Your Network" and "What You Can Ask of Your Industry Network."

How to Connect?

Choose your method of connection based on what you think they might prefer, or which method will put you in a good light.

- **Email:** Introduce yourself. Explain that you are doing a job search, and why you would like to talk with them. If applicable, tell them who recommended that you make this connection. Request time to discuss your list of questions and topics. Offer the alternative of connecting in person or virtually within the next month. Request their availability. Do not go into detail about when you are or are not available. Right now, just get a YES, and work out the details later. See the sample contact note in Figure 6-1.

- **Phone:** Before you call, outline what you will say (a) if the person answers the phone, (b) if you get their voice mail, and (c) if a receptionist or office administrator answers the call and is willing to set up a time and place. Don't expect to talk to your connection right then; plan to set up a convenient time to call back or meet in person. However, be prepared with your questions in case they suggest that the two of you talk right now.

Social Media: See "Email" above. You might need to shorten the message if the social media platform limits the number of words per message. If so, take it in steps. First, who you are, why you are contacting

Figure 6-1 Sample Contact Networking Notes

Sample Meeting Request

Dear [Mr./Ms. Contact Name],

I was recently referred to you by Grace Santana of Fairfield Tech. She recommended you as an excellent source of information about the physical therapy field.

I am a student at Fairfield Tech about to begin a search for a position as a physical therapy assistant, and I would welcome the chance to hear your advice about our career field and get your feedback on my qualifications and skills.

Do you have 30 minutes available to talk with me in the next two weeks, either in person or on the phone? Thanks in advance for your insights. I look forward to meeting you.

Sincerely,

[Your name and contact information]

Sample Thank-You Note

Dear First Name [or Mr./Ms. Contact Name],

Thank you again for taking the time to talk with me today about our career field and my career objectives. I enjoyed hearing about your job at Woodside Physical Therapy, and I appreciate your advice about the upcoming national exam. I'm looking forward to reviewing the online resources you suggested.

As you requested, I have attached my resume. Thank you in advance for your generous offer to give me advice about improving it.

I will be in contact from time to time to keep you updated on my job search. Thank you again for all the valuable information.

Best regards,

[Your name and contact information]

them, and whether they would be willing to connect. Next, talk about how to connect, either in person or virtually, including when and where. Finally, outline your goals for getting together.

Accept or Decline?

Remember that your connections are **doing you a favor** by helping you with your job search. Make it easy and fun for them. Don't push to meet in person if they prefer to talk by phone, and do be prepared to change your schedule to accommodate theirs. Smile as you talk or type; this brings out your positivity, and others are more likely to be attracted to your positive attitude. Whether they accept your request or not, always thank them for their time.

When and Where?

If the connection agrees to get together with you to discuss your questions, gently encourage a face-to-face meeting. In-person Career Network Meetings are best because body language communicates so much of the message. Offer to meet at a coffee shop or a local lunch spot where you can sit across from each other without too much noise. Settle on a place and a time that are convenient for your connection. It might be inconvenient for you, but that's the price for getting some of their valuable time.

No matter what, always thank them for their time.

Be Prepared for Your Career Network Meeting

Getting ready for your Career Network Meeting involves these things:

- **Be physically prepared.**
- **What to wear.** Dress like you have a job in the industry already. Be professional. (Tip: do your laundry the day before.)
- **Plan your trip.** Make sure you have a way to get to the meeting place. (Tip: have the car gassed up, the route mapped out, and time it so you arrive 15–20 minutes early to allow for the unexpected.)
- **What to bring.** Be ready to pay for your own drinks or lunch. Print two copies of your resume and put them in a folder. Also, bring your list of questions, with space for taking notes. (See "Good Questions to Ask in a Career Network Meeting" on page 173). A pen or pencil, even if you are using a tablet or iPad, so you can make a note on a business card or your resume.
- **Be emotionally prepared.** Be prepared to talk about your efforts in positive terms; don't whine about how long you have been looking for a job or how many bills you need to pay. The people who give you leads may be taking a risk with their own reputation, and they expect you to make a good impression on the people they refer you to. Never forget about what kind of the impression you are making when you meet with people in your Career Network and talk about your job search.
- **Do your homework.** Know something about the person you are meeting and the company where they work. Look at your connection's social media profile and their company website before the meeting so that you can ask questions or compliment the person or their company. This will help you demonstrate your interest and professionalism.
- **Prepare your questions and comments.** As you prepare your questions, you are mentally rehearsing your Career Network Meeting. Start with some warm-up questions that help you break the ice. Include your Personal Brand Statement or a 30-Second Commercial. List questions related to your goals for this meeting. Finally, list some wrap-up thoughts and questions. See "Good Questions to Ask in a Career Network Meeting."

Meet With Your Connection

Here is the general flow for a Career Network Meeting.

Introductions. Meet or call your connection. "Hi, I'm [name], are you [their name]?" Shake hands. Thank them for agreeing to meet with you, work on being likeable, by smiling, listening and being courteous. Seek out common interests. Use your warm-up questions to get things going.

Get to the Point. Shift quickly to the main part of the session by reiterating your goal for the meeting. You might say, for example, "As I mentioned, I'm about to graduate and am trying to better understand what companies might offer a good place for me to use my skills and education." Briefly tell them about your job search goals, using your Personal Brand Statement and 30-Second Commercial. Then lead with a question related to your goals for this meeting and listen to your connection. Let them dictate the flow of the meeting, but get it back on track with another question if there is a lull or the conversation is getting off track. Try to learn about their career, their company, the industry, and the business environment. Think of these meetings as practice runs for actual interviews. With each successive meeting, you will likely find that you can deliver your message smoothly in a very short time.

Listen. Listen. Listen. Listen for what employers need, descriptions of the work environment, the terms and language used by professionals in that field, examples of how career paths develop over time, and the process the company uses to fill job openings. Ask follow-up questions to clarify your understanding or to get deeper meaning. Then listen again.

If You Get a Job Lead. While you typically are not asking directly for a job, some connections may offer you information about a job that is posted or soon to be posted. Take accurate notes on how to find the job posting and/or how to apply for the job. Ask if you can mention their name when you apply for these jobs. Don't be disappointed if they say "no." It likely has nothing to do with you and more about company politics, procedures, or policy. Better yet, ask if your connection would be willing to pass on your resume directly to the HR or hiring manager. They might even be willing to act as a Warm Introduction at this point to another person you can talk to that is closer to the job opening. This may give you a higher chance at getting an interview and, ultimately, the job*. Keep your connection up to date about your job search, because that is the polite way to work with your network connections.

Wrap Up the Meeting. Respect the time limits that have been set. Busy employees can't take too much time from their workday. Try setting an alarm that will signal you 2–5 minutes before the end of your meeting. Use this time for any wrap-up questions you have prepared.

If you haven't done so already, ask if you can share your resume with them. If they say yes, offer a second copy of your resume and ask if they can pass it on to appropriate people in their company. This will be your Warm Introduction to their employer. Ask your connections if they can suggest other people who might help you learn more about career paths in your field. If you get a few names from every person you meet, your network will expand exponentially.

---

*Job seekers with personal referrals have about a 7%–20% higher chance of being offered the job. (Sources: (1) https://careerpivot .com/2017/employee-referrals-ticket-next-job/ (2) http://time .com/money/3994858/job-search-referral/)

Good Questions to Ask in a Career Network Meeting

Your list of questions should look professional (i.e., not scribbled on a piece of scrap paper). Leave space to take notes during the meeting or take notes on your device if you can do so without interrupting the flow of the conversation. Don't record the conversation, because you will need to have their permission and this can make the meeting too formal.

Here are some good questions to ask—but don't expect to ask all of them in 30 minutes. Let the conversation flow naturally, ask deeper questions based on their answers (known as active listening), and watch for cues that the person wants to end the meeting or phone call.

Conversation starters

- What drew you to this career field?
- Is this your first job in this career field?
- I see you have an award for ___. Can you tell me about that?
- How long have you worked at your company?

Job and career questions

- What is your typical workday like?
- Which parts of your job do you find most challenging? Most enjoyable?
- What is the culture like at your workplace/in this career field?
- What is a typical career path at your company or in this industry?
- What do you wish you had known when you started your career?
- What changes have you seen in this field? What changes do you anticipate?

Career advice

- What advice to you have for someone looking for a job in this field?
- Does my job goal seem realistic and achievable?
- Do you recommend any additional training or certifications?
- What professional, industry or other associations do you recommend joining?
- What publications or websites do you recommend?
- Who else would you recommend I speak with? When I call, may I use your name?

Wrap-up comments and questions

- Thank you—for your time and insights.
- May I call you if I have follow-up questions?
- When can I expect your feedback on my resume (or draft job application)?
- When do you think I should reach out to (name of person they agree to introduce you to)?
- May I share my resume with you? Here is an extra copy. Please share it as you see fit.
- I'll keep you up to date on my progress. It'd be nice to have you as a connection after I have a new job in the industry.
- Is there anything I can do for you? (If you think of anything later, please let me know.)

Summarize any agreements you two made during the meeting. Be sure to have their contact information so you can follow up with a thank-you note and update on your progress. Tell them how much you appreciate their time and give a short summary of what you learned from them. Thank them. Say goodbye with a smile.

Follow Up

If you made any agreements during the meeting, such as to send a digital copy of your resume of draft job application, follow up immediately! Preferably before 8:00 a.m. the next day. At a minimum, send a message summarizing your agreements, including dates by which you will complete your part of the agreement. Then send a thank-you note, message, or email within one day after the meeting.

You should also follow up with anyone who referred you to the connection and let them know how the meeting went. Your goal is to maintain your relationships and, ideally, get two more connections from every meeting. Keep your network up to date on your progress, especially if your goals change or become more specific. A well-written thank-you note creates a good impression and will remind your connections of your job search. If some new information comes to them, your thank-you note will remind them to share the information with you. See the sample thank-you note in Figure 6-1 on page 171.

▶ *CAREER ACTION*
Complete Worksheet 6-2
Career Network Meeting Outline, page 187

▶ *CAREER ACTION*
Complete Worksheet 6-3
Hold a Career Network Meeting, page 189

Real World Scenario **6-1**   Ralph was feeling frustrated with his job search. He was sticking to his goal of applying for 15 jobs every week, but he hadn't gotten any positive responses from his applications. It was time for a strategy change. He looked at the local Chamber of Commerce website and saw that there were several business events coming up in the next two weeks. He registered and attended an event held in the evening, after his classes and part-time job were over for the day. He had an excellent conversation with the owner of a local business who was looking for more employees. The business owner suggested that Ralph call his site manager to set up a Career Network Meeting.

What opportunities do you have to get out from behind your computer and in front of a live audience? In addition to live meetings, how can you personalize your online interactions?

THE COLD LEADS STRATEGY FOR FINDING JOBS

While many jobs are never posted, a very large number of jobs *are* posted, as you can see by searching online. So, while you are waiting for your network connections and professional, industry, or trade groups to come through for you, get busy—take the search into your own hands and apply using the Cold Leads Strategy.

A Cold Lead is an opportunity for a job found through an impersonal source where neither the job seeker nor the recruiter or hiring manager know each other. You can find Cold Leads from several sources:

1. **Online job sites** are an impersonal technology-driven approach that reveals a larger set of job postings with specific job requirements. By using a job site's search

engines and job alerts, you are less likely to miss a good job posting. These sites post jobs that companies pay a fee to list. Examples are Indeed.com and LinkedIn.com/Jobs/. Also look at job sites provided by groups in your industry, profession, or trade. For example, RoofingContractor.com, MedTech.org, Project Management Institute and NewEngineer.com. See the next section for more on this very popular method of finding job postings.

2. **Employer websites** list available jobs and accept applications directly. Government agencies and most not-for-profit organizations frequently provide links to job postings.

3. **Government job information sites** can link you to jobs postings. Try usajobs.gov, or a state website such as ohio-means-jobs.

4. **Newspaper classified ads** have help wanted notices. While not as common as in the past, these have job postings that are close to home. But be careful! Spot phony ads. These may require you to pay a fee up front or give personal information such as your Social Security number. The more respectable newspapers (online or print) are more likely to contain legitimate job postings.

5. **College career center** have a wide range of services. The staff can help point you to job postings that match your skill set and needs. They can also help you prepare for the job search with such things as personal assessments, resume writing, mock interviews, thank-you notes, and customized advice. Some career centers help students network with alumni in their career field. If you are an alumnus, ask what job search resources are available.

6. **Private employment agencies** can help you find jobs with a particular employer, especially if the agency works in your field or has a long-term relationship with a specific employer. Some agencies find employees for companies, while others actually hire the employee and contract that person to the company. Some charge employers for finding full-time employees (commonly called head-hunters), while others charge the job applicant. Research the agency to make sure they are legitimate. Do an online search to uncover lawsuits against agencies, and read independent reviews by people who have used the agency. Before you sign a contract, reach out to your network and have them read the contract to look for red flags.

Use Job Sites Selectively

Some people on the Job Search Journey believe that if they simply post their resume to an online job site, recruiters will come to their doorstep with job offers.

Many people on the Job Search Journey think that finding a job is as simple as searching online and applying to as many jobs as possible to assure they get one. However, this is a very time-consuming approach. Research shows that, on average, it takes at least 10 minutes to complete an application, and some require up to 50 minutes!* Also, since a lot of job seekers rely on the Cold Leads Strategy, there is a lot of competition!

Obviously, you want to use your time wisely and focus on finding those jobs that are an ideal match for your personality and preferences, your skills and qualifications, and your interests. Find job postings that are a match to your Job Target.

Be aware that there are two types of online job sites. Both are useful, but it helps to know which you are dealing with. (See "Apply Quickly and Directly" to understand how this makes a difference for you.) One type uses a job search engine to aggregate job listings from thousands of job boards, career sites,

---

*Source: http://blog.indeed.com/2016/08/15/fastest-job-application-process/.

and recruiter listings. Job postings arrive here a few days after the post is initially put online. So, job search engine sites are a bit behind on bringing you the latest job openings. The other is a job board where companies and recruiters pay a fee to list job postings. If you tap into these, you'll be one of the first to see the posting. The downside is that there are so many of these. And then, some online job sites do both! There are four types of online job sites: keyword-based, industry-based, location-based, and employer-based.

- **Keyword-based job sites** are the most commonly used methods for finding job postings today. Indeed.com, SimplyHired, Career-Builder, ZipRecruiter, and Monster are a few good ones, but there are many, many others. Choose just one or two sites so that you are not overwhelmed with too much information or duplicate postings. (The same job can appear on many sites.) In addition, companies are actively posting jobs on social media. See "Jobs On Social Media."

- **Industry and trade group job boards** post only jobs for your industry, so there are fewer to cull through. Ask people in your Industry Network which industry job boards are most helpful. Sign up for several of these. If the job board offers an alerts feature, use it.

- **Location-based job sites** are sponsored by a state, city, or country as a way to attract or keep talent in their location. If you are trying to stay local, or are focused on a specific location, using these might be better than that second keyword job board you were going to look at.

- **Employer-based job boards** list available jobs and accept applications for that company only. These may also be found on the "Careers" page of the target employer's website. If you have your heart set on working for a specific company, search this one regularly or set up an alert if available.

Also, if you find a job posting on one of the many online job sites, try to find it on the target employer's job board and apply directly. You may get preferential attention.

Compare Job Postings to Your Job Target

This part is covered under "Identify Which Job Postings Are a Good Match" later in this chapter. It is also covered in Career Worksheet 6-5.

Apply Quickly and Directly

See Chapter 7 about applying for jobs. For now, it's worth knowing that recent research shows that job seekers can spend up to 15 hours a week searching online for jobs. That's a lot of time, so be sure to streamline the process by following the steps suggested for the two strategies: Network Strategy and Cold Leads Strategy.

When you find a posting that is a good match, apply now (after reading Chapter 7). Do not procrastinate. Research also shows that half of the people who eventually got the job had applied for it in the first week after it was posted. With all the preparation you've done in Chapters 1–7, you can go quickly when it comes to applying so you get interviews!

Keep Track of Applications and Selectively Follow up

With so many options to find leads and apply for jobs, it is easy to get overwhelmed. You can find jobs through your network or through Indeed, Monster, LinkedIn, and the company's website, all for the same job! Savvy job seekers keep track of each critical job lead and especially those that they apply for. As you finish reading Part 3 and Part 4, it will become clear why tracking is so important. For the latest on how to keep track of your Job Search Journey, do a search on "how to organize your job search." Here are some popular ways to stay on top of it.

Jobs on Social Media

Most social networks have a job search feature. Three popular ones are described below, but there are others. Use one of these, along with the other job boards listed above, with the caution to avoid applying for the same job twice.

LinkedIn: Use the menu to search for jobs. (Can't find it? Do a search on how to find jobs on LinkedIn for the latest set of directions.) When you find a job you're interested in, you can apply through LinkedIn or the company site. Sometimes, you can even see the recruiter who posted the job and follow up with him or her directly. LinkedIn Premium Membership allows you to message people you may not have access to otherwise, as well as access information such as wages or salary range for a specific job. Additionally, you can view how you compare to other applicants for the job and apply with more confidence. It's a little pricey, so maybe just do it for a month, then cancel your subscription.

Twitter: Many companies have job-related Twitter handles that you can follow for the latest updates on jobs. Handles refer to Twitter usernames, which are preceded by the @ symbol.

Facebook: "Jobs on Facebook" became a thing around 2017. It continues to grow. Learn more directly on the Facebook platform. In addition, you can *like* a company's page and engage through its posts. When you *like* a company, this demonstrates agreement and is shared with your social media network. Another approach is to see who in your network works at companies you are interested in.

Rawpixel.com/Shutterstock.com

1. Use a spreadsheet or document table. Include the following:
   - **Company Name** you applied to
   - **Contact** at the company, often a Director of Human Resources
   - **Contact Information** for your contact, such as email and phone number
   - **Date Applied** and how you applied (paper, or the online site used)
   - **Application Package Summary** (Chapter 7), including which file you sent as your resume, application, and, if applicable, cover letter or any additional materials, like a portfolio or reference list
   - **Interview Date**
   - **Follow-Up,** such as when you sent a thank you email or letter

   - **Status**, such as if you were rejected, offered the job, asked in for a second interview, asked to take additional tests, including drug tests, etc.

2. Use an online job tracking service. Consider using an online job tracking service such as JibberJobber or StartWire to manage your job search (jobs you apply for, contact information, etc.). These services have a free level, but each one has a learning curve. As JibberJobber's CEO Jason Alba says: "In my job search I didn't think I'd need a job search organizational tool, but as my job search went on, and I continued to network and apply for jobs, the need for a tool like JibberJobber grew exponentially—because the amount of data I was collecting grew exponentially!

OVERCOMING BARRIERS
Dress Like You Have the Job

When you meet with a network contact, dress almost as if it were an interview—professionally and conservatively. Follow these simple tips to make a good impression:

- Be neat. Even the nicest clothes look unattractive when stained, wrinkled, or covered with dog hair.

- Pay extra attention to good hygiene. Simple things make a difference, like using mouthwash and cleaning under your fingernails.

- Avoid revealing or tight clothing such as tank tops, shorts, or low-rise jeans. Showing skin is not appropriate in most workplaces, even if it is in style.

- Choose neutral tones and solid colors over prints and bright colors. Help them focus on YOU, not your clothes.

- Unless you are applying for a job at the gym, leave the athletic wear and yoga attire in your gym bag.

- Don't accidentally offend someone by wearing clothes with political or religious slogans or advertisements.

- Typically, it's best to cover up or downplay body art such as visible tattoos and piercings.

It's easy to get buried under the data and miss follow-up opportunities."*

3. Use an App. Many of the online job sites offer well-rated apps. Examples include Indeed Job Search, CareerBuilder, Glassdoor, Snagajob, and more. Research online to discover the latest and currently most popular apps for your industry. Look for those that show a history of your interactions for the jobs you apply for.

Keep good records of your online searches. All too often, job seekers spot something on the Internet and can't find it again. When you find a good site, use the bookmark function or the method of your choice to save the site and plan to check it regularly for updates.

For your most favorite top 3–10 jobs, follow up! Your goal is to set yourself apart from the applications that get submitted to online job boards. Two ways to do this are first, by having a Warm Introduction who knows your personality and initiative, and second, to send a Job Application Package. You'll read more about this in Chapters 7 and 11.

*Statistics show that job seekers who apply before 10 a.m., and in the first days after a job is posted, are five times more likely to get an interview.***

▶ CAREER ACTION
Complete Worksheet 6-4
Research Job Postings, page 191

Winners in all fields agree: Perseverance is a major factor in their success. When they meet an obstacle, they find a way around it.

*Source: https://www.thebalancecareers.com/organize-your-job-search-2060710.

**Source: https://talent.works/blog/2017/10/19/youre-5x-more-likely-to-get-job-interview-if-you-apply-by-10am/

IDENTIFY WHICH JOB POSTINGS ARE A GOOD MATCH

How will you compare these jobs? It's no problem if you have 20 or so jobs that are a current career fit. Apply for all of them. It ought to take only about 7 hours. However, with your expanding Career Network and good job search practices, your list of job leads and job postings can quickly expand to two or three times that many. You need a way to sort through the job postings and find the best ones to focus on.

Evaluate Your Qualifications for Job Openings

In Part 1 of this book, you spent time thinking about your career goals. In Part 2, you documented your qualifications in your resume. Now it's time to begin to compare job openings to your qualifications. Try it now by completing the first part of Career Action Worksheet 6-5 on page 193. Start with the handful of job postings that you found in Worksheet 6-4. Have your resume in front of you so you can see which qualifications are listed. Now evaluate each job posting and decide if it is a (1) stretch job, (2) job target, or (3) contingency job.

1. A **stretch job** is the hard-to-get "dream job" you would like to have in the near future. It might be in a competitive company or field that does not hire many applicants; it might offer exceptional compensation and benefits, or it might offer a desirable location. Since we are "our own worst critics," it is well worth it to apply for a job higher than you think you can achieve to "test the waters." Be confident and put your best efforts into a great cover letter and resume. You may be more competitive than you realize, and you might even get the job! Even if you are not fully qualified for the job yet, by reaching for these "stretch jobs," you get exposure and experience that can move you toward higher career goals in the future.

2. A **job target** is a job that is ideal for you right now. It suits your view of your current qualifications and interests, matches your compensation and work environment preferences, and provides a challenging and interesting work situation. You believe you have a realistic opportunity at being hired for such a job. (Just be careful that you aren't underestimating yourself!)

3. A **contingency job** is your backup plan. You could easily get this job, most likely because you are overqualified. It is a "safe bet." It is not your first choice because it might lack the compensation or work environment that you want, or it might not be in your preferred career area. It offers security by giving you a compensation and the opportunity to develop your workplace skills, but it is usually the job you take when you have exhausted other options. A contingency job should never be the end of your job search. If you are overqualified or unhappy, you can continue your Job Search Journey and eventually leave this job for a better one, but without burning bridges with the contingency employer. (See Chapter 13.)

Now use Career Action Worksheet 6-5 Part 2 to double-check your assessment against your qualifications. Have your resume in front of you for this one. By comparing your qualifications to each job posting, you confirm that it is worth applying for the job. If there is too big a gap, perhaps this is a dream job. Dream jobs take extra follow-up effort, as described elsewhere, such as a Warm Introduction, and personal delivery of your application package so that you can get the employer's attention. This double-check is also helpful to make sure you are not aiming too low in your job search.

> ▶ *CAREER ACTION*
>
> **Complete Worksheet 6-5**
>
> Compare Job Postings to Your Job Target, page 193

Determine the Best Match for You

Once you find job postings for which you are qualified, take the next step. Evaluate them against factors covered in Chapter 3, including your personal preferences, the workplace culture, and the employer/employee relationship. In Career Worksheet 6-5, Part 3, rate job postings for fit—great, okay, no match. Focus on the "great" ones first. (Before you apply, see Chapter 7, Apply for Jobs.)

Now look at several of the jobs that you rated as "great" or "good," that is, job postings from which you are qualified and are a good match to your job target. The next step is to compare these jobs and pick the top ones.

To do the comparison, make a list of the things that are most important to you on a job. Maybe it is compensation at a certain level, or avoiding travel. Using a simple 3, 2, 1 approach, rate each job in each category and sum up the total. For example, if you don't want to work on weekends, give a 3 to the job listings that indicate there is no weekend work, a 2 to the jobs with occasional weekend work, and a 1 to the jobs with regular or significant weekend hours.

After rating each job for the things that are important to you, add up the ratings. The jobs with the highest ratings are the ones you should focus on. If your ratings don't match your "gut feeling," it is time to talk with someone and review what you wrote down as being important. It is common to need to think through "what is important to me?" several times to better understand your own internal motives. Don't hesitate to go through the process a few times on paper or spreadsheet. After all, this assessment is much easier to do on a chart than in real life, jumping from job to job.

> **Real World Scenario 6-2**   Diana just completed her first Career Network Meeting with someone she met through online networking—and it was great. She had found Erik through LinkedIn and was intrigued because his job sounded like her ideal stretch job. Although she hadn't heard of Erik's company, what she learned about his day-to-day tasks and the most important qualifications for his job was promising. Even though she didn't meet all the qualifications, Diana had great examples from her current job proving her ability to do the day-to-day tasks and meet similar challenges. Erik gave Diana his department manager's name and email address, and told her to use his name in her email. Diana feels much more confident about applying for a stretch job like Erik's and is ready for her next Career Network Meeting.
>
> *What qualifications might be negotiable in the jobs you're interested in? How can you learn more about the day-to-day tasks? How can you find similar jobs you might be qualified for?*

Make the Best Match Job Postings a High Priority

When you find a job posting that feels like a best match, the employer is more likely to see the fit, too! Your resume and personal brand will naturally align well to what they are looking for and you will be more likely to hear a response. As you search for job postings and apply for jobs, be aware of the balance between stretch, target, and contingency jobs. It is important to have a few possibilities in each category, but most of your leads should be for jobs in the realistic job target category.

MAKE IT A HABIT
Schedule Time to Network

One of the biggest mistakes job seekers often make is focusing their job search strategy on applying to X number of jobs a week through online job boards such as CareerBuilder. While job boards are a critical resource, make it a habit to strategically connect and network with real, live people behind the job listings. When you create your Job Search Journey goals, include time every week for networking activities:

- **Reach out to your connections, both new and old.** Take time every week to keep your existing connections up to date on your progress, and follow up with your new connections, through posts, messages, emails, or phone calls.

- **Search for new connections.** Actively consider who could be your next lead-providing resource. Think about people in the "real world" and people you meet online.

- **Schedule Career Network Meetings.** Schedule several of these meetings each week or month with people who work in your career field or who can help you in other ways.

- **Go to events.** Schedule and attend career fairs and industry events, such as trade shows. Make these a priority on your calendar.

- **Find ways to be helpful, and interested.** Always listen to your connections with the intent to learn how you might be able to help them. Networking is not about talking and taking; it's about giving and building a trusting relationship. For people in your Industry Network, send them links to articles that relate to their work or some other topic they expressed interest in. Some people in your network may also be searching for a job. Stay in touch by sharing job leads that aren't a good fit for you or by inviting someone to attend a networking event with you.

Make it a habit to get out from behind your devices and showcase your personality, qualifications, and professionalism in person.

Chutima Chaochaiya/Shutterstock.com

Don't fall into the trap of focusing only on the dream jobs. Likewise, don't fall into the trap of "settling" by focusing only on contingency jobs. This second trap is common when a person lacks confidence or is afraid of failing. If this is you, talk to a trusted friend or ask a career counselor to help you stay focused on jobs that are a good fit for your current qualifications.

Chapter Checklist

Check off each item you can do. Reread sections in this chapter to help you complete the checklist.

☐ Explain how having a Career Network can help me find a job.

☐ Describe the four steps in the Career Network Strategy for finding job openings.

☐ List the people who are part of my Career Network—people who can help me with my job search by providing career advice, job leads, referrals, and other assistance.

☐ Describe the difference between a job posting and a job opening and why it matters. **❶**

☐ List ways to expand my Career Network, and especially the part called my Industry Network. **❶**

☐ Describe one or more ways to keep track of all the people in my Career Network. **❶**

☐ Describe some of the things (other than a job) that I can ask of my Career Network. **❶**

☐ Prepare for and conduct effective Career Network Meetings with people in my career field. **❷**

☐ Describe the Cold Leads Strategy for finding jobs. **❸**

☐ List the sources of Cold Leads that I think I will use to find job postings. **❸**

☐ Categorize job postings in my career field as stretch job, job target, or contingency job. **❹**

☐ Determine the best fit job postings by rating them against my needs and preferences. **❹**

Critical Thinking Questions

1. Who is more likely to be helpful in your Career Network: neighbors and friends or people you meet at trade fairs and professional events? Explain your answer. **❶**

2. Which of the two strategies for finding job postings is most likely to help you on your Job Search Journey? Why? **❶❸❹**

3. Why is it so important to be polite and professional in Career Network Meetings? On online social media? **❶❷**

4. What are *your* goals for your next Career Network Meetings? Explain. **❷**

5. What barriers do you anticipate in scheduling Career Network Meetings? How can you overcome these barriers? **❷**

6. How can volunteer work help you in your job search? What are three local organizations that you could volunteer with? **❶**

7. Should you take the time to apply for stretch jobs? Why or why not? **❹**

Trial Run

Role-Play a Career Network Meeting **❶❷**

Use role-playing to practice for your next Career Network Meeting. If possible, pair up with a classmate in a related career field. The role-play has four parts:

1. Brainstorm good questions to ask. Print or copy Career Action Worksheet 6-2, Career Network Meeting Outline, on page 187 and fill it in together.

2. Take turns being the job seeker and the network connection, and role-play two meetings. The job seeker asked for the meeting, so he or she leads the role-play. Spend three to five minutes doing each role-play.

3. Evaluate how well each of you did in the role of job seeker.

4. Together, write a thank-you note. See the sample thank-you note in Figure 6-1 on page 171.

When it is your turn to role-play the job seeker:

- Introduce yourself professionally and quickly explain why you asked for the meeting.
- Be professional and courteous.
- Ask two questions from your networking meeting outline in Career Action Worksheet 6-2.
- Ask your connection for additional contact names.
- Thank your connection for her or his time.

Evaluate the job seeker on the following elements:

Rating Scale: 1 to 3 (1 = not done; 2 = done; 3 = well done)

Feedback for Job Seeker (completed by role-play contact)	**Rating (1 to 3)**
Stood up, shook hands, introduced self politely	_____
Asked good questions	_____
Demonstrated knowledge of the career/job	_____
Acted in a professional and courteous manner	_____
Smoothly requested additional contacts	_____
Ended meeting on time	_____
Thanked the connection for his/her time	_____

Job seeker's strengths:

Suggestions for improvement:

▶ CAREER ACTION WORKSHEET

6-1 Your Network List ❶

Complete items 1 to 3 now and do item 4 in a few weeks.

1. **Evaluate the size of your network today.** Your list should look like the sample below (template available online at www.cengage.com). Include names (or group names), what part of your network they belong to, and where you have their contact information recorded for easy access.

Name	Network Type Life	Work (if appl.)	Organization	Industry	Contact info location	Quality rating
TOTAL SIZE	309	21	28	16	≈374	
Alycia Shehan	X				phone	
Apolonia Pascarelli		X			phone	
Chere Smoot		x			phone	
Daniele Riva	x				phone	
Daniella Shiba	x		x		contacts	
Denn Chrzanowski			x		contacts	
Denna Tracy			x		contacts	
Earnest Daily				x	contacts	
Esperanza Riess	x				phone	
Evelyne Willer			x		contacts	
Facebook Friends	237				Facebook	
Instagram	48				Instagram	
Joanna Yun		x			missing	
LinkedIn	20	18	23	15	LinkedIn	
Virginia Gittens	x				phone	
Wilson Hoback			x		missing	

2. **Evaluate the quality of your network.** Rate how likely each person is to be able to help you in your job search. Add 1 point for each item; each person will have from 1 to 11 points. Fill in the right column of your chart (use averages or approximations for large groups of people on social media).

_____ I have this person's contact information

_____ We have a contact in common

_____ We have met in person

_____ We are both members of the same group (volunteer, work, class, other)

_____ We are connected on social media (LinkedIn, Facebook, etc.)

_____ We have known each other for at least two years

_____ We regularly exchange information and resources

_____ We stay in touch during the year (via phone, email, social media, in person, etc.)

_____ We work in the same career field

_____ He/she works at a company I am interested in

_____ He/she has a high-level position in the company

_____ We would speak up for each other in a conversation

1. **Grow your network.** Reach out to at least five of your highest rated network connections and ask them for the names of two people they know who might be able to talk with you. Try to add at least two names for each person you contact. **Important:** You are not asking for the names of people who will give you a job. You are seeking career information and additional contacts.

2. How many people are in your network now? _____

Keep repeating Step 3. Continue to grow your network throughout your Job Search Journey. Grow both the number of people and the quality of your contacts.

Add your completed work to the "About Jobs" section of your Career Builder Files.

▶ *CAREER ACTION WORKSHEET*

6-2 Career Network Meeting Outline ❶

Develop a general outline for your Career Network Meetings that you can customize for each meeting. Start with the sample questions on page 174 and add questions that are relevant to you and your career field.

Conversation Starters (write at least 2 questions)

Job and Career Questions (write at least 5 questions)

Career Advice (write at least 5 questions)

Add your completed work to the "About Jobs" section of your Career Builder Files.

This page is intentionally blank.

▶ *CAREER ACTION WORKSHEET*

6-3 Hold a Career Network Meeting ❶

Use this worksheet to plan, schedule, and evaluate at least one Career Network Meeting.

1. **Identify at least two people in your career field.** Ask your college career center staff, instructors, family, and friends to suggest people to contact. Write each person's name, title, company, phone number, and/or email address here:

   _____

   _____

2. **Call or email the person and ask for a 30-minute meeting to learn about his or her job and discuss your job search.** Schedule a date, time, and place to meet. Outline what you will say in your email or phone call, or the message you will leave, here:

3. **Prepare for the meeting.** Print your questions from Career Action Worksheet 6-2 appropriately. Print two copies of your resume. Bring business cards if you have them and a few samples of your work, if appropriate.

4. **Act professionally.** Dress as you would for the job, and plan to arrive a few minutes early. Take notes, but do not let note-taking interfere with the conversation. Do not ask for a job or an interview during these meetings, and end the meeting on time.

5. Follow-up and evaluation. After the meeting:

   - **Follow up with a thank-you note or email** and send a note to the person who helped you get the meeting.

   - **Summarize what you learned** and store your notes in your Career Builder Files.

   - **Take the time to evaluate the process,** from greeting the person to saying good-bye. Think about what happened, what was different from what you expected, what went well, and what you would do differently next time.

Be prepared to tell the class about your meeting or write a short summary of the meeting.

This page is intentionally blank.

▶ CAREER ACTION WORKSHEET

6-4 Research Job Postings ❷❹

Use at least five sources to research job postings. Fill in the table and then answer the questions at the end of the worksheet.

Here are Ibrahim's notes to help you get started. Ibrahim is finishing his associate degree in accounting and volunteers as a bookkeeper for the EMT crew that's based in a nearby fire station. He hopes to find a job where he can combine his degree and his interest in the medical field by doing billing and accounting work at a hospital or medical facility.

Site/Location (or path)	Date of Search	Search Terms	# of Job Openings	Helpful? Y/N
Mercy South Hospital bulletin board	3/14	N/A [not applicable]	3	Yes; met Rita Wagner, head of volunteer services
Mercy South Hospital website	3/14	Accounting Insurance Billing	8 2 6	Yes
SimplyHired.com	3/19	Hospital billing	528	Yes and no; must register to use advanced search to narrow down leads
Saylor College > Career Services > Resources > Career Specific Sites > Accounting	3/13	[name of city] hospital medical	0	No; did other searches too, but most jobs are not local

Save a least five job postings that you can use for Career Action Worksheet 6-5.

Site/Location (or path)	Date of Search	Search Terms	# of Job Openings	Helpful? Y/N

1. Which resource was most helpful? Why?

2. How long did it take to find a job posting that might be right for you? _____

3. What types of sites will you use to expand your search?

4. When will you schedule time to look for more job postings? _____

Add your completed work to the "About Jobs" section of your Career Builder Files.

▶ CAREER ACTION WORKSHEET

6-5 Compare Job Postings to Your Job Targets ❸❹

Use this worksheet to categorize five of the jobs you found in Career Action Worksheet 6-4 as a stretch, current, or contingency job target; then compare two jobs in terms of their fit with your needs, interests, and qualifications. Be prepared to report your findings in a PowerPoint presentation or short report.

PART 1: IDENTIFY AND CLASSIFY JOBS

List the job title and the company's name for five jobs that you found in Career Action Worksheet 6-4. Categorize each job as a stretch, current, or contingency job.

Job Title and Company	Stretch job, job target, or contingency job?
1. _____	_____
2. _____	_____
3. _____	_____
4. _____	_____
5. _____	_____

PART 2: RATE JOBS BASED ON A MATCH TO YOUR QUALIFICATIONS

Select two jobs above to compare. They should both be the same time of job (preferably two job targets, but could be two stretch or contingency jobs). Label these A and B. Rate how well your qualifications match the Job Posting requirements (3 = overqualified; 2 = well qualified; 1 = not qualified).

My Qualifications	Job A	Job B
Education	_____	_____
Work experience	_____	_____
Job skills	_____	_____
Transferable skills	_____	_____
Accomplishments and recognitions	_____	_____
Personal values	_____	_____
Personal traits	_____	_____
Other _____	_____	_____
Total ratings	_____	_____

PART 3: RATE THE MATCH BETWEEN JOBS AND YOUR TARGET JOB

Under "My interests and needs," list five things that are important to you in a job and rate each job on these items. For example, you might list challenging work, close to home, and flexible hours (see Career Action Worksheets 3-1 and 3-2 on your preferences). In the right two columns, rate how two jobs match your interests (3 = great; 2 = okay; 1 = no match).

My interests and needs	Job A	Job B
1. _____	_____	_____
2. _____	_____	_____
3. _____	_____	_____
4. _____	_____	_____
5. _____	_____	_____

PART 4: THINK ABOUT IT

Answer these questions:

1. Based on your answers above, which job do you think you would spend more time pursuing?

2. What did you learn about how to compare job postings as you completed this worksheet?

3. How can you use this knowledge on your Job Search Journey?

Add your completed work to the "About Jobs" section of your Career Builder Files.

Write Job Applications

OVERVIEW

You will be offered job interviews based on the quality and effectiveness of your Job Application Package: job application, resume, and, optionally, cover letter, business card, and/or portfolio. This chapter presents tips and activities for successfully completing job applications and, when appropriate, adding optional items to your Job Application Package.

OUTCOMES

1. Describe how to apply for jobs, page 196
2. Use best practices to complete online job applications, page 197
3. Apply best practices for other types of job application forms, page 203
4. Describe how to create and use a Job Application Package with a cover letter, page 206

CAREER ACTION WORKSHEETS

WHERE ARE YOU ON THE JOURNEY?

PHASE 1: Prepare for the Journey
- *The Job Search Journey*
- *Know Yourself to Market Yourself*
- *Picture Yourself in the Workplace*

PHASE 2: Create Your Resume
- *Plan Your Resume*
- *Write Your Resume*

PHASE 3: Apply for Jobs
- *Find Job Openings*
- **Write Job Applications**

PHASE 4: Shine at Interviews
- *Know the Interview Essentials*
- *Prepare for Your Interview*
- *Interview Like a Pro*

PHASE 5: Connect, Accept, and Succeed
- *Stay Connected with Potential Employers*
- *Dealing with Disappointment*
- *Take Charge of Your Career*

PHASE 3 Apply For Jobs
Step 2, *Write Job Applications*

Your goal in this chapter is to complete job applications accurately and to use search optimized keywords that grab attention.

When you're doing something tedious, that's when you should check, double check, and triple check before calling it complete.

APPLY FOR JOBS

Throughout your networking, you will encounter many leads for jobs. Some of these leads may also be found through job boards, social media platforms, or directly on a company's website. Once you find a job posting, the next step is to complete the job application. Even though you may have sent your resume to the hiring manager through a Warm Introduction, you likely will still have to complete a job application. Chapter 7 covers the following topics:

- Best practices for completing job applications using your resume as a basis
- Creating customized Job Applications Packages with a cover letter,

Your application is critical. As discussed in Chapter 4, employers use applicant tracking systems (ATS) to screen online applications. The ATS is set to look for keywords and phrases that demonstrate an exact match to the job posting. If there is a match, then employers see the application and may be willing to invest the time and money it takes to interview the applicant. Employers use job applications, resumes, and sometimes cover letters to weed out people who do not appear to be qualified or the best fit for the position.

Application Forms

Job application forms are designed to get the information needed to make hiring decisions. By using the forms, employers get the following:

- Consistent information from every applicant so that they can compare applicants accurately and objectively
- Information needed to evaluate an applicant's qualifications, cultural fit, and match with the job (for example, references, years of experience, or specific technical skills)
- Background and legal information needed to make a job offer, such as Social Security number, proof of citizenship or legal right to work in the United States, and information related to affirmative action and equal employment opportunity

The format, length, and complexity of applications forms vary greatly—from paper forms, to pdf fillable forms, to online forms, and from the average 10-minute forms to lengthy 50-minute forms. Some applications have questions that require detailed answers. Some employers ask questions that test applicants' knowledge of the job or career field. Treat every question seriously and answer it completely. Applicants who submit incomplete applications with mistakes are the first to be eliminated.

Real World Scenario 7-1 Louisa made a great impression at a recent job fair when talking to a recruiter. The recruiter left her a business card and a link to the job application on the employer's site. Louisa was so excited that she went home and filled out the application right away. She then followed up with the recruiter and provided a cover letter and resume, along with the job application in .pdf format. She was sure she had done everything correctly. However, she received a response from the recruiter stating that she had applied to the wrong job posting!

What impact did this mistake have on Louisa's impression as an applicant? How could she have avoided this issue?

Preparation and Practice

Search for an application you can use as a practice version and save it off line (or print it). Read the instructions carefully and *follow them exactly* because following directions is important to assure that the ATS won't throw out your application. *Read the entire application* to see how sections are related and which sections require more detailed answers.

YOUR CAREER NETWORK: The Give and Take of Networking

Networking is about building relationships and involves a mutual give and take. Here are the kinds of things you are "taking" at this point in your Job Search Journey:

- Reviews and feedback on resume, cover letters, job applications
- Suggestions on where to find jobs
- Warm Introductions to potential employers
- Insights into your chosen industry and what it is like on the job
- Feedback on your 30-Second Commercials
- Suggestions on answering tough job application and interview questions

But what can you give at this point in your Job Search Journey?

- Say thank you. Say it in person, in texts; as many ways as you can without boring them.
- Give them a big compliment by using their feedback or advice and telling them what you did and how it worked out.
- Mention them kindly when speaking with others in your network and theirs. Your kind words may filter back to them, and your attitude influences how these contacts will interact with your contact.
- You can always offer a free lunch or coffee.

You have more to give than you may have realized.

Before you start filling out the form, realize that you may be filling out 10, 20, maybe more of these application forms. To make it easier, create a plain text application data sheet from which you can copy and paste all the information. Career Action Worksheet 7-1 has a table with commonly requested information that is not already included in your resume. Also pull out the plain text version of your master resume that you created in Chapter 5 so that you can copy and paste answers from it as well into the application as needed.

> ▶ *CAREER ACTION*
> **Complete Worksheet 7-1**
> Create an Application Data Sheet, page 219

ONLINE JOB APPLICIATIONS

This section has guidelines for completing typical online application forms. Applying online is part of the Cold Leads Strategy for finding jobs and can be part of the Warm Introduction Strategy (See Chapter 6). For the Cold Leads Strategy, you might be applying through a job search engine, a job board or directly on a company website. If you have a Warm Introductions for a job posting, apply on the company website, unless your network contact suggests otherwise.

Most online job sites are free to job seekers but may require that you set up a profile before you apply for a job posting. If the online job site is password protected, be sure to make a secure record of your username, password, and the email name and phone number associated with your account.

Profiles may include contact information, job objective, career field, and skills and qualifications. Your profile may be posted on the site where employers can find it, so use as many of your industry keywords as you can. Make sure your profile is consistent with your Application Data Sheet and LinkedIn profile. If a resume is part of your online profile, update that as well. Be warned that some employers and ATS insist that details, like exact dates of employment, are a perfect match across all platforms and documents. From the employers' perspective, if you can't take the time to get the application right, they will wonder why they should trust that you will take the time to do any job well.

As a guide, refer to the completed sample application in Figure 7-1 on pages 199–200. You can fill in most of the fields by pasting in text from the Application Data Sheet you created in Career Action Worksheet 7-1. Use your Application Data Sheet to make sure you accurately and exactly enter the information. Do not leave any section of a form blank. Enter "NA" or "N/A" (not applicable) if a question does not apply to you.

Personal Information

Provide your name, address, contact information, Social Security number, etc. If the application asks for a current address and a permanent address, but both are the same for you, you can repeat your current address in the permanent address section rather than leave it blank. If the form asks for a second phone number, list a phone number where messages can be left, or repeat the first phone number here. Provide a working email address that you check daily.

Start Date

If you can start work right away, enter "Immediately" for Date Available. If you are currently employed, think about the amount of notice you will give (typically two weeks). You may be asked about your available days, hours, or shifts and your willingness to relocate.

The application may also ask how you heard about the position. Mark "Other" and name a referral if you found out about the position through a Warm Introduction.

Education

List all schools/colleges attended, your major, your degree/diploma, and your graduation dates. Figure 7-1 lists one high school and one community college.

- If you attended more than one high school, list the most recent one you attended and indicate the year you received your diploma. List your GPA only if it is requested or if it is high.

- If you have attended more than one post secondary educational institution, list the most recent one first and work back to the first one you attended.

- If necessary, attach a separate list of additional schools you attended.

If the form has a space to list additional information, include items such as subjects of study, research, special skills (such as a foreign language), or other activities; also give examples of your capabilities and activities that relate to your job objective. Emphasizing foreign language skills can be a very valuable asset to potential employers. If you do speak a language in addition to English, make sure to highlight this in the appropriate section. Sometimes the application will specifically ask if you speak other languages. Other times, you may be able to include this information in the Education section or Special Skills section. Summarize the information and use abbreviations if space is tight.

Employment History

List your most recent job first. Be exact about dates. It's often checked by employers. The dates on your LinkedIn profile must match

Figure 7-1 Sample Job Application Form

JOB APPLICATION
ABC Company

This application is used in the selection process and both pages <u>must</u> be completed. Attach extra sheets if necessary (references to resumes are <u>NOT</u> acceptable).

APPLICANT INFORMATION

Last Name Martinelli	First Elizabeth	M. I. S.	Social Security Number 999-00-0088	Home Phone 208.555.0106	Alternative Phone 208.555.0170

Permanent Address – No. & Street 6518 Willow Way	City Boise		State ID	Zip 83706	Date 01/15/--

Have you previously ☐ applied to OR ☐ been employed by ABC Company?   Where and when? **N/A**   E-mail Address **emartinelli@provider.net**

Do you have relatives working for the ABC Company? ☐ Yes ☒ No If yes, give names and departments where they work.

POSITION

Position Desired **Sales Supervisor**	Salary Desired (per month) **Negotiable**

Willing to relocate? ☒ Yes ☐ No   Do you want ☒ Full-time ☐ Part-time   Date Available for Work **Immediately**

EDUCATION

Highest Educational Level Completed:

Name of School	Location	From	To	Degree or Diploma	Major	Minor
High School **Idaho Falls High School**	**Idaho Falls, ID**			**Diploma**		
Community College **Central Community College**	**Boise, ID**	**9/08**	**1/10**	**A.A.**	**Marketing**	
College or University						
Graduate School						
Special Training						

Languages Other Than English (if required in employment announcement):	Speak **Spanish**	Read **Spanish**	Write **Spanish**

EMPLOYMENT HISTORY & RELATED EXPERIENCE
List present or most recent experience first. Include armed services experience and volunteer work.

Employer Name **Kevington's Emporium (Part-time)**	Employer Address **3315 Front Street Boise, ID 83705**	Dates (Mo./Yr.) From **12/08** To **Present**
Position Title **Assistant Sales Supervisor**	Supervisor **Charlie Wu**	Phone **208.555.0131** Ext. **125**
Reason for Leaving **Still employed**	Salary: Start **9.00/hr** End **11.58/hr**	No. Hours Per Week: **20**

Duties:

Training, supervising, and scheduling staff of six

Promoted to Assistant Sales Supervisor after only six months

Employer Name **Crown Sportswear (Part-time)**	Employer Address **1800 Orchard Street Boise, ID 83704**	Dates (Mo./Yr.) From **5/08** To **11/08**
Position Title **Sales Clerk**	Supervisor **Connie Pratt**	Phone **208.555.0114** Ext. **418**
Reason for Leaving **Took new job**	Salary: Start **8.50/hr** End **8.50/hr**	No. Hours Per Week: **10-15**

Duties:

Sales, customer service, and design and setup of all merchandise displays

Performed managerial and closing duties for store three nights a week

Figure 7-1 *(continued)*

JOB APPLICATION

Employer Name	Employer Address 460 Park Way	Dates (Mo./Yr.)
Value Market Variety (Part-time)	Idaho Falls, ID 83402	From **12/05** To **3/08**

Position Title	Supervisor	Phone
Salesclerk	**Tevia Levitt**	**208.555.0199** Ext. **420**

Reason for Leaving	Salary: Start **7.00/hr** End **8.25/hr**	No. Hours Per Week:
Moved to college location		**15**

Duties:

Sales, customer service, and inventory stocking tasks

Selected "Customer Service Employee of the Month" twice in one year

Employer Name	Employer Address	Dates (Mo./Yr.) From To
Position Title	Supervisor	Phone Ext.
Reason for Leaving	Salary: Start End	No. Hours Per Week:

Duties:

REFERENCES

Name	Address	Telephone	Occupation	Years Known
Charlie Wu (**Kevington's Emporium**)	**3315 Front Street** **Boise, ID 83705**	**208.555.0131** **Ext. 125**	**Sales Manager**	**2 years**
Tevia Levitt (**Value Market Variety**)	**460 Park Way** **Idaho Falls, ID 83402**	**208.555.0199** **Ext. 420**	**Supervisor**	**3 years**
Dr. Robert Cornwell	**Business Department** **Central Community College** **8500 College Way** **Boise, ID 83704**	**208.555.0143**	**Professor, Marketing and Sales**	**2 years**

ADDITIONAL INFORMATION

Φ Are you currently employed? ☒Yes ☐No   May we contact your employer? ☒Yes ☐No   May we contact your former employers? ☒Yes ☐No

Can you (if accepted for employment) provide proof of your legal right to remain and work in the U.S.? ☒Yes ☐No

A separate affidavit on felony and misdemeanor convictions is REQUIRED to be completed on the attached form.

I hereby certify that all statements on this application are true and complete to the best of my knowledge and belief. If employed, I understand that any untrue statements on the above record may be considered grounds for termination.

Date *01/15/--*   Signature *Elizabeth S. Martinelli*

those on your application. Most forms ask for the month and year you started and stopped each job, and some ask for the day. If the application does not have a separate section for military service, list it in your employment history.

References

In Chapter 4, you began to consider who in your network could serve as a reference. Although references are not included in your resume, they are usually requested as a part of the job application. Use Career Action Worksheet 7-2 to create your reference list. Consider the following when choosing references:

- **Right number:** Provide the number of professional or personal references requested. Employers may ask for three to five references. Find both personal references (people who vouch for your good character) and professional references (people who vouch for your work skills and qualities).

- **Right relationship:** Employers may specify the relationship they would like you to use as a reference. Whenever possible, tie your references directly to your work experience. Most employers value good references from former reputable employers because former employers know firsthand how you performed at work. In Figure 7-1, notice how the first two references are the applicant's coworkers at previous jobs.

- **Former direct managers:** It is generally better to request a recommendation letter when leaving a job and then keep it in your files. Always try to leave on good terms and stay in touch with previous managers, including keeping contact information current.

- **Former coworkers:** Again, maintain positive relationships with former coworkers. You never know when they can help connect you to a job or act as a reference.

- **References not related to work experience:** Consider teachers, members of volunteer

MAKE IT A HABIT
Respect Your References

A person cannot be a reference for you without providing a phone number for potential employers' use. Whether or not you discuss privacy issues with your references, they expect you to guard this information.

When you complete an application and send a copy of your resume, do not include your references' phone number or attach a reference list with their phone numbers. Instead, enter "Upon request" in the field or on the list. Employers will not call your references before meeting you, and you can provide the phone numbers during the interview.

Due to hacking issues online, do not include your references' email addresses in an application. When a site will not accept an application without references'

email addresses, one job applicant enters "uponrequest@uponrequest.com" in these fields. She has been selected for phone interviews by employers when she has done this. During the interview, she gives the phone numbers verbally so that the interviewer can include them in the interview notes.

StanislauV/Shutterstock.com

organizations, and members of your network who know your skills and capabilities.

- **Permissions:** Remember to talk to your references in advance and get their permission to list them on an application. Thank them for allowing you to do so.

Watch out for the following when you develop your reference list:

- Use only those references who would recommend you highly from firsthand knowledge and with whom you have a good relationship and regular communication.

- Because legal constraints may restrict your previous employers from giving a reference, ask former coworkers. They may be more willing to give you a recommendation.

- Do not use relatives as references.

- It is inappropriate to use someone you have not spoken to in years as a reference. He or she may not have enough information to provide an accurate view of your qualifications. To maintain your references, stay in touch via an occasional email or phone call with regular updates on your job status and career goals.

Potential employers will check your previous employers and your references. Previous employers might only confirm your dates of employment, References may be asked to respond to questions about your attitude, work history, job performance, ability to work with others, and work habits. Coach your references accordingly. You can't control what your references will say about you, but you should give them information about the jobs you seek and the skills required so that they will be able to emphasize your qualifications and abilities.

▶ *CAREER ACTION*
Complete Worksheet 7-2
Create Your References List, page 221

Difficult Job Application Questions

Employers may ask additional questions throughout the application or in an "Additional Questions" section. Consider carefully how to handle challenging questions.

Contacting Your Current Employer

If an application asks permission to contact your current employer, answer yes only if your employer is aware of your job search and approves. Otherwise, protect your current job by answering no.

Legal Status

You will be asked for information that protects the employer if you are hired. Be truthful about your status as a U.S. citizen or having the legal right to work in the United States.

Law Violations

You may be asked about any past criminal record (convictions, not arrests). As of this writing, 17 states have laws removing this check box from the standard job applications. Check applicable state laws before responding. If you have been convicted of a felony or misdemeanor (excluding minor traffic violations), you may be asked about it. A typical background check by the employer would reveal a conviction. Answer truthfully and indicate "will discuss at interview." Your best option is to explain any negative history in person, take responsibility for your actions, and explain what you learned in the process. Any misrepresentation on your part would be identified, and you would be eliminated from consideration for the job.

In some states you may be able to expunge your record or obtain a Certificate of Good Conduct (for multiple offenses) or Certificate of Relief that can help reduce the legal barriers to employment.

Whether or not you have a law violation on your record, you may still be asked if you are willing to take a drug test. While it may seem unfair, saying "no" could cost you the job.

Reasons for Leaving Prior Job

Answer this question using positive, growth-oriented language. Do not criticize your former employer and do not use reasons that may indicate you may be unreliable or a poor fit for the job. For example, "Seeking advancement" is a positive reason compared to "Company refused to promote me."

Real World Scenario 7-2 Danilo recently had been laid off from his job. He needed to find a new job soon. There were several people in his division who were laid off. In his case, it was because he was a good but average performer. He wasn't sure how to talk about his lay off in a positive way. On his application, he decided to be as truthful and positive as possible. He outlined the financial difficulties in his division but did not go into detail regarding his performance. He mentioned that he could discuss this further at the interview if requested. He was sure that his previous manager would still provide a reference because his performance problems had not been serious. He felt comfortable about not going into detail in his job application for this reason.

How can you put a positive spin on any difficult questions you encounter on job applications?

Desired Salary

Because salary is such an influential factor, say "negotiable based on job responsibilities and total compensation package," or "the market value of the job." Don't risk eliminating yourself before you have a chance to present your qualifications in an interview. Save any discussion about compensation until the employer has expressed a definite interest in you. If you are required to enter a salary figure, use the following tips:

- If the job is posted with a set, nonnegotiable salary, list that figure.

- List a range based on your compensation research. Review Chapter 11 for more information on how to research compensation ranges, including using the salary information provided by some online job sites.

- If you are not allowed to type a range, pick the midpoint of the range and list that figure.

Sign the Application or Submit It

Because a job application is a legal document, when you sign the form or check the box indicating that the information is correct, you literally take an oath that the information you provided is true and accurate. (On a more practical note, unsigned applications cannot be processed. You may lose valuable time—and face—if the company has to take extra steps to ask you to sign your application.)

Applying Using a Common Application

In general, while job search engines help aggregate job postings from a wide variety of sources, you may still have to fill out a unique application form for each employer. However, a few sites such as LinkedIn use a "common application." For employers that choose to use this feature, you can apply using the same LinkedIn form for every application. Similarly, Indeed.com offers the *Easy Apply* feature, and CareerBuilder offers *Quick Apply* (once you create an account). In contrast, this feature does not exist for Monster.com.

Recruiting technology is advancing very quickly, so other job sites might add this feature in the near future.

OTHER TYPES OF JOB APPLICATION FORMS

When applying for jobs at smaller businesses, you may need to request an application either in person, by phone, or via email. You

OVERCOMING BARRIERS
The Myth: I Can't Apply Yet!

It's not uncommon for job seekers to want to put off applying for jobs. They may want to be perfectly ready, or wait for the perfect time. Below are a few common myths.

I Can't Apply Because:

- ***The application requires a degree and I'm still in my final year of school.***
  Here's what you do. Enter the name of your college, your major, and the words "*Degree in Progress.*" If there is a space for date, enter the month/year when you started, and the future month/year when you expect to graduate followed by the word "Anticipated." For example: Miami University, CBS Communications, 9/2019 to 6/2021 (anticipated).

- ***It's the wrong time of year to apply.*** The best time to apply is within the first few days that a job is posted. There are seasons with higher numbers of job postings, but there are always some postings out there, so get started.

- ***I'm too busy with work and school to apply.*** Even if your school work is intense, for the right job, consider squeezing a few more hours into your schedule to apply and, if it's a good fit, interview for the job. The alternative is spending months after graduation searching instead of earning.

Sigrid Eriksen/Shutterstock.com

might have learned about the job through a Cold Lead—such as a sign in the window or a newspaper classified advertisement—or through a Warm Introduction—someone in your network indicated the company was looking to hire people. If you have a Warm Introduction, mention your contact's name when you request the job application.

Paper Forms. If you are given a blank paper application form, take it home to fill out. First, make (or request) several copies. One copy will be used to draft your application. Other copies are in case you make errors and have to start over, so that your final application looks neat and readable.

Digital Forms. You may be asked to complete a digital form. Either you will find it online or the potential employer might send it to you via email. You can print it out and fill it out as a paper form (see above). Depending on the type of form provided, you may be able to fill it out using your computer. Typically, the form is either a Microsoft Word .docx file or an Adobe .pdf file. Test the type of form by typing in a few answers and saving the form under a name like "test-application for John's shop." Close the file, then reopen it to see if the information you typed in was saved or not. If not, print and fill out like a paper form. If it is saved, then continue to complete the form using your computer. Save the file using a file name that contains YOUR name, so the potential employer can easily identify your file when you return it via email. For example: "Chip Davis Mechanic Application February 2020.pdf"

General Tips. Follow these tips to make the best impression when you are requesting a job application.

- If you go in person.
  - **Look the part and be ready to interview.** If you are visiting the employer's place of business, dress conservatively and looking professional (business casual is

fine). You could be invited to meet the manager and even interview on the spot. Be sure you get the manager's full name. Be especially courteous to the receptionist. Prepare by studying the interview chapters in this book, Chapters 8–10.

- **Bring identification** such as your driver's license.
- **Come alone and do not conduct any business during your visit.** Do not order food or come to the customer service desk carrying a bag of purchases.
- **Allow enough time for your visit.** You may be asked to take a survey or an employment test, so allow plenty of time for your visit. You do not want to miss out on an opportunity because you have to rush to another obligation. Ask to meet the manager either when you pick up the application or when you return it. State your interest in the job. Mention how you heard about the job, and ask open ended questions such as "what can you tell me about the position?"

- **If you call,** be professional. Call from a place without distracting background noise. Be ready to take notes in case you are asked to call another person on another extension at another time. When the person answers the phone, state your name and ask if they can help you get a job application for the xxx job. You will either get help or be transferred to someone who can help you.
- **Position information.** List a position title or job reference number from the job posting so the employer knows which job you are applying for.
- **Proofread your application carefully.** The application is your "ambassador"; make sure it represents you well. Check it for accuracy, neatness, completeness, and the quality of your answers.
- **Promptly return the completed form** with a customized version of your resume and, optionally, a cover letter and your business contact information card. If you submit the application via email, use these tips:
  - Put the title or number of the job listing and your name in the email subject line.
  - Copy your cover letter (see Outcome 4 below) into the email message. Attach your resume and completed job application.
  - Before emailing your application to the employer, send it to a friend or different email account to see how the documents look after transfer. You may need to modify the spacing and formatting. Always proofread your attachments before clicking "Send."
  - Because no one wants emails with a lot of attachments, attach only what is requested by the employer. Save portfolio items for the interview.
- **Keep a copy of the application.** Create a filing system for all of your paper job applications. Include a page with the manager's name and contact information along with any notes about the application process.
- **Check back in a week if you don't hear from anyone.** Call, or if you really want the job, go in person and leave a Job Application Package.

▶ *CAREER ACTION*
Complete Worksheet 7-3
Complete Other Types of Job Applications, page 223

Figure 7-2 shows the first page of a job application at an employer's website.

"To get noticed, begin by noticing others first. To encourage others to care about you, begin to care about them first. What you do reflects back toward you."

Figure 7-2 First Page of Application on a Company Website

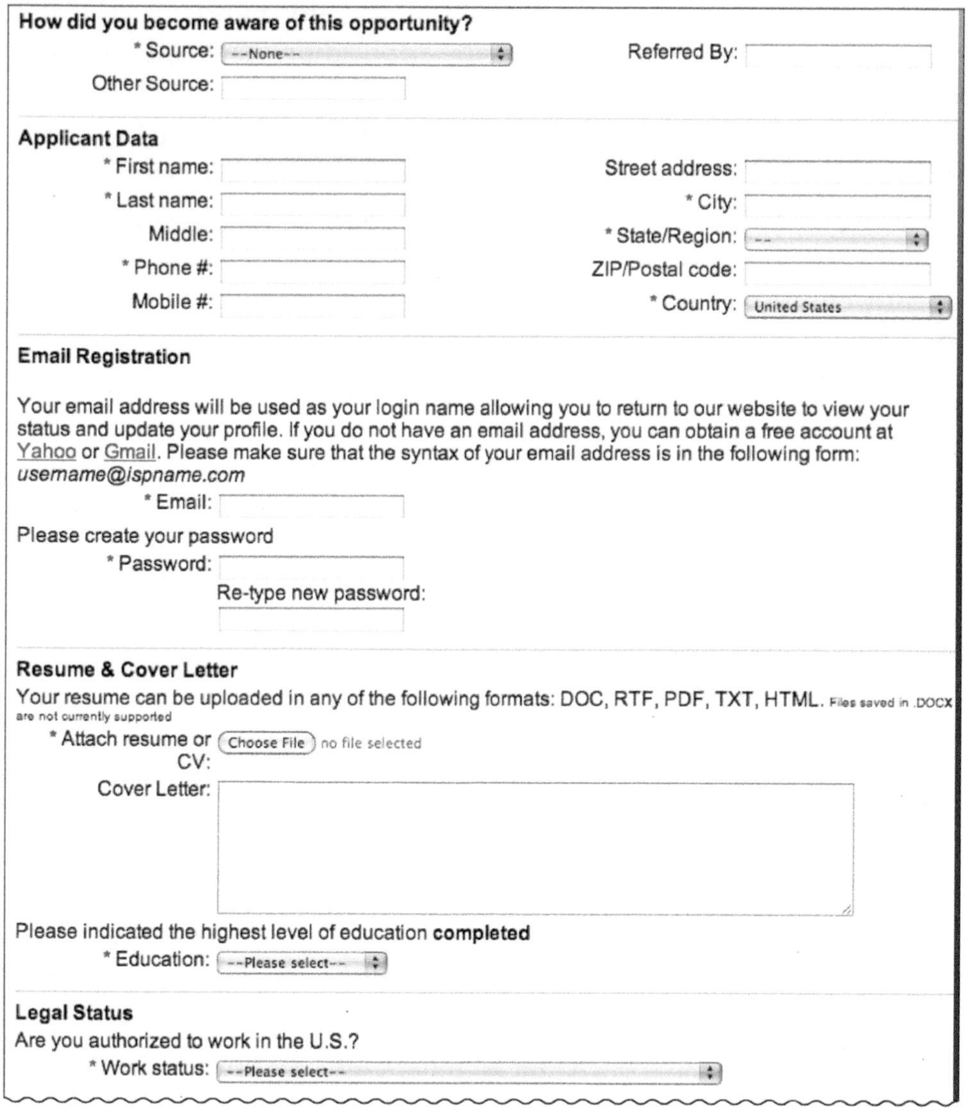

How did you become aware of this opportunity?

* Source: `--None--`   Referred By: [   ]

Other Source: [   ]

Applicant Data

* First name: [   ]   Street address: [   ]

* Last name: [   ]   * City: [   ]

Middle: [   ]   * State/Region: `--`

* Phone #: [   ]   ZIP/Postal code: [   ]

Mobile #: [   ]   * Country: `United States`

Email Registration

Your email address will be used as your login name allowing you to return to our website to view your status and update your profile. If you do not have an email address, you can obtain a free account at Yahoo or Gmail. Please make sure that the syntax of your email address is in the following form: *username@ispname.com*

* Email: [   ]

Please create your password

* Password: [   ]

Re-type new password: [   ]

Resume & Cover Letter

Your resume can be uploaded in any of the following formats: DOC, RTF, PDF, TXT, HTML. Files saved in .DOCX are not currently supported

* Attach resume or (Choose File) no file selected
CV:

Cover Letter: [   ]

Please indicated the highest level of education **completed**

* Education: `--Please select--`

Legal Status

Are you authorized to work in the U.S.?

* Work status: `--Please select--`

JOB APPLICATION PACKAGE WITH A COVER LETTER

OUTCOME **4**

What Is a Job Application Package?

A Job Application Package is a powerful tool to get potential employers' attention during your Job Search Journey. A Job Application Package consists of a job application, cover letter, resume, and may include your business card and copies of a few items of your work from your career portfolio. By pulling all this together into a nice package—either in an email or physically in an envelope—you are showing potential employers that you are willing to go the extra mile, and you are making life easier for them by pulling all the pieces together for them to see.

Pulling together a Job Application Package, complete with customized cover letter (see below), takes time, so reserve this tool for those jobs for which you have a Warm Introduction and those for which you are an excellent match to your job target or stretch job, as described in Chapter 6. Your package can give you an edge over other applicants.

Your job application may have been submitted online already. Make a copy and include it in the Job Application Package. It's okay if your job application information is received in multiple ways—online, email, and physical mail. You want to use the methods that help you stand out from the crowd. Also consider what method is the easiest for the recipient to handle or to pass on to others in their company who might be interested in you. Ask your network about the normal approach for your industry, and advice on how to stand out.

When you send your Job Application Package, send it to a real person, not to a general email or to the HR department. To find the right person, use your network and research on LinkedIn. Be aware that some companies block emails with attachments. If you know this to be the case, copy/paste your files directly into an email, and take the time to reformat. If this become impossible, instead send just your cover letter in the body with a link to your LinkedIn profile and mention your online job application number so they can find it in their applicant tracking system.

Here are two other ways to use your Job Application Package:

- For job interviews, take several copies of your Job Application Package and hand a copy to each person who interviews you.
- As a physical "thank-you package" after a phone interview, use a paperclip to attach your handwritten thank-you note to your package. Slip this into an envelope and send it to the interviewer.

Write Cover Letters

A **cover letter** is a letter that introduces you to a potential employer for a known job opening or asks about openings in the company. Most important, the cover letter answers the questions every reader has: "Who is this person, and how will this person help us?" and "Should I take the time to look at this resume or application?"

Some job sites have a check box or area for a cover letter, In these cases, a cover letter should be viewed as required, not optional. Wherever employers offer an opportunity for you to showcase your personality, you should!

Effective cover letters make an excellent first impression. They are well written, get the reader's attention and interest, and convince the reader to read the attached resume and offer an interview. An effective cover letter highlights your most important qualifications and emphasizes how those qualifications can meet the employer's needs. You can also use your cover letter to address things in the job posting where your ability to perform the job may not be obvious from your resume.

Cover letters are short—one page with 200 to 300 words total—and have similar structures. Figure 7-3 shows a standard cover letter. Additional examples are at the end of this chapter. The following describes the parts of a cover letter.

Top Part: Address, Date, and Salutation. This draws attention to your name and contact information. Next, for both email and printed letters, type the employer's name, title, company name, and address. Skip a line, then use a formal salutation or greeting such as "Dear Ms. Och," followed by another blank line. If you are using email, some of this is already done for you, so you start at the greeting line. See Figure 7-4 for an example of an email cover letter.

Content of the Cover Letter. The body of the cover letter includes three short paragraphs: opening, sales pitch, and closing.

The Opening. Introduce yourself and state your purpose. Mention by name the position you are applying for if one has been made

Figure 7-3 Structure of a Cover Letter

Your Name as a title or header
Your physical mailing address
Your email address | Phone number with area code

Today's Date

Mr./Ms./Capt./Chef/Dr./Prof./Rev. [last name]
Person's job title
Name of person's company
Street address at the company (or PO Box number)
City, State abbreviation, Zip code of company

Dear Mr./Ms./Captain/Chef/Dr./Reverend [last name],

Content of letter that includes three parts. First and opening line to introduce yourself and explain in a sentence why you are contacting them. (Tips: Use only your name, not Mr., Ms., or Mrs.) Specifically mention a job title if one exists that you are aware of.

Content continues with you marketing yourself by explaining why you are a good fit for the job, or why you would be a good employee at this company. Use your Personal Brand Statement in a way that flows smoothly in the letter.

Content wraps up with a closing that summarizes what you hope to achieve as a result of this letter—a phone call, meeting, email, or reference.

Sincerely,

[your signature]

[your printed name]

Enclosure

Figure 7-4 Sample Email Cover Letter with Resume inside Body of Email

EXPERIENCED ADMINISTRATIVE ASSISTANT, JOB #4864-10

File   Edit   View   Insert   Format   Tools   Message   Help

From:	Kimi Okasaki <'kimi.okasaki@email.com'>
To:	'hiring.manager@megamallmanagement.com' <'hiring.manager@megamallmanagement.com'>
Cc:	
Subject:	EXPERIENCED ADMINISTRATIVE ASSISTANT, JOB #4864-10

Dear Hiring Manager:

Please accept my application for the administrative assistant position advertised on the *Arizona Bugle* website. As secretary-treasurer of the Valley Elementary School Parent-Teacher Organization, I appreciated MegaMall's offer to let us hold our promotional event in the center of the mall last fall at no charge. I would welcome the chance to work in a civic-minded organization.

I am an energetic, detail-oriented person who has strong administrative and computer skills, retail and community service experience, and the ability to work well with others. I have held positions of responsibility in three community organizations over the last three years.

As you can see from my resume below, I thrive in a busy atmosphere that involves many different tasks, the opportunity to work with people, the satisfaction of meeting deadlines, and the chance to excel. I would enjoy the opportunity to talk with you about how I can help MegaMall Property Management with its administrative needs. I will call you next week to request an appointment, or you may call me at your convenience at the number below. Thank you for your consideration.

Sincerely,
Kimi Okasaki
kimi.okasaki@email.com

===

Kimi Okasaki Resume
Kimi Okasaki
148 Barrister Street, Tucson, AZ 85726, (520) 555.0136
kimi.okasaki@email.com, linkedin.com/in/kimi.okasaki

PROFESSIONAL PROFILE
Seeking Administrative Assistant position at mid-size organization. Detail-oriented professional with exceptional customer service, communication, and relationship building capability.

QUALIFICATIONS
• Skilled presentation, newsletter, and report designer
• Advanced software skills in MS Office, Adobe Acrobat, FTP, and QuickBooks
• Database design and maintenance using Access and Oracle
• Keyboarding at 75 words per minute
• Proven external relationship builder

EXPERIENCE
Community Volunteer, Tucson, AZ. December 2009 to December 2015

   Served as a volunteer in various roles for three well-known organizations that contribute significantly to the community.

• National Diabetes Foundation. Reduced fundraising reporting time by 50% by developing and customizing Excel spreadsheet report to track three fundraising activities
• Secretary-Treasurer, Valley Elementary School Parent-Teacher Organization. Designed and published monthly electronic newsletters for organization using MS Publisher. Passed yearly CPA audits with excellence through tracking of budget in QuickBooks Pro.
• Meals on Wheels. Developed and maintained Access database for survey responses from 1,200 participants.

Katz Department Store, Tucson, AZ. March 2009 to December 2010

   Department Supervisor, Part-time.
   Perform basic supervisor responsibilities, manage inventory, and meet target sales goals.
• Attained highest part-time sales volume through personalizing customer interactions
• Trained 4 new sales clerks who achieved target sales goals by end of first month by using good coaching skills
• Had <5% losses on computing daily cash receipts, balancing registers, and coordinating weekly deliveries by using detailed organization systems and strategies

Value Variety, Tucson, AZ. Summers 2008, 2009
   Sales Clerk
• Given positive feedback as a provider of complete customer service in sales and returns

EDUCATION
Associate of Applied Science, A.S.A., 2015, Westfield Community College, Tucson, AZ
Major: Administrative Office Technology, GPA 3.6

===

public. Explain why you are interested in the company or this type of job.

Figure 7-5 is an excerpt from a prospecting cover letter by Kimi Okasaki. You can see the associated resume in Chapter 4, Figure 4-2 on page 96. Kimi mentions Carmine Garduno, a person who is well known to the addressee. Carmine told Kimi it was okay to use her name in this cover letter.

The Sales Pitch. This is the heart of your letter. A sales pitch refers to communication you use to market yourself. It's similar to your 30-Second Commercials. Focus on what you have to offer—your most relevant qualifications for the job. Include two to four results-oriented, bullet point descriptions of capabilities and accomplishments that show how you can benefit the employer and handle the job. These might be restatements of things you have already written in your resume and application, but tailored to the job posting. For example, you might highlight a few critical examples of experience from your resume that match with the skill requirements in the job description. It's okay to use similar wording. Be sure to include elements of your Personal Brand Statement. Be truthful and remember that you must be able to verify these accomplishments during an interview. Express interest and enthusiasm for the job

Figure 7-5 Opening of a Prospecting Cover Letter from Kimi Okasaki

Carmine Garduno from the Health Services Bureau recommended that I talk with you about the possibility of your needing an administrative support person with experience in educational and community activities. I am confident that my experience as a volunteer in the Valley Elementary School Parent-Teacher Organization (VES-PTO) and the Diabetes Foundation would be useful in helping you achieve success with your new five-year education and community plan.

and focus on your strengths, experience, and achievements.

Somewhere in the letter, refer to the job description or something specific you know about the company's activities or requirements. This demonstrates your initiative and interest in the company. It demonstrates that you care enough to do your homework and learn about this company and this job.

Write one to three lines to highlight the qualifications you want to emphasize. See Figure 7-5 for an example. An alternative, easy-to-read style is to use a bulleted list. As shown in Figure 7-6, the left column lists

Figure 7-6 Example of Sales Pitch for Use in Cover Letter

Job Requirements	My Qualifications
GPA of 3.0 or higher	I completed an Associate of Science degree, majoring in Information Management Technology, with an overall GPA of 3.5.
Interest in health and disease prevention	Through my volunteer work at the Diabetes Foundation, I learned about the disease prevention techniques your department teaches to day care workers. I am highly motivated by the desire to help families and fight disease.
Community involvement	I am actively involved in community volunteer work and serve as Secretary-Treasurer of the VES-PTO. I use Word and Excel to generate and track correspondence with more than 500 families.

the key job requirements (quoted exactly from the job listing using the company's language), and the right column describes your matching experience.

The Closing. Ask for a meeting, phone call, or an interview—not a job—and indicate when you would like to connect. State that your resume is attached or enclosed. Then add a courteous sentence that expresses appreciation or thanks. Set a goal on your calendar to follow up by phone or email to check availability and interest. See Figure 7-7 for a good example.

The Bottom Part: Closing, signature, contact info, closing. Skip a line and type a phrase such as *Sincerely*, or *Kind Regards* followed by a comma. For printed letters, leave a few blank lines for your signature, then type your name (your formal name used on the resume and application). Use a black or blue pen and sign your name. Also for printed cover letters, type the word Enclosure at the bottom of the page to indicate that there should be other pages that go with this letter. For email letters, type your formal name, and below that, type your contact information—phone number with area code, and LinkedIn Profile URL and/or web resume URL. For email only: If you use a standard email signature—a block of text that is appended to the end of your email—make sure it is appropriate for this use, or change it now. Alternately,

Figure 7-7 Example Cover Letter Closing

My resume is enclosed for your review. I would appreciate meeting with you to discuss the possibility of our working together. If you are interested, what does your availability look like for a 30-minute call next week? I would welcome the opportunity to contribute to the exceptional community outreach efforts of the Department of Disease Prevention. Thank you for your consideration.

start using an email account that you set up exclusively for your Job Search Journey.

Tips for Writing Effective Cover Letters

Start by writing a master cover letter. Make it as perfect as you can. A good master cover letter makes it easier to customize every letter for each specific job listings and get great results in less time. Keep in mind the writing tips from Chapter 5, "Write Your Resume." The advice to write clearly and concisely also applies to your cover letters. Here are additional tips:

- **Use a template.** Look online for free, standard cover letter templates. By using a template, you can rely on the template to get the format right so that you can focus on crafting great content.

- **Answer the basic three questions.** Write the content so that the reader can quickly answer these three questions: Why are your contacting me? What's in it for me? and What do you want me to do next?

- **Use your Personal Brand Statement.** You've crafted your story. Now is the time to use it. Be sure your letter does it consistently with your resume. No contradictions! Use a conversational tone and tell a cohesive story or paint a vivid picture of your abilities and experience.

- **Be positive.** Share your positive qualities. Project confidence and show interest in the job. Ask friends to see if they can find any negative tone in your cover letter, then delete it!

- **Write clearly and concisely.** Use short sentences, short paragraphs, and short words. It makes it easier for the reader. Then make sure every word counts in your master cover letter.

- **Be truthful.** Never misrepresent yourself or encourage a reader get a false impression.

MAKE IT A HABIT
Show Off Your Writing Skills

Use your cover letters to show employers that you have business writing skills. Re-read your letter (and get help from your network) until it is concise, articulate, and convincing. An error-free, grammatically correct letter shows that you are conscientious and detail-oriented.

Never allow slang, informal language, or texting abbreviations to sneak into your job search correspondence.

Use well-crafted sentences and businesslike language to demonstrate your professionalism and readiness to communicate in the workplace.

You can write more concisely if you avoid clichés, dated expressions, and "inflated" words. Here are some common examples and alternatives:

Clichéd/Dated	Concise	Complex/Wordy	Concise
At this point in time	Now	Advantageous	Helpful
Ballpark figure	Estimate	Attempt; endeavor	Try
Explore every avenue	Explore the options	Equitable	Fair
In a timely manner	On time; promptly	Initiated	Started
In the event that	If	Possess	Have
In the near future	Soon	Proficiency; proficient	Skill; skilled
Last but not least	Finally	Regarding	About
State-of-the-art	Latest	Remainder	Rest
		Timely	Prompt
		Transmit	Send
		Utilized	Used

wavebreakmedia/Shutterstock.com.

Be honest about your education, background, experience, and interests. On the other hand, don't go overboard to tell all your faults and fails. Everyone has them, so drop it and move on. Be positive.

- **Do your research.** Make sure you have researched the company and/or the job enough to make informed comments.

- **Read the letter aloud.** Listening to your cover letter will give you distance from your writing and help you judge the letter from the reader's perspective. Do you sound likable and sincerely interested in working for *this* company? Would *you* be

convinced to take time to read the application and resume?

Customize the Content

The recipient of your cover letters should feel as if you took the time and effort to write this letter especially for him or her. This is not hard to do if you start with a good master cover letter and customize small parts for each recipient. The impact can be worth the little extra time. Here are the types of things you should customize.

- Show your fit with this job. First, tailor the letter to emphasize your fit with each particular job you are applying for. Edit the text to match the job title and use the same job requirements wording as is listed in the listing. Matching their words is one way for you to begin to show that you can fit in with the people at this company.

- Get an edge through research. Demonstrate your knowledge of the company or industry. Use your company research to personalize the letter. Mention your interest in a new or popular product or service; the expansion of the firm; recent accomplishments; the company's reputation (for example, the quality of its products or services, excellent customer service, or community involvement); or a special achievement of the person you're writing to or the company in general. Mention only one thing and keep your praise short.

- Incorporate specialized terminology from your industry and job target where appropriate. Be sure to use the terminology correctly.

- Emphasize how you can meet the employer's needs. Restating the duties and qualifications in the job listing shows how you meet them. For example, consider an applicant who has the education and work experience to apply for customer support jobs and IT jobs in both the accounting and insurance industries. Each letter (and resume) should use concrete, specific terminology and examples that highlight the writer's qualifications, experience, education, and training in the field (customer support or IT) and the industry (accounting or insurance) of the job opening.

- Edit the text carefully. Check every part of the letter, including the date, inside address, salutation, name of the company, and job title. Starting fresh with a master cover letter each time can reduce errors.

Customizing will take time, yet it reflects your genuine interest in the company and the position. Plan accordingly.

Real World Scenario 7-3 Deidra applied for a job position that stated the importance of being able to manage multiple priorities and organization skills multiple times throughout the job description and qualifications. As Deidra customized her cover letter, she used a bullet point format. She highlighted three examples of when she had to manage multiple priorities and in some cases, delivered before the deadline or under budget. She included an example from when she successfully managed an important school project deadline and planned a school organization's event. She even considered various formats of her cover letter that would display her organization skills best.

How can you customize your cover letter for your ideal job position?

Follow Up with the Employer

After you have sent your cover letter and resume to get a job interview, don't just sit around and wait for the phone to ring. Applicants who follow up to request an update demonstrate initiative and increase their name recognition.

- If you applied by mail, contact the person you sent your application to.

- If you applied through the company's website, contact the human resources department and tell the receptionist which position you applied for (have the reference number when you call) and ask for the hiring manager's name, phone number, and email address.

- If you applied through a career site for a job listing that includes that hiring manager's name, contact the manager directly.

- If you applied for several jobs through a career site or if the job listing did not include the manager's name, decide whether getting the information is the best use of your time.

Keep the conversation or email brief. See an example of a phone call:

> Hello, _____. Thank you for taking my call. I'm Jennifer Ortiz calling from Raleigh. I applied for the system support programming job and wanted to make sure you received my resume and job application.

Sample Cover Letters

The following sample cover letters are on pages 215–217:

- Figure 7-8. Sample Application Cover Letter (uses paragraph style for qualifications)
- Figure 7-9. Sample Prospecting Cover Letter (uses the bullet style for qualifications)
- Figure 7-10. Sample Prospecting Cover Letter (uses two-column, comparison-list style)

▶ **CAREER ACTION**
Complete Worksheet 7-4
Write Cover Letters page 225

Figure 7-8 Sample Application Cover Letter

Kimi Okasaki

148 Barrister Street • Tucson, AZ 85726

(520) 555.0136 • kimi.okasaki@email.com • linkedin.com/in/kimi.okasaki

April 20, 20—

Mr. George O'Donnell
Office Manager
MegaMall Property Management Company
P.O. Box 555
Tucson, AZ 85726

Dear Mr. O'Donnell:

EXPERIENCED ADMINISTRATIVE ASSISTANT, JOB #4864

Please accept my application for the administrative assistant position advertised on the *Arizona Bugle* website. As secretary-treasurer of the Valley Elementary School Parent-Teacher Organization, I appreciated MegaMall's offer to let us hold our promotional event in the center of the mall last fall at no charge. I would welcome the chance to work in a civic-minded organization.

I am an energetic, detail-oriented person who has strong administrative and computer skills, retail and community service experience, and the ability to work well with others. I have held positions of responsibility in three community organizations over the last three years.

As you can see from my resume, I thrive in a busy atmosphere that involves many different tasks, the opportunity to work with people, the satisfaction of meeting deadlines, and the chance to excel. I would enjoy the opportunity to talk with you about how I can help MegaMall Property Management with its administrative needs. I will call you next week to request an appointment, or you may call me at your convenience at the number above. Thank you for your consideration.

Sincerely,

Kimi Okasaki

Kimi Okasaki

Enclosure

Figure 7-9 Sample Prospecting Cover Letter

Kate Foresman
2689 Canyon Avenue
Riverside, CA 92502
(951) 555.0179 | kforesman@email.com
linkedin.com/in/katelouiseforesman

June 29, 20–

Ms. Stephanie Nolan
Manager, Auditing Staff
Nolan Henry O'Leary Public Accountants
1410 Granada Avenue, 7th Floor
San Francisco, CA 94115

Dear Ms. Nolan:

Meagan Gerena at Smythe and Associates indicated that you are interested in hiring an experienced accounting graduate. My degree and special interest are in Accounting/Information Systems. Please consider me for a place on your well-respected auditing team, which the *San Francisco Business Reporter* recently named one of the Top 10 auditing firms in the area.

During the last two years, I have worked for a CPA firm where I developed a wide range of accounting and accounting-related skills. My accomplishments included:

- Received excellent ratings for speed and accuracy as a full-charge bookkeeper with duties such as opening, posting, and closing the books; completing federal and state corporate tax returns; and creating error-free Excel templates used by myself and others.
- Assisted a consultant in upgrading software for a customized accounting system by applying my knowledge of both accounting and IT, to meet in-house needs on schedule.
- Created a procedures manual for operating, maintenance, and troubleshooting situations that can occur between the two operating systems that users say helps them identify and fix problems quickly, resulting in fewer calls to the help-line.

During my senior year at the University of Los Angeles, I led an internship research team. We studied the operations of a local accounting firm and assisted its auditors in the audit of several clients. These experiences cemented my interest in auditing as a career.

I am confident in my ability to make a positive contribution to Nolan Henry O'Leary Public Accountants and am enclosing my resume for your review. I will call next week about your interview schedule, or you may reach me at the contact information above. I look forward to meeting you.

Respectfully,

Kate Foresman

Kate Foresman

Enclosure

Figure 7-10 Sample Prospecting Cover Letter

TAYLOR WHITAKER

10806 Delaware Avenue | Camden, NJ 08105
[856] 555.0195 | taylor.whitaker@email.com
Linkedin.com/in/taylor.whitaker

January 10, 20–

Mr. Gary Whaley
District Sales Manager
Computeriferals Company
1 Computer Way
Camden, NJ 08102

Dear Mr. Whaley:

Computeriferals has earned my respect. I have used and repaired peripherals from most of the leading manufacturers in my studies as a Business Systems/Computer Repair major and in my job as a sales representative at ComputerChoice. I know you build quality products, and I want to sell quality products—Computeriferals.

Careful review of my qualifications and the requirements of a sales representative at Computeriferals suggest that I am well qualified for a sales position with your organization.

Your Requirements	**My Experience**
• Ability to handle multiple prospects	• Expanded customer base from 137 to 183 accounts in the past year—a 34% increase
• Proven ability to meet sales goals	• Increased yearly sales from $743,000 to $1,236,000—exceeded goal by 66%
• Ability to expand sales in existing accounts	• Negotiated a new $250,000 service contract for an existing client with five locations
• Strong communication and follow-up skills	• Attained 100% customer retention through a service-first approach and frequent communication

The expanding market for Computeriferals presents an appealing challenge. Even if you have no current sales openings, I would appreciate meeting with you to discuss your requirements. My resume is enclosed for your convenience. I will call next week to request an appointment, or you may reach me at the contact information above. Thank you for your time.

Respectfully,

Taylor Whitaker

Taylor Whitaker

Enclosure

Chapter Checklist

Check off each item you can do. Reread sections in this chapter to help you complete the checklist.

☐ Describe how to get a job application and fill it out.

☐ Fill out job applications using good practices and with a positive self-representation. ❶

☐ Identify at least five good-quality references. ❷

☐ Describe how to answer challenging questions on job applications. ❷

☐ Be ready for any possibility when applying in person, including an on-the-spot interview. ❸

☐ Create a Job Application Package and describe when to use it.

☐ Write a master cover letter and describe how to customize it to demonstrate my knowledge of and interest in their company.

Critical Thinking Questions

1. What are the possible consequences of not filling out a job application completely and according to the instructions? ❷

2. Should you mention a salary figure in an application? Explain. ❷

3. What are the consequences of choosing the wrong references? ❷

4. What are the consequences of not notifying your references of their inclusion in your job application process? ❷

5. How is an online application different from a print application? Describe what you will do differently with each one. Then describe how an employer might use these differently. ❹

Trial Run ❷❸❹

Job Application Challenges

Work with a partner. Consider the following tough job application questions and brainstorm answers that would represent an applicant in the best light possible. Write a three- to five-sentence answer or explanation for each question.

1. Why do you want this job?

2. What is your desired salary for this position?

3. Why did you leave your previous employer?

▶ *CAREER ACTION WORKSHEET*
7-1 Create an Application Data Sheet ❶

A preprinted application form requires information that will not be on your resume. Below, you will create an application data sheet. When you fill out multiple job applications, this will allow you to easily copy and paste the information from this application data sheet and your plain-text resume.

PART A: Use this Career Action Worksheet to collect commonly requested information. The textbook companion site has a form for recording the information.

Remember: A completed job application form is an official document, and you can be denied employment or fired if you aren't truthful about the information you supply, including details about previous jobs. Your signature indicates that the information is complete and accurate.

Name		
Street Address		
City		
State		
Zip Code		
Social Security Number		
Email Address		
Phone Number		
Days Available to Work		
Hours Available to Work		
If Not a U.S. Citizen, Type of Visa and Expiration Date?	Type of Visa	
	Expiration Date	
If Armed Forces:	Specialty	
	Date Entered	
	Date Discharged	
Criminal History	Conviction	
	Nature of Offense	
	State Where Offense Occurred	
	Sentence	

Foreign Language Skills	Language	
	Skill Level	

PART B: Find several job application forms for jobs in your industry, either from online or paper copies from local employers. As you review these applications, find three more items that you can add in the left column of your application data sheet. Then fill in your data on the right.

In addition to your master resume, this Career Action Worksheet will allow you to easily copy and paste information into multiple job applications.

Add your completed work to the "About Jobs" section of your Career Builder Files.

▶ CAREER ACTION WORKSHEET

7-2 Create Your Reference List ❷

Review your network and identify the following possible references who you think would be able to vouch for you, professionally or personally:

Relationship	Name	Phone Number Email Address	Agreed?
Former Managers			
Former Coworkers			
Instructors and Other Academic Mentors			
Organization Presidents or Leaders (Volunteer, School, etc.)			

Reach out to these references with an email or phone call and ask if they would agree to be a reference as you continue your job search. This conversation is a good time to bring them up to date on what you're doing and catch up on their activities as well.

Add your completed work to the "About Jobs" section of your Career Builder Files.

This page is intentionally blank.

▶ *CAREER ACTION WORKSHEET*

7-3 Complete Other Types of Job Application ❸

If possible, obtain a job application form from an employer in your target industry—even one from your target employer. Using an application from your target industry provides the best preparation and practice. If one is not available, search the Internet for "sample job applications." Complete the application for practice and use it as a model when you fill out actual job applications. Consider trying a paper form (filled in by hand), or one of the two types of digital forms—a fillable PDF or an MS Word form.

Add your completed work to the "About Jobs" section of your Career Builder Files.

This page is intentionally blank.

▶ CAREER ACTION WORKSHEET

7-4 Write Cover Letters ❹

PART 1: Outline Your Cover Letter. Use this worksheet to organize and outline your master cover letter. Don't try to write a perfect letter at this point; just work on getting the essence of your message on paper. You will refine it later. Use the samples in this chapter for guidance.

Part 1: Cover Letter Outline	
Text for your letterhead: (your name, address, phone number, email address, and LinkedIn URL)	
Date:	
Inside address: (recipient's name, title, company, and address)	
Salutation: Dear (put a colon after the person's name; use the right honorific such as Ms. or Dr.)	
Paragraph 1 (opening): (include the name of the job position and of a referral if you have these)	
Paragraph 2 (sales pitch): (tailor it to the job listing; where appropriate, use bullets or side-by-side columns to highlight strong job-relevant qualifications; see cover letter examples in this chapter)	
Paragraph 3 (closing): (mention your attached or enclosed resume and request a meeting or an interview; include your phone number and email address if not already provided on this page; thank the reader)	
Complimentary close: (leave enough room for your signature and type your name under it)	Sincerely, _____ (type your name here)

PART 2: Write a Master Cover Letter. Using your cover letter outline, compose a master cover letter. Make it concise and courteous. Most importantly, make sure it demonstrates how you can benefit the employer.

PART 3: Customize Cover Letters

Find two job listings that you might be interested in applying for. Now customize a cover letter for each job. When you are done, you should have three documents: your master cover letter, a cover letter for the first job listing, and a cover letter for the second job listing. Now answer the questions below.

1. About how much of the core content did you need to change?

For the first job listing: [ ] some of it   [ ] half of it   [ ] most of it

For the second job listing: [ ] some of it   [ ] half of it   [ ] most of it

2. What types of changes did you make?

a.   For the first job listing: [ ] match job posting language? [ ] describe why I am a good fit for the job? [ ] something else? (describe)

b.   For the second job listing: [ ] match job listing language? [ ] describe why I am a good fit for the job? [ ] something else? (describe)

3. Based on having customized two cover letters, what would you tell a friend or fellow student about how to customize cover letters quickly and effectively to encourage the reader to give them an interview?

PART 4: Outside Review of Master Cover Letter and Job Application Package. Get a final review of your master cover letter with the entire Job Application Package.

A. Assemble your Job Application Package, including your master cover letter, a job application (sample only), master resume, business card, and, if appropriate for your field, select career portfolio items. Choose either to do a digital package, such as in an email or a flash drive, or do a printed-out package.

B. Ask an outside critic, perhaps someone in your Career Network, to comment on (a) overall impression of your package and (b) how to make your cover letter clearer, better, and more convincing.

C. Revise and save. Decide what changes you will make based on the input you receive. Then make the changes. Save the file using a name that helps you find your final master cover letter and other documents.

Add your completed work to the "Master Career Portfolio" section of your Career Builder Files.

PHASE 4:
SHINE AT INTERVIEWS

Shine at Interviews

PART 4 Learn how to shine at the most important business meetings you'll ever attend: your job interviews. Learn how to get interviews, prepare for the many types of interviews, showcase your Personal Brand Statement, manage all the questions, and even ask a few questions of your own.

CHAPTER 8	Know the Interview Essentials
CHAPTER 9	Prepare for Your Interview
CHAPTER 10	Interview Like a Pro

**DEDRA
PERLMUTTER**

*Senior Career Coach,
JVS Career Services*

ADVICE FROM THE EXPERT

After 13 years in human resources helping employees navigate the workplace, Dedra Perlmutter changed direction and decided to help job seekers become employees through her work at the Cincinnati Career Network. She stresses that it is not a job placement agency. Instead, clients attend small-group workshops and get one-on-one counseling on any part of their job search. Dedra believes that "it's essential to find a 'go-to person' you feel comfortable with and who will be honest and helpful."

Dedra stresses "the power of networking—everywhere you go!" She emphasizes that networking is about giving and receiving and reminds job seekers to communicate their appreciation to the people they meet. She also promotes "LinkedIn as an important tool for both job seekers and recruiters."

Dedra advises job seekers that "the interview starts in the parking lot, continues with the receptionist, and doesn't end until you send your thank-you note."

Dedra's most heartfelt advice is to keep reminding yourself that "rejections are not personal! Seek out others who are going through the same thing and share your experiences, disappointments, and successes."

The Cincinnati Career Network is a free, not-for-profit career center. "Most communities have an agency like ours. Call the library or United Way to find the one near you—and go!" Dedra knows that every job search is unique and is constantly changing, as is the job market. "Please," she says, "find a counselor who can coach and guide you through the process."

PLAN for Success

Success is more likely when you have a written plan. Use the online template *Plan for Success* to create your own written plan for successfully completing Part 2, Chapters 4 and 5.

"Don't tell me how talented you are. Tell me how hard you work."

—*Arthur Rubenstein*

STORIES FROM THE JOB SEARCH

JENNIFER PIRINO
Senior Business Operations Coordinator

Jenn Pirino earned an Associate of Arts in Communication and worked in banking. After five years, she realized that her job was a dead end, with no pay increases or chance for promotion or development. An internal manager–mentor agreed with her assessment, but had no internal jobs for her. Desperate to get out of her situation, Jenn initially made heavy use of online job sites, putting in lots of time, but with no results.

Jenn then reached out to friends, and her mom connected her with a family relative who is a recruiting expert. From her friends, Jenn learned what it was like in different jobs at other companies. She studied project management and other books to help increase her understanding of the work she preferred. From her new mentor, she received the book, *Your Career: How to Make It Happen,* and began going through all the Career Action Worksheets.

"The *Your Career* book helped me refine my resume, learn how to leverage my social network, and gave me confidence that I deserved the change in jobs that could start a career for me. I had been stuck with my old job for so long that I was feeling very weary of the whole process of job searching. By working with a mentor and using the *Your Career* book, I was able to get my feet back under me and get back to the job search."

"Much of the coaching I received helped me in feeling more confident going into the whole process. It helped to know I had my resume well designed and well worded. The suggestion to have business cards on hand was a surprising confidence builder and very helpful. I felt and acted like a true professional. I started applying for jobs directly on company websites. And when I got called for interviews, all of that preparatory work going into the application and interview process helped me feel confident and well prepared."

"In the end, I think I interviewed well, and the job I interviewed for was a natural fit for my skill set. My interviewers saw it too. They saw that I was comfortable and confident and knowledgeable. They also knew I was the right person to offer the position to."

"My job at UnitedHealth Group is going extremely well! This continues to have been just an incredibly natural fit for me in terms of my skill set and how my mind works. I was chosen by my boss to serve in a leadership position, leading classes for clinicians whom we assist with setting up new nursing licenses. As a result, I have also been given the opportunity to travel for work to different UnitedHealth Group and Optum locations around the country, leading groups of clinicians through the application process for new licenses. It has been an excellent learning experience, as I've never traveled for work before, and it grants me the ongoing opportunity to refine my skills as a leader and presenter. It's been nearly a year now, and my supervisor agrees that it's time to interview for my next step up within the company. I am on a good career path now, and am very happy."

Know the Interview Essentials

OVERVIEW

After applying for jobs, it's time to prepare for interviews. In Chapter 8, learn interview preparation basics, how to ask for and get interviews, and how to continue the Job Search Journey even while waiting for invitations to interview.

OUTCOMES

1 List the key elements of successful interviews, page 231

2 Describe strategies for getting interviews, page 238

3 Discuss steps to stay on the Journey between interviews, page 244

CAREER ACTION WORKSHEETS

8-1: Body Language Self-Assessment, page 249

8-2: Research Potential Employers Online, page 251

8-3: Develop Your Request for an Interview, page 253

8-4: Stay on the Journey While You Wait, page 255

WHERE ARE YOU ON THE JOURNEY?

PHASE 1: Prepare for the Journey
- *The Job Search Journey*
- *Know Yourself to Market Yourself*
- *Picture Yourself in the Workplace*

PHASE 2: Create Your Resume
- *Plan Your Resume*
- *Write Your Resume*

PHASE 3: Apply for Jobs
- *Find Job Openings*
- *Write Job Applications*

PHASE 4: Shine at Interviews
- **Know the Interview Essentials**
- *Prepare for Your Interview*
- *Interview Like a Pro*

PHASE 5: Connect, Accept, and Succeed
- *Stay Connected with Potential Employers*
- *Dealing with Disappointment*
- *Take Charge of Your Career*

Interviews are about the complete package—not just the answers you give.

PHASE 4 Shine at Interviews
Step 1, *Know the Interview Essentials*

Your goal in this chapter is to prepare for interviews by practicing basic interview success skills, learning how to ask for and get interviews, and learning how to keep your Job Search Journey moving forward even while waiting for the invitation to an interview.

KEY ELEMENTS OF SUCCESSFUL INTERVIEWS

No one ever gets a job without having some type of interview. The interview is the doorway that every job seeker must be prepared to walk through on the way to successful employment. Think of it as a very important business meeting—maybe the first one with your new employer. Your goal is to learn about the job and the company. The interviewer's goal is to learn about your abilities and potential. Both of you are evaluating whether you are a good match.

If you have done your homework well, you will know the name of your interviewer, and the interviewer will be aware of your personal brand through a Warm Introduction or your Job Application Package. The interviewer will likely have looked at your application and be familiar with your education, work experience, and qualifications.

The interview is your chance to market yourself as someone who can help the employer achieve its goals. A successful interview has many elements, some of which are more important than you may realize. Your confident attitude is the biggest factor determining your success, and it comes through in many ways, including your appearance, body language, how you speak, and your manners. Your confident attitude comes through in the way you describe your job qualifications and tell examples of your experience. Start practicing now! Demonstrate your confident attitude at every networking meeting and interaction.

Your Attitude—The No. 1 Factor

Attitude is the number 1 factor that influences an employer to hire. Here are some ways you can exhibit a good attitude:

1. **Concentrate on being likable.** As simple as this may seem, research proves that one of the most essential goals in successful

When They Can't See You

Many of your interactions and some of your interviews will be by phone. Your voice conveys much more meaning than the words alone. Use these tips for success by phone.

- **Do a tech check.** Whether it's a simple phone call or a video call, check your tech. Do you have enough bars? Is the background noise level low? Can you minimize the risk of a dropped call?

- **Have a positive attitude.** Your attitude shines through in your voice. Start with a smile. You will sound friendlier. Try it. Read something aloud to a friend with a smile and without a smile. Can they hear the difference?

- **Take a power pose.** Instead of sitting down for a call, try standing up. Stand tall and strong. You might even pace a bit (but don't get out of breath). Standing gives you more vocal energy and has the psychological effect of boosting confidence.

- **Establish rapport.** There is a person, not just a voice, on the other end of the call. Try having a photo image of the person in front of you to help you be more personable. Be sure to say "thanks" at the start and end of the call.

- **Convey your emotions with words.** While your voice conveys emotions, don't hesitate to say how you are feeling, For example: "I am very interested in this position at your company." Or "When I saw this job posting, I just knew I had to call. Your company is one I'm very excited about because of your strong reputation for producing good products."

interviewing is to be liked by the interviewer. Interviewers want to hire pleasant people whom others will enjoy working with on a daily basis. Many interviewers use this question as a guideline: "If I was stuck in an airport with this person overnight, would I enjoy it?" Build rapport with your interviewer by bringing energy to your interview and smiling. At the end of the interview, ask a question to get to know your interviewer better such as "How long have you worked here? How did you arrive at this company?"

2. **Project an air of confidence and pride.** Act as though you want the position, are capable, and deserve the job—not as though you are desperate. However, do not act as though you already have obtained the job.

3. **Demonstrate enthusiasm.** The applicant who demonstrates little enthusiasm for a job will never be selected for the position. Genuinely show excitement for the role by sharing how you will grow from the job. Show your passion for the career field you have chosen.

4. **Demonstrate knowledge of and interest in the employer.** Saying "I really want this job" is not convincing. Explain why you want the position and how it fits into your career plans. You can cite opportunities that may be unique to the company or emphasize your skills and education that are highly relevant to the position.

5. **Perform at your best every moment.** There are no time-outs during an interview. From the parking lot to the waiting area to the interview room and on your way out, treat everyone courteously, like you would like to be treated. Learn and use the assistant's or receptionist's name. An interviewer often requests this person's opinion of the applicants and hears reactions from others.

6. **Understand that an interview is a two-way street.** Project genuine interest in determining whether both you and the employer can benefit from your employment.

Dress for Success

By the time you have walked in the room and sat down, the interviewer has decided whether you will be considered for the position. One way your attitude is projected is the way you dress. Your image and appearance help determine the all-important first impression you make. That impression may count for as much as 25 % of the employer's positive or negative hiring decision.

Dress Conservatively

Wear businesslike clothes when you apply for office or professional positions. Review the box in Chapter 6 titled "Overcoming Barriers: Dress Like You Have the Job." You can start planning now by shopping for sale prices on clothes that are appropriate, fit you well, and are comfortable.

Look the Part

If you have a Career Network contact inside the company, ask for suggestions for what to wear and what to expect. A word of caution: even if an employer permits casual dress on the job or if employees wear uniforms or safety gear, you should still dress formally for an interview to show that you take the opportunity seriously. T-shirts, jeans, tennis shoes, and other casual items may cost you the job. Avoid trying to make a bold statement with your attire. Instead, show that you conduct yourself professionally and dress accordingly.

Use Active Listening Skills

When the interviewer is speaking, listen carefully to what they are saying instead of trying to figure out how to answer the question. Even your body language indicates if you are listening or not. Make eye contact, lean forward, give short verbal comments like "I see," "thank you," "I understand." Reflect back to confirm understanding, or clarify a complicated or long question, by summarizing or rewording it and asking if you understood correctly. Don't interrupt, but do make head nods. Active listening takes practice, so start now to practice on friends, instructors, family members, and at networking events.

Use Positive Body Language

Your body language speaks louder than your words. Through our life experiences, we become experts at sending and interpreting nonverbal messages. You may be speaking persuasively, but body language that conveys arrogance, lack of enthusiasm, excessive nervousness, or other negative messages will drown out your words. Start now! Practice confident body language.

▶ *CAREER ACTION*
Complete Worksheet 8-1
Body Language Self-Assessment, page 249

Appear Relaxed

Your body language will immediately notify an employer if you are overly tense. Be well rested before an interview so that you will be alert and, if possible, exercise by running, stretching, or doing yoga on the day of the interview. Exercise is one of nature's best techniques for relaxing your body and your mind. Try to allocate adequate time in your day—especially during your job search—to do some form of exercise. And be sure to eat something light and healthy before your interview so that you don't feel hungry or tired.

During the interview, occasionally change your position in your seat; this relaxes muscular body tension and breaks the rigid feeling that nervousness can cause. Breathe deeply and don't hurry your movements; this will project confidence and will reduce your anxiety. If a question arises that you cannot immediately answer, pause and take a breath

to think about it. If possible, give a genuine smile! It's an effective tension breaker for both you and the interviewer.

If you think you don't have any physical mannerisms or don't know what they are, spend a day watching the body language of the people you interact with. Then, become more aware of your physical responses—look in a mirror or ask trusted friends what they notice about you.

Develop Assertive Body Language

Concentrate on sending assertive messages with your body language. Your intent is to appear as though you believe that you are the top talent among all job applicants and they would be lucky to have you join the company. Assertive body language is relaxed, open, and confident. Your posture and gestures support your words and convey credibility and self-assurance. Be careful not to cross the line into arrogant body language. An example of an arrogant posture is one in which you approach the company as though you already work there. Another is if you exhibit a frustrated or even angry posture that conveys "you should have given me the job already."

- **When you meet the interviewer, give a firm handshake and make eye contact.** This immediately communicates intelligence, competence, and honesty.
- **Walk briskly.** You'll look confident and show that you're ready for the meeting.
- **Sit, stand, and walk with your head up and your back straight.** Good posture conveys that you're composed, respectable, alert, and strong. Slouching conveys that you're bored, disinterested, lazy, or unintelligent. Crossing your arms and legs may be interpreted as being closed or stubborn.
- **Make eye contact.** Making good eye contact is essential to achieving effective communication. It conveys that you really

care about what the person has to say. It also conveys confidence, intelligence, competence, and honesty. This doesn't mean that you should glue your eyes to the interviewer; it means that you should look at the interviewer, especially when he or she is talking. Break eye contact at natural points in the discussion. If you are extremely uncomfortable looking directly into the eyes of the interviewer, look at his or her forehead. This gives the impression of looking into his or her eyes. In a group interview, periodically make eye contact with each person. Avoid letting your eyes dart back and forth around the room.

- **Aim for a pleasant, uplifted facial expression.** Occasionally nod your head and gesture to convey agreement and emphasis. Avoid frowning, clenching your jaw, and making other negative expressions.

- **Don't fidget.** Fidgeting is distracting and makes you look nervous, self-conscious, and unsure of your ability to get the job. Keep your hands apart to avoid fidgeting. Rest them on the arms of the chair and keep them still. Keep your hands relaxed, not in tight fists.

- **Watch the interviewer's body language.** The interviewer may lean forward, signaling you to expand on what you are saying. If the interviewer shuffles papers, looks around the room, or gives other nonverbal cues that you should finish speaking, heed the signal. Continue listening and watching to determine whether what you are saying is clearly understood. Retreat from a subject if you observe that it's not being well received.

- **Subtly mirror the interviewer's communication behaviors.** Some people have intense, highly energetic body language and voice qualities, while others are more relaxed. Subtly match your interviewer's style, speed, and tone of voice—but don't overdo it. Do not mirror negative behavior.

Real World Scenario 8-1 Diane just finished interviewing Marcus for a nurse position at her hospital. She was impressed with his answers based on his previous experience concerning how he handles stress, challenges, and multiple priorities. These are all important skills for a nurse. However, customer service and bedside manner are also important characteristics, and Diane was not sure that Marcus would be a good fit. He often looked down when answering questions and had a hesitant, nervous manner. Nurses needed to be able to reassure patients with confidence and positivity. If Marcus wasn't able to exhibit positive behavior during an interview, how would he handle stress with a seriously ill patient? Diane placed Marcus's folder on the "reject" pile, picked up the next resume, and resumed her search for the best fit candidate.

What would have helped Marcus in his preparation for the interview? What unconscious body language do you send out that you would like to change?

Speak Well for Yourself

You're dressed for the part; your positive attitude is shining through; and your body language shows that you're confident, relaxed, and enthusiastic. What's next? Speaking, of course. Even though research shows that body language can carry more influence than words can, you need good verbal communication skills to make a strong case for yourself and to get the information you need.

It's How You Say It

Follow these general tips about voice quality to build on the great first impression you made.

- **Use an energetic, pleasant tone of voice** to convey a positive attitude and to enhance your likability. View some TED Talks videos to find a few role models of energetic voices.

Phone Calls: Sound Impressive by Sounding Prepared

- **Identify yourself.** "Hello, this is Brenda Bernstein." Personnel who screen calls are suspicious of callers who don't give their names or state why they are calling. Be straightforward to eliminate any suspicions instantly.

- **Explain why you are calling.** Emphasize your qualifications before you make a request so that your listener has a reason to answer yes. Ask for an interview or use a practiced indirect strategy for getting through to the employer.

- **Get the name of the person who answers.** Ask, "Could I please have your name in case I need to talk with you again?" Write down the name. Using this person's name may make him or her more receptive to helping you.

- **Ask whether it's a good time to talk.**

- **Clarify the details.** Clarify any follow-up activities you are instructed to complete (for example, pick up an application, supply additional information or references, or keep an appointment). Verify the time and place of any meetings and get the correct spelling and pronunciation of the names of the people you will meet.

- **Thank the person you speak to by name.**

© Felix Mizioznikov/Shutterstock.com.

- **Modulate your voice.** Don't speak in a monotone or speak too slowly or too rapidly. Speak loud enough to be heard, but not too loudly. Evaluate your tone and speed by recording and listening to yourself as you practice your opening lines and your 30-Second Commercial.

- **Don't slur your words.** Speak distinctly and clearly. No one likes to ask a person to repeat something.

- **Use positive words and phrases.** One of the most important interview goals is to keep the content positive so that the interviewer's final impression is "Yes, this is the person for the job." Use a positive vocabulary and eliminate all negative terms. For example, instead of saying, "I haven't done that exactly," say, "I've done something similar" or "That sounds like something I would enjoy doing."

- **Use proper grammar.** Use correct grammar, word choice, and a businesslike vocabulary, not an informal, chatty one. Avoid slang and never use profanity or derogatory terms. When under stress, people often use pet phrases (such as *like* and *you know*) too often. Ask a friend or family member to help you identify any speech weaknesses you have, and start now to practice good interview language.

It's What You Say

Be clear about your key messages in advance of the interview. Communicate your 30-Second Commercial, how you are a good fit for the job, and how you are interested in

OVERCOMING BARRIERS
Choose Your Words Carefully

Avoid using words and phrases that make you sound indecisive or unbelievable. Eliminate the following credibility robbers from your vocabulary:

- **Just or only.** Used as follows, "I just worked as a waiter" or "I only worked there on a part-time basis" implies that you are not proud of your work or that you don't consider the work meaningful. All work is meaningful; it demonstrates initiative. Leave out these credibility robbers.

- **I guess.** This makes you sound uncertain.

- **Little.** Don't belittle your accomplishments, as in "This is a little report/project I wrote/developed."

- **Probably.** This suggests unnecessary doubt: "The technique I developed would probably be useful in your department." This statement sounds more convincing: "I believe the technique I developed would be useful in your department."

This is a small sample of words and phrases that can diminish your image. Ask members of your support system to help you identify other verbal credibility robbers and to remind you when you use them.

---

learning enough to assure yourself that the company is a good fit for you. Here are some tips you can practice.

- **Start off right by greeting the interviewer by name.** This conveys respect, which enhances your likability. If more than one person is conducting the interview, learn and use everyone's name.

- **State your name and the position you're seeking.** Begin with a friendly greeting, such as, "Hello, Ms. Ong. I'm Bella Reyna. I'm here to interview for the accounting position." Identifying the position is important because interviewers often interview for many different positions. If someone has already introduced you to the interviewer, simply say, "Good morning, Ms. Ong. I'm pleased to be here today."

- **Emphasize how you fit the job.** Near the beginning of an interview, as soon as it seems appropriate, ask a question similar to this: "Could you describe the scope of the job and tell me what capabilities are most important in filling the position?" Listen carefully and jot down a few notes if needed. The interviewer's response will help you focus on emphasizing your qualifications that best match the needs of the employer.

- **Keep the interview businesslike.** Do not discuss personal, domestic, or financial problems.

- **Don't ramble.** Be concise—but not curt—with your replies. Answer questions with required information, adding anything you think is relevant or especially important; then stop talking or ask your own question.

- **Concentrate.** An interview isn't just about talking. Listen to the interviewer carefully to learn important details about the job requirements, the company, and the department so that you can respond appropriately. See "Become a Good Listener" in Chapter 9 on page 268.

- **Come prepared with stories.** Practice giving examples of situations where you used a variety of skills relevant to the job. You should have many of these stories that are so well practiced that they are part of your normal conversation by the time you get to an interview (See Chapter 9 for more on this.) Practice your 30-Second Commercials.

- **Emphasize your strengths—even when discussing an error you made.** Although you want to avoid bringing up past shortcomings, do not try to dodge one that comes out during an interview. Face it head-on and explain what you learned from the experience. If the interviewer asks you about the circumstances, explain briefly; don't make excuses or blame others. You will create a better impression by being honest, candid, and sincere. Remember: the interviewer is human too and has made his or her share of mistakes.

- **Do not lie during an interview.**

- **Be prepared to state why you left a previous job if asked.** Do not speak unfavorably about your former supervisor or company. Interviewers may believe that you would do the same after leaving their companies. Speak only well of others, and stick to facts. Practice this in advance.

- **Focus on your goal.** Keep coming back to the main purpose of the interview: determining how both you and the employer can benefit from your employment. One way is to get feedback from the interviewer by asking such questions as: "Do you think my skills in that area would be helpful to you?" If the answer is yes, you know you're on the right track. If the answer is no or unclear, get clarification on the qualifications needed for the job, and reintegrate your own qualifications while expressing willingness to continue growing on the job.

Find Out the Basics Online

Before an interview, learning and being able to speak about the employer is a great way to stand out. With so much information available on the Internet, employers expect you to be aware of the basics about the company. Use the employer's website to research the employer thoroughly before any interaction. Here are some things you should know:

- Formal company name, address, locations, contact information, hours of operation

- Industry, products and/or services, competitors, and customers

- Advertised job openings (with salary ranges)

- Number of employees, departments, and managers

- Corporate culture, code of ethics, and statements of purpose or vision

- Reputation and history (past successes, challenges and awards, industry ranking)

- News (Have they been in the news lately? Why?)

Using social media is a quick way of staying relevant and up-to-date on news about your potential employers and the industry. Instead of spending hours researching and reading news articles, consider using some social media shortcuts to speed up the process:

- Review the Twitter feed of your potential employer. Anything exciting on the horizon?

- Visit the site of a news aggregator such as Reddit or Digg. Search for your industry to find headlines quickly.

- Search on the company name in the "News" feature offered by Google or Yahoo!, for example.

Sometimes just knowing the headlines is enough to get a conversation started. For more information on how to research a company in depth using social media, read the Appendix. The next time you're heading out the door to a networking opportunity or interview, take a few minutes to check social media sites to keep yourself sharp!

▶ *CAREER ACTION*
Complete Worksheet 8-2
Research Potential Employers Online, page 251

Be Aware of Business Etiquette

Business etiquette is the expected professional behavior in the workplace, and it is based on common courtesy, manners, and cultural and societal norms. Etiquette blunders include leaving your cell phone ringer on during a business meeting and using your napkin to wipe your nose during a business lunch.

Your behavior in an interview gives your potential employer clues to how you will treat clients and customers. So brush up on etiquette now by researching the topic as it applies to your industry. You can research online and with people in your network who are in this career field.

GET AN INTERVIEW

If you have been doing Career Network Meetings, you have already had pre-interviews. Now it's time to get official interviews that can lead to signed paperwork

MAKE IT A HABIT
Practice Assertive Behaviors in Every Interaction

Don't wait until interview day to become a master at your body language, dress, communication capability, and etiquette. Every interaction, from Career Network Meetings to connecting with an old friend to discover potential job leads, is an opportunity for you to practice and perfect your professional, confident presence. Often, you don't know how you appear from a third-party perspective and what changes need to be made. If you wait until the interview day, something that could have been modified earlier may become the deciding factor between you and the next top candidate for the job.

Give your old friends confidence that they can refer you to other businesspeople by amping up your professional presence when you meet with them. Although it may take them by surprise, it will shift their perspective about how serious you are about your job search.

Wow recruiters, associates, and new connections at Career Network Meetings and job/career fairs by coming prepared with a confident, assertive approach, including tone, body language, and dress.

Ask for feedback from those you feel comfortable approaching. Ask questions such as "What could I have done better? Did I seem prepared, confident, and engaging? Was there anything I did that gave you a pause?"

You can improve your image and approach before you start doing interviews. Sometimes minor changes in your style is all it takes to make a big difference.

© AnneMS/Shutterstock.com.

making you an official employee. To get an interview, ask for one, either directly or indirectly.

Direct Requests for Interviews

First, find out WHO to talk to for an interview, that is, get the name and contact information of a person who would interview you and have authority to offer you a job. If you are working through a recruiter, this part is done for you. Otherwise, a good way to get the name of your interviewer is to ask your network contacts, especially one who already works in the company. Alternately, search online to find the name of a person in the department where you want to work, or the head of human resources (HR) or recruiting. If you can't get a name, contact the receptionist, front desk, or someone at the workplace, either in person or by phone, and request the name of the person you should talk to about an interview for a job.

When requesting an interview, it's best to meet face to face or talk over the phone. Don't email when you can call and don't call when you can make a personal visit. If you can't visit or call, a standard letter or email is appropriate. Tailor your request for an interview to each potential employer by emphasizing your strengths and experience that are most relevant to the employer's needs. See Chapter 7 on prospecting cover letters for more on this topic.

Request an Interview in Person

Requesting an interview by making a personal visit is the most successful method of getting an interview. It is difficult for people to ignore you when you are standing in front of them. If you make a good impression, you have already achieved a major goal in the interview process. Follow these guidelines:

1. **Research the firm** thoroughly beforehand. Career Action Worksheet 8-2 provides a guide.

2. **Dress for the part.** Dress and groom yourself as though you are going to an actual interview.

3. **Be prepared.** Use the Interview Preparation Checklist (see Chapter 10) to make sure you have everything you need, including your resume.

4. **Pay special attention to the gatekeeper** (the person standing between you and the employer). This may be a front-line staff member, an administrative assistant, a supervisor, or a human resources staff member. Actively and courteously seek that person's help.

5. Present a concise, action-packed version of your 30-Second Commercial; then request an interview.

6. **Thank your contact by name** for his or her time and consideration.

If you don't get an interview, ask for a referral to another department or company that may need your abilities. Remain courteous and professional throughout the conversation.

Study the example of a request for an interview made during a personal visit to an employer in Figure 8-1. The applicant is applying for an administrative support position in a medical center. Note how he highlights his qualifications, demonstrates his knowledge of the employer and the industry, and expresses his interest in a job—just the right approach.

Request an Interview over the Phone

Your phone communication skills will affect your success throughout your career. You can develop these skills just as you develop any other skill. Your voice is your personality over the phone. You want to use your voice to project confidence and enthusiasm and make a positive impression. Follow these guidelines:

1. **Know why you are calling.** Is your purpose to get the name of the hiring individual? Is it to request information about the position? Is it to request an interview?

Figure 8-1 Sample In-Person Request for an Interview

The Opening. "Hello, Mr. Washington. My name is Stephen Rogowski. My instructor Phyllis Johnston recommends your Information Services Department at St. Mary's Hospital for its well-organized systems design. I recently completed my education at Mesa College, earning two A.S. degrees—one in information management technology and another in medical administrative assisting."

The 30-Second Commercial Excerpt. "My ability to organize and communicate information in an easy-to-understand way has been a big asset in my previous work. I worked for 18 months as a clerical assistant in the Business Office at Lewis State College while attending school. I'm proficient in Office 2019 and SharePoint software and have my Microsoft Office User Specialist (MOUS) certification in Office 2019. I operate personal computers, networks, and general office equipment. I also key 70 words per minute and am skilled in English usage."

The Request. "I've developed time-saving methods for creating templates and macros that may be appropriate for your department. Would you have time today for me to review them with you, or would a day next week be more convenient?"

The Close. "Next Tuesday at 10 a.m.? I appreciate your willingness to meet with me so soon, Mr. Washington. I look forward to meeting with you then. Thank you. Good-bye."

2. **Research the firm beforehand.** Get the name of the person you need to contact before you call to request an interview, as suggested above.

3. **Write a script or an outline before you call.** This helps you organize your message, making you sound intelligent and well prepared. List the information you need to obtain from your contact before the phone call ends. Pattern your script after the samples in this chapter and use your 30-Second Commercial.

4. **Don't read from the script during the call.** Practice what you want to say ahead of

time until you are comfortable saying it. During the call, use your script or outline as a checklist to guide you from one idea to the next.

5. **Speak clearly and get to the point.** Any long pauses could cause you to be put on hold or transferred to voice mail before you have had a chance to make your pitch.

6. **Don't do anything else.** Listen and respond to the person on the other end of the line. Give the phone call your complete attention. Don't chew gum or drink while talking on the phone.

7. **Stand up, speak directly into the mouthpiece, and smile while you talk.** The muscles used to smile relax your vocal cords and create a pleasant tone of voice. Standing up gives your voice more energy. Start with, "Hello, this is xxx, and I'm calling to …." We are all comfortable saying our own name, so this is a smooth way to get started.

Study the phone request for an interview in Figure 8-2. Note how the applicant incorporates her qualifications, knowledge of the employer and the industry, and interest in the employer.

▶ *CAREER ACTION*
Complete Worksheet 8-3
Develop Your Request for an Interview, page 253

Write an Email or Letter to Request an Interview

If you can't meet or call, use the written word to request an interview. Review the guidelines in Chapter 7 for preparing and distributing a Job Application Package with a customize cover letter. You may use both an email and a letter to give extra emphasis to your message and increase the likelihood that your request will be read.

If you don't receive responses from your Job Application Package within 10 days,

Figure 8-2 Sample Phone Request for an Interview

> **The Opening.** "Hello, Ms. Hope. This is Jaleesa Williams. I recently completed research comparing the product quality and service records of computer network manufacturers. I'm impressed with the results XYZ Company has achieved, and I'm interested in learning about a possible sales representative position."
>
> **The 30-Second Commercial Excerpt.** "I've become fascinated with the impact that service can have on sales. I'm completing my degree in sales and marketing at Fairmount State College and have two years of successful retail sales experience. I also was the advertising assistant for our school paper and increased sales by 18 % this year."
>
> **The Request.** "Would it be possible to arrange a meeting with you to discuss your sales goals and how I might contribute to them?"
>
> **The Close.** "Thank you, Ms. Hope. I look forward to meeting with you next Tuesday, the 18th, at 2:30. Good-bye."

reinforce the request through a phone call, personal visit, or, if needed, a one-time follow-up email.

If you decide to call, before doing so, review the "Phone Calls: Sound Impressive by Sounding Prepared" box in this chapter.

Indirect Strategies for Landing Interviews

Using an indirect strategy is really simply an extension of your Warm Introductions strategy to find job openings and your ongoing networking efforts. (See Chapter 6.) The difference is that the goal is to get an interview rather than more connections or job opening leads. The indirect strategy can create opportunities to meet people in your target company who can arrange an interview for you. To reach an employer, to bypass a gatekeeper, to find the hidden job market, or to get around the office receptionist, consider using the indirect strategy to land an interview.

Get Through to an Employer

When job competition is high for a specific company or job posting, employers are flooded with applicants. In response, they may issue a temporary no-hire policy, which makes personal contact difficult because employees are instructed to notify applicants that no interviews are being scheduled at that time.

In a situation like this, use your initiative and persistence. Develop a persuasive reason to contact the person with hiring authority in your target company. See the "Ask…" examples below.

While you should not make a direct request for a job during a meeting that is arranged indirectly, you can discuss your experience and abilities. By doing so, you may convince your contact that you would be an asset to the company, which is exactly your intention. Also ask whether the employer may need your skills in the future or if your contact could suggest another company or department that may need someone with your qualifications.

Ask for Professional Advice

One effective indirect strategy is to arrange a brief meeting or phone call with a potential employer to discuss professional issues and to ask for advice about additional preparation to make you more employable.

Ask About Professional Organizations

Ask for recommendations about professional associations, industry trade groups, and publications in your field. Consider asking the following questions:

- What professional association(s) would keep me informed of industry developments, technological advances in the field, and emerging trends?
- Which professional publications or Internet resources deal specifically with our field?
- Who else could I speak to for further advice on this topic?

Please Leave a *Good* Message

- Make notes about what you want to say before you place the call.

- Have a plan for a conversation if the person answers the phone.

- Listen carefully to the person's voice mail greeting. The person you are trying to reach may be on vacation or may ask callers to send an email instead of leaving a message.

- Use a pleasant, professional speaking voice. Your voice *is* you to the person who has never met you. Sound confident and helpful; avoid sounding needy or pushy. Encourage the listener so that they want to call you back.

- Speak slowly. Speak more slowly than you ordinarily do so that the person can take notes without having to listen to your message more than once.

- Pronounce your name clearly. Clearly say your name and spell your name if it is commonly misspelled. For example, "Hello this is Ken Owens, that's Owens with an s."

- Say your phone number clearly and slowly. Your listener is writing down your number, so don't mumble or rush. Be sure to give the area code. Remember that many work place land-lines do not have an auto callback feature, nor do they record the phone number that called.

- Leave *yourself* the message before you make the real call. Practice makes perfect, so call yourself from another phone and leave the message on your own voice mail.

- If you speak English with an accent, ask a friend to listen to your message and tell you if any parts of it were hard to understand. Speak slowly and clearly. Being able to be under-stood is much more important than speaking quickly or demonstrating difficult vocabulary.

- Repeat your name and phone number at the end of the message. For example, "I look forward to hearing from you. Again, my name is Ken Owens (with an s) at ###."

© auremar/Shutterstock.com.

Ask for Help with Career Planning

If you have not completed your education or have limited experience related to your job tar-get, ask for help in choosing your course work or with career planning. Your conversation could be similar to this example. (See Figure 8-3)

Ask for Help with Your Resume

If you are seeking help in developing your resume into one that employers will want to read, you can place a phone call to an employer and ask for his or her help. See Figure 8-4 for an example of what you might say.

Develop a Relationship with Your Target Employer

The **gatekeeper** (the administrative support person, receptionist, or human resources staff member) who must screen all job applicants can help, hinder, or ruin your chances of obtaining a job with the company. Because this person's

Figure 8-3 Sample Request for Career Advice

"Hello, Mr. Cuervo. This is Cecilia Lee. I'm completing an assignment for a career planning course and would appreciate your assistance with some of my research. I'm seeking opinions from people who are recognized and experienced in the field of (your field)."

"My skills are in the area(s) of _____. Could you please help me identify positions in (your career field) for which these skills would be most useful?"

"I'd also appreciate your recommendations about any additional course work and preparation I may need."

Figure 8-4 Sample Request for Resume Advice

"Hello, Ms. Pappas. This is Nhon Tran. You've been highly recommended to me by Dr. Ivarsen of the Computer Information Systems Department of Nevada College. I'm developing a professional resume and would very much appreciate your critiquing it."

influence on your job search can be considerable, use good diplomacy when communicating with him or her. Follow these guidelines:

- Express respect for the employer, perhaps referring to its reputation for professionalism, reliability, or leadership.
- Find common ground in an effort to establish a good rapport with the gatekeeper. If he or she likes and trusts you, you may learn valuable information about what it is like to work for the company and whether you will fit in.
- If it seems feasible, ask for the person's help in arranging a meeting with the appropriate staff member. Indicate your awareness of everyone's busy schedules and ask the gatekeeper the best time to contact the employer. Ask if you could speak with someone else who can tell you more about your areas of interest.

- Before leaving, thank the person by name for his or her time and assistance.

When making the first contact with a potential employer, remember that if you are successful in your job search, you will be working with the people you meet. You cannot afford to be ill-mannered, unprofessional, or overbearing with anyone you encounter during the first phone call or step through the door.

Your Career Network: Who You Know at the Company

When a company offers you an interview, who you know at that company can make a difference. Here's what you want to know and how you might get answers using your Career Network.

What you want to know

- Who might be interviewing you and what is known about this person that might help the two of you connect better during the interview?
- What are the norms for interviewing at this company?
- Can I get a Warm Introduction or LinkedIn recommendation from someone in the company to help me stand out?

Who in your network can help

- Go through your network and see who works for this company.
- Use LinkedIn to find out who you know who knows someone inside the company. Ask for an introduction.
- Use LinkedIn to find people in the company and read through profiles to find something you have in common. Use that commonality to give credibility to your request to connect.

Other Indirect Strategies

Try following tried and true strategies for getting interviews. Refer to additional sources of job leads in Chapter 6.

Go Through the Human Resources Department

If your target employer has a strict policy requiring all applicants to be processed through the human resources department, follow the required procedure. You can expect the first step to be submitting an application, a resume, and a cover letter. If you are selected, you will be invited to a screening interview with a member of the human resources staff. This interview may be in person or over the phone. (The screening interview is covered in Chapter 9.)

Real World Scenario 8-2 Lily had created a list of her ideal employers in her area, following the guidelines in Chapter 3. Even though she hadn't seen job openings posted, she knew, through her research, that she could contribute greatly to these companies and would fit well with their culture. Using LinkedIn, she found the name of a manager in the department where she would like to be hired. She went in person to the office and asked to schedule a meeting with the manager. She casually asked the administrator what it was like working in the department, and she was excited to hear that several people had recently left the department. Although the jobs were expected to be filled internally, this was just the opportunity Lily was looking for. She was able to schedule the meeting and began to prepare to market herself effectively.

What are some conversation starters that will help you discover the hidden job market? What indirect strategies can you use to create interview opportunities?

If you perform well during a screening interview and you appear to be qualified, you may be scheduled for a departmental interview. If the employer doesn't have an opening in your area, find out how to keep your file active and how you can stay informed about the hiring status for the position.

Use a Private Employment Agency

If you plan to use employment agencies, staffing agencies, or employment contractors in your job search, they will arrange your job interviews. Read the agency's agreement thoroughly to be certain you are satisfied—and comfortable—with their procedures, including interviews.

Request Interviews at Career Fairs

Employers use job fairs to show off their businesses and to actively seek resumes and contacts. Job seekers can meet dozens of potential employers in one location, so bring several copies of your resume. Ask company representatives about hiring procedures, their opinion of industry trends, and the types of employees they typically hire. Try to arrange a follow-up Career Network Meeting with an employer, using the name of the person you meet as your contact. Keep your contact's business card and use it to follow up within the week with a thank-you note or phone call.

Show the interviewer the type of employee you will be. Give solid, to-the-point answers. Ask thoughtful questions and never interrupt.

STAY ON THE JOURNEY BETWEEN INTERVIEWS

Getting interviews can take a long time. The hiring process typically lasts several months. Don't expect to hear immediately from employers. While getting an interview and a job may be your top priority, recognize and respect the fact that employers have other business to attend to. Make good use of the time while waiting for interviews by advancing your Job Search Journey in other ways. Here are some suggestions.

Get Closer to People in Your Career Field. Look back at the suggestions in Chapter 6 about joining professional associations and trade groups, taking on internships or cooperative jobs, and doing volunteer work. This is a great way to get experience and expand your network. You might even run into your potential employer in the process.

Keep Applying for Other Jobs. Until you have a job offer in hand, your Job Search Journey is not over. Even if you have a possibility or strong lead, do not stop finding and applying for other leads.

Follow Up. Call your target employer regularly, especially if you sense that there has been a favorable change in the job market. Ask whether the employer would consider reevaluating your qualifications in light of your new experience.

Take Another Job. You may need to take another job while you wait for your best fit job position to become available. This work experience can increase your value. Use the experience to polish your current skills, develop new ones, and establish a reputation as a valuable employee. Then follow up on your best fit jobs every 6 to 12 months.

Check Back Periodically. Call the human resources department to remain informed of the hiring status and to reaffirm your interest. This may help you be first in line for openings.

If you consider more than one company to be a prime employer, don't let one discouragement slow you down. Review the techniques in this chapter and rally your efforts toward your next target. Preparation, practice, action, and perseverance will pay off. Keep at it until you get several interviews, and ultimately, the job you want.

▶ *CAREER ACTION*

Complete Worksheet 8-4

Stay on the Journey While You Wait, page 255

Chapter Checklist

Check off each item you can do. Reread sections in this chapter to help you complete the checklist.

☐ Describe how to start practicing now for interviews by working on my attitude and body language, and what I say about myself. ❶

☐ Conduct online research of potential employers. ❶

☐ Prepare to request an interview in person, by phone, or in writing, as though it were the start of an actual interview, knowing that a first impression can influence the outcome. ❷

☐ Emphasize my qualifications before I ask for an interview, giving the listener a reason to answer yes. ❷

☐ Prepare a written script or an outline and practice asking for an interview before doing it. ❷

☐ Treat gatekeepers and other staff members courteously and professionally because I know they are often the key to connecting with the hiring authority. ❷

☐ Use my time effectively to continue on my Job Search Journey while waiting for the next interview. ❸

Critical Thinking Questions

1. How can a job applicant demonstrate a positive attitude during an interview? ❶

2. Why do interviewers respond positively to assertive body language? How can a job candidate demonstrate assertive body language? ❶

3. What negative nonverbal habits are most important for you to eliminate to improve your interview abilities? ❶

4. What method of making a request for an interview do you think will be most effective in your Job Search Journey? Why? ❷

5. What are some advantages to requesting interviews by phone rather than by in writing? ❷

6. Why is it important to establish a good relationship with the gatekeeper and other people you meet while you wait to be interviewed? List several strategies you can use to establish good rapport. ❷

7. What could happen when requesting an interview if a job applicant hadn't prepared a 30-Second Commercial? ❷

8. Get creative. Think of an employer you could realistically target for job openings that have yet to be posted. What are the needs of this employer based on your research? What special skills and knowledge do you have that suggest a unique job or position that you could perform to meet the employer's needs? ❷

9. If you have already scheduled or completed an interview with one company, why should you keep searching for jobs? Describe what could happen if you had multiple interviews. **❸**

Trial Run

Request an Interview ❷

It helps to be proactive and confident when using the strategies in this chapter. Before you try your approach on strangers, practice with your classmates and support team. Most of these approaches are new, so review the advice as a class to make sure you understand when to apply each suggestion.

Divide into teams of three or four students. Each team creates an interview request scenario and presents it to the class. Discuss types of employers, types of approaches, possible pitfalls, and follow-up. One student can play the role of the employer on the phone or in person, reacting to the request for an interview.

Use these criteria to evaluate each team:

☐ Verbal and language skills (in person, by phone, and in writing requests)

☐ Good use of a 30-Second Commercial applicable to job

☐ Alignment with the employer's style (attitude, dress, body language, how you talk about yourself)

☐ Reaction to rejection

Team's strengths:

Suggestions for improvement:

This page is intentionally blank.

▶ CAREER ACTION WORKSHEET

8-1 Body Language Self-Assessment

PART 1: Review the descriptions of nonverbal behaviors and voice qualities and check the box for each item that describes your body language habits. You also can do this Career Action Worksheet with a partner.

Definitions:

- **Assertive body language** is relaxed, open, and confident. It supports your words and conveys competence, self-assurance, caring, and credibility.

- **Passive body language** looks nonenergetic and diminishes your credibility by conveying insecurity, weakness, anxiety, and a lack of self-assurance and competence.

- **Aggressive body language** appears brash and overbearing and sends offensive messages that convey hostility, pushiness, intimidation, and a domineering attitude.

Review your answers and highlight your aggressive or passive habits. In Part 2, list the habits you think are most important to change. Finally, take action to correct these habits and ask others to remind you when you exhibit them.

POSTURE

☐	Comfortably upright	Assertive
☐	Relaxed, balanced	Assertive
☐	Open, not constricted	Assertive
☐	Overly stiff	Aggressive
☐	Arms/legs crossed	Aggressive
☐	Overbearing, intimidating	Aggressive
☐	Wooden, tight	Passive
☐	Slumped shoulders	Passive
☐	Slumped back/spine	Passive

HANDSHAKE

☐	Appropriately firm	Assertive
☐	Connect between thumb and first finger	Assertive
☐	Shake from elbow through hand	Assertive
☐	Held for appropriate length of time	Assertive
☐	"Bone-crushing" grip	Aggressive
☐	Held for too long	Aggressive
☐	Limp	Passive
☐	Shake from wrist through hand	Passive
☐	Held too briefly	Passive
☐	Grasping fingers only	Passive

FACIAL EXPRESSION

☐	Open, relaxed, pleasant	Assertive
☐	Frowning	Aggressive
☐	Moody, sulking	Aggressive
☐	Tight upper lip, pursed mouth	Aggressive
☐	Clenched jaw	Aggressive
☐	Wrinkling forehead	Passive
☐	Biting or licking lips	Passive
☐	Continual smile	Passive

EYE CONTACT

☐	Comfortably direct	Assertive
☐	Staring off; bored expression	Aggressive
☐	Sneering, looking down nose	Aggressive
☐	Direct stare	Aggressive
☐	Constantly looking down	Passive
☐	Blinking rapidly	Passive
☐	Frequently shifting focus	Passive
☐	No eye contact; avoidance	Passive

VOICE QUALITIES

☐	Distinct and clear	Assertive
☐	Controlled but relaxed	Assertive
☐	Warm, pleasant tone	Assertive
☐	Energized; suitable emphasis	Assertive
☐	Too rapid	Aggressive
☐	Too demanding or urgent	Aggressive
☐	Too loud	Aggressive
☐	Arrogant or sarcastic	Aggressive
☐	Dull or monotone	Passive
☐	Whiny tone	Passive
☐	Too soft or too low	Passive
☐	Too nasal	Passive

GESTURES

☐	Natural, not erratic	Assertive
☐	Occasional gestures to emphasize	Assertive
☐	Occasional positive head nodding	Assertive
☐	Open hand (conveys trust)	Assertive
☐	Leaning toward speaker	Assertive
☐	Pointing finger	Aggressive
☐	Hands on hips	Aggressive
☐	Wooden gestures	Passive
☐	Tilting head to one side	Passive
☐	Bringing hand to face	Passive
☐	Nodding head too much	Passive
☐	Fidgeting	Passive

DISTRACTING NONVERBAL HABITS

☐	Drumming fingers	Passive
☐	Use of fillers (*um, uh, you know*)	Passive
☐	Jiggling leg/arm	Passive
☐	Fiddling with hair or glasses	Passive
☐	Fiddling with an object	Passive
☐	Rubbing beard or mustache	Passive
☐	Biting nails	Passive
☐	Scratching	Passive

PART 2: In order of importance, list the negative nonverbal habits you plan to change.

My Goals for Improving My Nonverbal Communication and Voice Qualities

1. _____

2. _____

3. _____

Add your completed work to the "About Me" section of your Career Builder Files.

▶ CAREER ACTION WORKSHEET

8-2 Research Potential Employers Online

Learn the basic information about a potential employer using your online resources.

1. Choose one of your target employers. Company name: _____

2. Research online to answer the following questions. Use the company website, news websites, and general search engines (Google, Bing, Yahoo!, etc.)

a.   Official company name: _____

b.   List three of the company products or services.

    1. _____

    2. _____

    3. _____

c.   Describe or name several of their customers, such as other companies or types of people (examples: pet owners or fitness enthusiasts).

d.   List 3 competitors.

    1. _____

    2. _____

    3. _____

e.   Summarize the company values and culture, based on their website, Glassdoor, Facebook, LinkedIn, Twitter, or other social review website (examples: innovative, casual, competitive, cost-driven, quality-driven, people/relationship-driven).

f.   Read items in the news about this company and, from what you read, describe the company's current successes, concerns, and/or goals.

    1. _____

    2. _____

    3. _____

g.   Why is it important to be informed about a company prior to your interview?

This page is intentionally blank.

▶ *CAREER ACTION WORKSHEET*

8-3 Develop Your Request for an Interview ❷

PART 1: Read the sample request for an interview in Figure 8-1, then write an outline that would be appropriate for you to use when requesting an interview. Next, read the sample phone request in Figure 8-2 and determine what would be different in your outline if you were making this request by phone rather than in person.

The Opening:

The 30-Second Commercial Excerpt:

The Request:

The Close:

PART 2: Turn to your support system for assistance. Do some role-playing, following the guidelines below. Deliver your request for an interview to someone in your support system. First as if you were in person, and then by phone.

1. Critique your delivery and improve on it. It helps to record your delivery and play it back.

2. Have your helper ask you questions that lead to your sharing more information about your qualifications.

3. Practice responding when your helper makes excuses for not scheduling an interview. (Remember to stay cool and positive, and be courteous to the gatekeeper.)

4. Practice presenting your qualifications persuasively, using your 30-Second Commercial.

5. Practice turning objections into acceptance.

Add your completed work to the "About Jobs" section of your Career Builder Files.

This page is intentionally blank.

▶ *CAREER ACTION WORKSHEET*

8-4 Stay on the Journey While You Wait ❸

While waiting for the next interview request, continue your Job Search Journey. Use this worksheet to discover more jobs that you are qualified to do. Refer to your completed Career Action Worksheets in Part 1 to help complete the following.

1. List the benefits of working at a job related to your career field that may be an untraditional use of your talents.

2. Find and list three jobs that you are currently qualified to do that you have not previously applied for.

3. Describe your action plan for interacting more with people in your chosen career field. Describe how you could strengthen relationships with people you already know.

4. Find and list three jobs that you are currently overqualified to do. Describe why you haven't applied for these jobs, and at what point you would apply.

Add your completed work to the "About Jobs" section of your Career Builder Files.

This page is intentionally blank.

Prepare for Your Interview

OVERVIEW

You can improve your chances of success in an interview if you prepare for different kinds of interviews, practice answering interview questions, learn to ask appropriate questions of your own, and practice good listening skills.

OUTCOMES

1 Prepare for pre-employment tests, page 258

2 Prepare for common interview styles, page 260

3 Prepare answers to typical interview questions, page 265

4 Ask good questions to stand out, page 274

CAREER ACTION WORKSHEETS

9-1: Research Pre-employment Test Types, page 279

9-2: Research Interview Styles, page 281

9-3: Create a Question-and-Answer Planning Sheet, page 283

WHERE ARE YOU ON THE JOURNEY?

PHASE 1: Prepare for the Journey
- *The Job Search Journey*
- *Know Yourself to Market Yourself*
- *Picture Yourself in the Workplace*

PHASE 2: Create Your Resume
- *Plan Your Resume*
- *Write Your Resume*

PHASE 3: Apply for Jobs
- *Find Job Openings*
- *Write Job Applications*

PHASE 4: Shine at Interviews
- *Know the Interview Essentials*
- **Prepare for Your Interview**
- *Interview Like a Pro*

PHASE 5: Connect, Accept, and Succeed
- *Stay Connected with Potential Employers*
- *Dealing with Disappointment*
- *Take Charge of Your Career*

Those who prepare show the best of themselves when put to the test.

PHASE 4 Shine at Interviews
Step 2, *Prepare for Your Interview*

You are in Phase 4, *Shine at Interviews*, at Steps 1 and 2, prepare and practice and take pre-employment tests. Your goal in this chapter is to prepare and practice for common interview questions and pre-employment tests.

PREPARE FOR PRE-EMPLOYMENT TESTS

Before you are even considered for an interview, you may be asked to take pre-employment screening tests. Some tests are requested only after you have successfully completed a screening interview. To help you feel confident and to do your best, it helps to know what to expect. Here are some common types of tests.

The Personality Test

The **personality test** is the exception to the "do your homework" rule. Because this type of test is usually designed to determine whether your personal and behavioral preferences are well matched to the work involved and company culture, advance study doesn't apply. Technically, there are no wrong answers in these tests. Personality tests can measure, for example, your solitary or social tendencies, your relative need for stability, your preference for efficiency or creativity, your style of goal achievement (flexible or fixed), and your tendency to accept others' ideas or stick to your own. Answer all questions honestly. If your personality doesn't match the culture of the employer, you won't be happy in it.

The Skills Test

If you will be taking a general **skills test,** start to review, practice, and improve your skills today. Try to learn what is covered in advance of the test, for example, grammar, spelling, math, typing or computer skills, or something else. No matter how good your skills are, you can improve them with practice, which increases your employability. Another benefit of polishing your skills is that you'll be able to start your new job with more confidence. However, stop preparing one or two days before you take a skills test. Cramming until the last minute increases anxiety and often results in poorer performance.

The Technical Test

The purpose of a technical test is to find out how much you know about a subject related to your job. Try to get samples of the technical questions that may be asked through the employer's human resources department, other employees in the company, people who have taken the test, and people who have taken similar tests in your field. Libraries, bookstores, and websites may also have sample tests.

If you find sample questions, write out answers to the questions as a way of practicing. The important thing is to be as complete as possible in your answers.

The Computerized Test

The computerized pre-employment test is useful for screening large numbers of applicants because it saves time and other expenses. The test may be general in content, or it may be a skills or personality test.

Typically, you take this test at the employer's site or at an employment agency. You may also be asked to log on to an employer's website and take the test online. You receive instructions on how to use the computerized test program and are given a specific amount of time to complete it. The results are usually scored electronically and generated in a report. They are then analyzed by human resources personnel. The best advice for performing well on a computerized pre-employment test is relax, do your best, and don't try to outwit the test by overthinking the questions.

Taking Employment Tests

Employment testing may be an important factor in an employer's hiring decision. Follow these guidelines to perform at your best:

- Try to find out in advance what will be tested and how. Is it a written, oral,

Take Drug Screening Seriously

Applicants who test positively for drug use or who admit to using illegal drugs may be screened out of the job immediately. Never give flippant answers to questions about drug use. They could be interpreted negatively.

Policies for drug screening vary considerably from one employer to the next. As part of your employer research, find out the drug screening procedures and requirements. Check with employers directly and with people who work for them. Schools' career services counselors often have information about drug testing procedures and may be familiar with the procedures that local employers use.

To protect yourself, before you are tested, report to the employer any prescription or over-the-counter drugs you are taking. Some of these can result in a false-positive test.

Be aware that even if marijuana use is legal in your state, employers may have a policy prohibiting use by employees. Do your research; don't assume.

iStock.com/Justin Horrocks.

computerized, or combination test? Does it test technical knowledge, skills, manual dexterity, personality, special abilities, or other job-related capabilities? Prepare accordingly.

- Eat properly before the test and be well rested. A sluggish body and brain can diminish your performance.

- Do some physical exercise or yoga before the test to improve your circulation and your ability to relax and concentrate.

- Arrive 10 minutes early to avoid feeling rushed or tense.

- Ask exactly how much time is allotted for the test. Take your time and don't rush into poor performance.

- Read the test carefully to clarify the instructions and to determine how many points are assigned to each question. If the points aren't indicated, ask the person monitoring the test how the questions are weighted.

- Read each question multiple times to make sure you understand what is being asked. If you have a question, ask the test monitor if possible.

- Ask whether points will be deducted for questions you don't answer. If they will, answer every question. If not, don't spend a lot of time on questions you can't answer easily. (Save those for last.)

- Many tests are objective, often including multiple-choice questions. In true-false questions, extreme statements are frequently false (for example, choices that contain the words *all, never,* or *always*). Moderate statements are often true.

- Double-check to be sure you didn't skip any questions. Because your first response is usually the correct one, don't change answers unless you made a careless mistake.

Jacob was never a good test taker. When he heard his upcoming interview required a basic math test using Excel, he was nervous. The week of his interview, he set aside time every day to practice using sample tests he found on the Internet. He limited his studying to one hour a day and aimed to finish six samples tests prior to the interview. The day before the interview, he took the last sample test in the morning and then decided to relax the rest of the day. Prior to the interview, he reviewed a few notes of the common errors he had made during the sample tests. He took a deep breath and felt calm, knowing he had done the best he could to prepare for the test.

What tactics help you to be calm during times of stress and pressure? How can you apply these tactics when preparing for pre-interview tests and the interview process overall?

- On general math tests, expect some simple addition, subtraction, multiplication, division, fraction, percentage, and decimal problems. Many math tests also include word problems.
- Advanced math tests will be geared to your field (engineering and statistical analysis, for instance). Consult others who have taken similar tests to determine what you should review. Your education and work experience are your primary preparation for advanced math tests.

Once you have successfully completed pre-employment tests, you are on your way to the next steps in your Job Search Journey.

▶ *CAREER ACTION*

Complete Worksheet 9-1
Research Pre-employment Test Types, page 279

PREPARE FOR COMMON INTERVIEW STYLES

OUTCOME **2**

The traditional style of interview is a one-on-one meeting. You might be nervous—most people are—but less so if you know what to expect during the interview and have practiced your answers to the most likely questions. There are two basic styles of traditional interviews that you should be prepared for:

- **Structured:** In these interviews, all the job candidates are asked the same or similar questions. This allows the employee to compare candidates more easily.
- **Unstructured:** These interviews might follow a pattern or outline but can "go with the flow" to get to know the candidate and assess their fit for the company and the job.

You may receive a request to schedule an interview at any time. The request can come by email, standard mail, or phone. In case the request comes by phone, have a businesslike outgoing voice mail message that includes your name, and make sure anyone who may answer the phone knows to answer professionally and take a complete message. If a call comes at an unexpected time, politely ask if the caller can hold for a moment while you move to a quiet location. When you get an interview request, respond promptly with your availability.

In general, for any interview, use the following tips.

1. **Be prepared.** Have a copy of your resume and any other materials you would like to use during the interview. Have paper and pen so that you can write down names and information.

2. **Focus on why you are interested in working for the potential employer** on the basis of your research and understanding of the employer's products or services, current developments, philosophies, mission and

values, and so on. Talk about your qualifications that make you a good fit.

3. **Be professional, courteous, and friendly;** let the caller lead the conversation but ask questions of your own.

4. **Be factual in your answers; be brief yet thorough.** Avoid yes/no answers; they give no real information about your abilities.

5. **If you need time to think about a question, avoid using repetitive phrases to buy time.** Instead, simply say, "Let me think about that."

6. **As the interview wraps up, ask what about next steps.** Tell the interviewer that you are available for a follow-up interviews, if needed. Get an approximate date when you can expect to hear from the company again about this job.

7. **Follow up.** Contact the interviewer one or two days later to say thank you for his or her time, and restate your interest in the position. You can leave this message by voice mail or send an email.

While there are only two basic styles of interviews—structured and unstructured—there are many types of interviews. These vary based on where the interview takes place, who conducts the interview, and the intent of the interview—to screen potential candidates or to make job offers. Get familiar with all these types so that you can recognize which type of interview you are doing and be prepared and relaxed for this all-important meeting.

Screening Interview

Large employers often require applicants to go through a **screening interview** to screen out unqualified applicants and identify candidates—qualified applicants—who will be invited for the next level of interviews. Screening might be done by phone, in person, or in a group interview. Screening interviews might be outsourced to recruiting agencies or done by human resources people.

The interviewer may use a rating sheet to evaluate each candidate. Your goal in a screening interview is to be given a second interview. Make sure you state your qualifications clearly and concisely. Ask what to expect next, who is responsible for making a hiring decision, and when this decision will be made.

Computer-Based Interview

Computer-based interviews may be part of the application process to screen candidates. The candidate logs onto a password-protected website with instructions on how to complete the interview. The interview may consist of 50 to 100 multiple-choice and true–false questions and be timed, so start the interview only when you can have uninterrupted time. Some programs search for contradictions by asking you the same question several times in different forms; so be consistent in your answers. Some computer-based interviews include open-ended questions that are reviewed by recruitment specialists or managers. Answer questions just as you would in a face-to-face interview. Use correct grammar and strong written communication skills. Emphasize your related skills but don't exaggerate. Be concise, and be positive in your responses. Your goal is to get through this screening process by demonstrating your skills, honesty, and qualifications.

Campus Interview

Campus interviews, generally scheduled through a school's career center, are typically structured screening interviews averaging 20 to 30 minutes. Because the interviewer must evaluate each candidate quickly, you should keep your remarks concise and to the point. Let the trained interviewer guide you through the fact-finding process. Respond concisely without omitting pertinent information about your qualifications. Smile and be pleasant in order to build rapport with the interviewer.

Phone Interview

A **phone interview** is a cost-effective screening technique. For this type of interview, be sure to have a quiet place without distractions. Have all your materials ready—resume, pen, paper, and so on. Stand up, speak directly into the mouthpiece, and smile while you talk. This gives your voice more energy and a pleasant tone. Never smoke, eat, or chew gum while on the phone. Be sure to listen as well as talk. Pay extra attention to articulating your words clearly.

Video Interview

A two-way **video interview** uses technology to conduct a "face-to-face" interview over the Internet. Video interviews are used with increasing frequency. You should practice with this type of technology, such as Zoom, to be sure to be at your best. Test your video setup and connectivity in advance. Make sure lighting and sound quality are set up properly. You should have a light in front of you so that your face is not shadowed. Your face should be centered with your chin clearly in the picture. Try to find a plain wall or background to sit in front of so that the background is professional, not distracting. Find a quiet place with no interruption from children, pets, or phone calls. Dress appropriately, project energy, and maintain eye contact with the camera. Use positive body language and good posture, and avoid fidgeting. Ask if it is okay to take notes, and then do so as needed.

MAKE IT A HABIT
Collect Your Stories

It takes planning and preparation to be able to discuss your strengths persuasively and explain how they can benefit an employer. Throughout your experiences, consider the positive capabilities and personal qualities your coworkers, managers, instructors, and others have recognized in you. Consider times when you have made a big impact or achievement:

- Examples that demonstrate your organizational skills and orderly mind
- Examples of improved methods of performing tasks
- Examples of motivating people successfully
- Examples of leading a team or being an effective team member
- Examples of effective problem solving
- Examples that demonstrate your creativity
- Examples of handling detailed assignments carefully and accurately
- Examples of being dependable and flexible
- Examples of working independently without regular supervision

Make it a habit to collect stories as they happen during your career.

Robert Kneschke/Shutterstock.com

Try to practice your interview skills using the video-conferencing technology available today, regardless of the technology that will be used for the interview. You can learn a great deal by using any two-way video technology such as Skype or Zoom (the free version) or other technology. Ask a friend or colleague to do it with you. It's a great way to prepare for the real interview. Many of these technologies have an option for recording your interview. You can even ask a small group to watch it and provide critique.

One-way video interviews are a newer, and increasingly popular option for employers. Typically, these are used to confirm that a candidate meets the basic requirements for the job. If you are offered a one-way video interview, the following will help you prepare.

- Read the interview instructions carefully and follow instructions exactly.

- Pay attention to the employer's deadline for submitting your answers. Don't wait until the last moment, because technical difficulties that night might prevent you from completing the interview.

- Have your interview answers ready. Review them before you answer each question. You don't want to sound or look like you are reading your answers. You want to respond as if a person were sitting in front of you asking the questions. That means, most of the time you are looking at the camera, not your notes.

- Practice. Practice. Practice.

- Follow all the other advice in this chapter and Chapter 8 for preparing for an interview.

- Watch the time. There may be cut-offs or time limits. These should be described in the instructions. Try to end sooner rather than use all the time allowed. Remember that someone has to take the time to listen to your answers, so keep it concise.

- Use keywords in your answers. Get these from your knowledge of the industry and from the job posting itself. Be aware that there is an emerging technology that will "listen to" your video interview and rate your responses for the employer. Just like the ATS systems for job applications, without the right keywords, your interview could be declined before you even get to a real person. Use the keywords!

Behavioral Interview

The **behavioral interview** is based on the premise that past performance is the best predictor of future behavior. The interviewer asks questions aimed at getting the candidate to provide specific examples of how he or she has successfully used the skills required for the target job. This helps the interviewer evaluate the candidate's experience and predict future on-the-job behavior. Take time to prepare for behavioral interview questions, covered later in this chapter. The examples you give about your past success can be useful in most every other type of interview.

Panel Interview

In a **panel interview** (also called a **board interview**), more than one person interviews you at one time. Although this situation can seem more difficult than a simple one-on-one interview, it can play in your favor because you have the opportunity to appeal as a strong candidate to multiple people on the panel. Focus on the person questioning you at the moment, but don't ignore the others. Appearing relaxed and projecting a self-assured attitude is important. Before a board or panel interview, try to obtain and memorize the names of the panel members. During the interview, draw a diagram of the seating arrangement and label seats with interviewers' names. At the close of the interview, shake hands and thank each interviewer by name as you leave. Leave your business card with each person, if possible. A key to success is being personable.

Team Interview

A **team interview,** or **Day Visit** (if conducted on-site), is a series of three to five interviews with different people in the company. The candidate meets individually with each person. The interviewers might be your peers or managers, if you are given the job, so building rapport and leaving a positive, likeable impression is key. Team interviewers often meet before the interview to decide who will cover each topic. The team members may ask a few common questions to give the candidate more than one opportunity to cover a particular topic. After the interview, the team members meet to discuss the candidate's

performance and identify the best candidate. Before a team interview, learn the names of the members and, if possible, learn something about their areas of expertise. Use this information to enhance your performance. Be sure to give consistent answers to the individual members' questions.

> ▶ *CAREER ACTION*
> **Complete Worksheet 9-2**
> Research Interview Styles, page 281

Investigate the Interview Process Online

When a company offers you an interview, use your online resources to learn what to expect, both from the interview process and the types of questions. Start with your LinkedIn connections to help you set up Career

The Stress Interview

Stress interviews are generally reserved for jobs that involve regular pressure. They are designed to test the candidate's behavior, logic, and emotional control under pressure.

A skilled interviewer may combine some stress techniques with an unstructured interview approach to get a well-rounded picture of your personality. Some techniques used in stress interviewing include (a) remaining silent following one of your remarks, (b) questioning you rapidly, (c) placing you on the defensive with irritating questions or remarks, and (d) criticizing your responses or remarks.

Some stress questions are routinely asked in other types of job interviews—even informal

ones. Every job has an occasional crisis situation. An interviewer may also use a stress technique unintentionally. Do not react negatively. Take a deep breath, demonstrate control, and be courteous.

PathDoc/Shutterstock.com.

Network Meetings with existing employees at that company in order to gain insights into the interview process. Then learn more about the interview process through sites such as Glassdoor.com, Quora, or other platforms.

Social media can provide more insights. Search social media platforms for people who work for the company. Then pay attention to employee profiles, including noticing the background they use in their profile photo, the level of professionalism presented, their posts about the company. These sorts of details can help you understand what to expect when entering their company atmosphere for an interview. If the culture appears formal, be overprepared and buttoned-up. If the culture appears to be informal, plan to dress more formally than current employees as a courtesy, and be prepared to adjust to a more informal culture through your language, tone, and attitude. Cultural fit is a key qualification. Eighty percent of recruiters on LinkedIn and 50 % on Twitter look for cultural fit when evaluating candidates.*

PREPARE FOR TYPICAL INTERVIEW QUESTIONS OUTCOME 3

The core of a job interview is the question-and-answer period. Generally, you should let the interviewer take the lead. Interviewers usually consider a candidate's effort to control the interview to be rude or aggressive.

Questions asked by interviewers generally fall into five categories:

- General information questions
- Behavioral questions
- Character questions
- Difficult or "stress" questions
- Inappropriate questions

*Source: JobVite's 2014 survey. https://www.jobvite.com/wp-

Your Career Network: How Do You Say "I Got the Interview!"

Be careful about sharing information about your interviews on your social media profiles. Never announce which companies offered you an interview. While it is nice to celebrate, steer clear of doing so online until you have accepted a job offer and have started working at your new workplace. Sharing specifics beforehand is a red flag to most recruiters and HR resources. You might harm your chances of moving forward. Share your joy privately until your job search is complete.

If some of your Career Network connections provided Warm Introductions, or leads for this job posting, reach out to them privately to thank them. Ask if it would be alright to mention their names during interviews.

You can also ask individuals associated with the company to provide insights into the interview process, including answers to questions such as:

- How many rounds of interviews is typical before landing the job?
- What questions do they remember being asked? What questions were the hardest?
- Are there any tests? What suggestions do you have for preparing for the tests?

Tell your connections the date of your interview, and be sure to follow up again with a "thank you" when the interview is complete.

Start preparing for your own interview by studying the following lists of the most common questions and suggested answers. Keep your Personal Brand Statement and 30-Second Commercial handy while preparing for interviews because these contain the key message and impression you want to leave your interviewer with. Your answers to most questions should continue to reinforce your Personal Brand Statement and 30-Second Commercial.

General Information Questions

General information questions are asked to obtain factual information. They usually cover your skills, work experience, education, interests, and so on.

1. **Why do you want this job?** Be prepared; every employer wants to know the answer to this question.

   Suggested answer: "My skills and experience are directly related to this position, and I'm very interested in this field because _____." Position your answer as a win-win situation: You have skills and talent that will benefit the company, and you have a long-term interest in the position because of your personal development goals. If applicable, relate examples of your experience, education, and/or training that relate to the job you are seeking. Never say that you want the job because of the pay and benefits.

2. **What type of work do you enjoy most?**

   Suggested answer: Play your research card; name three of the top types of tasks that are involved in this job and demonstrate how you are qualified for the position.

3. **What are your strongest skills?**

   Suggested answer: Review your abilities and accomplishments and your 30-Second Commercial to develop your answer. Describe three of your skills that directly relate to those required for the position.

Be specific and focused, and avoid overwhelming the interviewer with too much or appearing vague.

4. **Are you a team player?**

   Suggested answer: The ability to collaborate and get work done through others is highly valued in today's workplace, so a positive answer is usually a plus. Give examples of your successful team roles (as a leader, a member, or a partner) from school, previous jobs, volunteer work, or sports, in which you demonstrated the ability to work well with, communicate, influence, and lead others.

5. **What are your long-term career goals, and how do you plan to achieve them?**

   Suggested answer: Emphasize your strengths, state that your goal is to make a strong contribution in your job, and explain that you look forward to developing the experience necessary for career growth. Employers are impressed with employees who show initiative and a desire to learn because they perform better than those who have no plans for self-improvement. Mention your plans to continue your education and expand your knowledge to become a more valuable employee.

6. **Do you have a geographic preference? Are you willing to relocate?**

   Suggested answer: Your research should let you know in advance if this job requires travel. Have your answer ready in advance. If you have no objection to relocating, make this perfectly clear. If you do have objections, be honest in your answer; otherwise, you will no doubt be unhappy in the job.

7. **With what type of manager have you had the best relationships?**

   Suggested answer: "I've had good relationships with all of my managers. Communication is so important; I make sure I understand what I'm supposed to do.

Become a Good Listener

You may think of the interview primarily in terms of talking, but listening carefully is just as important. So that you can respond appropriately, you need to listen to the interviewer carefully to learn important details about the job requirements, the company, and the department.

Follow these tips to become a more effective listener:

- Give each question your undivided attention. Don't formulate your response while you are listening.

- Nod as appropriate.

- Repeat or summarize the main ideas.

- Ask questions when you need to clarify what the interviewer means. If you don't understand a question, ask for clarification instead of talking and hoping you answered correctly.

- Listen "between the lines" for the underlying messages.

- Don't argue or interrupt.

- Maintain eye contact (but not too intensely).

- Maintain an "open" position (don't cross your arms or legs; keep your hands unclenched).

- Maintain the same eye level as the interviewer (sit or stand as appropriate).

That's especially important when I've been given new responsibilities so that we can get off to a good start. I think managers appreciate someone who takes responsibility for his or her job." Then give an example. This is also a good time to use your research on the company culture. For example, if you are aware that the culture is to work under tight deadlines, share your willingness to work with managers on communicating and delivering results frequently. Caution: avoid any reference to a bad manager, and instead talk about what type of supervision you prefer.

Behavioral Questions

Behavioral questions probe a candidate's specific past performance and behaviors. The interviewer wants details of experiences that illustrate how you perform or behave on a job or in stressful environments.

To prepare for behavioral interviews, recall scenarios from your experiences that illustrate how you have performed or behaved on the job. Write out examples that demonstrate good performance. Also, be ready to describe how you have handled difficult situations. Students with little work experience should focus on class projects and group situations that illustrate their task performance and interpersonal behavior. These four steps provide a good model for your answers to behavioral questions:

1. Describe the situation. (What)

2. Explain the actions you took. (How)

3. Describe the outcomes. (Importance)

4. Summarize what you learned from the experience. (Insights from you)

Does this sound familiar? It should! This WHII method is an expanded version of the WHI (What, How, and Importance) model introduced in Chapter 2. Now, you have a chance to go into the details of the concise story you have already shared and add some new examples, too.

Example: Describe an accomplishment that demonstrates your initiative.

Suggested answer: "While I was working part-time as a computer lab technician for Seattle Technology College, our department received several complaints about service response time. I set a personal goal of answering all troubleshooting calls within 90 minutes. I recorded the exact response time for each call and maintained the goal of a 90-minute response time for one full semester. I was awarded the Customer Service Certificate for this performance. I learned that by making a plan to address an issue, I can be more effective."

Whenever possible, give positive examples that demonstrate measurable achievements. Or when describing a less positive experience, emphasize what actions you took to correct weaknesses or poor performance. By giving specific examples, you establish credibility and believability that can translate into a job offer.

Prior to the interview, practice your stories. You should have at least eight stories describing such things as times where you went above and beyond in completing a task, or used your leadership skills, or handled a difficult situation, or used your talent to contribute to a goal or project. By rehearsing so many examples and stories, you will be ready to answer a wide variety of questions using stories during a behavioral interview. These stories give the interviewer confidence in your answers and can help you earn the job.

You can expect questions such as "Describe the most challenging assignments you've had. How did you handle it?" followed by "Explain what problems you encountered. How did you overcome them?" Some behavioral questions probe for negative experiences. Use the WHII method to frame your answer: **What** you did, **How** you did it, and the **Importance** of the results, then add **Insights** you gained, what you learned from the experience, or what actions you took to improve the situation.

As you prepare your stories and examples, be sure to include the following content:

- **Your work skills:** Work-specific skills, such as computer programming, CAD, and medical transcription.

- **Your functional and transferable skills:** Skills used with people, things, or information, such as good communication, organizational, or planning skills. These skills are valuable from one job to another.

- **Your self-management skills:** Personal characteristics such as being a dependable person, a team player, a self-directed worker, a problem solver, or a decision maker.

Review the activities in Chapter 2 to help you prepare for behavioral interview. Your 30-Second Commercial can be used as an answer to these questions, especially if it contains proof-by-example descriptions of your capabilities that are relevant to the job.

Here are some common questions you should be prepared to answer:

1. **Tell me specifically about a time when you worked under great stress.**

   Suggested answer: Be careful to choose a relevant example that would be considered stressful in a work environment, such as working under pressure of time. Quickly describe the elements that made it stressful for you and how you maintained your cool and got the job done.

2. **Describe an experience when you dealt with an angry customer or coworker.**

Suggested answer: Give an answer that highlights how you value communication and know that conflict can lead to personal growth and opportunity. Discuss your ability to maintain a calm and positive attitude. Your reply also should include how you turned the situation from negative to positive.

3. **Give me an example of your ability to adapt to change.**

Suggested answer: Choose a time when there was a significant change at work, school, a club, or a volunteer organization. Explain what the change was, and focus on sharing how you quickly and successfully adapted to the change.

4. **Explain what problems you have encountered. How did you overcome them?**

Suggested answer: Some behavioral questions probe for negative experiences. In responding to these, focus on what you learned from the experience or what actions you took to improve the situation. The intent of the interviewer is to discover how you turn negative situations into positive results.

Do you see any recurring themes in the suggested answers? Turn negatives into positives and focus on your strengths.

Write the answer to every question you think you may be asked—and every question you hope you won't be asked.

Character Questions

Character questions are asked to learn about your personal attributes, such as integrity, personality, attitudes, and motivation. Be prepared to answer these common character questions.

1. **How would you describe yourself?**

Suggested answer: Emphasize your strongest personal attributes and focus on those that are relevant to your target job. Review your capabilities and accomplishments. Examples: "I'm punctual and dependable.

At my current job, I haven't been late or missed one day in the last two years." "I get along well with others; in fact, my coworkers chose me to represent them in our company's monthly staff meetings."

Give specific examples of your strengths. Don't just say, "I'm a hard worker" or "I'm dependable." Other leads include "I learn quickly," "I like solving problems; for example ...," "I like contributing to a team," and "I like managing people." Use a relevant example that shows that you know what is important in a work environment.

2. **What rewards do you look for in your career?**

Suggested answer: Don't make financial rewards your prime motivator. Emphasize your desire to improve your skills, make a valuable contribution to the field, and become better educated. These answers show initiative, interest, and professionalism.

Real World Scenario 9-2 Sam sat comfortably in a meeting room, ready for his interview. He was careful to exhibit positive, assertive body language by keeping his hands relaxed in his lap, sitting up straight, and having a smile on his face. He had carefully prepared and practiced eight stories showcasing his strengths, experience, and results. He felt so familiar with the stories because of course they were his life! He was the expert! Regardless of the question asked, he knew he could tailor at least one out of the eight stories to create a great answer. He also had researched the company on Glassdoor and through his Career Network Meetings and had questions prepared for the interviewer as well. As soon as the interview ended, Sam knew the preparation paid off when the interviewer said they would get back to him within the week and they were excited to have had the opportunity to interview him.

What are your best stories that are "multiuse" and can be tailored to answer a variety of questions?

Be Prepared for Silence

Be prepared to handle silence. The interviewer asks you a question, you answer, and the interviewer does not respond.

Interviewers sometimes use this technique to test candidates' confidence and ability to handle stress or uncertainty. Do not retract your statement; just wait calmly. You have no obligation to continue talking if you answered adequately. By doing this, you will pass the "test" and project a mature, confident image. Break a long silence by asking whether the interviewer needs more information or by asking a related question.

You also can use silence. If you are asked a difficult question, answering too quickly without enough thought can be detrimental. You're entitled to think carefully about a question and to prepare a response. The employer wouldn't want you to solve problems on the job without adequate thought and planning.

Avoid long pauses in a phone or video interview, however. When the interviewer has fewer "clues" about you as a person, long pauses may be perceived as slow thinking abilities.

pan_kung/Shutterstock.com

3. **What accomplishment are you most proud of, particularly as it relates to your field?**

Suggested answer: Relate an accomplishment that shows special effort and initiative. "I recognized the need to improve communications [between two departments]. I designed a questionnaire that was completed by representatives from each department. Management made several of the changes, and communications were improved in those areas."

4. **Do you work well under pressure?**

Suggested answer: You may be tempted to answer with a simple yes or no, but don't. Yes and no answers reveal nothing specific about you. Don't miss an opportunity to sell yourself.

Be honest in your answer. If you prefer to work at a well-defined job in an organized, calm atmosphere (rather than one that involves constant decision making and pressure), say so. Otherwise, you may end up in a job that is a constant source of tension. If you enjoy the challenge of pressure, either in decision making or in dealing with people, make this fact clear.

Keep in mind that a large company may have more than one working environment. For instance, an administrative support job in the customer relations department would likely involve more interactive pressure with the public than a support job in the data processing department.

Difficult or "Stress" Questions

Difficult or **"stress" questions** are asked to understand deeper motivations and identify a possible mismatch between you and the company, such as being overqualified or underqualified or lacking dependability (if your resume shows many different jobs). They also provide the opportunity for the interviewer to determine whether you are good at making decisions, solving problems, and thinking under stress.

OVERCOMING BARRIERS
Tell Me About Yourself

Sometimes an employer will start an interview by taking a few minutes to establish rapport or make small talk and then say, "Tell me about yourself."

Experienced interviewers say that this question stumps many candidates. They either don't know what to say to get started, or, if they get started, they don't know how to stop, and go on and on using up all the valuable interview time.

Be prepared to handle this type of interview effectively. Once the interviewer makes this request, he or she might comment just enough to encourage you to keep talking. The purpose is to see whether you focus on your qualifications for the job and how the employer would benefit by hiring you. Do not ramble on about your life history; this is a sure way to disqualify yourself on the spot. Remember all the hard work you did on your Personal Brand Statement and 30-Second Commercials. You spent a lot of time creating a concise message of your secret sauce. This a great time to expand a little bit more about your journey as a professional, while still keeping it short. If it seems like the interviewer isn't moving on to a more specific question, ask questions such as "What exactly would you like to know about [my work experience, educational experience, skills, or extracurricular and community activities]?"

Your objective is to highlight your positive qualities (personal attributes, accomplishments, skills, pertinent training, work experience, etc.). After you think you have covered these topics, ask, "Would you like me to clarify or expand on any area for you?" This helps you focus on the information the interviewer wants.

Remaining Cool Under Stress

Take three to five calming deep breaths and tell yourself, "I can do this." After using Career Action Worksheet 9-3, you will be prepared to answer difficult questions. Make sure to rehearse your answers.

However, if you are asked a question that you are totally unprepared for, don't ramble through an answer. Pausing to think is perfectly fine. Use the "That's a good question, let me think about it for a minute" technique. Your goal is to demonstrate that you can handle stress—that you don't just react, but instead think through the situation and remain composed.

When describing a less positive experience, emphasize what actions you took to correct weaknesses or poor performance, and what you learned from the experience for next time. Be prepared to answer these common difficult or stress questions.

1. **Why do you think you are the best candidate for the job?** *or* **Why should I hire you?**

   Suggested answer: Summarize what you believe the important objectives and challenges of the job are. Ask the interviewer for confirmation that you have a good understanding of what the job entails. Then explain how you can handle them. Focus on how you can benefit the employer, citing examples of increasing productivity, saving money, increasing sales, and so on. Summarize your accomplishments, skills, and experience that are pertinent to the job. Then ask, "How does that fit your requirements?" This shifts the focus from you to the interviewer, helping reduce stress for you.

2. **Why do you want to leave your current job?**

   Suggested answer: This question will likely be posed to determine whether you have a problem with your current job. Accentuate the positive—for example, you are seeking a new challenge, you have mastered your present job and are seeking advancement, or you want to work for a company with stability. If you have a problem with your current job or boss, do not discuss it. Do not be specific or emotional in your response to this question. Be prepared by practicing your answer to this question in advance.

3. **Why have you held so many jobs?**

   Suggested answer: Employers like to see a work history that implies stability and dependability. People often have valid reasons for holding numerous jobs that don't necessarily imply immaturity or an inability to commit. Be factual and emphasize that your current goal is to apply yourself to long-term employment and the development of a career. You can also describe the skills you learned from the variety of jobs that will be beneficial on this job.

MAKE IT A HABIT
Savvy Q&A Strategies

- **Pause to think before you reply.** If you're uncomfortable with a question, go back to the familiar. Stress your assets. Use a "thinking pause" to buy time to answer the question well. For example, "Could we return to this question? I'd like to think about it for a moment" or "That's a good question" or "Let me see ..." (This works if you need only a little extra time.)

- **Be candid and honest.** Be realistic when expressing your preferences and dislikes. You won't be happy in a job that isn't a good fit. Honesty also naturally builds trust and rapport.

- **Understand the motive behind the question.** Listen actively when the question is asked and try to answer what they are really looking for. For example, asking about a challenging project is usually not just about the results that were achieved, but what leadership skills and creative thinking you displayed in overcoming challenges.

- **Give appropriate context.** Don't assume the interviewer knows the full background or needs to know all of the details. Practice telling the right amount of relevant background.

- **Fill in the gaps.** If you sense that the interviewer thinks you have an area of weakness, communicate how you plan to eliminate the weakness or round out your qualifications—perhaps by completing research or course work in the area.

wavebreakmedia/Shutterstock.com.

4. **What is your greatest weakness?**

   Suggested answer: Either describe something that is not needed for this job or a skill that you are working on improving. "My weakest area is foreign language, so I am focusing on a career that is more geared to mathematics at national companies." Or "My weakest area is accounting, so I am taking a course in beginning accounting at the community college. It's going well, and I plan to take the advanced course next semester." The objective is to acknowledge a weakness that is low on the employer's list and to explain your steps to improve or manage the weakness.

5. **Have you ever been fired from a job?**

   Suggested answer: If accurate, use less negative terms such as *laid off, let go,* or *employment ended.* Be honest, but not too specific about the reason for your termination. Use phrases such as "the job was not a good long-term fit" or "my career goals no longer aligned with the company goals." Be truthful, yet brief. Briefly describe the situation; explain what you learned from the experience and how you could have handled the experience differently. Take responsibility for past mistakes but end your response on a positive note. Your goal is to give some assurance that the situation will not be repeated.

6. **Does your current employer know you are planning to leave?**

   Suggested answer: If your current employer is aware of this fact, say so. If not—and especially if you depend on your current income—make this clear. Say that you prefer your current employer not be informed of your job search until a firm offer is made and that you will give two weeks' notice before leaving. Consider it a good sign that the interviewer is asking this question—you are probably close to being offered a position.

Explaining Gaps in Employment and Reasons for Leaving a Job

- Use brief, positive phrases to explain reasons for leaving a job and periods of unemployment: "returned to school," "changed careers," "reorganization," "employment ended," "business closed," or "took a position with more responsibility."

- Avoid negative language ("couldn't find a job," "quit," "personal conflict," "fired for no reason") that may lead an employer to question your abilities and judgment.

- If you were fired from a job, be as brief and positive as possible and leave longer explanations for the interview.

- Be prepared to describe what happened using unemotional and professional language.

- Take responsibility for your actions (don't blame others), explain what you learned from the situation, and explain how you could have handled the situation differently.

It may help to write out an explanation, but your best chance of getting a job will come from explaining the situation in person. It also will be essential to have a reference who will give you a solid recommendation.

g-stockstudio/Shutterstock.com

Inappropriate Questions

The interview is going along well, and then it happens: "Do you have any children?" or "How long has your family been in this country?"

On the surface, questions such as these seem innocent enough. Yet the structure and format of the questions may be illegal or, at the very least, inappropriate. When you are in a situation where the person asking the question has the power to decide whether you will get the job, this information can be used to discriminate against you or other candidates.

Questions that focus on age, gender, race, marital status, language, children, criminal record, national origin, religion, or disability are inappropriate in a job interview.

So you've just been asked an inappropriate question. What do you do? How do you respond?

The most effective approach is to answer the question in a polite, honest manner. Don't offer detailed personal information. Instead, steer the conversation back to your ability to meet the employer's expectations, by stating simply "This issue does not affect my ability to perform the job" or "I am confident I will be able to perform the duties of this job."

ASK GOOD QUESTIONS TO STAND OUT

The interview is not only a chance for the employer to learn about you but also for you to learn about them. Treating the interview as a two-way communication process is important because it displays confidence, genuine interest in a best fit match, and preparation. Prepare to ask three to five well-chosen questions to help you learn about the employer, company culture, and position.

Don't ask all of your questions at the end of the interview. Interject them naturally at appropriate intervals throughout the meeting unless you're told you will have the opportunity to ask questions at the end. Keep your questions positive. Also, do not discuss salary until a job offer has been made. The best scenario is to first have the company share the salary range with you before you share your expectations.

Good Questions to Ask

Asking appropriate questions demonstrates interest and confidence, showcases your knowledge, and gives you an active role in the interview. Study the following sample questions carefully; then write your own questions as part of Career Action Worksheet 9-3.

1. **Do you have a training program for this position? If so, will you describe it?**

   Why it works: This question demonstrates interest in the job and a desire to perform it well.

2. **Can you tell me about the duties and tasks of this position in a typical workday?**

   Why it works: The answer will help you better understand the scope of the job and if it is well matched to what you want to do.

3. **May I have a copy of the written job description?**

   Why it works: Getting a job description can help you tie your qualifications to those required for the job in follow-up emails or later interviews. Of course, if the job description was online or you already have it, don't use this one!

4. **Will the responsibilities of this position expand with time and experience on the job? Can good performance in this job lead to opportunities for career growth?**

   Why it works: The answer to this question will help you determine whether this is a dead-end job or whether employee career growth is encouraged.

5. **If I were the *best* employee that ever had this job, what would that look like?**

   Why it works: You get instant insight into how to succeed when you get the job offer. Or you learn that the bar is very low or too high for the type of job you want.

6. **Can you tell me about the people I would work with? To whom does this position report?**

   Why it works: These answers can help you assess company structure and how you might fit into the company.

7. **Do you need any more information about my qualifications or experience?**

   Why it works: If the interviewer wants more information, you have an opportunity to clear up any misunderstanding or lack of information. It also gives you another chance to run your 30-Second Commercial, once again emphasizing just how well qualified you are.

8. **When will you be making your hiring decision? What does your hiring process and timeline look like? May I call you if I have additional questions?**

   Why it works: These types of questions help you judge when to follow up and will keep the door open for further communication.

Turnoff Questions to Avoid

Following are some questions that are most disliked by employers. Do not ask them; they will make you sound uninformed and diminish your likability.

1. **What does this company do?**

   Why to avoid: You should have done your research well enough to know what the company does. Employers are not looking for employees who know nothing about their business.

2. **How much sick leave and vacation time will I get?**

   Why to avoid: This question gives the impression that you are looking forward to being off of work, rather than on the job. Ask this and other benefits question only before making a final decision about a job offer. Employers understand the importance of major benefits to potential employees.

3. **Will I have an office?**

   Why to avoid: This suggests that you care more about where you will work than about what you will do.

4. **What time do I have to be at work in the morning? How long do you allow for lunch?**

   Why to avoid: These questions do not project an enthusiastic interest in the work and suggest that you might have personal business that will distract you from work.

5. **How long do I have to work before I am eligible for a raise?**

   Why to avoid: This question tells the employer that you are more interested in the salary than the job.

▶ *CAREER ACTION*

Complete Worksheet 9-3

Create a Question-and-Answer Planning Sheet, page 283

Chapter Checklist

Check off each item you can do. Reread sections in this chapter to help you complete the checklist.

☐ Prepare for different types of pre-employment tests. ❶

☐ Prepare for different types of interviews. ❷

☐ Focus on responding persuasively to questions about my qualifications and abilities; cite examples of applying my abilities in work, school, and other activities. ❸

☐ Prepare and rehearse responses to typical interview questions. ❸

☐ Anticipate the stress of inappropriate interview questions and practice careful responses. ❸

☐ Prepare and practice responses to stress questions, while being calm and composed. ❸

☐ Prepare and ask appropriate questions. ❹

☐ Avoid asking questions that diminish my likability, including questions that are too direct, questions that my research should have answered, and questions that make me appear immature or uncommitted to the job. ❹

Critical Thinking Questions

1. How can you prepare for the different types of pre-employment tests? ❶

2. How will you benefit from knowing what style of interview your target employer typically uses? ❷

3. What style(s) of interviewing do you expect to be most prevalent in your job search? What techniques do you plan to use to maximize your performance in these types of interviews? ❷

4. What are the candidate's main objectives during the question-and-answer portion of the interview? What are the interviewer's main objectives during an interview? ❸

5. What specific types of questions do you most need to prepare for to be ready for your interviews? List two examples and include the answers you plan to give. ❸

6. How will you handle an illegal or inappropriate question from an interviewer? ❸

7. Why is it important for a candidate to ask some questions during an interview? ❹

Trial Run

Find Good Answers to Interview Questions ③

Divide into teams of four and make sure you have a sheet of paper.

Each person selects a type of interview question (general information, behavioral, character, or difficult/stress) and uses a sheet of paper to write two questions from the lists in this chapter:

- One question on side A
- One question on side B

Pass the sheets to the left.

- Take two minutes to write an answer to the interview question on side A.
- When time is up, pass the sheets to the left again and answer the question on side A of the second sheet of paper.
- Do this until each person on the team has answered all four interview questions on side A.

Repeat the exercise with the questions on side B.

When all A and B questions have been answered by each team member, compare answers and discuss which is the best. You can do this by reading each question and the four suggested answers aloud. Critique the answers and decide which one is the best choice or how a combination of the answers would be most appropriate. Be creative.

If possible, have someone record all of the questions and answers and distribute them to the group.

This page is intentionally blank.

▶ *CAREER ACTION WORKSHEET*

9-1 Research Pre-employment Test Types ❷

Use Your Career Network contacts for research.

Contact at least two companies in your field that are similar to your target employer and arrange a brief meeting with someone at each place to research the company's use of pre-employment tests. Make sure the person understands that this is not a request for an interview. Follow the guidelines for conducting a Career Network Meeting in Chapter 6, as well as these steps. During your meetings, ask your contacts to describe the following:

1. Types of pre-employment tests

2. How the test answers are used to select employees

3. What they recommend as ways to prepare for these tests

Take notes of any information you find useful. As always, act professionally and thank the people who help you. Follow up by sending thank-you notes.

Add your completed work to the "About Jobs" section of your Career Builder Files.

This page is intentionally blank.

▶ *CAREER ACTION WORKSHEET*

9-2 Research Interview Styles ❷

Use Your Career Network for research.

Contact at least two companies in your field that are similar to your target employer and arrange a brief meeting with someone at each place to research his or her interview style. Make sure the person understands that this is not a request for an interview. Follow the guidelines for conducting a Career Network Meeting in Chapter 6, as well as these steps.

1. During your meetings, ask your contacts to describe the style of interviewing they use to evaluate candidates for positions similar to the one you are targeting.

2. Ask what criteria (skills, experience, education, personal qualities) they use to evaluate candidates.

3. Ask for specific examples of candidates' positive and negative actions and comments.

4. Take notes of any information you find useful.

5. As always, act professionally and thank the people who help you. Follow up by sending thank-you notes.

Add your completed work to the "About Jobs" section of your Career Builder Files.

This page is intentionally blank.

▶ *CAREER ACTION WORKSHEET*
9-3 Create a Question-and-Answer Planning Sheet ❷

Record the answers to typical questions you can expect to be asked during job interviews. Also write sample questions you can ask during interviews. Use the suggestions in this chapter and Chapter 8, as well as your 30-Second Commercials and Personal Brand Statement. Tailor your answers to your target job. Emphasize your qualifications for the job at every opportunity. Use positive, action-oriented words.

General Information Questions

Why do you want this job?

What type of work do you enjoy doing the most?

What are your strongest skills?

What are your long-term career goals? How do you plan to achieve them?

Do you think of yourself as a team player? If so, give examples.

Do you have a geographic preference? Are you willing to relocate?

Under what management style do you work most productively?

What is important to you in a company? What do you look for in a company?

Behavioral and Character Questions

What have you accomplished that demonstrates your initiative?

How do you deal with an angry customer or coworker? Describe an experience you've had.

How are you able to adapt to change? Give an example.

How would you describe yourself?

What rewards do you look for in your career?

What accomplishment are you most proud of, particularly as it relates to your field?

What do you think are the most important characteristics and abilities a person must possess to be successful? How do you rate yourself in those areas?

Stress Questions

Why do you think you are the best candidate for this job? Why should I hire you?

Why do you want to leave your current job?

Why have you held so many jobs?

What is your greatest weakness?

Have you ever been fired from a job?

Does your current employer know you are planning to leave?

What kinds of decisions are most difficult for you?

What is your salary range? (Although this is not strictly a stress question, being asked about salary expectations is awkward. Chapter 11 has advice about handling this common question. Hint: avoid giving a direct answer.)

Questions and Topics to Avoid

List several questions to avoid asking during an interview and explain why the questions are inappropriate.

Q&A Savvy Strategies

Review "Savvy Q&A Strategies" on page 273. List the strategies that are most applicable to your job search. Add others you found through your Internet research.

Your Questions

Now prepare questions of your own from three sources:

A. Review the sample questions in "Ask Good Questions to Stand Out" on pages 275–276. In your own words, write the questions you want to ask during your interviews.

B. Search the Internet and social media platforms (Twitter, Facebook, etc.) for current topics related to the company. Write any questions these news events might bring to mind. Stick to questions that might impact your decision to join the company if they offer you a job.

C. Ask a member of your support system to help you add questions that are pertinent to your job search and goals.

Add your completed work to the "About Jobs" section of your Career Builder Files.

Interview
Like a Pro

OVERVIEW

To interview like a pro you have to practice like one—mentally, emotionally, and physically. In this chapter, practice describing your ability to do the job through examples and stories, research companies so you can talk their language, prepare physically, and practice a strong close for your interview.

OUTCOMES

1. Express confidence after participating in practice interviews, page 286
2. List homework that is needed before every interview, page 288
3. Describe how to be physically prepared for the interview, page 292
4. Explain how to close an interview in your favor, page 296

CAREER ACTION WORKSHEETS

10-1: Arrange a Practice Interview, page 301
10-2: Participate in a Dress Rehearsal Interview, page 303
10-3: Summarize and Evaluate Your Interviews, page 305
10-4: Interview Critique Form, page 307
10-5: Do Your Homework Before Every Interview, page 309
10-6: Get Physically Prepared for Success with Interviews, page 311

WHERE ARE YOU ON THE JOURNEY?

The pros practice. Shouldn't you?

PHASE 1: Prepare for the Journey
- *The Job Search Journey*
- *Know Yourself to Market Yourself*
- *Picture Yourself in the Workplace*

PHASE 2: Create Your Resume
- *Plan Your Resume*
- *Write Your Resume*

PHASE 3: Apply for Jobs
- *Find Job Openings*
- *Write Job Applications*

PHASE 4: Shine at Interviews
- *Know the Interview Essentials*
- *Prepare for Your Interview*
- ***Interview Like a Pro***

PHASE 5: Connect, Accept, and Succeed
- *Stay Connected with Potential Employers*
- *Dealing with Disappointment*
- *Take Charge of Your Career*

PHASE 4 Shine at Interviews
Step 3, *Interview Like a Pro*

You are in Phase 4, *Shine at Interviews*, Step 3, *Interview Like a Pro*. Your goal in this chapter is to develop confidence and to do your homework before every interview so you are comfortable and natural at interviews.

PARTICIPATE IN PRACTICE INTERVIEWS

While some people may claim that they can walk into an interview and "wing it," do not try to be one of them. Interviews require practice. Because an interview is a dynamic exchange between two people, there will never be a list of "Interview Dos and Don'ts" that works in every situation. Instead, be at your best in every interview by giving yourself these three gifts:

- **Plenty of time** to prepare so that you aren't rushed or stressed the day before the interview

- **A competitive edge** through thoughtful, focused preparation and practice

- **Self-confidence** gained from techniques like positive visualization to feel ready for the interview

If you are asked to come to a job interview, the employer is interested in you. You are the focus of the interview. You will be evaluated on your past successes and mistakes and on your future goals and potential. You will be expected to give concrete examples of your skills and explain how they relate to the requirements for this job.

Any nervousness that you feel about an upcoming job interview is an appropriate response to a situation that will test your interpersonal, social, professional, and verbal and nonverbal skills. Preparation and practice can help you relax. Users of *Your Career: How to Make It Happen* emphasize that doing practice interviews improves their actual interview performance by as much as 100 %. They say that practice increases their self-confidence, improves the image of competence they project, and reduces their anxiety about the process—all of which improve their performance in actual interviews. Gain these valuable advantages yourself by doing practice interviews.

Real World Scenario 10-1 Out of all the steps in the Job Search Journey, Sara was most scared of the interview. It was easy to stay behind the computer or network at events, but the pressure of making a mistake during an interview after all that hard work was nerve-racking. She decided to reduce her anxiety by scheduling practice interviews, starting with a friend who knew her very well and ending with someone she recently met at a career networking event. By the end of her practice interviews, she was more confident presenting herself and her strengths to a stranger and had gained valuable feedback. For example, when the "interviewer" asked a question, she learned to listen actively to the question being asked instead of focusing on how she was going to respond. Honing her active listening skills helped her answer questions better and with more confidence and relevance.

What interview strategies do you need more practice in? How can you reduce interview-related anxiety?

Set Up Practice Interviews

Schedule a practice interview with a friend, family member, or acquaintance, preferably someone who is experienced in interviewing, knows you personally, and is comfortable providing impartial, honest, objective feedback. Ask someone else to observe the practice interview and get recommendations from both people—the practice interviewer and the observer—for improving your performance. If you don't have a friend or family member who can help, do a search online. Websites like myinterviewpractice.com generate interview questions for you to use for practice.

If possible, video-record the practice interview. You can use video recording technology such as the camera on your phone. You can also use Skype, Google Hangouts, FaceTime, Zoom, or another video-conferencing technology to practice

Figure 10-1 How You Are Rated During an Interview

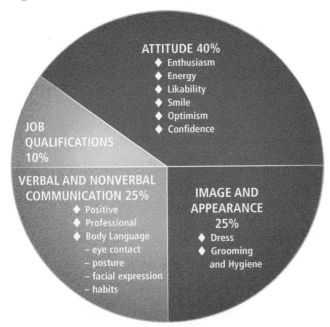

with a friend. Watching yourself firsthand may be the most valuable performance feedback you can get. Use the Chapter 8 Career Action Worksheet 8-1 to assess your body language and try to improve it.

Figure 10-1 shows the areas that employers consider when they are evaluating you as a possible fit for their company. Practice being a pro in each of these areas.

> ▶ *CAREER ACTION*
>
> **Complete Worksheet 10-1**
> Arrange a Practice Interview, page 301

Interview with Someone in Your Career Field

Once you feel comfortable with your performance in the practice interview, schedule a dress rehearsal interview. This is best done with an employer in your field, but is typically done with a Career Network contact who is working in your career field, or with a recruiter or professional career coach.

Some people receive job offers as a result of dress rehearsal practice interviews; others obtain leads that result in jobs. Everyone gains helpful interview experience. When making an appointment for a dress rehearsal interview, do the following:

- Explain that the interview is a course assignment and that you would appreciate the employer's help in completing it.
- Say that you would like the interview to be as realistic as possible.
- Ask what the protocol is for real candidates and follow each step. If there is an application form, pick it up ahead of time and complete it carefully (see Chapter 7).
- Prepare using your Interview Preparation Checklist (described later in this chapter) and use it appropriately.

When you attend the practice interview, do the following:

- Be dressed and groomed as if this were a real interview. You have practiced this already for your Career Network Meetings, as described in Chapter 6.
- Show up for the interview a few minutes early and dressed as if it were a real interview.
- Practice interacting with any "gatekeepers" as described in Chapter 9.
- Ask the person or people who interview you to evaluate your performance and give them a copy of the Interview Critique Form in Career Action Worksheet 10-4.
- Be sure to follow up with a thank-you note. Chapter 11 shows an example thank-you note in Figure 11-1.

Remember that your intent is to practice an interview, and that any job offered during a practice interview should come spontaneously from the employer. Asking directly for a job contradicts your request for help in practicing your interviewing skills. If your contact makes an offer or provides leads or suggestions, however, follow up

MAKE IT A HABIT
Reduce Stress on the Interview Day

Many things can derail you on the day of the interview. Using advance preparation and managing your schedule well can eliminate stress and risk during interview day. Consider the following strategies:

- **Limit the number of interviews scheduled in one day.** After two interviews, a candidate's performance level typically drops. Don't jeopardize your chances of getting a job because you are tired.

- **Know where you are going.** If the interview is in an unfamiliar area, be sure you have directions and know how long it will take to get there. If possible, go to the location a few days before, at the same time of day, to look for construction delays and traffic jams. Alternatively, take public transportation and use the time to relax and rehearse.

- **Never be late for an interview.** Plan your commute to arrive about 10 minutes before the interview in case something goes wrong. If you are early, sit in your car or find someplace else to wait until a few minutes before it's time to go in. Being too early for an appointment may create some awkwardness with the receptionist and/or the interviewer, who may be busy until the time of the interview. Take your cell phone so that you can call the interviewer if you will be late. (Be sure to turn it off during the interview.)

© Michaelpuche/Shutterstock.com.

immediately if you are interested. After each practice or real interview, use Career Action Worksheet 10-3 to do a self-evaluation and make plans for gradually improving your performance over time.

> ▶ *CAREER ACTION*
> **Complete Worksheet 10-2**
> Participate in a Dress Rehearsal Interview, page 303

> ▶ *CAREER ACTION*
> **Complete Worksheet 10-3**
> Summarize and Evaluate Your Interviews, page 305

DO YOUR HOMEWORK BEFORE EVERY INTERVIEW ⟨OUTCOME 2⟩

If you do your homework before every interview, you will give yourself a competitive advantage and be more confident during the interview.

Demonstrate That You Are Interested

You want the interviewer to be interested in you. It helps if you can reciprocate by demonstrating that you are interested in the company. Use these three tips to help you do just that.

Show that you read and understand the job posting or job description. While this seems obvious, you will give yourself a competitive advantage by going through the job posting line by line. As you do this, make a note of how your qualifications fit each item or where you are missing skills or requirements that you will need to address. Prepare your example stories to demonstrate that you have these qualifications or transferable skills. Confirm that you know what each word means. If you don't know, ask someone in your Career Network, or, if necessary or if the word seems important, ask the interviewer to explain. Your interest in understanding the company lingo may impress them.

Read the company website. Find out everything you can about how the company started, where they are located, their major clients, products, names of their leaders and owners, and their mission statement and values. Check out Wikipedia, Facebook, and LinkedIn too for more information.

Search for the company in the news. If you search for the company's name or the name of the CEO, owners, or leaders, you can learn about the current events that are important to the company. Using social media can also be a quick way of staying relevant and up-to-date on news about your target employers and the industry.

- Review the Twitter feed of your target employer. Anything exciting on the horizon?
- Visit the site of a news aggregator such as Reddit or Digg. Search for your industry to find headlines quickly.
- Did you know that you can specifically search News on Google? Do a quick search on Google and then narrow the results by clicking on News, located below the Search bar.
- You might also look at online reviews, such as Angie's List, Better Business Bureau, Consumer Reports, Best Doctors, the local newspaper, and industry newsletters.

While you may see negative press, stick to the positive while being aware of potential areas of concern for the company.

Learn about your interviewer. If you don't already know about your interviewer through a Warm Introduction, use social media platforms. Search for your interviewer on LinkedIn, Facebook, and Twitter. You just might learn something you have in common that will help build positive rapport during the interview.

- Alma mater: Did you go to the same school, college, or high school?
- Hometown or state: Did you grow up in the same town or state?
- Previous job experience: Have you worked in the same company or do you know someone who worked in his or her that company in the past?
- Volunteer/organization experience: Do you share a common interest in a community, nonprofit, or association?

Start by saying, "I viewed your profile on LinkedIn [or from your Twitter feed] and saw that we have... in common." This opening lets them know you did your research but doesn't get too personal. Having something in common with the interviewer creates the feeling that you already belong. It furthers your likeability and positive rapport with the interviewer—both of which are critical to a successful interview that leads to a follow-up interview or offer. As you learn more about the company, think about ways that you might use your new knowledge during the interview to demonstrate your interest in the company.

▶ *CAREER ACTION*

Complete Worksheet 10-4
Interview Critique Form, page 307

Your Career Network: Know What You Are After

While networking is extremely helpful during your Job Search Journey and throughout your career, use it strategically. When you are at the interview stage of your journey and are seeking to network with people within in the company, be very clear about what you hope to gain. After all, simply reaching out to people in the company does not give you any extra points at the interview. Here are valid reasons to connect:

- Mock interview practice
- Insight into the interview process
- Deeper understanding of the company culture to determine your "fit"
- Information about the interviewers or hiring manager to help establish rapport

---

Be Convincing with Your Examples and 30-Second Commercial

Look at the job posting and make a list of your qualifications. Before you walk into an interview, it helps to be very clear about what you offer and why you're the best person for this job. Once you are clear, select your best examples and stories for this interview. Your goal is to give the interviewer confidence, along with some examples about you that the interviewer can use to convince other people in the company that you are a good fit for this job.

Review your Personal Brand Statement and tailor your 30-Second Commercial to each employer so that it matches the requirements of this job. For example, if the job posting lists computer skills first, talk about your computer skills first. Use the wording and terms used in the job description. Practice saying it in several ways so that it rolls off your tongue smoothly in conversation. Here are things you can do to be convincing:

- **Be authentic.** Make sure your 30-Second Commercial represents you authentically. Don't "sell" what you can't deliver.

- **Include measurable accomplishments.** The key to an effective 30-Second Commercial is to provide examples of your capabilities. Pick the items that best fit the needs expressed by the interviewer. Example: "I can see that *xyz* is the most crucial challenge to your company. My skills can solve those problem areas because of my specific *xyz* experience."

- **Focus and polish the content.** Your aim is to prepare a brief, polished summary of your qualifications. The heart of your message should emphasize how you can benefit the employer. It is your interview "billboard" saying "Here's what I can do for you." This helps the interviewer focus on the strengths you have to offer.

- **Be ready for any situation.** Practice delivering 30-, 45-, and 15-second versions. Weave your commercial into the interview—perhaps a longer version first, followed later by a shorter one. Don't overdo it, however; twice is probably enough.

- **Don't bore your audience.** Observe the situation so that you know when to stop talking. Watch for signals that the interviewer wants to ask a question or move on to a different topic or wrap the interview.

Be Ready for an Offer

Your goal is to get a job offer, but few people think ahead about how to respond when the offer actually is extended! How will you respond if they offer you the job on the spot? There are three basic options: yes, I'd like to think about it, or no. Keep your answer short and sweet. Here are some examples:

- Thank you for the offer. I am happy to accept it.

- I am very excited about your offer. Once we work through the details, I look forward to being part of the team. ("Details" includes such things as compensation, contract, and start date.)

- I am very excited about this offer. When do I need to make my final decision? (This is a good answer if you have additional interviews pending.)

- I appreciate the offer, however, based on what I learned about the job in this interview, I'm not sure it is a good fit for me. May I have some time to think about it further? (Don't burn your bridges just yet. Think it over.)

If you want this job, and they offer it, what will you say if they say they want you to start immediately—today or next week? Plan your answer in advance. If you already have a job, it is common to say that you need to give your current employer two weeks' notice. What if the interviewer or recruiter says they are interested in you but can't make an offer for several months? A good response is to let the interviewer know that you would be very interested to hear from them when they are ready. They know, without your telling them, that they are taking a risk that you might accept another job while waiting for their offer. However, the old adage don't burn your bridges is a good one to remember at this point. It is not uncommon for a person to take another job and then discover it wasn't what was expected. When the delayed offer comes to you several months later, you might actually be in a position to take it!

© Minerva Studio/Shutterstock.com.

OVERCOMING BARRIERS
Avoid Interview Disqualifiers

Any one of these blunders during an interview could cost you the job:

1. Don't be late. It's hard to count all of the negative messages that being late sends—lack of respect, lack of genuine interest, personal disorganization, and on and on.

2. Don't be abrupt or discourteous to anyone you meet.

3. Don't sit down until the interviewer invites you to; waiting is courteous.

4. Don't bring anyone else to the interview; it makes you look immature and insecure.

5. Don't invade the interviewer's personal space by reading anything on the desk or putting anything on it.

6. Don't touch your cell phone or get distracted by other technology during an interview. Make sure your phone is on silent.

BE PHYSICALLY PREPARED FOR THE INTERVIEW

OUTCOME **3**

You have already practiced being mentally and emotionally prepared, that is, you have prepared what you will say and practiced body language that will convey that you are interested in the company and confident that you are the right person for the job. Now it's time to prepare the physical elements of an interview. This includes three things: reviewing the **Interview Preparation Checklist** with portfolio items or marketing materials that you can show to an interviewer, assembling an Interview Survival Pack to help you look and feel confident, and a final practice run with your props to ensure you can move smoothly through your interview.

Show portfolio items that highlight your hands-on experience in the areas that count the most. Do not use every item for every interview.

Review the Interview Preparation Checklist

Before each interview, review the Interview Preparation Checklist in advance. Select items from your Master Career Portfolio that relate to this particular job and job qualifications. Be selective; don't take everything. Put these items in a professional-looking binder or small attaché case. (A regular briefcase is overkill.) If you have more than 10 pages, use labeled folders to organize your materials so you can quickly find what you need during the interview. It may be a good idea to print or copy this checklist and use it before each interview.

Interview Preparation Checklist
General Job-Related Materials from Your Master Career Portfolio

☐ A copy of the job posting or description

☐ A copy of your application for this job posting

☐ Your customized resume—copies for the interviewer(s), yourself, and an extra

☐ A copy of your customized cover letter if you created one for this job posting

☐ Portfolio materials and job-related samples of your work

☐ Certificates, licenses, transcripts, and related documents

☐ Letters of recommendation (for this job or this specific type of work)

☐ Lists of references (general endorsement of your character, knowledge, and skills)

☐ Business or contact cards, if you have these, including your professional social media platform usernames

Marketing Materials from Your Master Career Portfolio

☐ A copy of your targeted 30-Second Commercial (for your use only)

☐ A reminder list of examples and stories you can tell (for your use only)

Organizing Materials

☐ A notebook with questions you can ask during the interview (see Chapter 9)

☐ A businesslike pen—not too cheap, expensive, flashy, or quirky

☐ A note pad to take notes (ask permission to take notes before doing so)

☐ Your appointment calendar (If you use your smartphone, turn the sound off before you even walk in the building!)

☐ A list of the names, titles, and phone numbers of people related to this interview

Create a set of portfolio items and marketing materials prior to every interview that is tailored to that particular job posting. Organize these documents in a professional-looking file, binder, or portfolio. Many of the items you've assembled in the About Me and Master Career Portfolio section of your Career Builder Files will be a good candidate to bring to the interview. If appropriate, create a Job Application Package for each interviewer. (See Chapter 7.) It will contain some of the items listed above.

Prepare an Interview Survival Pack

Feeling in control is one way to keep your cool in interviewing situations. If you can anticipate situations ahead of time, you can more effectively manage them. Prepare an Interview Survival Pack to help you. It should be in a small zippered pouch. It will contain items such as these:

- Personal hygiene items (toothpaste and toothbrush, comb, deodorant, tissues)
- Spare stockings or tie (in case of snags or stains)
- A Tide™ stain kit or similar product to take care of unexpected spills and stains
- Cash, coins, or credit card for parking or a bus
- A written map or directions to get to the interview
- A backup plan in case you need your smartphone and it fails or loses its charge
- Your normal "cure" for a headache or upset stomach
- Whatever else you need to look, smell, and be your best no matter what

While preparing your Interview Survival Pack, think through the entire interview event, not just the conversation with the interviewer. For example, if you're riding a motorcycle or bike, what will you do with your helmet? If there's two feet of snow on the ground, how will you carry your shoes into the building and where will you put your boots?

Also think through your attire. Select an outfit that fits well, is clean and pressed, and is appropriate for this interview and the weather. Make sure all the buttons and zippers are in good repair. Choose shoes that are shined, clean, comfortable, and suitable for the job and interview. If you are in a factory, do not wear sandals or open toes shoes. Ladies, leave behind that beloved ancient handbag you take everywhere, instead opting for a simple professional bag or attaché. If rain is in the forecast, take an umbrella and wear a raincoat—you do not want to walk into an interview dripping wet! Wear effective deodorant, but go easy on the after-shave lotion, cologne, or perfume. Be immaculately groomed from head to toe.

Using Your Marketing Materials

Use the marketing materials and portfolio items you've assembled using the Interview Preparation Checklist wisely, especially the job-related samples of your work. Before an interview, arrange the items in priority order based on the best examples of your work related specifically to the employer's needs. Ask if the interviewer would like to see samples from your portfolio before you display anything. Even if the interviewer prefers not to review them, having samples of your work with you makes a good impression and conveys that you are professional and organized.

During the interview, you may still have an opportunity to offer a portfolio sample if the topic suggests it. Simply turn to (or take out) the appropriate portfolio items that demonstrate your qualifications. This tangible evidence of abilities often gives candidates a winning edge in competing for a job. When employers ask questions about your resume, you can use your portfolio items to support your responses. Do not misrepresent yourself in the portfolio items; the work need to be your own. Be prepared to provide copies of the work if requested to do so.

Find It Fast

Your interview can come up fast! Here's a guide to the main topics so you can do a rapid review:

Develop your 30-Second Commercial, **CAW 2-7: Create Your 30-Second Commercials, page 61**

Review your Interview Preparation Checklist, page 293

Prepare an Interview Survival Pack, page 294

Make a good impression:

- Your appearance, Dress for Success, page 232
- Your body language, pages 233–234
- Your verbal skills, pages 234–236
- Your use of business etiquette, page 238

Know what to expect:

- Types of interviews, pages 261–266
- Typical questions (and answers), pages 266–275

- Good questions to ask (and avoid), pages 275–276
- Prepare for your interviews, pages 287–291

During the interview:

- Use the items you brought from your Interview Preparation Checklist, page 296
- Close the interview in your favor, pages 297–298

It's a mistake to rely only on your portfolio items to convince an interviewer of your qualifications. The focus of the interview is still on you. Your personal appearance, your body language, and your verbal communication skills are essential. The portfolio items are visual aids to support your qualifications. Using the Interview Preparation Checklist,

Real World Scenario 10-2 Walter was interviewing for a job as a marketer and had just been asked the question, "What's an example of a time when you received negative feedback? How did you handle it?" Walter had used his Interview Preparation Checklist to assemble the right marketing materials for the interview and this was the perfect opportunity to use it. He pulled out a *before* and *after* sample of branding work he had done as part of a project for a course. He showed his initial ideas and how they improved dramatically with the feedback he received. He highlighted how he incorporated the feedback and pushed the ideas further. By following the Interview Preparation Checklist, he was able to show how he handled negative feedback to create an even better final solution. Even though he didn't predict using his marketing materials for this question, it worked out perfectly.

What versatile samples will you include as you follow the Interview Preparation Checklist? How can you use your assembled marketing materials to highlight your skills and experience?

for each interview, select the items to match the specific employer and job. Be prepared to tell the story related to each item. Do not use every item for every interview.

▶ *CAREER ACTION*
Complete Worksheet 10-5
Do Your Homework Before Every Interview, page 309

Last-Minute Preparations

Even if you prepared well in advance of the interview, there are still a few things that can only be done at the last minute. Add to this list based on your own unique situation.

- Look at the Interview Critique Form in Career Action Worksheet 10-4 to remind yourself how you will be judged and to recall what you learned from your practice.

- Call someone from your Career Network for a last-minute morale boost before heading to the interview.

- Check the weather and the traffic, so you can be prepared and on time.

- On the day of the interview, take the time to look your best. Eat well and be rested, immaculately groomed, and appropriately dressed (Chapter 8). Consider the effects of coffee or other stimulating drinks prior to an interview and whether it is a good idea or not.

- Start using positive, assertive body language (Chapter 8), even as you travel to the interview.

- Use your voice well—what you say and how you say it (Chapter 8). Taking a few deep relaxing and refreshing breathes before an interview does wonders for good vocal control.

Using Your Marketing Materials

To capture an interviewer's attention early in the interview, refer first to a portfolio item that represents one of your most outstanding accomplishments or makes a point about your key qualifications. Use a strong item toward the end of the interview to leave a favorable last impression.

Practice using the marketing materials you've assembled using the Interview Preparation Checklist so that your delivery will be smooth. Have a friend give you a mock interview so that you can practice referring to your marketing materials at key points during the interview. Here is an example:

The interviewer asks, "How important do you think it is to keep up with changing technology?"

Destiny replies, "I think it is very important, and I regularly attend industry group meetings to update my software skills." She provides a brochure for a talk about Mobile Applications that she recently attended at a local chapter meeting of BDPA (Black Data Processing Associates). "Being part of BDPA is one way I stay up to date," she says.

- Review how to wrap up an interview in your favor (next page).
- Silence your phone before you go into the building for the interview.

Now that you are ready to interview like a pro, here is some last-minute advice: "Make up your mind to have a good time and *then* go to the party." Approach your interviews the same way and see how a positive attitude can strengthen your performance. Remember that the interview is a two-way process; you are there to learn about the company as much as they are there to learn about you. Try positive visualization and other techniques for managing stress to help you perform at the top of your game.

▶ *CAREER ACTION*

Complete Worksheet 10-6
Get Physically Prepared for Success with Interviews, page 311

CLOSE THE INTERVIEW IN YOUR FAVOR

Whether it's a practice interview or the real thing, be proactive and professional by influencing how the interview ends. For your own sake, clarify what to expect next in the process. Leave a positive impression by restating your qualifications and by closing the interview skillfully.

Clarify What to Expect Next
Before you leave the interview, clarify:

- What, if anything, you should do to follow up
- When a decision will be made
- How the interviewer prefers you to follow up (by phone, by letter, by email, or in person)

The following sample dialogue shows how to get this information.

Clarifying these details underscores your image as a professional who understands the importance of following through after important meetings.

Use Your Clincher
As you near the close of an interview, make a point of leaving your interviewer with a clear picture of how you fit the job. Bring the interview full circle by asking a question similar to this example in a courteous tone: "Would you please summarize the most important qualifications you're looking for in filling this position?"

Run the short version of your 30-Second Commercial to restate your skills, experience, and other assets that meet the employer's needs. This important clincher gives you one last chance to market yourself and your qualifications. People remember best what they hear first and last.

Close the Interview Skillfully
Some candidates lose the race for a job by not clearing the final hurdle: closing the interview skillfully. Don't let your posture, attitude, or verbal and nonverbal communication slip for even a moment. Use the following techniques to close an interview skillfully:

- Watch for signs from the interviewer that it's time to wrap up the interview. Signs include the interviewer asking whether you have any further questions, tidying up papers on the desk, pushing the chair back, or simply sitting back in the chair. Heed the cue. Don't make the interviewer impatient by droning on at this point.

- Ask the interviewer to notify you when a candidate has been selected. Imply that this is not the only job you are considering: "By what date will you make your decision on this position? I'd appreciate knowing within the next two weeks so that I can finalize my plans."

Following Up

You: When should I expect to hear whether I am selected for the position?

Interviewer: We'll notify all candidates of our decision within two weeks.

You: Do you mind if I check back with you?

Interviewer: I prefer that you don't until we notify you.

OR

Interviewer: No, I don't mind.

You: How would you prefer I contact you?

Interviewer: Please call my assistant.

- Before you leave, determine any follow-up activities the interviewer expects from you. If a second interview is arranged, check your calendar to make sure you are not scheduled for another interview at that time. Then write down the date, time, place, and names of all of the people who will be interviewing you. If you are expected to provide additional information, credentials, references, or work samples, make a note and verify what you are supposed to do and by when before you leave.

- If you're seriously interested in the job, say so! Just as in effective sales, the person who asks is the most likely to receive. Interviewers are impressed by candidates' expressions of interest; candidates who directly express their interest strengthen their position. Offer a simple statement—for example, "I'd be pleased to be a part of this organization" or "After talking with you, I'm convinced that this is the job I want, and I believe my qualifications would be an asset to the Acme Corporation. Please consider me seriously for this position."

- Finally, as you leave, remember to use the interviewer's name: "Thank you for interviewing me, Ms. Carpenter."

- If you haven't been given one, ask the interviewer for a business card. You'll need the interviewer's contact information so you can send a thank-you note.

- Be conscious of using positive body language. Keep your shoulders back and your head up when you stand and give a warm smile and a firm handshake. Once you leave the interviewer's office, you are still interviewing. Thank the receptionist or assistant by name and add a brief parting greeting.

Review Figure 10-1 on page 288 to reinforce your understanding of the areas that employers consider most important during an interview. With all your preparation, you will interview like a pro!

Chapter Checklist

Check off each item you can do. Reread sections in this chapter to help you complete the checklist.

☐ Schedule two practice interviews to improve my performance and confidence (an interview with someone in my Career Network and an interview with an employer in my target field). **❶**

☐ Ask interviewers to evaluate my practice interviews. **❶**

☐ Summarize every interview and evaluate my performance. **❶**

☐ Prepare for interviews by learning more about the company and interviewer. **❷**

☐ Have my examples ready to demonstrate how I am qualified and a good fit for this job. **❷**

☐ Prepare my response if I am offered the job. **❷**

☐ Assemble portfolio items and marketing materials using the Interview Preparation Checklist. **❸**

☐ Put together my Interview Survival Pack. **❸**

☐ Prepare physically for interviews to reduce my stress level and to appear organized. **❸**

☐ Use strategies to wrap up interviews in my favor. **❹**

Critical Thinking Questions

1. How have you used the success strategies described in Chapter 1 (maintain a positive outlook, set goals, manage your time, be proactive) to prepare for and participate in a practice interview? Which strategies are most useful? **❶**

2. Why is it important to prepare for and perform in a practice interview as if it were the real thing? **❶**

3. How can you let an interviewer know that you are interested in the company? Why does this matter? **❷**

4. What is the value of customizing your 30-Second Commercial for each interview? **❷**

5. What would you tell your friend to do to reduce his or her stress level in the days before an interview? The day of the interview? **❸**

6. What advice would you give your friend about wrapping up the interview skillfully? **❹**

Trial Run ❷

Prepare for Interviews by Reflecting on Your Job Search Journey

If you are using the chapters in order, you are likely to have found some job leads, applied for jobs, and had at least one practice and/or real interview. In this Trial Run, you take stock of your job search strategies.

Set aside at least two hours for this look-back and assessment. You will need this book, your Career Builder Files, and some blank paper. Find a quiet place to do this work. You can also work with a partner or in groups of three. Spend at least one hour evaluating each person's materials and progress in planning the next steps.

Remind yourself of the key points in Chapters 1–10 by looking at each of the Chapter Checklists and your Career Action Worksheets. Evaluate each area of your own Job Search Journey thoughtfully and honestly.

	What have I accomplished?	What advice or activity in the book has been most helpful?	Where are the gaps?	What advice or activity in the book (that I haven't done) could I apply?
Example: *Find job openings (Chapter 6)*	*Everyone knows I'm looking for a job; contacts in Ashland & Paducah*	*Very prepared for network meeting with Ms. Garcia; sent her thank-you note*	*Need job leads in small businesses; ask Anil and Jean how they found their jobs*	*Look at trade group sites and Chamber of Commerce sites*
Prepare (Chapters 1–3)				
Create Your Resume (Chapters 4 and 5)				
Apply for Jobs (Chapters 6 and 7)				
Shine at Interviews (Chapters 8–10)				

Trial Run ❷

Prepare for Interviews by Reflecting on Your Job Search Journey

If you are using the chapters in order, you are likely to have found some job leads, applied for jobs, and had at least one practice and/or real interview. In this Trial Run, you take stock of your job search strategies.

Set aside at least two hours for this look-back and assessment. You will need this book, your Career Builder Files, and some blank paper. Find a quiet place to do this work. You can also work with a partner or in groups of three. Spend at least one hour evaluating each person's materials and progress in planning the next steps.

Remind yourself of the key points in Chapters 1–10 by looking at each of the Chapter Checklists and your Career Action Worksheets. Evaluate each area of your own Job Search Journey thoughtfully and honestly.

	What have I accomplished?	What advice or activity in the book has been most helpful?	Where are the gaps?	What advice or activity in the book (that I haven't done) could I apply?
Example: Find job openings (Chapter 6)	Everyone knows I'm looking for a job; contacts in Ashland & Paducah	Very prepared for network meeting with Ms. Garcia; sent her thank-you note	Need job leads in small businesses; ask Anil and Jean how they found their jobs	Look at trade group sites and Chamber of Commerce sites
Prepare (Chapters 1–3)				
Create Your Resume (Chapters 4 and 5)				
Apply for Jobs (Chapters 6 and 7)				
Shine at Interviews (Chapters 8–10)				

▶ *CAREER ACTION WORKSHEET*
10-1 Arrange a Practice Interview ❶

Schedule a practice interview with your Career Network with (an interviewer and an observer if possible). Use the sample questions in Chapter 9 as a guide for your practice session. You can make a copy of them for the "interviewer." Be sure to include some difficult or stress questions that you want to rehearse. Encourage the interviewer to expand on the questions, if possible, tailoring them to your job target to give you relevant interview practice. If possible, arrange to have the practice interview video-recorded. If you can't find someone to interview you in person, you can use Skype or other video-conferencing technology. You may want to practice using this technology if you are participating in a video interview. If possible, make a copy of Career Action Worksheet 8-1 "Body Language Self-Assessment" and use it to assess yourself after the practice interview ask the observer for additional feedback following the practice interview.

This page is intentionally blank.

▶ CAREER ACTION WORKSHEET

10-2 Participate in a Dress Rehearsal Interview ❶

Contact an employer in your career field and ask for help with a course assignment. Ask the employer to conduct a practice interview and complete the Interview Critique Form (Career Action Worksheet 10-4).

1. Dress appropriately.

2. Take a copy of the Interview Critique Form with you and ask the interviewer to evaluate your performance by completing the form during or after the interview.

3. After the dress rehearsal interview, evaluate your performance using Career Action Worksheets 10-3 and 10-4.

4. Within two days of the dress rehearsal, send a thank-you letter to the person who gave you the interview.

This page is intentionally blank.

▶ *CAREER ACTION WORKSHEET*
10-3 Summarize and Evaluate Your Interviews ❶

Summarize every practice and real interview as soon as possible to avoid forgetting important details.

Duplicate and use this worksheet for your own evaluation and follow-up plans. Answer the questions as completely as possible.

Name of Company: _____ Date of Interview: _____

Location of Interview: _____

Name(s) and Title(s) of Interviewer(s): _____

Phone Number: _____ Email: _____

Summary Activities and Questions

On a separate sheet of paper, write every question you can remember being asked during the interview. Take your time and be thorough. Do this before answering the following questions.

1. Based on the knowledge you gained in your interview and research, which of your qualifications would be the greatest asset in this job? Which of these qualifications should be reinforced with the potential employer in your follow-up?

2. List any questions you think you answered inadequately. Write out the best possible answer to each question. Use additional paper as needed.

3. Did you forget to provide important information that demonstrates your qualifications for the job? Explain in detail.

4. What questions did you intend to ask but forgot or didn't have a chance to ask? Write them out now.

5. How could you have presented yourself more effectively?

6. In what area(s) do you think you performed the best in your interview? Why?

7. In what area(s) do you think you performed poorly? What steps can you take to improve?

8. Describe information you learned about the interviewer that may be helpful in establishing greater rapport in the future (for example, philosophy, current working projects, personal interests or hobbies, or mutual goals).

9. Is there any point of confusion that needs to be clarified for the employer? Explain.

10. Are you scheduled for another interview with the company? If so, record the date, time, place, and name(s) of the interviewer(s).

11. Record any other activities you offered to follow up on or were specifically asked to follow up on by the interviewer (for example, provide references, transcripts, certificates, or examples of work).

12. How does the interviewer prefer you to follow up (by phone, by letter, in person)?

13. When did the interviewer indicate the hiring decision would be made?

Add your completed work to the "About Jobs" section of your Career Builder Files.

▶ *CAREER ACTION WORKSHEET*
10-4 Interview Critique Form ❶

Give copies of the Interview Critique Form to the people who help you in practice interviews. You can also ask them to look at your completed Career Action 10-3 and offer suggestions. Before you give this form to someone, complete the first two lines below.

Name of Company: _____ Date of Interview: _____

Location of Interview: _____

Position Applied for: _____

To the Interviewer: Please check the rating in each category that reflects your opinion of the job candidate's performance. If you can add comments, it would be very helpful.

Documentation (resume, job application, business card, cover letter)

☐ Excellent   ☐ Very Good   ☐ Good   ☐ Needs Improvement

Comments or suggestions (optional): _____

Attitude (interested in position, self-confident, likable, pleasant tone of voice, smiling)

☐ Excellent   ☐ Very Good   ☐ Good   ☐ Needs Improvement

Comments or suggestions (optional): _____

Appearance (generally neat and tidy, appropriately dressed, alert, good hygiene)

☐ Excellent   ☐ Very Good   ☐ Good   ☐ Needs Improvement

Comments or suggestions (optional): _____

Job Qualifications (education, skills, and experience suitable for position; good personal attributes; human relations capability; dependable; punctual; industrious)

☐ Excellent   ☐ Very Good   ☐ Good   ☐ Needs Improvement

Comments or suggestions (optional): _____

Verbal Communication (speaks clearly with positive tone, uses proper English, avoids slang or repetitive words, emphasizes assets, is courteous, uses name of the interviewer)

☐ Excellent   ☐ Very Good   ☐ Good   ☐ Needs Improvement

Comments or suggestions (optional): _____

Nonverbal Communication (positive, assertive body language, good eye contact, does not fidget)

☐ Excellent   ☐ Very Good   ☐ Good   ☐ Needs Improvement

Comments or suggestions (optional): _____

Listening (does not interrupt or respond too quickly, asks to have a question repeated if necessary, takes time to think through important questions, calmly endures silence)

☐ Excellent ☐ Very Good ☐ Good ☐ Needs Improvement

Comments or suggestions (optional): _____

Enthusiasm (demonstrates interest and energy through verbal and nonverbal communication)

☐ Excellent ☐ Very Good ☐ Good ☐ Needs Improvement

Comments or suggestions (optional): _____

Please summarize any other observations you made during the interview, including several things that were done well and one thing that needs improvement.

Add your completed work to the "About Jobs" section of your Career Builder Files.

▶ *CAREER ACTION WORKSHEET*
10-5 Do Your Homework Before Every Interview ❸

Each time you receive a new job interview, use this form as soon as you can to help you prepare for this interview. Check off items you have completed and answer the questions.

Understand the Job Posting. Make a copy of the job description, and do the following:

☐ Circle words in the job description that are new to you or unique to this company.

☐ Look up the meaning of unfamiliar words in the job description to ensure you know what they mean for this career field and this company. Write the meaning on the job description.

☐ Number each job skill requirement (1, 2, 3, etc.), and on a separate piece of paper, write the numbers and a brief description of how you meet these qualifications. Outline your examples and stories related to this job that can give the interviewer confidence that you are qualified. Attach the separate pages to this worksheet.

Understand the Company. Find the company website, social media platform, or other resource and answer the following questions:

☐ When was the company started?

☐ Who are the owners/leaders of this company?

☐ What are the major products this company provides?

☐ Where is the company located? Is there more than one location?

☐ What is the company's stated mission or purpose?

☐ Does the company state its values or principles? If so, write them here or attach a copy.

☐   How might you work the information above into your interview discussion?

Identify Current Events for the Company. Do a general search on the company's name and the name of the top leaders or owners, then answer these questions:

☐   How recently was this company in the news?

☐   Is the news about this company generally favorable or not?

☐   What does this news tell you about the company?

☐   How might you be able to use this news in an interview discussion to demonstrate that you are the person they want for this job?

Learn About Your Interviewer. Try to find out the name of the person who will interview you. Do a general Internet and social media search on this person, and answer the following questions.

☐   What do I have in common with this person? Neighborhood? Schooling? Hobbies or Interests?

☐   Is this person someone who can offer me the job directly? Or is he or she someone who will recommend me to others?

☐   Is there a connection between this person and me? A mutual acquaintance? A friend of a family member or networking contact? If so, describe the connection.

☐   Have they recently posted an article or update that I can comment on?

☐   How might you use your knowledge of the interviewer in the interview discussion?

Add your completed work to the "About Jobs" section of your Career Builder Files.

▶ *CAREER ACTION WORKSHEET*

10-6 Get Physically Prepared for Success with Interviews ❸

Make a list of at least five portfolio items or marketing materials that you might include by reviewing the Interview Preparation Checklist. Many of these will come from your Master Career Portfolio.

To do this, read two or three job postings that you found earlier (see Chapter 6), and list items that demonstrate your qualifications for several of the job requirements. (For example, if you want to work as a cook or chef, include a sample menu, recipes, a nutritional analysis, and a cost analysis.) Be sure to include samples and examples of your career-related work and your transferable skills. (For example, if the job requires "superb customer service," include a thank-you note you received about your service, or a service award, or a letter from a person who recommends you for your attitude toward excellent service.)

1.

2.

3.

4.

5.

Optional: List other portfolio items you might want to bring to an interview, but be careful not to bring too many.

Add your completed work to the "Master Career Portfolio" section of your Career Builder Files.

This page is intentionally blank.

PHASE 5:
CONNECT, ACCEPT, AND SUCCEED

Connect, Accept, and Succeed

PART 5 This part provides tips for what to do after interviews to help you get the job and succeed in your career.

ADVICE FROM THE EXPERT

GINA ARENS

Owner, Little Sonoma Fine Wines

Gina Arens had a wide variety of experience working in all aspects of retail operation before starting her own fine wine retail store. She learned from the ground up what it takes to manage store operations, including purchasing, inventory management, marketing, sales, and supervision of staff.

From her experience of working with and managing new employees, her advice for succeeding at a new job is to "take time to learn and understand the business processes and procedures. Meet and exceed expectations that are set for you." She says the fastest way to appear unprofessional is to "show up to work with an untidy appearance and treat customers in a rude manner," whether these customers are internal or external.

If you do have problems adjusting, companies will help you improve job performance. Gina says for performance improvement, she will try to "meet and discuss on a regular basis and have someone work with the person to try to improve their understanding, skills, and performance." Additionally, timeliness is an important focus for performance. "We try to address performance immediately (good or bad) rather than wait for annual reviews." For new employees, the company enables success "by providing training and enrichment opportunities from seasoned employees and knowledgeable vendors."

When it comes to long-term success, Gina says, "Those who are promoted demonstrate a high level of commitment to the company. They are dependable, trustworthy, and hardworking. They are creative thinkers who solve problems and increase business in innovative ways." While promotion is demonstrated through talent, employees who are laid off or fired often make simple errors such as being "not dependable, not honest, and not productive." Often, they "may have lacked the skills we initially thought they had to do the job."

It's important to be cautious on the job as well. The office grapevine can often get you in trouble. Gina's advice is to "stay out of it! Be careful of people who try to draw you into commenting about other employees. You should never say anything about anyone that you wouldn't say to them directly. That includes electronic communication as well!" Another area that often poses issues is building a relationship with your manager. Gina especially highlights the need to be "careful about being critical of current business practices because you could be insulting your boss who initiated these practices and get off on the wrong foot with your relationship."

To make an impact at your job, Gina says, "Watch, listen, and learn before you start trying to reinvent the wheel. Try to understand why things are being done a certain way before making suggestions to do things differently. When you do, you will be able to address the objections that may come up and may just see some change happen!"

PLAN for Success

Success is more likely when you have a written plan. Use the online template *Plan for Success* to create your own written plan for successfully completing Part 5, Chapters 11–13.

"Never look back unless you are planning to go that way."

—Henry David Thoreau

STORIES FROM THE JOB SEARCH

Molly Cramer's major in leadership studies required an internship experience, and she learned of an ideal opportunity through word of mouth. She says, "A family friend had participated in the internship program and raved about the experience she had. I then searched online to learn how I could apply." Her proactive approach led to her paid internship at the JVS Cincinnati Career Network, helping members of the community search for sustainable employment.

Molly prepared for her first "real" interview by researching the company and reading about its staff on LinkedIn. She then "did a quick brain storming session of questions I thought the interviewer would ask me. I enlisted a friend to ask me the questions, listen to my responses, and give me feedback."

Molly's professional behavior and work habits had a positive effect on her workplace. She says, "I think I contributed to the organization because I brought a can-do attitude and executed a task—organizing a job fair—that would not have been accomplished without a capable intern."

Molly's advice to others is to "establish positive relationships with your supervisors, coworkers, and other personnel. You never know whether an internship could turn into a job down the line, so make every effort to be friendly and professional with everyone."

She now believes "there is nothing more fulfilling than helping others." Helping others find employment was deeply satisfying for Molly. "I know that whichever path my career takes, I will find a way to help others in the process," she says.

MOLLY CRAMER

Sophomore, University of Richmond, Psychology and Leadership Studies Major

OVERVIEW

After the interview, take steps to help you get job offers, understand what the offers really mean, negotiate the contract if needed, and respond to job offers professionally as you continue to make your career happen successfully.

OUTCOMES

1 Describe how to follow up after interviews, page 317

2 Evaluate job offers, page 322

3 Demonstrate how to respond to job offers professionally, page 328

CAREER ACTION WORKSHEETS

WHERE ARE YOU ON THE JOURNEY?

PHASE 1: Prepare for the Journey
- *The Job Search Journey*
- *Know Yourself to Market Yourself*
- *Picture Yourself in the Workplace*

PHASE 2: Create Your Resume
- *Plan Your Resume*
- *Write Your Resume*

PHASE 3: Apply for Jobs
- *Find Job Openings*
- *Write Job Applications*

PHASE 4: Shine at Interviews
- *Know the Interview Essentials*
- *Prepare for Your Interview*
- *Interview Like a Pro*

PHASE 5: Connect, Accept, and Succeed
- ***Stay Connected with Potential Employers***
- *Dealing with Disappointment*
- *Take Charge of Your Career*

Something that is seen repeatedly is more easily remembered. Be seen by your potential employers—in their email, in their workplace, on their phone. Be pleasantly persistent.

PHASE 5 Connect, Accept, and Succeed

Step 1, *Stay Connected with Potential Employers*

You are in Phase 5, *Connect, Accept, and Succeed*, at Step 1, *Stay Connected with Potential Employers*. Your goal in this chapter is to identify professional ways to ensure potential employers remember you, admire your persistence, and want you to join their workplace. Then, when the job offer comes, evaluate the offer and, if appropriate, negotiate to make the offer just a bit better.

FOLLOW UP AFTER THE INTERVIEW

Interview follow-up can increase your chances of getting the job, yet many candidates don't bother to do it! Interviewers often view follow-up by a candidate as a proactive step that shows initiative and interest.

Good follow-up reinforces your qualifications and helps you stand out favorably from

the competition. Be patient during this stage of the Job Search Journey. The hiring process takes longer than you want it to take, and often, longer than even the employer expects.

The key to follow-up is timely action: evaluate your interview performance and send follow-up messages to the interviewer.

Evaluate the Interview

At the earliest possible time, summarize and evaluate your own interview performance in writing. Use Career Action Worksheet 10-3. Keep in mind how interviewers tend to evaluate candidates during interviews, as shown in Figure 10-1 on page 288. This evaluation will help you do the following:

1. **Enhance your positives.** Note what you did well, and look for ways to reinforce these positives in your follow-up actions.

2. **Diminish your negatives.** Note what you forgot to say or did not express as well as you liked. These are areas you might be able to address or fix in your follow-up interactions.

3. **Follow up on commitments.** Did you agree to send something to the interviewer or the company? Did you agree to make a phone call or do something online? Maybe it was as simple as sending your business card or providing a current phone number for one of your references. It is critical that you complete each commitment on or ahead of schedule and communicate that you have completed the follow-up.

4. **Plan your schedule for follow-up.** The last two questions in the evaluation are about how the interviewer wants to be contacted and the timing for a hiring decision. These will impact your next step of mapping out your follow-up strategy.

Doing your evaluation immediately after the interview is critical. Don't even wait an hour or until the next morning. Why? Because it is too easy to forget little things that will make a difference. So do your evaluation

---

Your Career Network: Shift Your Focus

You can feel a lot of anxiety right after an interview! You're faced with a lot of unknowns at this point in your Job Search Journey. After so much work, you may wonder if it will all pay off. Your closest advocates in your Career Network can help you shift your focus away from anxiety and looking backward and toward keeping on track. Here's a few positive ways to reconnect with your advocates:

- **Express gratitude.** Consider how others have helped you on your Job Search Journey so far and take some time to thank them.

- **Share anxieties.** Sharing any feelings you have as you face the ambiguity can help get these feelings off your mind. Just make sure to stop if you start repeating yourself too many times! Use the positive visualizations you learned in Chapter 1.

- **Review next steps.** Your Career Network can provide feedback on any draft communications you've created as a follow-up to interviews.

By keeping your Career Network involved throughout your Job Search Journey, you keep growing relationships beyond acquaintances.

immediately, then review your worksheet the next morning and add anything else that comes to mind. Then start implementing your follow-up strategy.

Plan Your Follow-Up Tasks

Look at question 11 on your completed Interview Evaluation, from Career Action Worksheet 10-3. This question is about follow-up activities. Do these immediately. If you told the interviewer you would do something, consider this your promise. Keep your promises. This demonstrates your ability to follow through and is a crucial trait that employers look for.

Complete your interview evaluation promptly because some items might be best addressed in your follow-up thank-you note. Your thank-you note should be sent within a few days of the interview. The sooner, the better. See Figures 11-1 and 11-2 for examples of thank-you notes. You should write a thank-you note to every person who interviewed you. The letters can be basically the same, but try to vary each one by highlighting something specific each interviewer said in case the recipients compare notes.

Look through your interview evaluation notes for items that you want to follow up on,

Figure 11-1 Brief Thank-You Letter

2440 Observatory Boulevard, Apartment 34
Reno, NV 89511

July 2, 20—

Ms. Stephanie Nolan
Manager, Auditing Staff
Wyatt & Berkowitz Public Accountants
1410 Quarrier Street, Suite 700
Reno, NV 89503

Dear Ms. Nolan:

Thank you for the opportunity to interview for the Staff Auditor Level 1 position with you and your team. Your invitation to join the first hour of the weekly staff meeting made me feel especially welcome—and sent me to the library to brush up on the finer points of the state's tax credit program for employers who train welfare recipients!

I feel I have a good understanding of the requirements for the position, and I am very interested in joining your team. I look forward to the possibility of working with you. Please call me any time this week at 775.555.1537

Sincerely,

Max Wu

Max Wu

(775) 555.1537 | MaxWu@email.com | linkedin.com/in/MaxWu

Figure 11-2 Longer Thank-You Letter

3493 Huntington Heights
Denver, CO 80202
August 23, 20—

Mr. Frederick J. Gray Wolf
Normandy, Inc.
3500 Main Street
Boulder, CO 80302

Dear Mr. Gray Wolf:

The enthusiasm you shared this afternoon for the customer-centered philosophy behind the new Normandy Customer Care center is contagious! I know from experience how satisfying it is to make sure customers walk away with a great experience while still maintaining efficiency. The Normandy approach sounds unique, innovative, and challenging.

During our meeting, we discussed how I've been recognized for my ability to multitask, but we didn't have time to talk about my ability to ask questions. While I worked at the parts and service operations of Renaissance Business Systems, I received multiple testimonials from customers on my ability to get to the heart of their issue quickly. Asking the right questions can make customers feel cared about and understood. I have a passion and a strength for drawing out customer needs.

Thank you for talking with me about the new opportunities at Normandy. The company will be a great success in Boulder, and I would like to contribute to that success. As we agreed, I will call you next Thursday, but you can reach me before that at 303-555-0171.

Sincerely,

Francesca Elena Valdez

Francesca Elena Valdez

including information you need to clarify or reinforce with the employer, questions you want answered, areas of weak performance and suggestions for improving them, and specific actions you need to take. Jot down notes on how you might address these. Making a table, like the example shown in Figure 11-3, can be helpful.

In every follow-up interaction, plan to include some form of your Personal Brand Statement or one of your 30-Second Commercials that are customized for this job and employer. Your personal brand should always be clear and reinforce the job requirements.

Start with a draft Word document or draft email of all your follow-up communication to make sure you catch any errors and include everything you wanted. Make all your follow-up messages brief and polished. Include only the most important questions or information.

This is a good time to double-check your voicemail message to make sure it is business appropriate if someone calls you. If you do miss a call from a potential employer, be sure to return the call within 24 hours.

Now plan when you will do each follow-up. Figure 11-4 shows a sample schedule.

Figure 11-3 Example List of Interview Follow-Up Items, Noting Options for Follow-Up

What Needs Follow-Up	How I Might Follow Up
Reinforce that my experience training others on the JR-equipment can help them as they bring on additional staff	• In my thank-you note • Email • Phone conversations • Send copy of trainer certification as attachment to thank-you note
Forgot to say I really like fixing equipment, and studied the manuals on this	• During any interaction, say, "I like it when I can see the equipment manuals so that I can teach myself how to fix the equipment."
Need to know what their vacation plan is so I can take my annual mountain camping trip with my high school friends	• Wait until an offer is made • See if the answer is on the online site or on GlassDoor.com

Figure 11-4 Scheduling and Spacing Follow-Up Interactions

Follow-Up Items	Timing/Method
Send thank-you note	Today/physical card sent by U.S. mail
Send items requested by interviewer 1. List of my references 2. Copy of my training certificate 3. Email address of college instructor 4. My availability for pre-employment test	Tomorrow/by email (note: send scan of training certificate by email, and then send a hard copy by U.S. mail a few days later with an extra follow-up letter)
Tell them about my additional experience that we didn't discuss	For critical skill: Today in thank-you note For nice-to-know-about skills: Include in email if I don't hear from them within a few days of the date for a hiring decision
Improve my 30-Second Commercial to be more specific to the company's biggest challenges as described in today's interview	Follow-up interviews
Clarify that I taught myself about the topic I could not respond to during the interview	Today/in thank-you note
Take a drug test	This week, schedule an appointment at their preferred lab; mark calendar to confirm results are sent and received (call the lab, email the company to confirm)
Follow-up on "Did I get the job" (ask if there is any update on the hiring decision and can I provide any additional information to help them with this decision)	Only after the date for a hiring decision has passed/phone call (note: be prepared to leave a voicemail message too)

Be respectful of interviewers' time. Consider what their schedule might be. For example:

- Mondays and Fridays can be the busiest business days, so call on another day.

- Just before lunch and just before the end of the workday are usually inconvenient times.

- Different industries have different busy periods. Financial firms might be very busy at the end of the month. Tax firms are busy from January until April 15, and perhaps around July 1. Restaurateurs are busiest at meal times and when produce shipments are delivered.

When a first interview goes well, the potential employer may request one or more follow-up interviews and request that you take pre-employment tests. Start now to plan for these. A review of Chapter 9 can help you prepare.

Planning is just a way of thinking through what might happen in the future and dreaming up ways to respond. When you plan, you are always more prepared to be at your very best.

Craft Your Online Follow-Up Strategy

If you remembered to ask the interviewer how they wanted you to follow up, honor the interviewer's preferences and use that method. If you forgot to ask, send a follow-up letter or email rather than make a phone call, as these are currently viewed as less intrusive methods of communicating. If the interviewer approves of follow-up phone calls, use that method. A phone call is more personal and livelier and gives you quicker feedback. If you call, you should also follow up with a letter or an email because it serves as a reminder of you. Be

very cautious using text messaging. It usually is not professional or acceptable to text a potential employer.

More than likely, you will be sending your drafts and completing each follow-up through email or other online methods. Take a look at your list based on the example in Figure 11-3. Determine what method of follow-up is most appropriate for each item. Then, with each follow-up interaction, decide which items you can include from your list. You may not be able to cover all of them, so be selective.

Part of your online strategy is to stay connected with your potential employer. Use social media not only to stay informed but also to maintain a personal connection with interviewers and employees you met during your interview:

- Make sure to follow the company on LinkedIn and follow its Twitter feed if you haven't already.

- Connect with everyone you met—interviewers, possible team members, hiring managers, and recruiters—on LinkedIn.

- Mention latest company news or details from interviewers' profiles in your follow-up emails if the information adds value.

- Make sure to include a link to your own LinkedIn profile in your email signature when you send follow-up emails.

- Continue to stay on the company's social media radar by posting updates on your profile and commenting on discussions and updates shared by your new connections.

For all your follow-up communications, be ready to change your planned timing based on how the interviewer and employer respond. This might mean more communications upon their request, or a different method of communicating (for example, more email attachments instead of physical mail), or fewer communications. If the response to your follow-up messages is something like, "We will get back to you next month, as stated in the interview," that is a clear message to back off and let them run their internal process. Don't contact them again until a few days after the stated date. Connect with your Career Network again.

If a member of your Career Network is influential with your potential employer, contact him or her to ask for additional support. A friendly follow-up call from this person to the employer could tip the scales in your favor.

An alternative to the follow-up call by a network member is a letter of recommendation from one or more people who can confirm your qualifications. Some employers routinely request letters of recommendation from former managers of candidates. Arranging to have such letters sent on your own demonstrates initiative—another benefit for you.

▶ *CAREER ACTION*

Complete Worksheet 11-1
Follow Up After Interviews, page 333

EVALUATE JOB OFFERS

"We'd like to offer you the job." Those are the words every job seeker wants to hear. Because the decision to accept or reject a job offer affects your long-term career plans, consider this important decision carefully. Take your time to consider the job offer and stay away from accepting a job offer on the spot.

Consider the following factors when you evaluate a job offer:

- **The compensation:** Does the compensation package (wage and benefits) match your education and abilities and is it comparable with that of the competition? Does the potential for increases exist?

- **Entire compensation package:** This includes everything from the base wage to health insurance, education benefits, and retirement savings plans.

- **Career development opportunities:** Will you have adequate opportunities for professional growth (through training, increased responsibilities, and opportunities for advancement)?

- **The job itself:** Is the scope acceptable? Is the work interesting to you? Does the job fit into your work preferences (see Chapter 3) and long-term career goals?

- **Expense considerations:** If you have to relocate, will the company pay all or part of the moving costs? What is the cost of living in the new location?

- **The job market:** Are jobs in your field plentiful or in short supply?

- **The company and personnel:** Do you feel comfortable with the organizational structure and the people you met? Do the company's stated values and ethics align with yours?

The company expects you to have questions and may have a standard process for giving you the information you need to make an informed decision. This is the time to ask all those questions. You may be given access to a website for candidates, or a member of the hiring committee or the human resources department may contact you.

Be sure you understand all of the conditions of the job before you decide whether to accept the offer. If you have several offers, it often helps to make a chart so that you can compare the offers more visually. Selecting your next job based on a gut feeling alone has led more than one person to regret their choice. Be thoughtful, and engage your Career

Successful Follow-Up Phone Call

If your interviewer gave the go-ahead for a follow-up call, you can set yourself apart from the competition with a well-timed, well-prepared phone call.

- **Begin with a greeting and self-introduction.** "Hello, Ms. Nabavi. This is Greg Bell."

- **Demonstrate courtesy.** "Is this a good time for you to talk?" Call only during business hours. Pay full attention on the call; no multitasking.

- **Identify the position that you interviewed for and the date.** "I want to thank you for meeting with me yesterday to discuss the data processing systems analyst I position."

- **Provide important information you omitted.** "After reviewing our meeting, I realized that I hadn't mentioned some pertinent information regarding my (education, work experience, qualifications, certification, other)." Concisely give the specifics.

- **Reemphasize your qualifications.** If necessary, give a short, targeted version of your 30-Second Commercial, emphasizing precisely how your qualifications can benefit the employer.

- **If necessary, ask questions to clarify any points that were not covered adequately.** For example, a clearer description of the job responsibilities or clarification of work relationships.

- **Thank the interviewer, express your interest, and encourage a speedy hiring decision.** "Thank you again for the interview. I look forward to learning of your hiring decision soon. I believe we could benefit each other, and I'd be pleased to be a part of Mississippi Central Power Company."

oliveromg/Shutterstock.com

Network to help you look at the offers objectively. However, in the end, you are the one who will decide to accept or reject a job offer.

Negotiate a Good Compensation Package

Put yourself in a strong position to negotiate your compensation package by doing your research.

Become knowledgeable about the going salary ranges and the types of benefits being offered in your field. When you get an offer, take the time to understand the comprehensive benefit package. Don't let one company's high base salary fool you into thinking that theirs is the best offer. Other benefits, such as those listed in Figure 11-5, can have a significant impact on the overall value of the compensation package. Often it is easier to negotiate additional benefits than it is to negotiate wages.

Figure 11-5 Elements That May Be Part of a Compensation Package

Consider the following as elements of comprehensive compensation package:

- Wages or salary
- Performance reviews, raises, bonuses, profit-sharing opportunities
- Health, dental, and prescription insurance
- Retirement savings opportunities; companies may offer tax-deferred savings plans—known as 401(k) or 403(b) plans—and will contribute to your retirement savings if you participate in the company-sponsored plan through payroll deductions
- Vacation, holidays, personal, and sick days
- Flextime
- Onsite resources such as day care, gym, and cafeteria
- Lifestyle benefits such as maternity/paternity leave beyond government-required minimums, elder-care services, domestic partner benefits, and family-care leave of absence
- Relocation and business travel reimbursement, including personal use of loyalty points for hotels and airlines
- Flexible Spending Accounts; in addition to insurance programs, a Flexible Spending Account allows you to set aside pretax income to pay for medical expenses and dependent care and can lower your income taxes
- Insurance such as disability insurance, and long-term care insurance

OVERCOMING BARRIERS
Background Checks

Stephen Coburn/Shutterstock.com

A background check is a consumer report that employers use to screen potential employees. In addition to confirming your education and work history, employers may request a consumer report from a credit reporting bureau to check your social security number, credit payment record, driving record, or criminal history.

This type of background check is common for jobs that require government security clearance, but it may be used for any job.

Before employers can get your consumer report, they need to have your written consent, however. You always have the option of withdrawing your application if there is information you do not want to disclose.

The best way to prepare for a background check is to be truthful on all employment forms, maintain good credit, know what your references are going to say about you, and obtain copies of your personnel files from past employers. If necessary, get a copy of your credit report from a credit bureau and dispute any incorrect information.

Real World Scenario 11-1 Lee and Rose have both been applying for accounting positions at various companies and comparing notes on the offers they received. Lee was excited because he recently got a job offer for $15,000 more annually than Rose's offer. He encouraged Rose to try to get a job where he is going to work. But Rose has done her homework and knows that her employer contributes to her 401(k) retirement plan and provides a healthcare package that Lee won't get. When she calculated the annual savings with the better health insurance and considered the long term advantages of the 401(k), the total annual value was $25,000 more than Lee's offer. Plus there are three weeks of vacation instead of two weeks. Rose is sticking with her offer.

What factors are important for you to evaluate when looking at the overall compensation package?

Do be aware that sometimes salary and wages cannot be negotiated. Vacation and benefits may be off the negotiating table too. It often depends on such things as government laws and regulations, company policies, and union contracts. Talk to your network to learn more about what is and is not negotiable. See "Caution: When NOT to Negotiate" for more on this topic.

Research Compensation Trends in Your Field

Here are some places where you can find information about compensation trends:

- Talk with leaders in your field, people who hold positions that are similar to your target job, and a placement specialist.
- Search the Internet for salary and benefits information. Glassdoor.com, the BLS *Occupational Outlook Handbook,* Indeed, Google for Jobs, and other sites list salaries for specific companies and roles. Salary.com has a salary wizard tool that can be used as well.
- For part-time or contract jobs, use the full-time wage as a starting point. For part-time jobs, calculate the equivalent pay by dividing the full-time wage into an hourly rate and multiplying by the hours you expect to work. For contract jobs, divide the full-time wage by 2,080 hours, the average hours worked by contractors in a year.
- Ask your school's career services office for assistance.
- Check the websites of associations in your career field.

Some employers provide printed job descriptions that include a fixed salary listing, while others offer salary information on their websites. A job posting may include a salary range, or the salary may be open. You may be able to find the range or approximate salary for a position from the employer's human resources department. Some employers, however, don't give out this information. They may give you only the bottom of the range—rarely the top figure. Having a general idea of the range can help you evaluate a job offer.

Before you accept the job offer is the best time to negotiate the terms of your employment.

Salary Negotiation Tips

To obtain the strongest bargaining position, postpone discussion of compensation until you receive a job offer. Instead, focus on your qualifications. If the question of compensation comes up earlier, refocus the conversation using the following tactics:

- **If the interviewer brings up the subject of compensation before you are prepared to discuss it,** delay the topic by saying, "Actually, I'm more interested in learning about the position, than in talking about salary today. Could we discuss the position a little more?"

- **If the interviewer asks what salary you want, a good response is, "What figure or range is the company planning to pay?"** This gives you a starting point for negotiation. If it's higher than you expected, you help yourself by not stating a lower figure first. If it's lower, you now have a place to begin negotiations.

- **If the interviewer presses for your salary requirement, refer to your research.** "The national average for a person with my experience, education, and training is $_____. Considering cost-of-living factors, I would expect a salary in the range of $_____."

Whenever possible, let the interviewer bring up the topic of salary and benefits. These conversations are usually best held after you get an offer, or, at the earliest, during a second interview. Here is a sample dialog.

Joan: Thanks for coming in for a follow-up interview. Mick, the hiring manager, is looking forward to meeting you.

Juan: Thanks for asking me back, Joan.

Joan: Before we go to meet Mick, I'd like to talk with you about the compensation package. Let me ask you, what was your salary at your last job?

Juan: I am looking at jobs that are in the $60,000 to $70,000 range. And I'm looking for more than my current two weeks of vacation each year. I understand from reading the materials you sent that the compensation package is much more than just salary. Can you walk me through what a total package might look like?

Notice that in the above dialog, Juan does not directly answer the question about his salary from the previous job. As you negotiate, realize that you don't have to give direct answers to every question asked. Instead, keep the focus on your goals. When negotiating salary, use the following strategies:

- **Begin salary negotiations** by asking questions such as: "Thanks, is this the firm job offer?", "Is this negotiable?", and "Is this the base wage only?" These questions confirm you have received an official offer and indicate your interest in negotiating the full compensation package, not just salary or wages.

- **Aim for a salary that equals the peak of your qualifications.** The higher you start, the higher the offer is likely to be. State your requirement in arrange (upper twenties, mid-thirties), making it broad enough to negotiate. Don't specify a low end; if you do, the employer will likely select it.

- **Discuss the entire compensation package** during the discussion of salary. Your total take-home pay is greatly influenced by all benefits such as those listed in Figure 11-5. Review the offer package thoroughly and take the time to calculate the actual take-home pay after taxes. In some cases, a low salary is offset by low insurance premiums with high benefits coverage or pre-tax savings accounts such as the Health Savings Account option. In others, you may want to negotiate a higher salary due to the high cost of insurance, retirement benefits, lack of vacation, cost of living in that area, and so on.

- **Ask about the criteria used to determine compensation increases and the frequency of salary reviews.** Good benefits and salary increases can offset a lower starting salary. Directly ask, "How and when will I be evaluated, and is there a possibility of increase based on that evaluation?"

- **While discussing salary, return to your assets.** Review all of the benefits and qualifications you have to offer the company.

- **Once you state your salary range, do not back down,** particularly if you think it is equal to your qualifications. Base your range on careful research. The employer will respect your confidence in the quality and worth of your work.

- **Do not discuss any other sources of income and do not whine about your expenses.** Stay focused on the negotiation.

- **Get clear on benefit details and timing.** Ensure you understand when benefits will start, such as health insurance. If your previous insurance will run out prior to start of your new benefits, consider requesting your new employer cover any extension costs as a part of negotiations.

- **If the salary offer is made in a letter and the salary is too low, arrange an appointment to discuss it right away.** Bargaining power is far greater in person than it is by letter or phone.

- **If the salary isn't acceptable, state the salary you would accept** and close by reaffirming your interest in the company and the job. If the interviewer says, "I'll have to think about your requirements," wait one week; then call back. You may receive a higher or compromise offer. If the interviewer gives you a flat "no," express regret that you were unable to work out a compromise. Restate your interest in the job and the company; then send a follow-up thank-you letter within two days. This could swing the decision in your favor.

OVERCOMING BARRIERS
When NOT to Negotiate

Stuart Jenner/Shutterstock.com

There are some instances where you should not negotiate salary. You should always maintain the perception that you are acting in good faith and with integrity. Consider the following situations as times when not to negotiate the base wage offered:

- Do not negotiate just for the sake of negotiating. If you are happy with the offer and it meets the typical range for your role, review all the other benefits thoroughly, negotiate on these points if needed, and then accept the offer graciously.

- If a salary range was previously shared and you accepted the range, do not negotiate outside of the range. If you had accepted the range prior to doing adequate research or because you wanted to continue the process, you cannot go back on your acceptance of the salary range. This can result in removal of the offer.

- Do not negotiate salary without sufficient justification prepared.

- Do not negotiate salary if the range the company is sharing is vastly different from what you want. This will waste both parties' time.

Recall that outside of base wages, there are both costs, such as health insurance premiums, and benefits, such as paid vacation, that ultimately factor into how much you are earning. Consider negotiating in other areas if base wages are non-negotiable.

As you negotiate, consider the people and use your emotional intelligence to help you get a better compensation package. Here are some things to consider:

- **Be likeable.** The people you are talking with are more likely to work harder to maximize your package if they view you as a person they like.

- **Be attainable.** This is not a time to play hard to get. Communicate with body language and your words that you are seriously considering accepting this position provided the negotiations are satisfactory. Make sure you are not wasting their time.

- **Understand their side.** The employer has constraints. Try to understand what they might be. It can be a legal issue, a union contract, or a concern about setting a precedent for all employees.

- **Know the decision maker.** Often you are talking with someone who cannot make the ultimate decision. In some cases it might be the HR department, other times it is the hiring managers. Frequently it is someone higher in the company or even the legal department.

- **Know when to stop.** Pay attention to the mood of your contact. If they appear tired, frustrated, or seem to have other work to attend to, suggest that both of you take a break, and think about this for a day or a week. You never know; the answer might be different on a different day.

> ▶ *CAREER ACTION*
> **Complete Worksheet 11-2**
> Internet Research on Salary Information, page 335

> ▶ *CAREER ACTION*
> **Complete Worksheet 11-3**
> Salary and Benefits Planning Sheet, page 337

RESPOND TO A JOB OFFER PROFESSIONALLY

A job offer may be made in person by phone, face-to-face, or in writing by email or letter. If the offer is made in writing, you have more time to think it over carefully and less emotionally than you do if it's made in person. Respond to the offer quickly so that you don't jeopardize it in anyway.

If the offer is made by phone or in the interviewer's office, request time to think it over. You may want to discuss the job offer conditions with a member of your Career Network and family.

It's in your best interest to take at least one day to consider the advantages and disadvantages of the job offer. This gives you time to understand fully the compensation package and address any remaining questions you have.

Important: Be sure that waiting one day won't be an imposition or affect the job offer. Don't put yourself in the position of returning the next day to accept the offer only to find that someone else has the job.

When the Answer Is Yes

If you accept the job offer verbally, follow up immediately in writing. Summarize your understanding of the conditions of the offer and state the position title, starting date, salary, and other pertinent items. (Your employer may do the same, but this helps ensure mutual agreement about all of the conditions of the offer.) If a formal contract is given, review thoroughly, sign, and return. Request your new employer to provide you next steps and what to expect so you can come prepared to your first day on the job.

If you are waiting to hear about more than one offer, tell the other companies you interviewed with that you have accepted a job. You may deal with these people in your new job or you may want to contact them in the future regarding employment.

Contact your references and other people who helped with your job search to tell them about your new job and thank them for their help. People you thank are more likely to help in the future when you seek a new position or advancement in your career.

When the Answer Is No Thanks

If you decide this is not the job for you, first notify the employer by phone if possible.

Then politely decline the offer in a letter, thank the employer for the job offer, and wish the employer future success.

> ▶ **CAREER ACTION**
> **Complete Worksheet 11-4**
> Plan for Dealing with Job Offers, page 339

Real World Scenario 11-2   Jonas received his first job offer after three long months of searching for a job. He was so excited, he almost accepted it on the spot! But then, he remembered he was waiting for a response from another interview he had recently gone to. He asked for a few days to consider the offer and went home. He contacted the other possibility and let them know that he had received an offer. He made sure to share he was still interested in hearing the decision and they agreed to provide a decision in the next 48 hours. Two days later, Jonas had two offers to consider! He compared the full compensation package from both and began his negotiations.

What items can you clarify or negotiate when you take time to review your job offer?

MAKE IT A HABIT
Be a Gracious Winner

The Job Search Journey certainly takes a lot of work, but it is not a paying job. The time will come when you need to stop looking for a job and start working at one. Your final decision about accepting a particular job may well be influenced by economics—the need to earn a living.

If a job offer meets most of your requirements but is not your first choice or is not a perfectly logical career step, you may still decide to accept it. If so, take the job with a determination to excel. It is an opportunity for you to establish your reputation—while at the same time taking home a regular salary.

Accept the challenge and view it as preparation for the next step in your career development.

iStock.com/nyul

Chapter Checklist

Check off each item you can do. Reread sections in this chapter to help you complete the checklist.

☐ Use my interview evaluation (Career Action Worksheet 10-3) to make my interview follow-up plan. **❶**

☐ Make a strategic plan to follow up after every interview. **❶**

☐ Involve my Career Network in helping get a job offer after the interview. **❶**

☐ Consider all aspects of a job offer—the job and company, the compensation package (salary and benefits), growth opportunities, etc. **❷**

☐ Conduct research about salary ranges and trends. **❷**

☐ Develop a strategy for salary negotiations. **❷**

☐ Accept or decline a job offer professionally. **❸**

Critical Thinking Questions

1. What would you say to a friend to convince them to complete their own interview evaluation as soon as possible rather than wait a day or two? **❶**

2. How might a thank-you note sent to interviewers make a difference in getting a job offer? List three or more ideas. **❷**

3. List five reasons a lower salary/wage offer might be better than a higher salary/wage offer. **❷**

4. If economic conditions require you to accept a job that is not exactly what you are aiming for, how can you best approach the new job? What are the benefits of doing so? **❷**

5. What is an appropriate response when an interviewer asks what salary you are looking for during your initial interview? Would the response change if you'd been given an offer? **❷**

6. Base your answers to the following questions on your salary research: (a) What is the entry-level salary for the job you are seeking? (b) What salary range do you plan to seek in your job search? (c) What is this range based on? **❷**

7. Why is it important to act professionally when turning down a job offer? **❸**

Trial Run

Study the Local Economy ❷

Pay scales and benefit packages are affected by larger economic issues. Divide into four teams and research the employment conditions in your area. Use anecdotal information and your own observations and check the websites of the local newspaper, business journal, chamber of commerce, and television stations.

Start by having a class discussion about what you want to learn from your research. For example:

- How have the students in this class been affected by economic changes?

- What can older workers tell you about past economic down turns or economic bubbles?

- What is the relative impact of national and local factors?

- What is the local unemployment rate? How has it changed in the last two years?

- How long do people report taking to find a new job in their field? Are people changing fields or taking contingency jobs?

- What are the elected officials predicting? What are business leaders predicting?

- What advice do you have for your community leaders?

Team 1. Research the two or three largest employers in your area. How have they been affected by the national economy? Have there been layoffs? If so, have these jobs been shifted to other parts of the country or to other countries or eliminated altogether? Have programs been put in place to attract more people into certain fields of work or into an area that needs more workers?

Team 2. Research the local stores or branch offices of national companies. What is the reason behind any new storefront openings or closures; for example, did the national company close low-performing stores, or has its business model changed to focus on suburbs rather than cities? How many people have lost their jobs? How many new jobs have been created?

Team 3. Research small, locally owned retail businesses. Have any small businesses near your school closed? Have new businesses opened? What has happened in the neighborhoods you live in?

Team 4. Research locally owned service businesses. Include companies that provide services to consumers (such as drycleaners and nail salons) and business-to-business companies (such as janitorial services and restaurant supply companies).

This page is intentionally blank.

▶ CAREER ACTION WORKSHEET

11-1 Follow Up After Interviews ❶

After an interview, you will follow up at least once, and likely several times. Think about a real or practice interview you have done, as you write the drafts and scripts below. (Use a separate page or file for your work.)

PART A: Draft a thank-you letter.

PART B: Write a script for your follow-up phone call to provide additional information.

PART C: Draft a follow-up email to kindly request information about the job posting now that the date for filling the position has passed.

PART D: Ask someone to review and comment on your letter, script, and email. Revise them based on their comments and feedback.

PART E: Stay connected online. Follow the company on LinkedIn and Twitter. Connect with individuals you met on social media.

Add your completed work to the "About Jobs" section of your Career Builder Files.

This page is intentionally blank.

▶ *CAREER ACTION WORKSHEET*

11-2 Internet Research on Salary Information ❷

PART 1: Compare the websites PayScale.com and Salary.com. Use one site's salary calculator to compute the average salary for a field of your choice for two cities in different parts of the country where you might consider working. Look for difference in cost of living. What are some other factors to consider? Print the results.

PART 2: Visit the *Occupational Outlook Handbook* at the Bureau of Labor Statistics site and complete the following steps, recording your work on a separate page or file.

1. Select a title that closely matches your occupation.

2. Summarize the wage ranges for the occupation and the expected education and experience.

3. Find the wage ranges plus education and experience for at least five more occupational titles that are either similar or that interest you.

Add your completed work to the "About Jobs" section of your Career Builder Files.

This page is intentionally blank.

▶ *CAREER ACTION WORKSHEET*

11-3 Salary and Benefits Planning Sheet ❷

Contact two employers in your field to learn about the salary ranges and benefits they offer for the type of job you are seeking. Ask the following questions.

PART 1: Negotiating Salary and Benefits

Does this position have a fixed salary or a salary range?

If the salary is fixed, would you tell me the amount?

If the salary is in a range, would you tell me the range?

Is the salary negotiable?

What criteria are used for determining the salary for this position?

Are salary raises awarded for excellent job performance? If so, what criteria are used in this process?

What is included in the typical complete compensation package (salary and benefits)?

PART 2: Summary of Strategies for Negotiating Compensation

Review the strategies in the section "Negotiate a Good Compensation Package." On the back of this page or in a separate document, summarize, in your own words, the tactics you plan to use when negotiating a compensation package (salary and benefits). List any additional tips you have found in your Internet or other research.

Add your completed work to the "About Jobs" section of your Career Builder Files.

This page is intentionally blank.

▶ CAREER ACTION WORKSHEET

11-4 Plan for Dealing with Job Offers ❹

Respond to the following.

1. List factors you should consider when evaluating a job offer. Be thorough in your answer. You may want to talk with a member of your Career Network, a placement counselor, or both. Address the factors that are specific to your personal Job Search Journey, as well as general factors.

2. Explain how you can best respond to a job offer made in person:

   a. If you think you want the job

   b. If you are sure you want the job

   c. If you don't want the job

3. How can you best respond to a job offer made by phone?

4. List the follow-up steps you should take when accepting a job offer.

5. What should you do to reject a job offer in a professional manner?

Add your completed work to the "About Jobs" section of your Career Builder Files.

Dealing with Disappointment

OVERVIEW

Getting a good job often requires interviewing with more than one company; in fact it may take several tries before you land the job you want. Think of it as a learning experience as you continue on your Job Search Journey. Chapter 12 highlights practical strategies for managing a rejection notice, recharging your motivation, and trying new angles to land a top job.

OUTCOMES

1 Develop strategies for increasing your chances of getting interviews, page 342

2 Develop strategies for improving your interview performance, page 343

3 Explain strategies for managing a rejection notice, page 346

CAREER ACTION WORKSHEETS

12-1: Internet Research on Handling Job Search Rejection, page 351

12-2: Action Plans for Improving Your Job Search Campaign, page 353

WHERE ARE YOU ON THE JOURNEY?

PHASE 1: Prepare for the Journey
- *The Job Search Journey*
- *Know Yourself to Market Yourself*
- *Picture Yourself in the Workplace*

PHASE 2: Create Your Resume
- *Plan Your Resume*
- *Write Your Resume*

PHASE 3: Apply for Jobs
- *Find Job Openings*
- *Write Job Applications*

PHASE 4: Shine at Interviews
- *Know the Interview Essentials*
- *Prepare for Your Interview*
- *Interview Like a Pro*

PHASE 5: Connect, Accept, and Succeed
- *Stay Connected with Potential Employers*
- ***Dealing with Disappointment***
- *Take Charge of Your Career*

Just like in the fable of Goldilocks and the Three Bears, some jobs may be "too hot or too cold," some may be "too soft or too hard," and, as you continue your search, you will find the one that is "just right" for you.

PHASE 5 Connect, Accept, and Succeed

Step 2, *Dealing with Disappointment*

You are in Phase 5, *Connect, Accept, and Succeed*, Step 2, *Dealing with Disappointment*. Your goal in this chapter is to turn any rejection notices you might receive into tools to help you improve and move forward on your Job Search Journey. Sometimes it takes a few iterations to get your message right or to find those jobs where you are the best fit for the position.

Persevere for Success

No one is right for every job. The right person for a job doesn't always get the job. The best prepared and most determined person often does, however. While you may be partly responsible for an initial rejection, you have the power to turn the situation to your favor. All of the strategies in this chapter have been used successfully by other job seekers to win a good job offer, despite previous rejections.

IF YOU DON'T GET INTERVIEWS

There are many reasons you may not be getting interviews. If you have applied for more than 10 jobs and not received a response, it may be time to rethink your strategy.

More Sources

You may need to use more sources. The Bureau of Labor Statistics has compiled data showing that people who use many resources for finding job leads find jobs faster than people who use only one or two resources. If you are relying on Monster and Craigslist for job leads, look at the many sources of leads in Chapter 6 and expand your search options. According to Jobvite, only 14.9% of hires are made from a job board and 39.9% are made through employee referrals. Reconnect with your Career Network—so you can tap into a full 50% more jobs you may be qualified for. Remember, people hire people they have a connection with. Use the tactics in Chapter 6 to tap into your Career Network positively and effectively to supercharge your Job Search Journey.

Right Jobs

It could be that you are applying for the wrong jobs. It could be that you are applying for jobs that do not match your qualifications.

Look carefully at the requirements for several jobs you have applied for. If your skills and qualifications are at the low end of the requirements, this could explain why you aren't getting interviews.

Fewer Applications

You may be applying for too many jobs or through a method that has too many applicants, such as a job search engine. Job search engines make it easy to respond to job postings, and employers get more applications this way than through other sources. As mentioned in Chapter 6, try applying directly through the company website or start applying for jobs that have been posted for less than a few days. A more effective, personal way to reach potential employers is through your Career Network. Alternatively, focus on fewer jobs that are a great fit for you and your qualifications, and follow up with cover letters and phone calls. Review tips for follow-up from Chapter 11.

Real World Scenario 12-1 Stewart was having a hard time with his Job Search Journey. He was trying to balance school, a part-time job, and family commitments while trying to apply for jobs. His initial strategy was to submit his Job Application Package for five openings every week and to go to a career-related event once a month. After two months, he still hadn't heard back from any companies. He was getting frustrated, especially after he noticed that he spent an average of an hour on each application. He stepped back and reflected on his strategy. He decided instead of spending five hours per week on applications, he would spend two hours at an event or conducting Career Network Meetings per week and two hours applying to more targeted job opportunities. Stewart started getting responses with his new strategy!

How can you become more strategic in how you spend your time during the Job Search Journey? How can you increase the probability that the actions you take will deliver the opportunities you are looking for?

To counter natural feelings of rejection, the best approach is taking immediate positive action.

- Maintain a positive attitude.
- Evaluate your performance, your Personal Brand Statement, and your Job Application Package.
- Connect with your network for support. Update your contacts list.
- Plan your next job search steps and follow through. Keep moving forward and don't spend too long looking back!

Taking a short breather helps renew your energy and enthusiasm. Allow yourself one day—but no longer—to do something you enjoy and to relax. Then jump back into your Job Search Journey. Rejection is not an excuse for giving up.

Review Chapters 2 and 3, including your Career Action Worksheets with your self-analysis forms (talents, skills, qualifications, special accomplishments, and personal attributes). Visualize yourself performing successfully in your next interview and on your new job. Make a conscious effort to think and act positively and to use positive self-talk and affirmation statements.

Jupiterimages/Stockbyte/Getty Images

Customized Packages

You may need to spend more time customizing your master resume and cover letter to match the requirements in the job posting. Convince the hiring committee that you are interested in *this* job and *this* company.

Refreshed Resume

You may need to give your resume a face-lift. Print a copy of your master resume and compare it with sample resumes online. Review Chapters 4 and 5 for improvement ideas. For example, highlight and count the action verbs and search-optimized keywords and make sure you are using them effectively. Request feedback on your resume from your Career Network contacts, such as people who are already in the job you would like.

If these strategies do not seem to help, get professional assistance to reenergize your Job Search Journey. Make an appointment with a career counselor to get a professional appraisal of your job search strategy and recommendations for new strategies. Work with a resume adviser to make sure your resume stands out in appearance and content.

IF INTERVIEWS DON'T LEAD TO JOB OFFERS

Getting an interview indicates that you were one of the top candidates for the job. Every time you make it to the next stage in the job application process, take a moment to celebrate. Getting interviews is a positive sign—it means your resume, application, and network are working for you.

Most people have several interviews with multiple companies before they are offered a good job. Each company may have a process that includes multiple rounds of interviews.

Take what you learned from each interview to the next one, and use it in your favor. Getting a top-notch job is a full-time job that usually requires several interviews and some rejections.

If you receive a rejection, always ask the interviewer for feedback so you can learn and improve. Try to get a detailed answer. If you weren't the right fit, why? What else were they looking for? See Outcome 3 for more on this topic.

Also consider your interview performance. Do any of these items apply to you?

☐ Was not physically prepared for the interview (on time, well groomed, had copies of Job Application Package, body language, etc.)

☐ Was not mentally prepared for the interview (hesitated over many answers, didn't prepare questions to ask the interviewer about job, forgot interviewer's name, etc.)

☐ Did not show awareness of the company's current situation or industry issues

☐ Did not convince the interviewer that there is a match between qualifications and job requirements

☐ Did not give well-thought-out examples that showed in concrete, measurable way how previous work helped a previous employer

☐ Did not build positive rapport with the employees and support staff

☐ Answers were too long or rambling; gave too many details

☐ Said something negative about a previous employer

☐ Did not convince the interviewer that there is a match between you and the culture of the company

To improve your interview performance, take these actions:

- Review and use Career Action Worksheets 10-3 and 10-4 to evaluate your performance and recall interview details.

- Make notes about the ideal answer to each question you were asked.

- Video-record yourself answering the questions to provide practice and a chance to see how you look to an interviewer.

The Bad Interview

Some interviews are not good; in fact, some are grim. After learning the details of a job, you may be convinced that you don't want it. The interviewer may be inept at interviewing, making it difficult for you to perform well.

Do not stop trying. Do your best to be professional in every interview. You can always learn something beneficial or use the opportunity to polish your interviewing skills.

Never give up *during* an interview. Besides being unprofessional, it could cost you a future reference or a good job lead from the interviewer.

Eviled/Shutterstock.com

OVERCOMING BARRIERS
It Isn't Always About You

yanugkelid/Shutterstock.com

An application for a job can go flat for reasons you cannot control. Be careful about taking rejection personally. Instead, consider these possible alternatives:

- The company may implement a hiring freeze before the position is filled, or the decision maker may decide that the department doesn't need to fill the position.

- The hiring committee may be told to give preference to current employees and local candidates, or they may already know who the "best candidate" is.

- For political reasons, the person who interviewed you may want to defer to the candidate that another member of the committee recommends.

- The last job search may have backfired, and the hiring committee may decide that none of the candidates is a perfect fit.

- The hiring committee may decide, or be told, to postpone the job search. Overall, fewer jobs are filled in May and June, at the close of the current fiscal year.

- The committee may get applications from overqualified candidates and decide to redefine the job responsibilities.

Taking something personally only serves to hurt you—it demotivates you and makes it more difficult to be positive about the next opportunity that comes your way.

- Ask at least one person you do not know well to give you a mock interview.
- Follow the advice in Chapter 10 to prepare for different types of interviews and interview questions.
- Remember what you learned from interviews and use it the next time.
- Do your homework before the next interview!
- Review tips in Chapter 11 about what to do between interviews.

Winners in all fields agree: Perseverance is a major factor in their success. When they meet an obstacle, they find a way around it.

Manage Your Online Presence

So you found a great company, you got an interview, and you did your absolute best but still didn't get the job. Rule 1—don't take it personally! And whatever you do, don't air your disappointments on a social media platform.

When you're frustrated, it's only natural to turn to your social network for moral support, but it's best to keep your venting local and off the computer. What airs on Facebook doesn't always stay on Facebook—or on Twitter or YouTube or anywhere else online. Keep your negative comments to yourself.

Don't assume that just because you didn't get the job the company didn't like you. Perhaps you weren't right for the position, but who's to say you won't be a perfect match for the next opening? Keep your options open and your bridges intact. Leaving things on a positive note shows professionalism and an optimistic outlook—traits that employers appreciate. Here are some steps to take after an unsuccessful interview:

- Write a positive Facebook status update about your experience, mention how you'd like to be considered for future opportunities, and tag the company in the text.

- Send out tweets commending the company on a great interview process.

- Write a note of thanks to everyone who interviewed you. If you don't have their email addresses, search for them on LinkedIn and Facebook.

STRATEGIES FOR BETTER OUTCOMES

After receiving a rejection notice, don't take it personally. Instead, take action!

If you're not sure why you were not selected for the job, call the interviewer and ask for an honest evaluation. You may very well learn that the selection had nothing to do with your interview performance or job qualifications. If you are aware of the perceived shortcoming based on the interview or your Job Application Package, it can help to prepare a strong written clarification that you can refer to while making this follow-up call.

The interviewer may be willing to tell you if they consider you to be lacking in any area of skill, training, or experience. This information may be the starting point for an update of your skills or interviewing technique before your next interview.

Some employers are reluctant to offer specific opinions and are justifiably cautious about being sued by job applicants for unfair hiring practices. Even if you don't get concrete help, express your thanks. Remember, if an employer had one job opening, it is possible that they will have another in the future.

Prepare and Respond

If the interviewer is willing to evaluate your performance and make suggestions for improvement, listen carefully and take notes. Accept the concerns expressed, even if you disagree with the observations or opinions. The important point is that they represent problem areas in the interviewer's perception of you.

Real World Scenario 12-2 Larissa had one goal in mind for the Interview stage of her Job Search Journey: follow-up. Whether she was okayed to move forward to the next round of interviews or if she was rejected, she made sure to follow up in a timely fashion. If she received a positive response, she made sure to follow up with a thank-you note and relevant details to reinforce her qualifications and fit. If she received a negative response, she made sure to follow up with a thank you and two quick questions about what she could do to improve her performance next time and whether the interviewer had any possible referrals for other opportunities he or she could share. Larissa felt like following up was the most positive way to deal with any situation the Job Search Journey brought her way.

What is a positive way you can handle any rejection you receive?

If you like the company and you want the job, be prepared to *briefly* clarify your qualifications or clear up any misunderstanding. Use a friendly tone and do not react defensively. Remember that you asked for the opinion. If the interviewer seems receptive, explain that you didn't convey your qualifications as completely as you had planned and suggest that you meet once more to review them. Handled well, this approach demonstrates confidence, competence, and assertiveness and can even give you a second chance, if the job is still open or another position becomes available.

Consider Other Departments

Emphasize your enthusiasm for working for the employer and ask whether you are more qualified to fill another position. This strategy encourages the interviewer to give you more consideration and may land you a "hidden job."

Ask for a referral to another employer. Employers are impressed by candidates who demonstrate initiative and confidence. If you project confidence and competence, you greatly increase your chances of convincing others of your potential.

Your Career Network: Anything NOW?

It's probably been a while since you've asked your Career Network about any job openings they've seen. Reflect on what you'd like to share with them about the outcomes of your interviews or job search so far. What is valuable for them to know that might help them help you?

Then, take a moment to reach out and see if there are any new:

- Warm Introductions that you can connect with and find new sources for jobs

- Job postings they've come across at their workplace that might fit you

- Job targets they think you might not have considered

Keep your conversation focused on what you've learned from the process so far. Don't get bogged down in self-defeat or blame the employers you've tried. Recognize it's a success to have gotten in the door! Your Career Network will appreciate your positive attitude and be more likely to support your ongoing journey.

Don't Be Afraid to Reapply

If you don't get a job with a preferred employer now, don't give up. You never know how close you were to being hired. You might be at the top of the list the next time an opening occurs. You'll have the advantage of being known by the employer because a known applicant saves valuable time in recruiting. Stay in touch with the recruiter, HR resource, and interviewer.

Keeping your name in front of the employer can put you first in line for the next opening. One way you can do this is by calling the interviewer every couple of months just to check in. Keep the phone call brief and polite. Your purpose is to keep your name at the top of the list of applicants.

Be Persistent

Be persistent in pursuing your preferred job. Stay focused on your goal and consider all of the factors that may affect the status of the position. Changes in business conditions may affect the status of your target job. Consider how these changes may also present new opportunities to you as a job seeker.

Many companies keep applications in their active file for a specific period of time. If you are interested in a position with a particular company, find out their policy for keeping applications active. You may need to call a target employer periodically to keep your application active and to remind the company that you are interested in new job openings.

▶ **CAREER ACTION**
Complete Worksheet 12-1
Internet Research on Handling Job Search Rejection, page 351

▶ **CAREER ACTION**
Complete Worksheet 12-2
Action Plans for Improving Your Job Search Campaign, page 353

Chapter Checklist

Check off each item you can do. Reread sections in this chapter to help you complete the checklist.

- [ ] Take concrete action to recharge my motivation and improve my chances of getting interviews. ❶
- [ ] Reevaluate your job search strategy. ❶
- [ ] Improve my interview performance so that I get job offers. ❷
- [ ] Ask each interviewer to evaluate my performance so that I can identify any areas that I can improve. ❸
- [ ] Ask for referrals to other departments within the company. ❸
- [ ] Reapply at a later date and call back periodically to check the company's hiring status. ❸

Critical Thinking Questions

1. Which strategies will you use to improve your chances of getting an interview? ❶
2. What specific steps will you take to improve your interview performance? ❷
3. If your friend got a rejection notice after a job interview, what three things could you say to encourage your friend to continue on the Job Search Journey? ❷
4. What can you gain from seeking an evaluation of your interview performance from an interviewer who did not hire you? ❸
5. If all of your efforts fail to result in a job offer, what last request should you make of an interviewer? ❸

Trial Run

Write Yourself a Letter ❸

The search for a new job is challenging and often frustrating. This activity may help you put things into perspective and renew your energy.

Take written notes during each part of the activity.

The activity starts in the present day. Jot down words and phrases that describe the general business climate in the country and your community and the key issues in your career field and in your own career.

Think back five years and repeat the activity. Break into teams of people with related career interests. Take notes during the discussion. Reflect on the changes in your career field.

How many of the changes were deliberately planned for and implemented? How many changes were unexpected? How did the larger business environment affect your industry? What things that seemed small five years ago turned out to have big consequences? What big things turned out not to be so big after all?

In teams or as a class, project ahead five years. Take notes during the discussion. What changes do you predict in the general business environment and in your career fields? Where do you expect the most changes? How confident are you about these predictions? What are the implications of these changes for the public and for the people working in the field? If what you expect and what you hope for are far apart, what can you start doing to bring them closer together?

Think about these discussions for a few days and reflect on your own career five years ago and five years from now. Write yourself a letter to be opened in five years:

- Describe the circumstances leading to this letter: this assignment, your work situation today, your current plans, recent setbacks, and so on.

- Record your predictions about your situation in five years.

- List helpful actions and "attitude adjustments" you have decided today to take. Be specific about your plans so that in five years, you can judge how well you succeeded.

- Include anything else in your letter that you believe you will enjoy reading in five years or that you believe will be helpful to reflect on.

Put the letter where you will find it or give it to someone who can mail it to you.

This page is intentionally blank.

▶ *CAREER ACTION WORKSHEET*

12-1 Internet Research on Handling Rejection During a Job Search ❶❷❸

Search the Internet for additional tips on persevering after being rejected for a job. Use the search phrase *job search persistence* or *rejection* or go to job sites and blogs you bookmarked in earlier research. What speaks to you? Summarize your findings below, on a blank sheet of paper, or in a text file.

Add your completed work to the "About Me" section of your Career Builder Files.

This page is intentionally blank.

▶ *CAREER ACTION WORKSHEET*

12-2 Action Plans for Improving Your Job Search Campaign ❸

To assess your progress and develop improvement plans, take a look back at your Job Search Journey so far. Answer the following questions, including specific action plans you will take to improve your job search to get the results you want. Check off each item as you complete the actions.

☐ **Self-Analysis** After reviewing your self-analysis activities in the Career Action Worksheets from Chapters 2 and 3, have you overlooked anything important that supports your Job Search Journey? (List the items and describe any needed research or changes.)	
☐ **Your Network** Have you checked with your Career Network members to find out whether they have any new job leads? (List them here and follow up immediately.)	
☐ **Tailored Resume** Could your resume be tailored to a new job target? How could it be improved? Who could do a good job of helping you with it?	
☐ **Reconnect** Should you make additional phone calls/ personal visits or write additional letters to potential employers? (List details on a separate sheet of paper and begin following up today. Don't put off these actions.)	
☐ **Cover Letters** Could your cover letters be improved? How could they be strengthened? Who can give you advice?	

☐ **Follow-Up** Have you followed up on the cover letters and resumes you have sent? Have you followed up on all job leads? Have you followed up on every interview? (List any follow-up needed in these areas.)	
☐ **Research** Have you done thorough research on your current job leads—enough to talk intelligently and persuasively about how you would fit in with the company? (List any research that must be completed.)	
☐ **More Sources** Have you tried a broad range of job sources? (Refer to the list of suggested job sources in Chapter 6. List any you could use now.)	
☐ **Reapply** Should you reapply with any employers? If so, when?	
☐ **Search Time** Have you scheduled your job search on your daily and weekly calendars?	

Add your completed work to the "About Me" section of your Career Builder Files.

Take Charge of Your Career

OVERVIEW

Chapter 13 has guidelines for succeeding in a new job and growing your career long term. Successfully onboarding to a new job includes developing good work habits and building relationships. As you adjust to and become a master at your new job, you can consider growing your career through pursuing advancement, seeking new challenges, and transitioning to even more fulfilling roles.

OUTCOMES

1. Develop strategies to onboard quickly to your new job, page 356
2. Explain how to build successful relationships, page 359
3. Describe ways to manage your career, page 364
4. Identify signs that it is time to change careers, page 369

CAREER ACTION WORKSHEETS

13-1: Planning Your Work, page 377

13-2: Learn About Your Job Checklist, page 379

13-3: Learn About Your Company Checklist, page 381

13-4: Internal Resource Network Map, page 383

13-5: Prepare for Advancement, page 385

WHERE ARE YOU ON THE JOURNEY?

PHASE 1: Prepare for the Journey
- The Job Search Journey
- Know Yourself to Market Yourself
- Picture Yourself in the Workplace

PHASE 2: Create Your Resume
- Plan Your Resume
- Write Your Resume

PHASE 3: Apply for Jobs
- Find Job Openings
- Write Job Applications

PHASE 4: Shine at Interviews
- Know the Interview Essentials
- Prepare for Your Interview
- Interview Like a Pro

PHASE 5: Connect, Accept, and Succeed
- Stay Connected with Potential Employers
- Dealing with Disappointment
- **Take Charge of Your Career**

Landing the job is just the beginning. The opportunities to grow are limited only by your ability to dream big.

PHASE 5 Connect, Accept, and Succeed

Step 3, *Take Charge of Your Career*

You are in Phase 5, *Connect, Accept, and Succeed,* at Step 3, *Take Charge of Your Career.* Your goal in this chapter is to start your new job and grow your career successfully.

ONBOARD QUICKLY TO YOUR NEW JOB

All workers who start new jobs have one challenge in common: adjusting to the new workplace and the new job. This adjustment includes learning to perform specific tasks, learning how your job relates to the business as a whole, learning to work with others, and understanding the formal and informal rules and ways of doing things. Mastering these elements takes time, effort, and training assistance from your employer.

Don't expect to achieve top efficiency or have a high impact overnight. It doesn't happen because everyone has a learning curve prior to contributing at the capability level expected for your role's responsibilities. Experiencing some anxiety while trying to learn so much new information and so many new procedures is normal. Maintaining enthusiasm, an eagerness to learn, and a positive attitude will help you adjust successfully. The attitude you want to display to your new employer is, "I'm ready to take on the challenge. I'm excited to be here. You made the right choice!"

The following steps will help you adjust to a new job quickly and set yourself up for long-term success.

Project a Positive, Competent Image

From Day 1 on the job, your goal is to project and maintain a positive, competent image. Transition yourself from the "looking for a job" mindset to the "I got the job!" mindset. Even though you are new on the job, your immediate manager and new coworkers should walk away from every interaction with the perception that you are willing, able, and excited to succeed on the job.

Prepare for your first day by getting into the right mindset. Your image projects from three sources: your inner confidence, your outward appearance, and your verbal and nonverbal communication.

- **Your inner confidence:** Project a positive "can-do," ready to learn attitude. Remember, they hired you because they believe in your ability to get the job done. At the same time, don't start making suggestions on Day 1 of what could be done better or assume you already know everything. Review and practice the tips on self-esteem in Chapter 1, "Maintain a Positive Outlook," on page 11.

- **Your outward appearance:** Plan to show up on time, or even a bit early, on the first day. Prepare the night before with the right clothes, lunch, and transportation. Try to ensure you know where to go and who you will meet first. Bring any forms or additional information requested. Review Chapter 8, "Dress for Success," on page 232.

- **Your verbal and nonverbal communication:** If you project a negative attitude —insecure, bored, unenthusiastic, unfriendly, too passive—through your speech, appearance, and actions, you will be perceived negatively, even if your work is excellent. Maintain friendly, interested language and posture. Review Chapter 8, "Use Positive Body Language," on page 233.

In addition, developing and displaying good work habits also contribute to a competent image. Be ready to do the following:

- Show up to work on time or early, and avoid absenteeism. Always communicate unavoidable absences and avoid surprising your immediate manager.

- Practice punctuality for meetings, deadlines, and assignments. Value others' time and hold yourself accountable to meet goals. Don't procrastinate.

- Keep your work area neat. Organize your space so what you need is easy to find.

- Plan how you will use your time. Don't rely on your immediate manager to keep you on track. Start Day 1 with a planner or other means to keep track of assignments and milestones.

Projecting a positive, professional, and competent image from Day 1 gives you a competitive edge. For example, if you make an error, your professional image may influence people to view the error as a part of learning rather than a sign of incompetence. If you start your relationships on the right foot, coworkers and your immediate manager will be more willing to help you succeed, and your learning curve will be accelerated.

> ▶ *CAREER ACTION*
> **Complete Worksheet 13-1**
> Planning Your Work, page 377

The First Weeks, Step by Step

Once you have the right mindset to approach your first day at work, quickly ramp up your skills and knowledge within the first week and month on the job. During a job interview, you learn general information about the position and the job duties. To perform the work, you need more detailed information. Ask questions during your first month, especially during your first week, to learn about the following four areas: your job, skills/processes needed, your company, and your key relationships.

Learn About Your Job

First and foremost, you need to gain a complete understanding of your role, including what the basic tasks are, what success and poor performance look like, and what you need to accomplish the tasks. When you meet with your immediate manager and even peers who are in similar roles, make sure to ask and understand the following:

- **Basic equipment:** Make sure you receive all the equipment you need to perform your job as soon as possible. Even if this may be your employer's job to do for you, sometimes you have to proactively ensure everything is in place by contacting administrators and HR resources yourself.

- **Job description:** Ask for a job description if you don't already have one. A job description typically identifies the specific duties and responsibilities of the job, the skills and **competencies** required, the equipment and tools to be used, the expected outcomes and contributions to the company, and the relationship of the position to other positions within the company.

- **Success measures:** Ask your immediate manager (your main customer, who will be responsible for evaluating your performance!) what success looks like for your job description, as well as what it would look like to go "above and beyond." How can you excel? How does your role help your immediate manager achieve success? How does your role help the company achieve success?

Career Action Worksheet 13-2 provides a detailed checklist of questions to ask to learn about your job.

> ▶ *CAREER ACTION*
> **Complete Worksheet 13-2**
> Learn About Your Job Checklist, page 379

Learn What Skills and Processes You Will Use

As you learn more about what your job entails, you will also discover what skills are needed and what processes govern your role. Some work processes may directly enable you to get your job done quickly, while other process may be in place to help you succeed and ensure compliance in the workplace with federal or local regulations and laws.

- **Training:** Ask about any training you will receive. Your employer expects you to have the basic knowledge and skills you need to do your job, but you may need additional training for certain tasks.

- **Technology and standard procedures:** Most roles have certain procedures and systems they have to use when performing key tasks. The tasks may also require the use of particular software or technology. Ensure you receive training materials and step-by-step guides for any technology and standard procedures that are critical for performing your role.

- **Policies:** Most companies have a written **employee handbook** that covers policies and procedures such as work hours, the probationary period for new employees, pay and benefits, and rules about using employer equipment and email. Learn the rules and follow them.

- **Performance evaluation:** Ask how and when your job performance will be evaluated. See "Prepare for Your Performance Evaluation" on page 370.

- **Confidential information:** You have a moral and legal obligation to protect internal employer information that is considered confidential. Ensure you understand what confidential information you will encounter in your role and what procedures to follow to protect such information. When you are hired, you may be required to sign a nondisclosure agreement that defines the type of information that may not be shared with outsiders and the penalties for violating the agreement. Employers dismiss and often sue employees who are found to have leaked confidential information, even if done accidentally.

Learn About Your Company

Becoming a great employee who is recognized and rewarded often comes from developing a deep understanding of how your role contributes to the employer's success. When you first join a new company and start a new job, you have a great opportunity to ask as many questions as you want—because it is expected! Learn as much as you can about your employer, including:

- **Company and departmental values, mission statement, and goals:** Take the time to understand how your role aligns with not only your department's goals but also the broader employer's goals. Understand what business results are measured and what business results your work directly contributes to.

- **Employer culture:** In addition to concrete business metrics, every company has a unique personality and culture that is expressed in many ways, from the employer's mission statement to the way employees dress for work. To enhance your success, learn and adhere to the culture's values, including the expected work ethic and the customs and rules for interacting with coworkers and customers. Many of the elements that make up "how things are done" are not spelled out. Observe your coworkers and ask a trusted coworker for advice.

- **Products or services, industry, and competitors:** What business is your company in? What products and services do they offer to customers? Who are they competing with? What products and services are you working on in your role?

- **Future vision:** Request the latest annual report and organizational targets for the next year and next five years if available.

- **Company history:** Understand the major changes that have shaped your company culture.

► *CAREER ACTION*

Complete Worksheet 13-3

Learn About Your Company Checklist, page 381

Learn About Key Relationships

Similar to finding a job, succeeding in a job often hinges on knowing the right people. Furthermore, in a job, it is even more important to spend time developing and building these relationships. Below are the relationships that are important to establish during onboarding in your first weeks. These are people who belong in your Network—both the Organization Network and Industry Network. (See Chapter 1, page 10 for the four network groups.) In Outcome 2, you will learn in detail how to build those relationships over the life of your career.

- **Immediate manager:** Your immediate manager guides and designs your work plan, measures your performance, and enables you to deliver results.

- **Immediate coworkers:** Your immediate manager may have multiple direct reports in similar roles to you. You may or may not work directly with these coworkers on projects and assignments.

- **Team members:** Who will you be working with to deliver results, if any? Your role may be very individual. In other roles, for assignments and projects, you may have team members that report to other immediate managers in your company.

- **Internal customers:** Who does your work impact when you deliver tasks and results? These are your internal customers.

- **Coaches or mentors:** Who will be training you initially? Who can you go to when you have questions? Coaches and mentors may be informal and people who, in your initial introductions, showed interest in helping you find your way around and learn your

role. They may also be formally assigned by your immediate manager. You may also ask your immediate manager for coaches and mentors if you'd like help and don't know who would be a good resource.

- **HR/administrative support:** Who do you go to when you have questions on benefits and policies? Who do you go to when you need equipment or technical support?

- **Leaders:** Who is your immediate manager's boss? Who are the top leaders in the company?

Create a map of your network using Career Action Worksheet 13-4. Then update your Career Network list using Career Action Worksheet 6-1. By now, there will be dramatic changes to both your Industry and Organizational Networks. Your network continues to be an important resource, so pay attention to it, continue to grow it, track it, strengthen relationships, and give back to the people in your network.

► *CAREER ACTION*

Complete Worksheet 13-4

Internal Resource Network Map, page 383

BUILD GREAT WORK RELATIONSHIPS   OUTCOME ②

The ability to interact well with immediate managers, coworkers, suppliers, customers, and others is a critical skill in every workplace. There are very few roles that do not involve some kind of dependency on others to succeed. Your work is guided and reviewed by your immediate manager, is impacted by others' contributions to your tasks, and contributes to others' success as well. While it isn't necessary to be close friends with everyone at work, do not underestimate the importance of developing effective relationships at work.

Develop a Good Relationship with Your Immediate Manager

A good working relationship with your immediate manager is essential because you need your immediate manager's advice, help, and general understanding to do your work and because, ultimately, your immediate manager determines your performance review, rating, and career growth. Depending on your job, you may have day-to-day personal contact with your immediate manager or only occasional direct contact. Make sure to ask before assuming that more informal ways of connecting, such as texting or adding on Facebook, are appropriate.

When you are first hired, however, you can usually count on spending time together. Do not act flustered if you don't understand everything that is being explained about your job. Don't be afraid to ask many questions to ensure you thoroughly understand. At the beginning of your job, this is expected and shows you are motivated to be successful at your new job.

Your immediate manager's key responsibility is to ensure that his or her group produces the assigned amount of work on time and within acceptable levels of quality. To build a strong relationship with your immediate manager and perform well, consider the following strategies:

- **Deliver as expected.** When you receive an assignment, ensure you understand what high-quality results look like and that you have the resources you need to complete the task. Realize that delivering your results contributes to your immediate manager's goals as well. Find out what your immediate manager needs to meet the group's or department's goals and do what you can to provide it.

- **Learn your immediate manager's work style.** How does your immediate manager like to be communicated with? How often does he or she like status updates? Where do your styles align and where do they differ? Inform your manager how you best work and consider as much as possible what works best for him or her.

- **Balance priorities.** If you get a new assignment that will mean not meeting your deadlines for other work, ask your immediate manager which work should be completed first.

- **Resolve problems.** Before you approach your immediate manager about a problem, demonstrate your initiative by thinking of possible solutions. Even though your problem may seem like the biggest priority on your list, your immediate manager has many more priorities, so make it easy for them to help you. Offer your own ideas, but don't press for your opinion or ideas if other people have information that you didn't. Always do your best work to support the final decision, no matter whose idea it was.

- **Suggest improvements.** If you find a faster way to do your work—without cutting corners or having a negative effect on someone else's work—use a cautious approach. A process that may seem inefficient or that is different from the method used in your previous job may serve a purpose that is not immediately apparent to you. If you think a technique could be improved, request a meeting with your immediate manager to clarify the reasons for using it. Asking thoughtful questions is a good strategy for opening the discussion. Once you understand the reasoning behind the current process, if you still have ideas for improvement, move forward with sharing your suggestions.

- **Ask for feedback regularly.** At least quarterly, ask your immediate manager directly whether your performance is meeting expectations or if you need to improve. Ask for specific recommendations for improvement as necessary so you can make noticeable changes prior to your annual performance review. Learn to take feedback well—any feedback is valuable, whether it is negative or positive. Don't react defensively or blame others. Accept the criticism professionally and make improvements. To learn from your mistakes, ask for suggestions about how you can improve the situation. If you don't think the criticism is justified, tactfully present evidence that supports your opinion. If your employer or immediate manager continually criticizes you unfairly, particularly in front of others, request a meeting to discuss the reason for this behavior. If the criticism continues even though you make the recommended improvements, consider seeking assistance from a mentor or HR, before considering a position in another department or looking for a new employer.

- **Don't trash your boss or complain about your job online.** Many people have found themselves unemployed after this infraction. Even if you haven't "friended" your boss, you never know who in your network has, and your post will almost certainly get back to your employer.

By doing all of the above, you earn trust. Trust can make or break your relationship with your immediate manager. A trusting relationship depends on open and honest communication. Avoid surprises with your immediate manager and keep the focus on what will help you deliver the results you have been tasked to do.

Develop Good Relationships with Your Coworkers and Team Members

The way you relate to the people you work with will influence your career success as much as the quality of your job performance—no matter how skilled or educated you are. Studies repeatedly verify that job failure is most frequently the result of poor interpersonal skills (behavior and attitude), not lack of skill.

- **Learn the roles and priorities of the coworkers and team members you work the most closely with.** Understanding their barriers to helping you and how you can help them achieve their goals will enable you to succeed and build positive relationships.

- **Get to know your coworkers.** Be friendly and approachable; do not get a reputation as a loner. However, maintain stable emotions in the workplace, leaving your personal problems at home. Wait until you have a firmly established relationship and an understanding of the norms before connecting on personal social media platforms, like Facebook or Instagram.

- **Treat people the way you want to be treated.** Help others accomplish their assignments, compliment them on work well done, critique their work tactfully only when necessary, and listen to what they have to say. This behavior encourages others to treat you the same way.

- **Be accountable for your own work.** Check your work so that no one else has to correct it. Meet your deadlines and deliver outstanding work. Don't make excuses or complain about your workload.

- **Stay out of office politics.** Don't take sides when coworkers disagree about something that is not directly related to *your* work. Gossip is not harmless; misinformation and half-truths can damage a person's reputation and career. Develop a reputation for being discreet and courteous—your coworkers will respect you, and it's a good business decision. Don't look for problems or hold grudges.

- **Respect the work environment and culture.** Turn off your cell phone and conduct conversations privately, not over the tops of cubicles or while standing in front of someone's cubicle.
- **Demonstrate competence and trustworthiness.** If you commit to do something, do it. Do it on time. If you have a task to do, do it to the best of your ability and show others that you are working hard to continue to improve.

To be an effective employee (and for your own advantage), be aware of organizational politics. Every company has formal and informal politics. Learn who is respected—or even feared. These people often influence office politics. Learn to deal with them successfully. First impressions are not always accurate, so take time to observe and learn office politics. Avoid affiliating with "complainers" who are not in harmony with your employer's philosophy.

Develop Good Relationships with Internal Customers

You may work in a department where you do not interact with the people or companies that keep your employer in business by buying its goods or services. Nevertheless, you have internal customers—the people or groups that depend on your department (or on you) to help them get their jobs done.

If you work in the marketing department, for example, the product development group is your customer because it depends on you to develop effective marketing campaigns. Get to know who your internal customers are, what their needs are, and how they depend on you or your group; then go out of your way to provide great service.

Diversity in the Workplace

As you build relationships, it's important to respect diversity and use your communication skills to build bridges instead of creating divisions. Diversity is important in the workplace because it increases adaptability, allows for greater ability to meet diverse customers' needs, and increases the variety of solutions and ideas available. Do not exclude anyone or treat anyone differently because of factors such as race, gender, age, religion, or physical ability. People from a different background may have a different approach or understanding of tasks than you. It's important to keep in mind that often there is no wrong or right answer.

Real World Scenario 13-1 Mia was assigned to a project with a coworker she didn't know if she would get along with. In the past, the coworker often complained about assignments and accused others of not doing their fair share. Mia decided to take a different approach and try to set the relationship up for success from the beginning. Prior to her first meeting, she took a look at the work and determined what she thought a fair split would be based on time and her personal strengths. When she met with her coworker, she started by saying, "I haven't really gotten a chance to know you since I started here. Mind if I learn a little more about your time here?" She allowed the coworker to share her story and then they talked about the project at hand. She asked open-ended questions such as "What work would you most like to do?" and listened to the answer. It turned out that there were some items they agreed on and some they didn't. Mia first acknowledged where they agreed and then assertively explained her reasoning on the items they didn't. She made sure to document the final agreement and shared her approach with their immediate manager. She planned to keep her immediate manager informed on the status of the project and ask for help if needed.

How can you handle a difficult relationship with positivity and assertiveness?

People have different communication styles, including you! Even in the same culture, people have different communication styles. They process information differently, approach problems differently, want information given to them differently, and socialize differently. Learning the different styles of the people you deal with and adapting your style accordingly can be an important tool in resolving disputes and avoiding conflicts in the workplace.

Ethnicities in a diverse workplace often translate into working from a different set of assumptions of what is appropriate versus inappropriate in the workplace. For example, perceptions of time may be different between a person of an Indian background versus Hispanic background versus American background. Communication styles may be different—Europeans often have a much more direct style, and Asians may have a more subtle approach.

Gender has also been discussed heavily in the workplace. Perceptions of leadership skills and communication ability often differ based on gender. It's important to recognize there is often no right way of approaching work and that each approach has its own benefits.

MAKE IT A HABIT
Be a Lifelong Learner

Rapidly changing technology and a global economy have created a fast-changing world. Jobs and careers will continue to evolve. To have a successful career and distinguish yourself from the pack, you should keep your skills up to date, keep growing your network, and be prepared to learn new skills quickly. In short, you should make learning a lifelong pursuit.

There are many ways to continue learning and avoid being left behind. For example:

- Finish your college degree if you haven't already done so.

- Keep your licenses and certifications up to date. Expand you options by getting new certifications for your profession.

- Take continuing education courses.

- Use the resources of your professional association or industry trade group. Join the local chapter and attend meetings, subscribe to newsletters, and read blogs.

- Use free online training resources for software and for business topics such as teamwork and marketing.

- Follow industry experts on Twitter. Join LinkedIn groups that relate to your career field.

In all of these ways, you will also grow your network and meet people you can learn from and help. Share what you learn with your immediate manager and team. Your commitment to education and training will help you achieve career success.

Goodluz/Shutterstock.com

Another trending diversity topic is generations in the workplace. Currently, there are four generations working side by side in the workplace. These four generations span over 75 years of cultural influences and events that create traits and expectations in the workplace. A more tenured employee may have a certain way of doing things that a younger employee may need to understand. A younger employee may have different expectations given the state of the workplace today that an older employee may need to understand.

An important skill to develop when interacting in a diverse environment is active listening. Wikipedia defines **active listening** as a "communication technique that requires the listener to understand, interpret, and evaluate what (s)he hears." It is listening with the goal of understanding fully what the speaker intends and is a powerful tool for gaining information and solving problems.

In a conversation, give the other person your full attention. Focus on what is being said, look directly at the other person, and do not interrupt. Acknowledge that you are listening using body language such as nodding. Once the person has shared his or her message, rephrase what you heard in your own words. Ask questions to show the other person that you want to understand. A good rule of thumb is to listen twice as much as you talk. You do not have to agree on all items. However, you should be willing to respect disagreements and honor all viewpoints. Try to find at least one thing you can agree on and start from that point to move forward. Again, acknowledge that it is okay for someone to approach a task differently than you may approach it.

Finally, remember that your workplace relationships don't stop when you walk out the building. Your relationships also exist online. Be careful about the politics and views on diversity you post on your social media platforms. Don't post offensive photos or comments that will reflect poorly on your company. Your employer has a right to protect the company's name and reputation. Know the social media policy at the company. Don't release private information you learn on the job or through any of your accounts. A paramedic lost his job after tweeting about a call he went out on. Even though he didn't use the patient's name, the tweet was detailed enough that it constituted a violation of the patient's privacy and resulted in the paramedic's termination. Coworkers, managers, or leaders at your company could stumble across social media posts and if your updates violate policy, your job could become at risk.

MANAGE YOUR CAREER

Work takes up a large portion of the average adult's time. Use the following techniques to maximize the time you spend on work.

Learn About Your Compensation and Benefits

Take the time to learn about employee benefits and take full advantage of those that can help you save and invest your money, in both the short term and long term.

Enroll in benefit programs, including health, disability, and life insurance, at the start of your employment and update your benefit selections according to your employer's schedule (usually annually). Your employer subsidizes costs of these benefits, so generally it's more affordable than buying these benefits on your own. If your new position doesn't have all of the benefits you had hoped for, you may need to make alternative plans for health and disability insurance. These are available through professional organizations, credit unions, auto clubs, and alumni groups.

If you are fortunate to have a job, you owe it to yourself and to the people who depend on you to *get into the habit of saving money.* No matter how little, save money and deposit into a savings account out of every paycheck you earn.

Small savings add up. For a week or two, keep track of (1) how much you spend on food and (2) where you spend this money. Then make some of these changes and see how much you can save: eat dinner at home more often, make your own coffee, take your lunch to work twice a week, stay away from vending machines, and/or fill plastic water bottles with filtered water from your kitchen sink.

Finally, it is *never* too early to start saving for retirement, so take advantage of any savings and investment plans that your employer offers. Because you save your own money and often get contributions from your employer, this is one of the best ways to save for retirement. Depending on your plan, the amount you put aside can reduce your taxable income, the gains aren't taxed until you retire, and you may draw from the plan to pay for your education or buy a home.

You should also get investment and retirement savings advice from a financial planner or an investment banker who can help you establish an individual retirement account (IRA) if desired. Some companies offer access to advisers for their employees. Do your research on the opportunities your new employer offers!

Earn Your Advancement or Promotion

If you like your employer and want to advance in your career there, find out what it takes to get promoted or gain advancement. To grow in your career, you do not always have to move up. You can also move across to another role that may grow you in different ways than your career role. By mixing a variety of roles *laterally and vertically*, you will have a rich, satisfying career with new opportunities, growth, and recognition.

- **Tell your immediate manager that you are willing to take on new responsibilities.** Negotiate your work plan to include stretching goals or tasks that you are interested in. Demonstrate your ability to handle new responsibilities by acting professionally, working hard, and successfully taking on challenges on the job.

Real World Scenario 13-2 When Douglas first signed the job offer, he didn't realize there would be so many opportunities to take advantage of with his new employer. He always had a bank account, but now learned about two investments accounts he would like to set up for retirement planning. He also wanted to set aside money specifically for his daughter's college education. He didn't know where to start but he thought it wouldn't hurt to ask. So he asked his HR resource and his immediate manager for help. The HR resource took time to explain to him the different ways the employer incentivized establishing various accounts. His immediate manager gave him contact information for a financial advisor. Although Douglas knew it would take additional time and research, he wanted to set himself up for long-term success from the start of his new job.

What opportunities are you not taking advantage of that would jump-start your career success?

- **Learn about the new responsibilities you would have.** That way, your immediate manager will know that you are ready to be promoted because you understand the duties of the new position and can be trusted to become productive in that position quickly. For insight, talk to a mentor or employees who currently have the position you would like. If possible, talk to your immediate manager and take on projects that allow you to learn these new responsibilities or offer to help someone with their work in the role you are targeting. Often, if you can already do the job at the next level, it makes it easy for an immediate manager to promote you into that position.

- **Find a mentor.** A mentor is someone inside or outside your company who can advise and coach you—someone who is respected and knowledgeable in your field. Seek advice from mentors who are experienced in the areas you need to improve. Don't limit yourself to just one mentor. Look for people who are sensitive to your concerns, who help you learn new skills, and/or who take time to explain organizational dynamics. Strive to meet your mentors' expectations for your performance.

- **Increase your visibility.** Get involved in organizational committees and cross-team projects where you can excel. Meet people outside your direct line of management. Show extra initiative and demonstrate leadership. Develop your speaking abilities. Having multiple people who can positively speak on your behalf can really help you get a promotion or new role—think of these people as internal references, similar to the references you enrolled during your Job Search Journey.

- **Show initiative.** Personal initiative is a major factor affecting your immediate manager's opinion of your suitability for taking on more responsibility and being promoted. When you finish your assigned duties, don't sit and wait for more work to be assigned. Find an appropriate task to perform on your own, notify your immediate manager that you are ready for another assignment, or ask how you can help someone else. Think creatively about better ways to do your job. Then research and plan how to implement your ideas.

- **Maintain documentation.** Keep track of positive feedback you receive from internal and external customers on work you have delivered. You can use these as support when discussing opportunities for promotion.

Always display the qualities that your employer perceived in you when you were hired. Make your employer glad that he or she chose you.

- **Expand your knowledge and skills.** Identify your greatest working strengths and interests and build on them. Take advantage of all training in these areas. Become known for your special expertise. This will help focus your career in a direction that best suits you and will expand your career opportunities.
  - Stay current in your job and industry knowledge.
  - Get involved in professional groups, training, and education.
  - Learn all phases of the company, its goals, and how each job is designed to meet the overall goals.

- **Suggest ways to improve work procedures.** There is a right time, place, and method for presenting your ideas or suggestions to your immediate manager. Don't complain or criticize. Learn by observing how others present their ideas. Explain (and show) how your idea can improve a problem area (a cheaper vendor for office supplies, for example) and offer it as a suggestion for consideration. Do not try to bulldoze your ideas through.

YOUR CAREER NETWORK—Networking on the Job

Adding names to your Career Network list is easy when you're new and meeting a new circle of people. But building quality relationships takes time, and it is best to start now. Building relationships can increase your productivity, add contributions to the company, and even help the company itself to excel. (For more, read *Give and Take: Why Helping Others Drives Our Success*, by Adam Grant.) Here are good tips for a healthy, productive network.

- **LISTEN** to others. They are giving you valuable insights when they share their knowledge and experience. Also, LISTEN for what they might need or like to get from you. Listen with the intent of giving back in the future.

- **GIVE** but with balance. Being the newest person on the team may cause others to expect you to take on all the undesirable work. Do it—at least do some of it, and learn to set boundaries. How? By asking others in your network for their advice on setting boundaries. Their answers will give you great insights into the culture.

- **TAKE TIME** to be with others so that you can learn more about what they have to offer and what you can give back, whether it's lunch, walking together to the parking lot, joining an after-work sports team or an employees' parents group, or volunteering for a special project like running the department's United Way campaign.

- **SEEK DIVERSITY** by seeking out people outside your immediate department, and people who typically disagree with you. These people can offer you more insights because they are different. That's valuable.

- **YOUR PERSONAL BRAND** and your interests can guide you on when to help and when not to. If someone asks or seems to need something that is right up your alley, do it. Whether it's on-the-job expertise, or an interest in teaching or drawing, offer up what you do best. It can improve your reputation, your network, and your relationships.

- **Use subtle self-promotion techniques.** Sometimes it's not enough to perform well; you need to also make your superiors aware of your achievements—without bragging. Focus on your experience, not on yourself. Whenever you talk with coworkers and immediate managers, be positive and enthusiastic about your job and your projects. Speak with confidence about your experience and accomplishments, but avoid making too many "I" statements.

▶ **CAREER ACTION**
Complete Worksheet 13-5
Prepare for Advancement, page 385

Prepare for Your Performance Evaluation

Learn how and when you will be evaluated on your job performance so that you know where to focus your efforts to achieve a good evaluation. This will also help you avoid overlooking an area that is important to your employer.

Find out how heavily the employer weighs each performance area so that you can concentrate on the most important ones. If you don't receive this information with your other employment documents, ask your immediate manager or HR resource to explain the evaluation process.

If your employer uses an informal method of job evaluation, ask what is considered good job performance and what criteria are used in determining promotions and raises. This will

provide you with guidelines for your successful performance. As you become more knowledgeable about your job, show initiative by setting your own goals and deadlines for improving performance and growing in the job.

Kzenon/Shutterstock.com

Adapt to Changes in Your Employer and Industry

Your working life—the period of time in your life when you work—will last about 55 years, and maybe longer. Over the course of your working life, changes will occur in the companies you work for, in society, in your industry, and in every industry. Keep an open, flexible attitude toward changes at work. Don't make yourself obsolete through stubborn resistance; you may miss an open door to a career development opportunity.

Expect differences (some major) between the way your employer conducts business and the methods you learned in school or on another job. While schools often teach theories, employers interpret and apply theories and techniques (often developing their own) to accomplish specific work goals and tasks. Changes in technology make some textbook

theories obsolete. Personalities also influence work methods.

Continually update your skills and knowledge through education and training. Request training and if you are not able to participate, find informal ways to stay up to date using the Internet or outside of work resources such as professional associations. You are living in an economy that is based increasingly on knowledge and service and less on manufacturing and goods.

The Value of Staying Externally Connected

When you accept a job offer and start work at your new workplace, don't forget the strong social media presence you have built. Building a career is not just something you do between jobs. It should be something you think about even when you're happy in your work. It's important to keep your skills sharp, to stay up to date in industry advances, and to keep yourself relevant in the field. Social media platforms are ideal for ongoing career networking and development because they are free or low cost and require little investment of time. There's really no excuse not to take charge of your career online!

- Keep your LinkedIn profile updated and check in regularly to expand your network as you meet people in your line of work. Request recommendations from coworkers who can attest to your proficiency and professionalism and join groups that relate to your career field.

- Subscribe to email updates and newsletters for top industry blogs. Don't be afraid to comment on articles that interest you and share your own knowledge, within what your company guidelines allow.

- Do periodic searches on Twitter using industry-specific keywords. Respond to and retweet interesting tweets you find. Share articles you've discovered using Twitter and establish yourself as a knowledgeable professional.

- Leverage other social media platforms that are popular for your industry.

If social media participation is encouraged, show your support for your employer by speaking well of the employer and its personnel, products, and services. Stay active in your career field's community by continuing to share quality content and listening to thought leaders. There are several benefits to taking the time to maintain your online network:

- You may learn new information that you can bring to your workplace.

- Your passion for the field and personal growth will help you stand out as an employee and could propel you toward career growth in the future.

- Your Career Network will still be active if you need to find a job in the future.

- You can give back to others who are looking for jobs.

IS IT TIME FOR A CHANGE?

A job involves performing a designated set of responsibilities and duties for a specific employer. A career encompasses a family of jobs. Your career is your life's work. For example, a *high school history teacher for Washington High School* is a job and *teaching* is a career. Similarly, *evening wear salesclerk for the After Five store* is a job and *retail sales* is a career.

Many people don't understand the difference between a job and a career. As a result, they spend a great deal of time and money changing careers when they only need to change jobs. In other cases, people change jobs repeatedly and continue to be dissatisfied because they're not in the right career. Most people change jobs at least eight times during their working lives. With changes in technology and in people's values and interests, it's also common for people to change careers at least once during their lifetime.

If you realize that your current employment situation is no longer satisfying, consider whether the dissatisfaction is with your career or with the specific job. If you're unhappy with your immediate manager but enjoy your work, for example, you may need to change jobs. If you don't enjoy the type of work you do, however, you may want to consider a career change.

Think Carefully Before Changing Jobs

You may want to consider a job change if:

- Your current employer can't offer you job growth or advancement

- A poor economy requires layoffs or an entire class of jobs is being shipped overseas in an offshoring trend
- You want to move to a new location
- Your department is dissolving
- Your philosophy and values conflict with those of your current employer
- You want a new challenge

Give any change of job serious thought and planning. A job may look good, but without proper research, you could find yourself in a situation that is as bad as or worse than your current one. Evaluate your current job by asking yourself, "Is there room for advancement, or are other important opportunities available?" If the answer is no and you will not be happy staying in your current position, you have strong grounds for considering a new employer. If the answer is yes, there may be advantages to staying with your current employer.

Seeking advancement or growth with your current employer can offer many advantages, including the following:

- Staying is less risky because you are already established and don't need to repeat the process of adjusting to new surroundings and people.

- Your reputation for job stability is better if you stay rather than move frequently from one employer to another.

- In outsourcing and offshoring situations, some employers recognize the value of keeping their best employees. They may offer you retraining opportunities and help you transition out of a vulnerable position.

- You won't lose accumulated benefits such as vacation time, retirement, and profit sharing.

- If your current job offers important benefits such as healthcare coverage and life insurance, it can be risky to give them up. With today's rising cost of benefits, some employers are finding it too expensive to provide extensive coverage. When considering a job change, always consider benefits in conjunction with rewards and compensation.

Alternatively, changing employers can also offer many advantages, including the following:

- You increase your job engagement and motivation by becoming involved with new challenges, surroundings, and people.

- A job change may result in quicker advancement than you could achieve by seeking a promotion in your current company.

- You gain knowledge, broaden your experience, and increase your Career Network, expanding your career growth opportunities.

- You start with a clean slate as you develop your reputation for good job performance.

Strategies if You Want to Change Jobs

Before you quit your current job, make sure you follow these strategies:

- Reconnect with your network. To achieve the greatest levels of career success, stay in touch with your contacts so that you are ready the next time you want to pursue a career goal.

- Try to avoid quitting your job before you have a new one. If possible, complete your job change while you are still employed. Because being employed is current proof that you do a job satisfactorily, you're considered more employable when you're currently working.

Take Stock of Your Situation

Accepting a job or changing jobs is a big decision! On average, Americans who are fully employed spend 2,000 hours per year at work. When you consider a job offer, think about your current situation and your goals for the future.

If You Have a Job:

- Are you sure you want to change jobs?

- Why do you think the new job is a better opportunity?

- Does the work sound as interesting as you thought it would?

- Is the new job in a more stable industry or with a more stable employer?

- Will you have more opportunities for advancement or more interesting work?

- Do you like your future immediate manager and future coworkers?

- Does the new job have better benefits?

- Have you hit a plateau in your current job?

If You Are Not Working:

- How long have you been looking for a job?

- How much longer can you afford to look for a job?

- How many jobs have you applied for without getting an interview?

- How many interviews have you had without getting a job offer?

- What is the job market like where you live?

- Are you willing to take the risk of declining a job?

- What is your backup plan if you decline a job?

Ask a career professional and a trusted member of your network (or both) for help weighing the pros and cons of your decisions.

pan_kung/Shutterstock.com

- Do your current job to the best of your ability through your last day on the job. You're most likely to be remembered by how well you performed at the end of your employment. This can greatly influence the quality of future references from your current employer.

- Update your Master Career Portfolio before you leave. Assemble samples of your work and documentation of your achievements that are pertinent and exemplary. Update your master resume. Ask your coworkers and immediate manager to recommend you on LinkedIn. Add documents from each job you hold, such as your job description and performance evaluations. Print copies of emails commending your work and forward them to your personal email account.

- Plan for an orderly and efficient transition of your responsibilities to the person

OVERCOMING BARRIERS
Think Like a Free Agent

Monkey Business Images/
Shutterstock.com

An employer and an employee are partners in a contract that must work for both parties. A job may be temporary, so think about your options and be prepared to take the next step in your career. Being able to adapt to change is also a valuable life skill. If you lose your job and cannot find a full-time position, you may need to consider a series of part-time jobs until you find full-time employment. One of your achievements in this course is your Master Career Portfolio. You may also need to develop a "portfolio career"—a career made up of a variety of jobs and activities that capitalize on your strengths and provide an acceptable level of income. These may include part-time jobs, temporary jobs, contract work, and maybe even a hobby that you can turn into a home-based business.

taking your place. If you are asked to help train your replacement, be as thorough as possible, taking care to explain your duties clearly and completely.

- Give your current employer at least two weeks' written notice before you leave your job. This is common courtesy and is important in maintaining good standing with your employer. Giving less notice is considered unprofessional. You should submit a formal letter of resignation.

- Resign professionally. Make every effort to leave your current employer with good feelings; do not leave in anger or with hostility no matter how dissatisfied you might be. Throughout your career, references from your past employers will be requested each time you seek a new job. If possible, request a letter of recommendation prior to your last day.

Changing Careers

If, after thorough consideration, you decide that you aren't happy in your work and that a change to another job in the same field would not bring satisfaction, you may want to consider a career change. Ask yourself the following questions:

- **Have I changed positions several times only to find that I'm still unhappy?** Repeated changes of employment that don't improve your job satisfaction may indicate a career problem, not a job problem.

- **Are my problems the result of personality or philosophical conflicts with my immediate manager or coworkers?** If so, it's likely that you need a new employer rather than a new career. The exception occurs when the types of people usually found in your career field, regardless of the company, don't fit your personality or philosophy.

- **Am I unhappy with the work environment?** If you don't like working at a desk, for example, decide whether this is common to your career field or only to your job. Would you prefer outdoor work? You may want to look at other careers if your career doesn't provide the opportunity for the type of work you want. Is your problem with the work environment common to the career or only to some jobs in the career field?

- **Am I constrained in expressing my values?** Again, is this a function of your job or your career?

- **Is my position interesting?** What are your interests? Are you unable to satisfy them in your career or just in your current job?

- **Am I frustrated that I'm not using my skills and abilities?** Is this a job-related or career-related problem?

Even if you determine that your unhappiness is related to your career rather than your current job, you still have to weigh the pros and cons of making a career change. Rarely can you just jump into another career without making sacrifices, such as taking a cut in pay. You need to evaluate the advantages and disadvantages and decide whether you're gaining more than you're losing.

Reassess Your Situation

First, determine what alternative careers match your interests and abilities. Study the options to decide the career you think is the best match. Apply the strategies in Chapters 2 and 3. Then after you have selected an alternative career, find out what additional education or training you need, how long it takes to prepare for the field, and what it will cost. Also determine whether the education or training is available nearby and whether you can get the necessary skills while continuing your current job or if you need to return to school and/or relocate.

Be Realistic

What are the job opportunities in the new field? Are the jobs in a desirable location, and will the pay meet your requirements? Be aware that when you change careers, you often have to start over at the entry-level compensation.

What kind of risk taker are you? Are you willing to give up the security of your current position and career and take a chance? Do you expect to be significantly more satisfied in the new career? In the final analysis, decide whether the probable advantages of a new opportunity sufficiently outweigh the disadvantages and whether you are willing to assume any risk involved.

You should also be prepared to discuss your decision persuasively with potential employers who may question whether you will be happy with such a career change. It is important to convey to employers that you have considered and planned for this change carefully and that you believe the advantages outweigh the disadvantages.

Congratulations! You've come to the end of the Job Search Journey and the beginning of a career. You've done a great deal of work in the activities in *Your Career: How to Make It Happen.* The advice and cautions you have learned and the documents you have created can help you stay ahead of the competition throughout your career. Save the work you've done in this class—you'll be glad you did.

Chapter Checklist

Check off each item you can do. Reread sections in this chapter to help you complete the checklist.

- ☐ Transition my mindset from finding a job to confidently starting my career. **❶**
- ☐ Create a plan for my first weeks at work that include learning about my new role, skills needed, company, and resources. **❶**
- ☐ Discover what success looks like for my role, from my immediate manager's point of view and from the company's point of view. **❶**
- ☐ Identify who makes up my network at work; and map them within the four network groups. **❶**
- ☐ Know what is needed to build and develop long-lasting relationships at work. **❷**
- ☐ Understand how to work well and communicate with my immediate manager. **❷**
- ☐ Maximize my compensation and benefits to support my life and career. **❸**
- ☐ Expect changes in the workplace to occur and be flexible and adaptable when faced with changes. **❸**
- ☐ Take steps to become—and be seen as—promotable. **❸**
- ☐ Stay in contact with network members and add to my network. **❹**
- ☐ Evaluate whether it is time to change jobs. **❹**
- ☐ Evaluate whether this career is the best fit. **❹**
- ☐ Keep good records of job duties and accomplishments in every position and be prepared to begin a job search quickly and efficiently. **❹**

Critical Thinking Questions

1. What differences are there in mindset, habits, and approach between finding a job and starting a job? **❶**
2. What five things can you do to master a new job? **❶**
3. Why is it important to develop many positive relationships at work? **❷**
4. Why is it important to know how your performance will be evaluated? **❸**
5. Who is responsible for the growth of your career? What are five things you can do to help yourself stay satisfied? **❸❹**
6. Why is it essential to adapt to change? How can you demonstrate that you are flexible and adaptable? **❸**

7.   What additional training or course work could you take to increase your knowledge and skills? ❸

8.   Why should you be very careful when considering changing jobs or careers? What are the potential consequences? ❹

Trial Run

Follow Your Leader ❸

Every field has thought leaders or leading companies. For example, in accounting, every year there is a CPA Practice Advisor Thought Leader Symposium. Do an Internet search on your career path. Who are some of the thought leaders or award winners in your career of choice? Pick two thought leaders and review their bios. Take a look at their LinkedIn profiles and the latest updates on their social media platforms. Answer the following questions for each leader:

Question	Leader:_____	Leader: _____
1. Did they have multiple job or career changes?		
2. How did each job or career change contribute to their successful position today?		
3. What values and strengths do they have and/or admire?		
4. What surprised or inspired you about their career path?		
5. From your review, summarize how they achieved success in their career.		

This page is intentionally blank.

▶ *CAREER ACTION WORKSHEET*

13-1   Planning Your Work ❶

Most successful people have a written plan. Start your new job with a solid plan. Update your plan as you learn more on the job. Check off the following planning items as you put them in place during your first days at work.

Your organization systems: Starting a new job requires new organization systems.

☐ **Get a system.** Before your first day, get prepared by selecting some type of planner to organize your workweeks: a spiral-bound planner, the planner in your email program or some other planner on your computer, or a planner app on your smartphone.

☐ **Determine priorities.** Determine your priorities and plan your work around them. Ask your immediate manager and coworkers what tasks are most vital to the successful operation of your department. Prioritize your work based on their answers.

☐ **Form daily habits.** At the beginning or end of the day, take 5 or 10 minutes to plan the day's work. On paper or online, make a list of the things you need to do that day.

☐ **Diligently record.** Record appointments, meetings, assignments, deadlines, and reminders. Enter important tasks and dates as soon as you learn of them so that you don't forget to enter them later. Consider using one color for work obligations and another color for personal obligations.

Block off time to work on larger projects and longer-term assignments so that you don't end up having to do them all at once and miss deadlines for your ongoing work. For example, if you are giving a presentation at a meeting on Thursday, block off time to work on the presentation on Monday, Tuesday, and Wednesday. Make larger projects achievable by listing the smaller steps you need to do. Using to-do lists is a powerful, yet simple way to help you manage and achieve milestones in a large project. Here are some helpful approaches to to-do lists:

Manage Large Projects Well

- Put the most important tasks at the top of the list (tasks that need immediate attention or completion).

- List the tasks as you think of them and then label them A (most important tasks), B (tasks to do after you complete the A tasks), and C (tasks with no specific deadline).

- Beside each task, write the deadline for completing it and the amount of time you think it will take. Be realistic about time requirements, especially when you are new on the job, and ask your immediate manager or a coworker for advice.

- Group similar tasks and complete them in one block of time. This focuses your attention and enhances task performance. For example, schedule one block of time to prepare documents and another to place phone calls.

Reassess Priorities

As new tasks are assigned, periodically review your priorities with your team or immediate manager. Here are questions that you can ask to make the conversation go smoothly:

- Here are our top priorities as I see it for the next week. Do you agree with these?

- Help me understand what has changed that might impact our (or my) priorities.

- If this is our (or my) new set of priorities, can we change the due dates on these other items? If not, what additional resources can we get to assure we have capacity to meet the deadlines and the new priorities?

Add your completed work to the "About Jobs" section of your Career Builder Files.

▶ *CAREER ACTION WORKSHEET*

13-2   Learn About Your Job Checklist ❶

Use this worksheet as a template to ask questions and note answers as you learn about your role and the skills needed to perform your best.

✓	Question/Task	Notes/Findings
	Obtain a copy of your detailed job description.	
	Obtain and discuss your work plan with your immediate manager.	
	What are the primary individual assignments you will be spending the majority of your day on?	
	How is success measured for each assignment?	
	What tools will you need to complete each assignment?	
	Who will you interact with for each assignment?	
	How is success measured for your overall role?	
	What knowledge and skills are critical for you to deliver each assignment?	
	What gaps do you have in the knowledge needed to deliver each assignment?	

(Continued)

✓	Question/Task	Notes/Findings
	What training do you need to close each gap in knowledge? (Include both formal classroom training and informal training such as shadowing others along with coach, mentor, and immediate manager guidance and feedback)	
	What is the expected timeline for gaining the knowledge? (Put formal trainings on your calendar and note the expected time it should take for informal training to be completed)	
	When are you expected to be a fully functioning, high-performing employee? What is the expected length of onboarding time?	
	Have you filled out all the necessary HR paperwork and reviewed it carefully?	
	Do you have all the equipment necessary to do your job and access your work environment? (computer, phone, uniform, tools, security badge, etc.)	
	Have you been added to the appropriate lists for internal email conferences, information distribution, project teams, and so on?	
	Have you understood all employer policies, including confidentiality procedures, performance, payroll, vacations, and benefits?	

Add your completed work to the "About Jobs" section of your Career Builder Files.

▶ CAREER ACTION WORKSHEET

13-3   Learn About Your Company Checklist ❶

Use this worksheet as a template to ask questions and note answers as you learn about the company and how you will play a role in helping the company succeed.

✓	Question/Task	Notes/Findings
	What is the company's mission?	
	What are the company's values?	
	What is the company's vision? usually more future-focused than a mission statement	
	What are your direct department's vision and measurable goals?	
	How does your role contribute to meeting your department's goals?	
	How does your role contribute to meeting your company's goals?	
	What is the organizational structure? What are the different departments and levels that make up the employer?	
	What are the products and services my company sells? What is your role in these products and services (or details about one specific product/service you will be working on)?	

(Continued)

✓	Question/Task	Notes/Findings
	Who does your company compete with in the marketplace?	
	What is the history of your company? What major changes has your company been through?	
	Take a tour of the building.	
	What is the culture of your department? What is the dress code? What is the level of formality in the workplace? How hierarchical is the culture? How balanced are work and life? Do people bring their personality to the workplace? How well do people know one another?	
	What is your company's policy on employee use of personal social media during work hours?	
	What is your company's policy on employees' professional social media use regarding company matters?	
	Learn common acronyms and phrases used to describe the work.	

Add your completed work to the "About Jobs" section of your Career Builder Files.

▶ CAREER ACTION WORKSHEET

13-4   Internal Resource Network Map ❷ ❸

Fill out the map below by adding the names of key relationships important to the success of your work. If you have any gaps, try to learn who the right people are in your workplace and start building relationships with them. What are some internal and external thought leaders you would like to follow to stay informed and on the cutting edge? Put a circle or star next to the internal thought leaders you would like to follow. Go online and connect or follow the external thought leaders you think will help you stay current.

It may be helpful to ask your immediate manager, department administrator, or HR resource for an organization chart of your department. Also, you can create your own organization chart using PowerPoint or other Microsoft Office tools. Templates for org charts are available online.

Remember to add these people to one or more of your four network groups (work, organization, professional, life).

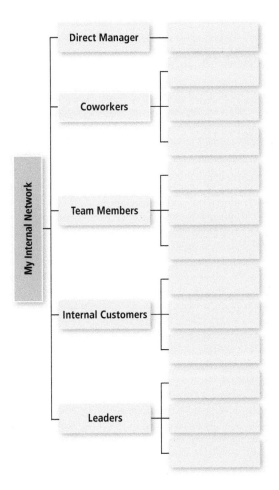

Add your completed work to the "About Jobs" section of your Career Builder Files.

This page is intentionally blank.

▶ CAREER ACTION WORKSHEET

13-5   Prepare for Advancement ❸ ❹

Career Action Worksheet 13-5 is a sample job performance rating form that is representative of the forms used by many companies. Typically, your immediate manager will rate your performance in the left column. If you don't have the performance template for your job, use the template below to help you think through the assessment process.

For this Career Action Worksheet, there are several parts:

A. Rating: Rate yourself in the left column. Assign yourself a score of 1 to 3 with 1 representing high performance and 3 representing low performance. Then chose two or three categories where you would like to do even be even better. Next, list action items that will help you improve your performance.

B. Overall: Consider your overall performance. Use an *X* to mark what you think your performance is. Mark with an *M* what you think your manager might rate you. Consider why this difference might exist and what you can do to ensure you both view your performance similarly.

C. Short Term: What would you like to be able to do in the short term, say, 6 to 18 months from now? A good goal is to become advancement-ready. Advancement is defined here based on your personal goals—whether that means being promoted, working more independently, moving laterally to another department or function, or becoming a master in your existing role. With your manager and/or mentor(s), list a few things you can focus on that will help you achieve your short-term goals.

D. Long Term: What would you like to be able to do in five to seven years? Again, with your manager and/or mentor(s), determine what things you can start doing now to meet this goal. Have a serious discussion about the probability of this goal becoming a reality, and if they view you as capable of even more or would advise you to take a different route. The primary value of this section is the discussion between you and others.

E. Manager's Summary: This is where your manager writes her or his viewpoint and signs it. You too may be asked to sign it. Be clear on whether you are signing to say "I agree" or "I have read this."

Rating[1]*	Performance or Behavioral Category	Action Items
	ABILITY TO ACQUIRE AND USE INFORMATION AND FOLLOW INSTRUCTIONS (Uses initiative in acquiring, interpreting, and following instructions and using references)	
	INTERPERSONAL SKILLS (Is tactful, understanding, and efficient when dealing with people)	
	BASIC SKILLS (Is proficient in reading, writing, mathematics, listening, and verbal and nonverbal communication)	
	JOB SKILLS (Demonstrates command of required knowledge and skills)	
	THINKING/PROBLEM-SOLVING SKILLS (Generates new ideas, makes decisions, solves problems, and reasons logically)	
	ABILITY TO COOPERATE WITH OTHERS (Works well with team members and under supervision, exercises leadership, and works well with people of diverse backgrounds)	
	QUANTITY OF WORK (Does required amount of work)	
	QUALITY OF WORK (Does neat, accurate, complete, and efficient work)	
	GOOD WORK HABITS (Maintains good attendance and punctuality, is dependable, and follows safety/work procedures)	
	ATTITUDE (Demonstrates enthusiasm, interest, and motivation)	
	TECHNOLOGY (Works well with technology —tools, computers, and procedures)	
	PERSONAL QUALITIES (Demonstrates responsibility, initiative, self-confidence, integrity, and honesty; practices good self-management; sets and maintains goals; exhibits self-motivation; and is cooperative)	
	LEADERSHIP SKILL (Demonstrates leadership and ownership of role)	

* Use a rating of 1 to 3, where 1 is best and 3 is not acceptable. Note that at many companies 80% of people are typically rated as average (or 2).

Overall Evaluation of Performance and Behavior

Your immediate manager will provide an overall rating of your performance based on the company's rating code (shown here as Outstanding, Very Good, Good, Acceptable, or Unacceptable).

_____ Outstanding _____ Very Good _____ Good _____ Acceptable _____ Unacceptable

Employee's Short-Term Goals (List your short-term job or career goals here and actions you and your manager can take now to help you reach each goal.)

Short-Term Goal	Action Items

Employee's Long-Term Goals (List your long-term job or career goals here and actions you and your manager can take now to help you reach each goal.)

Long-Term Goal	Action Items

Suggestions for Improving Performance or Behavior (While a typical performance evaluation will not have the right column "Action Items," there usually is a section for suggested actions to improve your work performance or behavior.)

General Comments About Employee's Job Performance (Your immediate manager will also add any other appropriate comments to describe the quality of your work performance.)

Signature of Immediate Manager (This is where your immediate manager would sign your performance evaluation.)

Note: Save your performance review documents to provide insights and reminders about where you have been on your career journey, where you are now, and where you might go next.

Add your completed work to the "About Me" section of your Career Builder Files.

This page is intentionally blank.

Your Career: Making It Happen

This guide contains helpful reminders and tips to help with your Job Search Journey. Tear it on the perforation or print out these pages and use it to complete job applications and prepare for interviews.

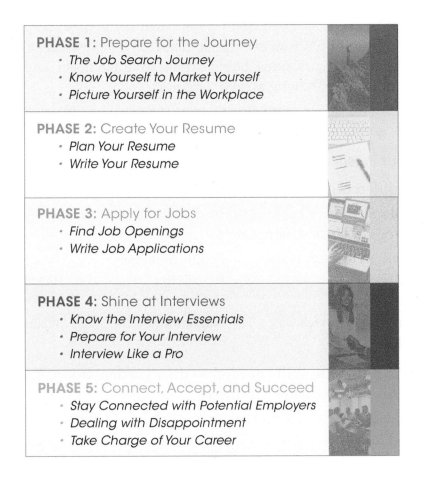

PHASE 1: Prepare for the Journey
- *The Job Search Journey*
- *Know Yourself to Market Yourself*
- *Picture Yourself in the Workplace*

PHASE 2: Create Your Resume
- *Plan Your Resume*
- *Write Your Resume*

PHASE 3: Apply for Jobs
- *Find Job Openings*
- *Write Job Applications*

PHASE 4: Shine at Interviews
- *Know the Interview Essentials*
- *Prepare for Your Interview*
- *Interview Like a Pro*

PHASE 5: Connect, Accept, and Succeed
- *Stay Connected with Potential Employers*
- *Dealing with Disappointment*
- *Take Charge of Your Career*

PHASE 1: PREPARE FOR THE JOURNEY

A. Organize Your Job Search by setting up your Career Builder Files using these three parts:

- **About Me:** This section contains a collection of records, awards, information about you, your thoughts about jobs and your career, and drafts of your Personal Brand Statement.

- **About Jobs:** Use this section to track job leads, contact information for people you talk to, your research about career fields and job listings, and your draft job applications and resumes.

- **Master Career Portfolio:** In this section, collect documents you will share with others, especially during interviews, such as your final resume and job applications, samples of your work, cover letters, and thank-you notes.

B. Assess and Market Yourself by creating a Personal Brand Statement based on your skills and strengths.

Personal Brand Statement Formula

1. What one or two words describe what you do in general terms (examples: thinker, doer, innovator, educator, caring person, organizer, actor, designer, worker)?

2. What are you known for (examples: delivering results despite challenges, balancing multiple priorities, being driven to finish tasks, knowing the right flavor combination, having an eye for color)?

3. What sets you apart from your peers (examples: speed, thoroughness, kindness, gentleness, logic)?

4. Write your Personal Brand Statement: I am a _____ that _____.

Recall there is a difference between transferable skills and job-specific skills.

- **Transferable Skills** are basic skills and abilities that can be applied to many different types of work. Examples:

Computer and technology skills	People Manager	Problem Solver
Multi-tasker	Researcher	Teach others
Project Manager	Skilled at Analysis	Use resources wisely
Skilled at Customer Service	Negotiator	Write clearly
Public Speaker		

- **Job-Specific Skills** are skills needed to do a particular job. These may often have a certification or license. Examples:

Take blood pressure	Drive a truck or vehicle	Give a customer a manicure
Operate a forklift	Create a balance sheet	Repair a dented fender
Frame a house	Train a police dog	

C. Explore Career Fields using your Career Network and websites provided by federal and state agencies such as the U.S. Bureau of Labor Statistics (BLS) or state business needs. A good example is the CareerOneStop website. Also use job boards like LinkedIn, Indeed.com, and other emerging sites.

PHASE 2: CREATE YOUR RESUME

A. Plan Your Resume
RESUME OUTLINE:

1. Contact Information
2. Professional Profile
3. Qualifications

4. Work Experience

5. Education

6. Optional Sections
   - Related Experience
   - Military Service

B. Write Your Resume

a) Use this guide to evaluate your resume:

Rating Scale: 1 to 4 (1 = not really; 2 = sometimes/somewhat; 3 = usually; 4 = definitely)

_____ **1.** The Objective or Professional Profile includes the job title or required abilities specified by the employer.

_____ **2.** Qualifications contain keywords that match requirements for the job.

_____ **3.** Qualifications are concise with three to five words per bullet point.

_____ **4.** Qualifications are relevant to the stated job objective. Major strengths are included.

_____ **5.** Work Experiences use the WHI method.

_____ **6.** Work Experiences focus on quantifiable achievements and results.

_____ **7.** Work Experience bullet points do not include long run-on sentences or unnecessary words.

_____ **8.** If work experience is limited, relevant paid and nonpaid internships and volunteer or other pertinent activities are included.

_____ **9.** The job seeker emphasizes courses, internships, degrees, certificates, and so on that best support the objective.

_____ **10.** The overall GPA or GPA in the concentration area is included (if impressive).

_____ **11.** The job seeker emphasizes involvement in professional and other organizations that support the job objective.

_____ **12.** Relevant awards, achievements, and offices held are included.

_____ **13.** The overall design is appealing.

_____ **14.** When you skim the resume for 30 seconds you get a feel for who the applicant is.

_____ **15.** The content is correct (grammar, spelling, and punctuation).

NOTE: The Internet offers up-to-date resume templates.

b) Use ACTION VERBS or power words that clearly describe your scope of responsibility and convey a sense of accomplishment:

Accelerate	Discover	Order	Repair
Advise	Distribute	Organize	Report
Analyze	Edit	Originate	Represent
Approve	Eliminate	Oversee	Research
Arrange	Enforce	Participate	Resolve
Assemble	Establish	Perform	Respond
Assist	Evaluate	Plan	Retrieve
Audit	Examine	Prepare	Review
Budget	Expand	Present	Revise
Build	Expedite	Prioritize	Schedule
Change	Forecast	Process	Select
Collaborate	Formulate	Produce	Sell
Collect	Generate	Program	Serve
Communicate	Handle	Promote	Set up
Complete	Identify	Propose	Solve
Compute	Implement	Protect	Specialize
Conduct	Improve	Prove	Start
Control	Increase	Provide	Streamline
Coordinate	Influence	Publish	Structure
Create	Install	Purchase	Study
Customize	Instruct	Raise	Supervise
Delegate	Integrate	Receive	Support
Deliver	Lead	Recommend	Teach
Demonstrate	Maintain	Reconcile	Test
Design	Manage	Record	Track
Detect	Monitor	Redesign	Train
Develop	Motivate	Reduce	Update
Diagnose	Obtain	Reinforce	Upgrade
Diagram	Operate	Reorganize	Write
Direct			

Optimize Your Keywords for search by including job titles, specialized skills and tools, industry buzzwords, jargon, acronyms, and words and phrases in job descriptions and listings. Employers and applicant tracking systems look for keywords that indicate the person is qualified for the job. Review the websites and publications of companies and professional associations in your industry.

PHASE 3: APPLY FOR JOBS

A. Find Job Openings using the Career Network Warm Introduction and the Cold Leads strategies.

    a. List your Network. It has four parts: Life, Work, Org, and Industry.

    b. Conduct Career Networking Meetings using the directions below.

  1. Identify at least two people in your career field.

  2. Call or email the person and ask for a 30-minute meeting to learn about his or her job and discuss your job search.

  3. Prepare for the meeting. Note the following questions and remember to bring your resume and business cards:

Conversation starters
- What drew you to this career field?
- Is this your first job in this career field?
- How long have you worked at your company?

Job and career questions
- What is your typical workday like?
- Which parts of your job do you find most challenging? Most enjoyable?
- What is the culture like at your workplace/in this career field?
- What is a typical career path at your company?
- What do you wish you had known when you started your career?
- What changes have you seen in this field? What changes do you anticipate?

Career advice
- What advice do you have for someone looking for a job in this field?
- Does my job goal seem realistic and achievable?
- Do you recommend any additional training or certifications?
- What professional or other associations do you recommend joining?
- What publications or websites do you recommend?
- Who else would you recommend I speak with? When I call, may I use your name?

  4. Follow-up and evaluation—send a thank you to the person you met with and to the person who helped you get the meeting. Summarize what you learned, evaluate your performance, and store your notes in your Career Builder Files.

    c. Apply the Cold Leads Strategy Use just a few online jobsites that are good for your industry. Keep track of all jobs you apply for and know which version of your resume and cover letter you sent.

B. Write Job Applications

Apply only to jobs that are a good match to your job target or stretch job descriptions. Be totally truthful and consistent with what is on your social media profiles. Apply quickly after the job is posted and follow instructions very carefully. Follow up.

Write Cover Letters when a job application has an option for this and for a few select jobs that you'd really like to have.

Create a Job Application Package with your application, job resume, business card, and select portfolio items. Send this for select jobs you are highly interested in, in order to gain attention.

PHASE 4: SHINE AT INTERVIEWS

A. Prepare and Practice before the interview, by doing these things: Research the company's website and search for them in the news • Know where you're going (address, location, maps, offices) • Research your interviewer • Review the interview preparation checklist • Practice your stories • Complete any pre-interview tests • Prepare and practice your body language • Check your appearance • Remember to use business etiquette • Practice good verbal skills.

B. Take Pre-Employment Tests and other screening tests and interviews. For each of these, do the following: Be prepared • Focus on why you are interested in working for the potential employer • Be professional, courteous, and friendly • Be factual in your answers, as well as be brief yet thorough.

C. Interview Like a Pro using the following checklists before, during, and after your interviews.

BEFORE YOUR INTERVIEW

General Job-Related Materials from Your Master Career Portfolio

☐ A copy of the job posting or description

☐ A copy of your application for this job posting

☐ Your customized resume—copies for the interviewer(s), yourself, and an extra

☐ A copy of your customized cover letter if you created one for this job posting

☐ Portfolio materials and job-related samples of your work

☐ Certificates, licenses, transcripts, and related documents

☐ Letters of recommendation (for this job or this specific type of work)

☐ Lists of references (general endorsement of your character, knowledge, and skills)

☐ Business or contact cards, if you have these, including your professional social media platform usernames

Marketing Materials from Your Master Career Portfolio

☐ A copy of your targeted 30-Second Commercial (for your use only)

☐ A reminder list of examples and stories you can tell (for your use only)

Organizing Materials

- ☐ A notebook with questions you can ask during the interview (see Chapter 10)
- ☐ A businesslike pen—not too cheap, expensive, flashy, or quirky
- ☐ A note pad to take notes (ask permission to take notes before doing so)
- ☐ Your appointment calendar (if you use your smartphone, turn the sound off before you even walk in the building!)
- ☐ A list of the names, titles, and phone numbers of people related to this interview

DURING YOUR INTERVIEW: Be prepared for the type of interview you will be participating in:

Screening Interview • Computer-Based Interview • Campus Interview • Phone Interview • Video Interview • Behavioral Interview • Panel Interview • Team Interview

Common Questions

General Interview Questions:

1. Why do you want this job?
2. What type of work do you enjoy most?
3. What are your strongest skills?
4. Are you a team player?
5. What are your long-term career goals, and how do you plan to achieve them?
6. Do you have a geographic preference? Are you willing to relocate?
7. With what type of supervisor have you had the best relationships?

Behavioral Questions:

1. Describe an accomplishment that demonstrates your initiative.
2. Tell me specifically about a time when you worked under great stress.
3. Describe an experience when you dealt with an angry customer or coworker.
4. Give me an example of your ability to adapt to change.
5. Explain what problems you have encountered. How did you overcome them?

Answering Behavioral Questions:

1. Describe the situation. (What)
2. Explain the actions you took. (How)
3. Describe the outcomes. (Importance)
4. Summarize what you learned from the experience. (Insights from you)

Character Questions:

1. How would you describe yourself?
2. What rewards do you look for in your career?

3. What accomplishment are you most proud of, particularly as it relates to your field?

4. Do you work well under pressure?

Stress/Difficult Questions:

1. Why do you think you are the best candidate for the job? *or* Why should I hire you?

2. Why do you want to leave your current job?

3. Why have you held so many jobs?

4. What is your greatest weakness?

5. Have you ever been fired from a job?

6. Does your current employer know you are planning to leave?

AFTER YOUR INTERVIEW:

Questions You Should Ask:

1. Do you have a training program for this position? If so, will you describe it?

2. Can you tell me about the duties and tasks of this position on a typical workday?

3. May I have a copy of the written job description?

4. Will the responsibilities of this position expand with time and experience on the job? Can good performance in this job lead to opportunities for career growth?

5. Can you tell me about the people I would work with? To whom does this position report?

6. Do you need any more information about my qualifications or experience?

7. When will you be making your hiring decision? What does your hiring process and timeline look like? May I call you if I have additional questions?

Before You Leave the Interview:

- Clarify what, if anything, you should do to follow up.
- Clarify when a decision will be made.
- Ask how the interviewer prefers you to follow up (by phone, by letter, by email, or in person).
- Make a point of leaving your interviewer with a clear picture of how you fit the job.
- Watch for signs from the interviewer that it's time to wrap up the interview, and run the short version of your 30-Second Commercial to restate your skills, experience, and other assets that meet the employer's needs.
- Ask the interviewer to notify you when a candidate has been selected.
- Determine any follow-up activities the interviewer expects from you.
- If you're seriously interested in the job, say so!
- If you haven't been given one, ask the interviewer for a business card.
- Finally, remember to use the interviewer's name: "Thank you for interviewing me, Ms. Carpenter."

PHASE 5: CONNECT, ACCEPT, AND SUCCEED

A. Stay Connected with Potential Employers by evaluating your interview performance, planning your schedule for follow-up, and sending prompt thank-you letters. Evaluate job offers based on the entire package, including how well they fit your long-term career goals. Respond to job offers professionally, whether accepting or declining.

B. Develop Strategies for increasing your chances of getting interviews, improving your interview performance, and managing a rejection notice.

C. Take Charge of Your Career over the long term by onboarding quickly to your new job; building successful relationships; managing your career path; and assessing when the time is right to change jobs and/or careers.

30-Second Commercials
verbal scripts or media based on your unique Personal Brand Statement that highlights your strongest qualities and shows how they will benefit the employer. It is used to capture the attention of target employers for jobs that are a good career fit for you.

A

About Jobs one of the three portfolios that make up your Career Builder Files: contains information about job leads, contact information for people you talk to about jobs, your research about career fields and job postings, and your draft job applications and resumes.

About Me one of the three portfolios that make up your Career Builder Files; contains a collection of records, awards, information about you, your thoughts about jobs and your career, and drafts of your Personal Brand Statement.

action verbs in a resume and cover letter, concrete verbs and phrases that reflect very specifically the action taken to meet a goal (for example, *build, prepare,* and *test*).

active listening a communication technique that requires the listener to understand, interpret, and evaluate what he or she hears; listening with the goal of understanding what the speaker intends.

applicant is a person who is applying for a job posting.

applicant tracking system (ATS) software that allows employers to automate recruiting processes such as receiving applications, reviewing resumes, ranking candidates, and tracking applicants throughout the whole process.

assertive behavior the ability to express oneself and to stand up for one's point of view without disrespecting others.

B

behavioral interview an interview technique in which the interviewer asks questions aimed at getting the applicant to provide specific examples of how he or she has successfully used the skills required on the job.

board interview see *panel interview.*

business etiquette expected professional behavior in the workplace based on courtesy, manners, and customs.

C

campus interview an on-site interview generally scheduled through a school's career center.

candidate a person who is being considered for a particular job, and typically has been offered an interview.

career encompasses a series of jobs in the same occupation or profession, either with the same company or with different companies.

Career Builder Files a filing system for collecting, organizing, and updating career and job search information with three sections or portfolios called *About Me, About Jobs,* and *Master Career Portfolio.*

Career Network the people you can contact who might support you in career-related situations; organized into four categories: Work Network, Industry Network, Organization Network, and Life Network.

Career Network Meeting a meeting set up by you to discuss career-related topics with anyone who is currently in your Career Network or who might be a good addition to your network.

character questions interview questions asked to learn about the candidate's personal attributes, such as integrity, personality, attitudes, and motivation.

cloud storage site a private, secure website where a user can store documents and files online; examples include Google Drive, OneDrive, iCloud, DropBox, and so on.

code of ethics written guidelines for employees, managers and vendors to follow; based on a company's ethical standards and values.

Cold Lead an opportunity for a job found through an impersonal source such an online or offline job board; when pursuing the lead, the person on the receiving end is unknown to the job applicant.

compensation both tangible and intangible benefits an employee receives from an employer for work provided to the employer; compensation may include a salary, wage, benefits (such as medical benefits, vacation, schooling training, sick days) overtime pay, and bonuses.

competencies the skills and traits that employers look for during job interviews and expect employees to demonstrate on the job.

computer-based interviews (a) time-based interviews in which applicants log on to a password-protected website with instructions on how to complete the interview; often consist of 50 to 100 multiple-choice and true/false questions. (b) online interviews using video software (such as Skype, or Zoom) either with a live interviewer asking the questions, or for recording the applicant while answering a set of questions sent in advance.

connect as used on the LinkedIn social media site, indicating a trusted contact who is a first-degree connection.

cover letter a letter of inquiry or introduction that introduces a job seeker to a potential employer.

E

employee handbook a written handbook that covers an organization's policies and procedures such as work hours, the probationary period for new employees, pay and benefits, and rules about using company equipment and email.

ethics guidelines or accepted behavior about what is right or wrong.

G

gatekeeper the person standing between you and the hiring manager, usually an administrative support person, receptionist, or human resources staff member.

general information questions interview questions asked to obtain factual information.

H

hidden jobs job openings that are not published and that a job seeker must uncover; studies show that 80% to 85% of job openings are hidden.

I

immediate manager the person who directly supervises or manages an employee's work and development, often called a supervisor, boss, or manager (differs from *one-up manager,* who is the boss's boss).

Interview Preparation Checklist a checklist of items to complete prior to an interview to ensure that you are ready to succeed during the interview.

J

job a role that involves performing a designated set of responsibilities and duties for a specific employer.

job application a form with a set of questions used to collect information about a job seeker's skills, qualifications, and experience.

Job Application Package the documents needed when applying for a job, including a job application, cover letter, and resume; may also include your business card and copies of a few select samples of your work from your career portfolio.

job description the detailed content describing the role, responsibility, and skills found in a particular job posting.

job posting an employer's description of a position that they would like to fill; often located on a job search engine, job board, or employer website.

Job Search Journey describes a typical job search process that has five phases with several steps within each phase.

Job Search Journey Map a graphic model showing the phases and steps of the Job Search Journey.

job target a desirable job or job description; can be further classified as a *stretch target* (hard-to-get "dream job"), *current target* (ideal for you right now), or *contingency target* (easy to get and for which you are overqualified).

job search engine a website that searches, aggregates, and displays job openings from other websites, such as company websites and job boards; examples include Indeed. com, Monster, Career Builder, and LinkedIn Jobs.

job-specific skills skills and technical abilities that relate to a specific job.

K

keywords in a resume or job application are words and phrases that recruiters or recruiting software (ATS) search for to score how well a resume matches a job posting. More keywords in the resume result in a higher applicant tracking system rating and improve the chances of getting an interview.

L

landing page a single page website.

Long-term goals targets for achievements that will take a long time to accomplish, such as greater than six months.

M

Master Career Portfolio one of the three portfolios that make up your Career Builder Files; contains documents you will share with others, especially during interviews, such as your master resume, job applications, samples of your work, cover letters, and thank-you notes.

master resume the finalized generic version of a resume that serves as the foundation for customized resumes.

mobile app a software application downloaded by users designed for use on devices such as smartphones and tablets.

N

Network See Career Network (includes Work Network, Industry Network, Organization Network and Life Network).

O

objective in a resume, a concise statement of the job seeker's job target.

P

panel interview an interview in which the job candidate speaks with more than one person at a time.

Personal Brand Statement a statement that summarizes the unique benefits you offer to an employer; the foundation for 30-Second Commercials and other marketing tools.

personality test a pre-employment test used to determine whether a job applicant's personal and behavioral preferences are well matched to the work involved.

phone interview a cost-effective technique for screening job applicants.

plain text cover letter a text file (.txt) version of a cover letter that has no formatting (no bold, no tables, no bullets, etc.) and is used as the source file for the cover letter in online applications.

plain text resume a text file (.txt) version of a resume that has no formatting (no bold, no tables, no bullets, etc.) and is used as the source file to copy and paste into online applications.

positive behavior purposely acting with energy and enthusiasm.

positive visualization purposely forming a mental picture of one's successful performance and recalling the image frequently.

positive thinking making a conscious effort to be optimistic and to anticipate positive outcomes.

proactive approach a focus on solving problems, taking positive actions, and taking responsibility for one's actions. Compare with *reactive approach*.

Professional Profile a two-sentence section of the resume that states your job target or objective and your Personal Brand Statement.

Q

qualifications in a resume, a bulleted list of skills that highlights why the job seeker is the ideal candidate for the job.

R

reactive approach a focus on problems and on avoiding difficult situations. Compare with *proactive approach*.

references people who are willing to vouch for a person's qualifications and recommend that person to potential employers.

resume a brief one- or two-page document of a job applicant's qualifications for a job.

S

screening interview an interview used to identify qualified applicants for the next level of interviews and to screen out applicants who do not have the basic qualifications for the job.

search engine a website or portion of a website whose function is to sort and filter through the information stored and provide relevant results to the user; some websites search the full Internet (for example Google, Bing or Yahoo), other websites have tools for just the information housed on their site (for example, LinkedIn search function).

self-esteem belief in one's abilities and worth.

Short-term goals targets for achievements that are expected to be accomplished in a short time, such as tomorrow or next month.

skills test a pre-employment test used to test for the skills needed for a job.

social media platform a virtual community including website and mobile apps in which users can engage in peer to peer communication, contribute content, and share information.

social media profile a page on a social media platform created by each user that captures and presents their personal details to the social media community.

social networking the actions taken to build relationships, both online and offline.

stress questions interview questions asked to determine how the job candidate performs under pressure and whether he or she is good at making decisions, solving problems, and thinking under stress.

structured interview interview technique using a predetermined set of questions for all candidates so that candidates can be more easily compared.

T

target employer an employer who you want to work for due to location, reputation, or other criteria.

team interview an interview given by a group of several employees; the candidate meets individually with each person; after the interview, the team members meet to discuss the candidate's performance (also called a Day Visit).

transferable skills abilities that can be applied in more than one work environment; the basic skills and attitudes that are important for many types of work.

U

unstructured interview an interview approach that is conversational in tone; used to get to know candidates and assess their fit with the company and the job.

V

values deeply held beliefs about what is important.

video interview uses two-way video to conduct a "face-to-face" interview over the Internet.

W

Warm Introduction personal introductions to a potential employer and possibly a job opportunity, often when a job opening isn't actually posted.

web resume a resume formatted in HTML and posted on the Internet.

WHI method a way to describe what you have done: what, how, importance; in other words, describe what you did, how you did it, and why the result you achieved was important to the business or organization.

work experience in a resume, the section that lists the job seeker's employment history; jobs are listed in chronological order starting with the most recent job.